Fredrika Bremer, Emily Nonnen, Charlotte Bremer, Fredr. Milow

Life, Letters, and posthumous Works of Frederika Bremer

Fredrika Bremer, Emily Nonnen, Charlotte Bremer, Fredr. Milow

Life, Letters, and posthumous Works of Frederika Bremer

ISBN/EAN: 9783337108922

Printed in Europe, USA, Canada, Australia, Japan

Cover: Foto ©ninafisch / pixelio.de

More available books at **www.hansebooks.com**

LIFE, LETTERS,

AND

POSTHUMOUS WORKS

OF

FREDRIKA BREMER

Edited by her Sister,

CHARLOTTE BREMER.

Translated from the Swedish by

FREDR. MILOW.

THE POETRY MARKED WITH AN ASTERISK TRANSLATED

EMILY NONNEN.

LONDON:
SAMPSON LOW, SON, AND MARSTON
MILTON HOUSE, LUDGATE HILL.
1868.

WHEN noble and distinguished individuals have fiinished their pilgrimage upon earth, a more general desire is usually felt to become acquainted with every thing relating to them — with every thing in connection with them — during their journey from the cradle to the grave. A wish has accordingly been expressed in the Old as well as in the New World, that a sketch of the life of Fredrika Bremer might be written and published by some person who was dear to her, — some friend, who fully understood how to judge of her and her writings, and who was perfectly acquainted with even the most trifling circumstances of her life, and able to represent the same faithfully.

It is a matter of great interest to contemplate, in remarkable characters, the innate natural disposition of the child, and to watch its development; but it is more interesting still to mark the outward relations of life, under which the child has grown up, — and which always have such a material influence upon the young mind, — the struggles and the trials it has had to undergo in the position in the world in which it has pleased the Almighty to place it, there to let circumstances and adversities, often not known by man, be its best teacher. Intellectual and highly gifted natures are always deeply sensitive; such, like the sensitive plant, shrinking under the slightest touch. If this touch be ungentle, it creates feelings of bitterness, of suffering, of pain. Even the mere sight of all the misery — misery both of body and soul — which exists in the world, is to them a source of painful, rebellious feelings and doubts,— doubts of the most precious treasure belonging to man, the belief in an all-wise, loving Providence and Supreme Ruler, guiding all created beings. These doubts, repeatedly combated and conquered, revive often in the breast of a reflecting and sensitive mind; cause inward conflicts, moments of anxiety and anguish; but eventually, after a persevering search after light and clearness, and by means of prayer to the Giver of all good, they change into a happy submissiveness to, and hopeful trust in, the mercy of the Eternal Creator, Redeemer, and Saviour.

These thoughts, these words, may perhaps with equal truth be applied to many noble and gifted minds. Here they apply to my departed, beloved sister, Fredrika Bremer.

Amongst the numerous friends who made her acquaintance in later years, or who know her only through her writings, she has in many called into life hidden or slumbering seeds of much that is noble and good, and they cherish therefore her memory in grateful hearts as a precious treasure. To these friends a sketch of her life, of the home of her childhood and of her youth (which by a strange dispensation was also to be her last home upon earth), is here given by her sole surviving sister, who for more than a quarter of a century shared with her under the parental roof the same solicitudes, the same education, the same instruction, and the good and ills of life.

During this time they became warmly attached to each

other. Separated in more advanced years, this sister received, almost every post-day, letters from her which best show her warm, loving heart, and with them much of what she wrote both in verse and prose. All this is too beautiful and too instructive to be withheld.

May it therefore be given to the world, and may she by these posthumous writings — perhaps amongst the best that have emanated from her pen — exalt and ennoble many a susceptible human heart.

It is possible, even probable, that the publication of these letters may call forth censorious remarks. The profoundly melancholy and sorrowful frame of mind, which most of them betray, shows the existence of disharmonies in her, home, — home — which always ought to be sacred from the intrusive eye of the stranger. But how could Fredrika Bremer's biography be written, and written faithfully, if the cause which so materially influenced the whole direction of her soul and her object in life — in a word, which made her what she became both as woman and authoress — were to be passed over in silence? It is therefore indispensable that she, who writes the biography of the dear departed one, should not only faithfully adhere to truth, but should also truthfully relate every thing that may exculpate and explain these incongruities.

It is also possible that some remarks may be made respecting the publication of letters so full of the breath of sisterly love, that she who wrote them saw in the beloved sister every thing *couleur de rose*, and that this sister, therefore, out of a feeling of modesty, ought not to have allowed them to be published. To these remarks it may be answered, that the omission of any part of the contents of these letters would be to deprive them of their heart, and of the essential characteristics of Fredrika Bremer. They resemble, in many respects, the well known letters of Madame de Sévigné to her beloved daughter, Madame de Grignan, — the same ease and grace of style, the same exclusive feeling for the persons to whom they are written. The letters of the former reflect motherly, those of the latter sisterly, love, which sees every thing belonging to its object in a beautifying and poetical light.

Here are also given some extracts of Fredrika Bremer's letters to a friend, who had the sorrow of losing two children. Perhaps the consolatory thoughts, with which Fredrika had the happiness to assuage the grief of this friend may bring comfort with them when read by a mother severely tried under similar circumstances.

To these letters are added some others which merit to be preserved, as showing Fredrika Bremer's views on some important subjects, and which are, besides, remarkable for the liveliness and grace of their style.

Amongst the papers left by my sister were also found several poems and writings, and some sketches more or less finished.

I have selected some of these to be published with the others, and I have besides inserted a few which were printed previously in some obscure annuals, but which were afterwards revised by my sister. Her Autobiography, the composition of which was interrupted shortly after my father's death, and shortly before she became for some time an inmate of my home, is with few omissions published here.

	PAGE
BIOGRAPHY	1
AUTOBIOGRAPHY	101
LETTERS	117
SKETCHES	268
My Dream	268
A Vision	270
A Violet, found in Stockholm in 1827	273
At Forty Years of Age	278
My Window, 1825. The Visitor	288
My Window, 1855. New Prospects. The Beggar-Woman	296
The Sisters	311
An Evening with the Sisters at Werna	320
The Morning	332
The Light-House	337
The Eagless	359
The Romance, the Epos of our Day	367
The Child's Prayer	372
May Thoughts	374
The Grateful Little Flower	376
The Ugly Hand and the Beautiful Hand	377
Christmas Eve and Christmas Matins	383
POEMS	407
Hymn	407
Gospel Tidings	407
The Lord's Supper	408
To my Sisters	410
The Cradle of Love	411
The Star	412
The Poetry of Spring	413
Autumn Sighs	415
The Cripple's Mission	416
The Song of the Weary One	418
Resignation	429

CONTENTS.

	PAGE
Consolation in Nature	420
Cradle and Grave	421
My Morning Song	424
Peace	425
The Volcano	426
Chilly blows the Wind	426
Had I Strong Faith	428
I Trust in Thee	429
The Sage and the Cataract	429
On reading Bishop Esaias Tegnér's Poem, "Resignation"	432
The Sound in Time of Peace	434
My Wrinkles	435
Summer Evenings	437
The Grave	438
The Last Song of the Lonely One	439

FREDRIKA BREMER was born in Tuorla Manor-house, near Åbo, in Finland, on the 17th of August, 1801. Her father, the Bruks-patron, or Iron-master, Carl Fredric Bremer, was descended from an ancient German noble family, which settled in Sweden in the reign of King Gustavus Adolphus the Great; her mother was Brigitta Charlotta Hollström. Fredrika's paternal grandfather, Jacob Bremer, had removed from Sweden to Finland, in which latter country he had, by commercial enterprises, ironworks, and factories prudently managed, succeeded in accumulating considerable wealth, while giving bread to several hundred industrious people, who had him to thank for their prosperity and comfort. Out of his rich store he gave liberally to the poor and needy, and at his death he was therefore generally regretted in Finland. He was twice married. In his first marriage with a young Lady Pipping, he had eleven children, of which only five survived him — three sons and two daughters. One of these daughters married the Governor of the county of Wasa, Krabbe; and the other, Baron Hisingör, a counselor of the Royal Court of Justice in Åbo. In his second wedlock with the young and handsome daughter of the Assessor of the Royal Court of Justice, Mr. Salonius, he had two children, Carl Fredric and Agatha. The latter was married at the age of sixteen to an old gentleman, Mr. Carleson, one of the court chamberlains; and when, at the age of twenty-one, she became a widow, and free to follow the dictates of her heart, she married General Baron, afterwards Field-Marshal Count Fabian Wrede.

Foreseeing the fate which was in store for Finland, his heart overflowing with grief, my father determined to remove to Sweden before the dreaded hour should arrive. After having sold one of his estates, he left Finland in the year 1804, together with his wife, his mother-in-law, and four children born in that country, and settled in Stockholm. The following year he purchased the estate of Årsta, in the parish of Öster-Hanninge, about three Swedish, or twenty English, miles from the capital. Little children of three years of age cannot have any recollections; and all that I can remember is, that we lived in Åbo, beside a market-place, in a house which belonged to my parents.

My mother had brought with her from Finland a young housekeeper, a Miss Louise Synnerberg, who became Fredrika's and my first teacher. From her we learned to read Swedish; and, in 1806, when I had completed my sixth, and Fredrika had not quite attained her fifth year, we had a governess whom we have to thank, not only for all that we have learnt, but also for her motherly tenderness and kindness towards us. The name of this friend so dear to, so beloved by us, was Sara Eleanore de Frumerie; she was descended from a French emigrant family. Having no property of her own, and having devoted herself to the calling of a teacher, she determined to drop the *de*, calling herself Miss Frumerie. Just, truthful, and God-fearing, she laid the foundation of all that was good in us. By her pleasant and judicious method of imparting knowledge to us, she made her pupils not only anxious to learn, the more the better, but also to find a real pleasure in learning. To her we came in all our troubles, and in her we placed an unbounded confidence,

At the time when Fredrika and I were children, there did not exist the same relation between parents and children as nowadays. Severe parents belong now to the exceptions; at that time they were generally severe, and children felt for them more fear than love and confidence. I remember still how frequently, when we heard the voices of our parents on their return home, we hastened to hide ourselves in our governess's room, or in that of our Finland nurse, old Lena. During the winters, in the first years of our residence in Stockholm, my parents used to be a great deal out in the fashionable world, and we children saw them rarely except at stated times in the day. At eight o'clock in the morning we were to be ready dressed, and had to come in to say " Good morning " first to my mother, who sat in a small drawing-room taking her coffee. She looked at us with a scrutinizing glance during our walk from the door up to her chair. If we had walked badly, we had to go back again to the door to renew our promenade, curtsey, and kiss her hand. If our curtsey had been awkwardly performed, we had to make it over again. Poor little Fredrika could never walk, stand, sit, or curtsey to the satisfaction of my mother, and had many bitter and wretched moments in consequence. Then we had to go to salute my father. When we entered his outer room, the footman laid down a large square carpet in the centre of the floor, and placed on it a chair, on which my father sat down, after having been enveloped in a large white cloak which reached down to the ankles. Mr. Hagelin, his hairdresser — a real original — in a light-gray overcoat, then made his appearance with a comb stuck behind his ear and a powder-puff in his hand, — himself powdered, bowing deeply and scraping with one foot, first to my father, and then to us little ones. He handed the powder-puff to the footman, who was to hold it, while he himself undid the ribbon tied round the pigtail, and then combed and replaited it. After that the powder-box was produced, the puff dipped into it, and Mr. Hagelin, like a true amateur, with a sweet smile on his countenance, his head inclined on one side, stepping back now and then to take a survey of the effect of the powdering process, powdered my father's head and face so thoroughly, that he was unable to open his eyes until the footman had handed him a basin of water and a towel. This ceremony amused us exceedingly, and we were permitted to look on for a short time. When we had curtsied to my father, we had our breakfast, and afterwards went to Miss Frumerie to read and work from nine till one o'clock.

My mother had laid down three inviolable principles for the education of her children. They were to grow up in perfect ignorance of every thing evil in the world; they were to learn (acquire knowledge) as much as possible; and they were to — eat as little as possible. The first of these principles was founded upon my mother's conviction that unacquaintance with all evil would preserve in her children an innocent mind, and accustom them to an atmosphere of purity, which would beneficially influence their whole development. I am grateful for this beautiful idea, emanating from my mother's own innate innocence, and I believe that it has in us led to purity of thought and mind; although, when we came out into the world, we found ourselves painfully deceived in all our imaginations, when one illusion after the other vanished. In order to gain the desired object, we were never permitted to remain in the drawing-room when my parents had any visitors or company, — at the utmost perhaps only a few minutes, — for fear that our innocent ears should listen to something which they ought not to hear; and we were strictly forbidden to speak to the servants, except to old Lena, who again was forbidden to tell us any thing.

We did not require any incitement to read or to learn; it was our, and especially Fredrika's, greatest pleasure. Within a couple of years we learnt to read and speak French, and we learnt to repeat by heart out of Madame de Genlis's plays, " L'Ile Heureuse," " La Rosière," " Les

Flacons," and others, such scenes in which only two persons appeared at a time; and these lessons we took so long, that " Bonne Amie," as we called Miss Frumerie, had not patience enough to listen to them to the end. Fredrika frequently knew a whole act by heart, and " Bonne Amie " exclaimed more than once, " *That* Fredrika, she is perfectly intolerable with her recitations; there is never an end to them!"

The third of my mother's principles, — that her children should eat as little as possible, — she had laid down partly under the conviction that if children are allowed to eat much, they become stupid and slow to learn; and partly from a detestation of strong, stout, and tall women. My mother read vast quantities of novels, and I suspect that the hope of one day beholding in her daughters delicate, zephyr-like heroines of romance, was constantly haunting her imagination. This principle certainly succeeded in making them short of stature, and not *too* strong; but with the prescribed diet it could not be otherwise. At eight o'clock in the morning we got a small basin — I have never seen such small basins — of cold milk, and with it a small piece of " knäckebröd.[1] If we were ever so hungry, which happened every day, still we did not venture to ask for any thing more to eat. Once or twice old Lena, when we told her of our distress, had given us each a piece of dry bread; but my mother having heard of it, Lena got such a scolding that she never dared to try that experiment again.

At two o'clock the dinner was always served in my parents' house, and that was indeed a glorious time for us hungry children. We were then allowed to eat as much as was considered necessary. Of the four or five dishes which, according to the fashion of the day, were put at once upon the table, we had permission to eat of three, and they tasted wonderfully good. After dinner we were

[1] A kind of very thin, hard, rye biscuit.

all assembled in the drawing-room to drink coffee, — we children of course only as spectators, — after which, at four o'clock, we went with "Bonne Amie" into her room to write, cipher, and work. My father, who was beyond description orderly and punctual, determined that every thing should be done by the clock, looked during the time repeatedly at his watch, and until it pointed at four exactly, nobody was allowed to leave the room, when he went to his own room to take a nap.

At six precisely, there came a knock at "Bonne Amie's" door, the footman announced that tea was ready, and we then marched, "Bonne Amie," Fredrika, and myself, through the dining to the drawing-room. There my parents, "Bonne Amie," and sometimes those who came to pay a visit, drank tea, while we were looking on, occasionally getting a rusk, with permission to go to the nursery to play, — for now the lessons were over for the day.

At nine, my parents, "Bonne Amie," and mostly some guests, were seated round a table in the dining-room covered with two or three warm dishes; but we children had already at eight o'clock had a small glass of cold milk and a small piece of knäckebröd. When we had finished our supper, we went to the dining-room, curtsied, kissed my father's and mother's hand, said "Good night," and proceeded to "Bonne Amie's" room, in which we both had our beds upon a corner sofa. Old Lena was there to undress us, and always used to hold a long lecture to Fredrika, who preferred running about the room and dancing with Lena to going to bed. After jumping and romping about for a little while, she usually got tired; but Lena fared far worse in the morning, when she wanted to dress her. The old nurse had then to run about to get hold of the little wild girl, who always bolted from her when she was going to be washed and dressed. Sometimes Lena was so angry with her that she got quite red in the face, and then she burst out with what I believe was her only article of faith: "Ah! *that* will be a nice one when she gets older; for certain it is, that the longer people live the worse they become!"

I am not quite sure, but I believe it was in 1806, when my maternal grandmother died. She lived with my parents, suffered a great deal from some painful internal disease, and was always confined to her bed. She was indescribably kind and tender to Fredrika and me, and always wanted to have us beside her during those moments when she was tolerably free from pain. It interested her much to hear what we had learnt; and if we read nicely to her, we knew that, one after another, we were allowed to put our hand into a large paper bag full of sweetmeats, which was lying upon the bed beside her, and take out of it as much as we could grasp. Otherwise I do not remember much of my kind old grandmother; except that on the day of her funeral we cried a great deal and eat a great deal of confectionery.

At midsummer, 1806, the whole family removed out to Årsta. Like all children, we were enchanted at being allowed to go on a journey — such a long journey — a whole twenty English miles! And during the preceding eight days we were busy, every leisure moment, packing and unpacking again and again all our toys and dolls. At last came the happy day, and in three large carriages the whole family proceeded to the country. I remember exceedingly well, that, on our arrival, both Fredrika and I thought that the large, palace-like edifice, with its projecting turrets, its uncommonly high, sloping roof, its high lattice windows, with small glass panes set in lead, and its dark walls, from which in many places the plaster had fallen off, did not look well at all. If we had understood the meaning of the word *awful*, we should certainly have thought of it on beholding the then dilapidated old Årsta, built nearly two centuries before by Mrs. Barbro Åkes's daughter,

Natt-och-Dag, while her husband, Admiral Bjelkenstjerna, was out in the German Thirty Years' War.[1]

When we had alighted from the carriage, and entered the spacious, vaulted hall, rising through three storeys, with its high stone pillars and double staircases, we were delighted, and asked permission to run up and down them, which was willingly granted, as being the best means of keeping us out of the way while every thing was taken out of the carriages. We must have been indulging in this pleasure of running up one pair of stairs and down another a long time, for I remember our being very hot and very tired when we were called in to eat our supper and go to bed.

Now came a happy time for us. When we had finished our lessons at one o'clock, we were allowed to go down into the large garden, and to take long walks in the afternoon with " Bonne Amie," after she had had her tea. We thought it wonderfully delightful to run out and play about. In town we had scarcely ever permission to go out. Happy beyond measure were we to hear the little birds sing; to gather flowers and fruit; but as happy as the curate's children, *that* we clearly saw we should never be. One day, when our carriage-horses had to be exercised,

---

[1] Årsta belonged in the thirteenth and fourteenth centuries to the German order of the Knights of the Sword. It was afterwards sold, and became in the year 1500 the property of Axel Laurson Tott, after which it became an heir-loom in the Bjelkenstjerna and Fleming families. — See *Groundrent Book of the County of Upland*, 1680, and Tham's *Description of the Province of Stockholm*.

In July, 1621, Gustavus Adolphus assembled his army and fleet to lead them in person across the Baltic to Riga. From the port of Elfsnabben, where the fleet was lying at anchor, detained by contrary winds, Gustavus Adolphus proclaimed his Articles of War, drawn up by himself, and written by his own hand. These Articles of War were read aloud for the first time by the Chancellor, Axel Oxenstjerna, to the army, consisting of 20,000 men, drawn up in battle array on the fields of Årsta. The whole royal family was there assembled on that occasion. — See Geyer's *History of the Swedes*.

"Bonne Amie" took us for a ride to pay a visit to the curate's wife.

In the little yard before the red-painted house lay a hillock of sand, and on it were lying four children, busy with large wooden ladles digging out walks and flower-beds. We were so fortunate as to be allowed to join in their play that afternoon, but never again.

The summer passed quickly away. We read and studied industriously, and were a great deal out in the open air.

On Sundays, the Countess F—— and her daughter, then sixteen years old, were almost always invited to dine with us. Countess F——, the former owner of Årsta, had, when she sold the estate, made it a condition that she should be allowed to remain there over the summer. She occupied one part of the lower storey, and my parents the other. The whole of the upper storey in the old house was unfurnished, and consisted of very large rooms with thick walls, and with heavy oak timbers across the ceiling. The largest of these rooms was forty-eight feet square, had nine high windows, and a gigantic chimney, upon the upper part of which were resting two massive blocks of stone, in which the Bjelkenstjerna's and the Fleming's arms were cut. The floor was inlaid with squares of polished oak. This room had in former times been the banqueting hall, and the heavy, clumsy, horseshoe table, which took up two entire sides of the room, was still remaining. On one of the small window-panes was scratched, —

"Lady Sigrid is a nincompoop,
So is also her beloved Soop."

All the rooms were nineteen feet high; every step awoke a loud echo; and the wind was incessantly whistling through the small window-panes, loosely set in their leaden frames. We were neither allowed, nor dared we go alone to the upper storey; but, whenever we could, we watched an opportunity for visiting the kind Countess F—— and her daughter, who were always so very friendly to us. We had then to pass through a large apartment, the walls of which were covered with gilt leather in sombre figures, and the floor was inlaid with large, square, polished stones. We were a little afraid of passing through this room; but we used to run as fast as possible, and in that manner always got through it without any adventure.

In a large apartment in that part of the flat which was occupied by my parents, were seen two well-painted portraits of the former owners of Årsta, — Mistress Barbro Åkes's daughter Natt-och-Dag of Göholm and Hedesö — a severe and sharp-looking lady; and her husband, Admiral Bjelkenstjerna, — the latter cased in full armor, looking very fierce. From this apartment we had a view of a long avenue leading down to a creek or arm of the Baltic, which could be descried only when the water happened to be very high. From most of the other rooms in the building, which stood on an eminence, the eye wandered over meadows, and fields, and villages belonging to the estate, stretching in one direction over nearly five English miles. Two churches raised their old-fashioned, high, pointed spires above the distant forest. They were the Öster and Wester Hanninge churches.

Only once during this summer my parents invited their relatives and friends from town to a so-called " hemkom-öl," or house-warming. Dinner was served in the banqueting-hall, and after dinner the guests drank coffee under the high, two hundred years' old maples, which, planted in two rows, divided the court-yard from the garden, forming a broad, shady walk.

When autumn and cold weather set in at last, my parents moved to town, and during several succeeding years we lived winter after winter, each week like the last: much reading, little eating, and rarely permission to go out. Another difficulty was now added to our other troubles. My mother considered it very wholesome that we should be thinly dressed, with bare neck and arms. We shivered with cold. It was probably cold in our rooms, which were large, and at that time double windows were unknown. I recollect very well that often, for days together, we could not look out of the window, the panes being covered with ice.

When I was eight and Fredrika seven years old, we had music and drawing masters. It was not expected in those days, as it is now, that a governess should possess all kinds of talent. Besides, our "Bonne Amie" would not have been sufficient for us all, especially as she had now to teach the younger children, Hedda and Claes, and three little future pupils had been added to our family up to the year 1810, so that she had a whole troop in perspective.

The good little Hedda had great difficulty in learning; but Claes could already, at the age of six, read both Swedish and French.

From seven till ten years of age, little Fredrika began to manifest strange dispositions and inclinations. Occasionally she threw into the fire whatever she could lay her hands upon — pocket-handkerchiefs, the younger children's night-caps, stockings, and the like. The servants complained to my mother, and Fredrika was interrogated. She confessed at once; and the only reason she could give for her delinquency was, "that it was so delightful to see the flames." In spite of scoldings and prohibitions, she frequently repeated this pleasure. If a knife or a pair of scissors happened to be lying about, they, and Fredrika too, disappeared immediately. She then walked about alone, meditating; and if nobody happened to be present, she cut a piece out of a window-curtain, or a round or square hole in the front of her dress. She looked very awkward if interrupted in her proceedings. One day, our parents being out, she fell upon the idea of quietly stealing into the drawing-room and double locking the door. Old Lena, suspecting that some mischief was on foot because Fredrika had disappeared, looked for her everywhere, and coming to the drawing-room, which she found locked, she knocked, calling to Fredrika to open the door. "Yes, immediately," answered Fredrika; but it took some minutes before she unlocked the door; probably she wanted first to finish her work. When she had unlocked the door, Lena went round the room to see what Fredrika had been doing, and was terrified when she discovered that she had cut a large round hole in the middle of the silk covering of one of the large arm-chairs, and had poked a piece of her own dress, cut out of the front breadth, into the hole.

With the knife she experimented upon the arms and legs of her dolls, to find out what they contained; and one poor doll had to lose its head. She wanted to find out what was inside of it. When Fredrika had performed any cutting or carving, and Lena was ordered to go and find it out, Fredrika always used to follow her, silently and calmly, as if she had done no wrong; and when Lena had found out what she had cut and chopped to pieces, and began to moralize, Fredrika walked up to Lena, stared at her and at her own handiwork, turned round and walked off without saying a word. If the discovery took too long, Fredrika lost her patience, and pointed silently in the direction in which Lena ought to go.

One day Fredrika and I had each got two beautiful figures of French porcelain as presents from one of my mother's friends. Before evening, Fredrika had tried whether one of these figures would break if thrown upon the stone flags lying before the stove; the brittleness of the other was tried upon a load of fire-wood, which the servant was carrying into a room to make a fire. Of course, she succeeded in smashing them both; but this did not in the least trouble her. Another day she came to my mother tendering a penny, the only one she had left in her little purse, asking at the same time her forgiveness for having broken a decanter and three glasses, for which she wished to make compensation with her penny. My mother could not help laughing. Fredrika got a slight scolding, and was allowed to keep her penny.

Fredrika and I had each three dolls, with very handsome wardrobes for them. As I was of a very quiet nature, and very orderly, my dolls were as carefully tended as if they had been little children, and I felt for them as a real mother. They were undressed every evening and put to bed, and were dressed again regularly every morning. Fredrika's dolls, on the contrary, were often much neglected. They remained occasionally dressed for a fortnight together; and if they happened to be once undressed, they usually remained undressed for an equally long time, and were then lying about in their chemises in the corners of the nursery. At last she got quite tired of her dolls, and I, who used to pity them very much, undertook to attend to them; but I got tired of this after some time, and complained that it was really too much for me to manage six children. Fredrika then made an agreement with little Hedda, that if she would take charge of her dolls, she should have a piece of gingerbread every time Fredrika got any, and also, now and then, a piece of confectionery; but not *every time* that Fredrika got any, because she was very fond of it herself. Hedda held boldly out for the confectionery, and the matter was ultimately arranged to her satisfaction; but Fredrika undertook to dress her dolls elegantly every time they were invited to a ball.

Every Christmas Eve, our parents had the kindness to give us as much pleasure as possible. In the large drawing-room a Christmas table was set out, literally covered with all kinds of good things. Each child had its jul-hög, or yule-heap, of saffron-bread, buns, and wheaten cakes, and, besides, plates full of raisins, almonds, nuts, and sweetmeats; and before every heap stood a three-branched wax candle.

A great number of Christmas-boxes, wrapped up in paper and sealed, were thrown into the room by a masked figure with horns on its head, called the yule-buck. We children ran a race after the various parcels dancing about on the floor, and great was the delight when she whose name was written on the parcel happened to pick it up herself. That evening was not like any other evening in the whole year, and I never saw my parents so happy as at the happiness which they gave to their children. We on our part were inexpressibly delighted and grateful. All fear of our parents was gone; we only ran about thanking them and kissing their hands for every new present we got. Besides many useful presents, we got also a great number of toys, which afforded us great delight during the whole of Christmas time; but Fredrika soon began making her experiments, and long before the next Christmas all her beautiful playthings were gone.

At eight years of age Fredrika wrote her first verses in French to the moon. She has unfortunately burnt them, and I remember only the first line:—

"O, corps celeste de la Nature!"

A couple of years later, she composed a little ballad, which she also destroyed, but of which she introduced the first verse in "The Home," where she describes herself in Petrea's person, letting her compose the same. It is as follows:—

"In the fine palace Elfvakolasti,
  Situated in some part of Sverge,
Once resided little Melanie,
  Only daughter of Count Stjerneberge."

About this time she intended writing a poem, the title of which, written in large letters, was, "The Creation of the World." The creation of the world began with —

CHAOS.

In clouds and gloomy darkness ever lying
Was all the world before,

> And ever all in vain, the minutes onward flying,
> Expected that this darkness would be o'er.
> The world to-day with men o'erflowing
> Was then a thing of naught;
> And all our lovely starry heavens glowing,
> They then no light had got;
> But He was who has been ever,
> Who is, and ever shall be.

"At this glimpse of light, the creation of the world was suspended," writes Fredrika in "The Home"; "probably doomed under Petrea's hand never to emerge out of Chaos."

Amongst my papers and letters from Fredrika I have found an old slip of paper, on which, in her childhood, she had written a couple of verses to Baron Wrede on the occasion, as it seems from their contents, of some little festival which she had arranged for him during one of his visits to Årsta.

This occurred probably in 1811, when Fredrika was ten years old, because my aunt is not mentioned. She died in 1810, and in 1811 Baron Wrede removed from Stockholm. At the top of the verses stands —

(AIR: *La Biondina.*)

> Flowers we here present, Your Lordship!
> They 're the produce of Fredrikaberg.
> Flowers we here present, Your Lordship!
> They have blossomed at Fredrikaberg.
> There we 've fruits and flowers ever,
> Winter, summer, failing never.
> 'T is, indeed, a splendid place!
> Berries in whole hillocks growing,
> Are varied by flowery ling.
> Sand and gravel, mines o'erflowing,
> Will make you as rich as a king.

(Repeat the second refrain.)

> Under lofty fir-trees' shadow
> Cows' and pigs' food can be had, O!
> Cows' and pigs' food can be had, O!
> Come, O! come into these regions,
> Where your numerous virtues' prize,

> Wreaths of fir in countless legions,
> Wait you in your Paradise.

(Repeat the second refrain.)

> Thus we greet you, Baron Wrede!
> Great and powerful Lord Manorial.
> Thus we greet you, Baron Wrede!
> Noble baron, this our present
> Can boast of little worth, 't is true.
> Give us yet assurance pleasant,
> That for our sakes 't is dear to you.

"Fredrikaberg" was a stony hillock lying on the verge of fertile meadows. Fredrika got this hillock as a present from my father on her birthday, with full right of possession. The previous year a similar hillock had been presented to me, in a place where the nature of the soil allowed of laying out walks, and where my father had ordered a large, round, wooden seat to be constructed. This hillock was inaugurated on my birthday by an invitation to several friends, who took their coffee there in the afternoon, after which my father made a speech announcing that this "Property" was to be called Charlotteberg, and should belong to his eldest daughter. I recollect well, even now, my delight. We had some presentiment that Fredrika, the following year, would also get such a hillock, to be presented to her with similar solemnities.

She got the hillock; but no wooden seat, no walks, no inauguration festival; and then, for the first time, the thought arose within her that she was less loved.

Amongst Fredrika's papers I found, in a very small old copy-book, a couple of verses which had escaped the fate of all her other earlier effusions, that were to be, as she used to call it, "destroyed as contraband." In this copy-book are found a few verses, remarkable only for being written by a little child, which one can see that she must then have been, from the great difference between the characters in which they were written and the verses which she wrote when ten years old. One might almost doubt that she was the authoress; but at all events they prove that woman's dependent and subordinate position in life had already made a deep impression on her childish mind. They are as follows, without either a comma or full stop: —

> can man not learn the art of saving
> could not our stronger sex be taught
> not from their poor wives all help craving
> to save their wages as they ought
>
> to give up cards and take to reading
> not novels — no — but books more meet
> and from mad scenes of mirth receding
> to fly from art to nature sweet

It does really seem as if the good Fredrika was ready to become, even as a child, the champion of her sex. I have heard it said that Fredrika was not an agreeable child. A child myself, I was unable to judge. Very kind she was always; "ready to give away indiscriminately the presents which had been given to her," as she says of Petrea in "The Home." In later years I found that her eyes were very handsome, thoughtful, and expressing goodness and vivacity; but the head was large in proportion to the small and slight figure; and the nose filled up a large place in her physiognomy. Her nose would probably never have been so large if she had not, from her earliest childhood, been displeased with its form, and therefore had determined to improve it; but all her experiments to this effect resulted in making her nose swell considerably, become larger and larger, and often very red. Fredrika had, when a child, an uncommonly low forehead. She had frequently heard my mother remark this, and she undertook, therefore, one day, to make it high, by cutting away the hair at the roots all round the forehead. While occupied with this operation, she heard my mother's step, and was as terrified as if she had committed a crime. My mother, who did not at once perceive what Fredrika had been doing, probably thought that she looked unusually well, and said to her later in the day, "Your forehead is, after all, not so very low," and Fredrika was enchanted with her successful handiwork. But in a few days the hair began to grow again, sticking out like bristles. Great was then her distress to find out how this was to be prevented in future, and Fredrika was obliged to walk about for some time with her bristles, until the hairs had grown so long that they could be seized with a pair of tweezers, when she tore them out, root and all. They continued, however, to grow; but Fredrika persevered patiently to pull them out, and produced ultimately in this way a fine high forehead, which became her much better than the low one which Nature had given her.

Fredrika was already, as a child, very inquisitive and eager for information. She wanted to know every thing; was very restless, and put all kinds of questions, especially on certain days, which I used to call her "inquiring days." "Bonne Amie" got tired, and told her to be quiet; and Lena also got tired, and gave her no other answer than "saucebox!" Fredrika was occasionally excessively wild and frolicsome, and then again she would dissolve in tears, especially if she had been scolded, — and scoldings she got, indeed, and plenty of them, particularly during our stay in the country. There we had permission to go out, and in our rambles Fredrika always managed to lose her pocket-handkerchief, gloves, or garters; or she tore her dress, or came home too late for dinner. She could never learn to be punctual, and in this my father was very strict; although she had an unusually good memory while studying, yet she could never remember what was told her in daily life. She was very anxious to please her parents, and it grieved her deeply that she could not remember what they told her, and to see them displeased with her. Her childish freaks to burn her things, cut her clothes to pieces, and so on, brought upon her many a severe scolding: this was also the case with her obstinacy. It was one of her juvenile faults, as also to give saucy and pert answers, which always irritated my father, so that he became excited and angry, and not able to correct the delinquent with gentleness. But poor Fredrika got indeed so many scoldings for mere trifles, that her mind became at times embittered.

My mother felt annoyed at all this, and Fredrika always forgetting the reprimands which she continually got, my mother treated her rather severely, believing that this would improve matters, and that, as Fredrika had an excellent memory for learning, she ought to have an equally good memory in every thing that was told her. Strange as it may appear, that memory can be as it were twofold; such was the case here, and Fredrika could not help it, that every thing which she was told to remember was forgotten a moment afterwards.

Notwithstanding my mother's severity, Fredrika entertained for some time a really passionate love for her, and tried every means to please her. My mother was always very elegant in her deportment and toilet; she had exceedingly agreeable manners, and Fredrika's admiring gaze followed her every movement.

My father was very taciturn and reserved, and his temper was melancholy and gloomy. During the disastrous war which was raging in Finland in 1808, and ended in its being lost to Sweden, he was more gloomy than ever. In the evenings he was in the habit of walking incessantly — sometimes for two or three hours together — up and down in the dark, in the dining-room in town, for he would not have the candles lighted; and we often imagined that we heard him weeping. " Bonne Amie's " room was next to the dining-room, and as long as my father was walking there, we did not venture to go through it. When tea was brought in at six o'clock, he broke off his walk, but he resumed it as soon as he had finished tea.

One day in 1809, while the war was still raging in Finland, a note was brought to my father while we were still at dinner. The contents seemed to surprise him, but he said nothing, and put the note in his pocket. Early on the following morning he entered " Bonne Amie's " room, after we had gone in to read, and asked her to let him have the two elder children for an hour or two.

" Bonne Amie " of course gave her consent at once, but seemed to be as much surprised as we girls. We followed my father, and when we had got into his private room, we heard a knock at the door of the outer room. All this appeared to us rather awful, and we did not know what to think of it. My father opened the door, and a man-servant in the livery of a Jägare-chasseur entered, saying that he had brought with him four soldiers of the guards, carrying two chests which he had orders to deliver to my father, handing him at the same time a sealed packet, with compliments from Count L——m, who would call upon my father about dinner-time. Two large iron-hooped chests were then carried in, which were placed in my father's outer room. When the Jägare had gone, my father double-locked and bolted, first the outer door leading to the hall, then the double doors, and lastly the door between his two rooms, all the time in profound silence and to our great amazement. This done, my father broke the sealed packet, took out of it two large keys, and applied them to the chests, which he unlocked and opened. They were full of small linen bags, and on each was written the initials of my father's name, C. F. B. We were now told to take out the bags and place them in rows upon the floor. These small bags were very heavy. When they had all been taken out, my father counted them, untying the string of one of them. We then saw that they contained large silver coin. My father then opened the door of a large closet or wardrobe, telling us to place all the bags in it; they were so many in number that, when piled one upon the other, they formed a large heap. When all this was done, my father locked the door to the wardrobe, took out the key, patted us, and told us not to mention what we had seen to any body, except to " Bonne Amie;" not to Lena, lest the little children should hear of it. We promised this, and kept our word.

Before the end of the year we heard it said, that, during the height of the war, Count Gustavus L——m had put the royal seal upon these chests, and had brought them over with him to Sweden, and that they contained the purchase money for a foundry and an estate in Finland, which my father had sold.

This or the following year, I am not quite sure which my father bought the estate of Nynäs, in the parish ot Ösmo, probably with the contents of the linen bags which we had taken out of the chests. My parents took up their abode at Nynäs the ensuing summer. The situation was exceedingly beautiful; but the principal dwelling-house, old and very decayed, contained only one floor, consisting of low rooms, so very different to those which we had been accustomed to at Årsta.

One thing very delightful at Nynäs was, that two glass doors opened out of a very large dining-room to the garden, into which we descended by two low steps. At the back of the dwelling-house was a spacious court-yard, planted all round with high, shady lime-trees, and opposite it was a beautiful chapel, in which divine service was held every Sunday. An arm of the Baltic came up close to one side of the fine court-yard, and we had there a splendid view of the wooded shores, and in the background, at some distance, was an island covered with stately oaks. Oh! how beautiful it was there, and on Sundays how solemn! Then, early in the morning, the people belonging to the estate were all assembled in the court-yard clad in their holiday dress; they seated themselves, some upon a row of benches placed on that side which was nearest to the water, and others under the lime-trees upon the grassy stone terraces. Waiting for the arrival of the clergyman and the ringing of the bells, the smartly dressed peasant women sat holding in their hands large bouquets of " southernwood." After the service, the clergyman came to see my parents. It was a custom from old times that he should dine at the Manor-house.

My father had purchased Nynäs of Count Mauritz Armfelt. I saw this favorite of Gustavus III., famous for his personal beauty, his wit, and his political intrigues, when he came one day to Nynäs. He was then already an elderly man, powerfully built, rather stout, but with an exceedingly beautiful head. My parents endeavored to persuade him to remain, at any rate, to dinner; but he declined their invitation, demanding only some luncheon, of which he would not partake in the dining-room, but alone, in his own former private apartment. This was a large room, and on the long wall hung a full-size portrait of the late King Gustavus Adolphus IV.

Immediately after luncheon, Count Armfelt returned to Stockholm. There was something so strange in his visit to Nynäs, that it gave rise to much surprise and many surmises. I heard subsequently that being a zealous adherent of the deposed king and his family, he did not consider himself quite safe in his native country, and that immediately after his return to the capital he had taken up his abode in the hotel of the Russian ambassador, Count Tuchtelen, where he remained until he went over to Finland.

Count Armfelt had left an *homme d'affaires* at Nynäs, who was to stay there over the summer, in order to settle all the accounts relating to the sale of the estate.

He was a Frenchman, an old Abbé, by name Gredaine. The good, hoary-headed Abbé soon became charmed with the little, witty, lively Fredrika, and said to her one day, " Mademoiselle Frédérique, je vous fais mon héritière universelle." The Abbé had had a summer-house fitted up for himself, which rested upon wheels, so that it could be moved wherever he wished; at present it was standing in the garden in the shade of beautiful trees, and he now made a present of it to Fredrika. She jumped and danced about with delight, patted and thanked the good Abbé, and was almost beside herself with joy. The good old man was quite as happy at seeing her happiness, and from that moment, whenever he met Fredrika he always repeated his " Mademoiselle Frédérique, je vous fais mon héritière universelle."

The Abbé dined frequently with my parents, and on such occasions the important question, relating to every thing belonging to the summer-house, sofas, chairs, table, &c., &c., was discussed in French, and when Fredrika was told that it all belonged to her, there was a fresh outburst of delight. After some time, and when the novelty had worn off a little, and the Abbé was one day again dining with us, Fredrika walked up to him asking if he had nothing else to give her. The good Abbé pretended to be angry, although it was easy to see that it was difficult for him not to laugh, and exclaimed, " Comment Mademoiselle Frédérique, vous êtes une ingrate! je vous fais cadeau de la plus jolie petite maison du monde, toute meublée, et vous n'êtes pas contente." Peace was, however, soon restored, and when the Abbé added, " Attelez quatre chevaux à votre petite maison, Mademoiselle Frédérique, et vous pouvez aller au bout du monde," Fredrika took this quite seriously, and invited me to be her travelling companion.

The happiest memories of my childhood I carry with me from Nynäs. I do not know whether Fredrika enjoyed as much as I the beautiful situation of this estate and the charming scenery of its environs; but I remember never having felt so grateful for every thing good, and so happy as then. So much singing of birds I have never listened to as there, and Fredrika was as much delighted at it as I, and at the delicious fragrance which the stately lime-trees diffused while they were in blossom. Grateful still for these moments of enjoyment, I remember even now many a beautiful Sunday morning — on the other days of the week we were not allowed to go out until one o'clock — when we used to wander through the park down to the sea, or sit under the old-fashioned porch facing the court-yard, looking at the church people as they assembled.

My mother, who looked upon us as too much of children to be able to understand a sermon, would not allow us to go to church. This was a great loss both to Fredrika and me, because we were then really seriously disposed, and wished so much to attend the service. But we soon fell upon the idea of seating ourselves upon a grass-sofa behind a hedge of lilacs.

Shaded by beautiful birch-trees, this sofa stood close to the chapel, on that side of it where the altar was placed. Seated there, we could hear the whole service, and we did not leave our place of concealment until the congregation had left the church.

Fredrika's tenth birthday, the 17th of August, was celebrated as all birthdays in our family, with a *gouter*, or luncheon, consisting of all kinds of nice things, — tea, lemonade, tea-cakes, sweetmeats, fruits, &c., &c. During the preceding winter I had conceived a bright idea. Fredrika had a real passion for sweetmeats, and I had proposed to Hedda and Claes that every time when, in the course of the winter, we should get any sweetmeats, we should eat only two or three of them each, and keep the remainder, in order to collect a large quantity for Fredrika on her birthday. I undertook to take care of the treasure.

They agreed at once to my proposal, but when it came to be realized, it frequently met with many difficulties. The little children wanted to eat up all that they got, and sometimes they seemed determined to besiege and storm the wooden box in which I had treasured the sweetmeats.

They were not quiet until I had given them each one, for all my remonstrances and beautiful speeches were in vain. At last came the 17th of August, and I took Hedda and Claes with me when I was going to put the sweetmeats upon the dining-room table, which was decorated with flowers and leaves in honor of the occasion.

To my great astonishment, I found that the contents of the wooden box filled four large plates, which were placed triumphantly upon the table. My parents were very much astonished, for nobody but "Bonne Amie" had been let into the grand secret.

They caressed and praised me and the little ones, who now made up for lost time. My mother's brother, who had spent a few days at Nynäs, entered in the midst of the rejoicings of the children.

Fredrika was delighted and happy on account of all the good things, and my uncle asked what was the matter? When the secret was revealed to him, he exclaimed, "They must be delicious, indeed, after being warehoused a whole year!" Then the truth flashed upon my mind, and I understood at once that the sweetmeats must be too old. All the almond confectionery was as hard as stone, and had to be pounded in a mortar; but then, we thought, it tasted deliciously.

In the autumn, it was very damp at Nynäs. I believe that the fine, high trees, with their rich foliage surrounding the old wooden mansion, were the cause of this. My parents, therefore, returned to Årsta early every autumn, I believe in September, where we remained a couple of months before we went into winter-quarters in town.

Extensive repairs and improvements in the whole upper storey in the mansion at Årsta had been commenced and were carried on until 1814, when the elegant and comfortable suite of apartments was finished.

We were very sorry to leave the country, for there we were allowed to go out. My parents, when in town, had always two pair of carriage-horses in their stables during the winter. My mother's, a pair of stately, beautiful "Isabelles," were used by her alone when paying visits, or when, with one of her friends, she took a drive out through "Norrtull," — in those days the favorite drive of the fashionable world. My father always drove his fiery, splendid black horses to run down to Årsta, or sometimes when he went out for an airing, which he preferred doing in the afternoon at dusk. He then always took two of the children with him, in order that they might breathe the fresh air, of which, however, they could not get much in a covered sledge with only one window let down. We did not particularly enjoy these excursions. Scarcely a word was then spoken, and we always went my father's favorite road, — from Regerings-gatan," where we then lived, past St. John's church-yard, and out through "Roslags-tull."

Between the age of nine and twelve, Fredrika and I studied the English and German languages; made great progress in history, geography, &c., &c., and underwent regularly every year an examination before my father's early friend, the Rector of St. Clara's Church, afterwards Bishop Franzén. He was pleased with our studies in general, but astonished at the progress which we had made in geography. This we owed to "Bonne Amie's" excellent method of teaching. On the map lying before us, she made us a present of empires and kingdoms in those parts of the world which we were studying for the time. When, for instance, I got France and Fredrika England, we were very anxious to become thoroughly acquainted with all the provinces, towns, and rivers, bays and boundaries of the country which we were governing, and this afforded us a great deal of pleasure. But Fredrika always knew all the *produce* of her kingdom much better than its boundaries; the latter she could never remember.

Fredrika had an innate aversion to all kinds of needlework. She turned upside down or inside out what she had to sew, constantly lost meshes when she was knitting, and would never take them up. When she dropped any meshes, she did not say a word, but, quick as lightning, she threw the stocking under her chair and ran out of the room. "Bonne Amie" used to be very much amused at this manœuvre. We knew perfectly well what was the matter, when Fredrika, silently and in haste, made off, and the stocking was lying under her chair.

"Bonnie Amie" had in her youth learnt to make very beautiful things in pasteboard. In order *to amuse us*, she taught us in the long autumn evenings, after we came to town, the art of making small work-boxes, baskets, needle-cases, &c., &c., which, succeeding more or less, were always admired by us; and *to educate us*, she proposed that we should sell these things, and, for the proceeds, buy stuff for shirts and clothes which we were to make up for poor children and distribute at Christmas. This proposal gave us a great deal of pleasure; and thus "Bonne Amie" gained her object, — to create in us a desire to assist those who were in want; to gain, by working, the means of doing so; or, by denying ourselves things that were not indispensably necessary, to apply our means in quarters where they were better wanted. We were astonished at the ready sale which our work met with, which we were told had been sent out to be sold. It was long before we discovered that my mother and "Bonne Amie" had bought most of it.

During three winters Fredrika, Hedda, and I took lessons in dancing, which delighted us very much. Fredrika was so weak about this time, that when, at the beginning of every lesson, she had to curtsey, standing behind a chair in all the five positions, she was often on the point of falling down; and her small feet were so soft and lissom that our teacher, when she was going to bend them, fancied they were broken to pieces.

It was the fashion in those days to make beautiful *pas* and *entrechats* when dancing *quadrilles*, as the modern *fran-*

çaise was then called; and young ladies learnt to dance the *gavotte*, the *shawl-dance*, and a kind of dance with a *tambour de Basque*, from which this dance derived its name. A first-rate *danseuse* from the opera came to our house twice a week, accompanied by an old gentleman, who played the violin while we were dancing, in order to teach us to keep time. This old gentleman stood in need of much patience, but this he had not. He became angry when, during every lesson, he had to play the same *reprise* over and over again; because we could never be ready with our steps when he began playing. He beat time with his foot louder and louder, then he grumbled in a half-suppressed voice to the tune of his violin, and now and then we heard him exclaim, as if to himself, " Devil's children!" We were very much offended at the old man's impoliteness; we dared not complain of it to our parents, but spoke, as usual, to "Bonne Amie," who gave us the prudent advice to do our best to fall into time at once, and to pretend not to hear what the old man was saying when he lost his temper.

I believe it must have been about this time, or when Fredrika was between nine and ten years old, that my parents, one beautiful day in spring, made an excursion with some friends to Skurö, a royal domain famous for its beautiful park. Before dinner, which was ordered at the neighboring hotel, the company took a stroll through some part of the extensive park, the intention being to take a longer walk through it after dinner; but after having sauntered about for some time, Fredrika was missing. We all returned at once to search for her, shouting her name in all directions, but in vain; Fredrika was not to be seen. Unacquainted with the large extent of the park, we did not venture to separate, for fear that any more of our party might be lost. It was, therefore, determined that my mother should return, with the greater part of the company, to the hotel, and from thence send out people to search for the lost one. Only my father, one of his friends, and myself continued to look for her, and to call her by name in another direction, along a path which we had crossed before, but which she perhaps might have followed. We soon came to more cross-roads, and having wandered about a long while, shouting her name, my father was getting fatigued, and was just on the point of returning to the hotel, when suddenly, at the turn of the road, we saw Fredrika walking quietly along. As soon as she espied my father, she ran up to him, exclaiming, —

"Oh, papa, papa, I have seen Pan, the sylvan god!"

"What do you mean by that?" asked my father.

"Why, he stands yonder," replied Fredrika, "playing his flute. I asked a strange gentleman, whom I met, to tell me who it was, and he said it was the wood-god Pan."

But Fredrika's delight at her new acquaintance, the sylvan god, was of very short duration; for now followed reproaches and scoldings for having so thoughtlessly strayed away from the company, who had been searching for her more than a couple of hours. We returned to the hotel; the elder ladies were fatigued and not inclined for any further walk, and we went back to town earlier than we intended doing.

In the spring of 1813 we returned to Årsta. My father had sold the beautiful Nynäs, to my great sorrow and regret. He found it too troublesome to attend to the management of two large estates.

Shortly after our arrival at Årsta, a strange gentleman called upon my parents with an unexpected message. The "Södermanland Regiment" had been ordered to embark on board a transport at Dalarö, to proceed, in company with several other regiments, to Germany, and this gentleman had received orders, I do not know from whom, to request that the officers of the regiment might be quartered at Årsta. My father, of course, willingly gave his consent, and in the following week there was a great deal of stir and bustle at Årsta, ordinarily so quiet. No less than ten officers, and amongst them the commander, General R——, were quartered at the mansion, together with the band, and one thousand men were quartered in the villages and farms belonging to the estate.

We children thought this exceedingly delightful. Every morning and evening the reveille and tattoo were sounded in the spacious court-yard. My father renewed his acquaintance with an early friend, Lieutenant-Colonel H——. They had studied together in Göttingen, and had not met since. This company remained more than three weeks at Årsta. Payment was made to cottagers and peasants for the common men. I remember well that there was also a question of remunerating my father; but this he would not listen to. I remember also General R—— being very much annoyed at not receiving orders to embark his men, and that he went two or three times to Stockholm to inquire how matters stood and push them on; but he always returned vexed, apologizing to my parents for all the trouble which he and his officers involuntarily gave them.

When all these guests were gone, Årsta relapsed again into its usual quiet and silence. We children missed especially the military band, and not hearing the reveille and tattoo, and after that the solemn "chorum," the singing of a psalm or evening hymn.

Twice a week a messenger was sent to town with the produce of the estate, and on his return we received letters and newspapers. My father read these latter aloud after supper. They were full of news from the theatre of war. Most of the European nations rose to grapple with the hitherto invincible Napoleon, who was now retreating after his defeat and enormous losses in Russia. Under the command of the Crown-Prince of Sweden, Bernadotte, in whom the nations saw one of their liberators, a part of the Swedish army had crossed over to Germany.

Then new ideas and feelings were awakened in Fredrika. She wept bitterly for not having been born a man, so that she could have joined her countrymen to fight against the general disturber of peace and oppressor of nations; she wanted to fight for her native country; longed to distinguish herself to win renown and glory. She felt that she would not be wanting in courage, if she could only get over to Germany. There she would disguise herself; perhaps be made page to the Crown-Prince. With her head full of these dreams, and how, to begin with, she was to get to Stockholm, she one day took her little shawl upon her arm, and set out upon the high road to the capital, in the hope that some chance — but of what kind she did not know — might favor her design. She got no farther this time than to the so-called "red gate," a short distance from Årsta. Thence she returned home, unhappy that she had failed in her attempt, and revealed to me in the evening all her plans. I prayed her by all means not to entertain such a silly idea, representing to her that she could do nothing as a warrior; and I spoke of the sorrow which she would cause our parents. But she was not at all convinced that she could not, with the courage which she felt herself to possess, distinguish herself in war; and once again in the summer she set out, trusting that chance this time would be more favorable to her.

She continued her march about a mile. Here she remained standing for nearly half an hour, in the expectation of seeing some family with whom she might be allowed to go to town. Disappointed in this hope, she returned home. "No carriage, not even a cat," had she seen during her walk. A long time did these warlike notions occupy her mind, but at last they gradually died away.

In the large dining-room in my parents' house in town, a luncheon-table was always spread for my father at eleven o'clock. It stood in a corner near the door opening from "Bonne Amie's" room. Upon this table, covered with several delicacies on small dishes, we trespassed on several occasions. We suffered afterwards many pangs of conscience; but this did not prevent us sinning again when the temptation offered. Deeply repentant, as if we had been guilty of some dark crime, we hastened always to confess our sin to " Bonne Amie."

On Sundays we had permission to run about and play in the dining-room. One day Fredrika said to us, " Now we shall play at theatre." We placed some chairs along one side of the room. " Now, Charlotte, Hedda, and Claes must sit upon those chairs and pretend to be asleep, and I shall run across the stage." We did so; but, all remaining silent a good while after we had heard Fredrika run across the stage, we looked up, and exclaimed simultaneously, "Ah, Fredrika!" There was Fredrika standing at the luncheon-table, swallowing as fast as she could what my father had left on the sundry dishes.

Fredrika's childish desire to cut things to pieces in order to examine and experimentalize upon them, had by this time given way to a desire to try practical jokes and harmless tricks; and nobody was so frequently her butt as my brother's tutor, the good Mr. R——. " Bonne Amie" and Mr. R—— used often to play at chess, and fell always to disputing during, as well as after, the game. " Bonne Amie" could not bear to have Mr. R—— capture the pieces which she had exposed, and Mr. R—— remonstrated and tried to prove that the game would never finish unless he captured all the pieces which " Bonne Amie" had endangered; and after the game there were long discussions how he or she might have avoided becoming checkmate. Fredrika availed herself of these opportunities to play her tricks. One day, while Mr. R—— was standing demonstrating before " Bonne Amie," Fredrika took a heavy leaden pincushion, belonging to my mother, stole behind Mr. R——, and dropped it quietly into one of the pockets of his dress-coat. His coat was drawn all on one side, and Mr. R—— looked quite woful, but did not take any notice of it. Fredrika was very much astonished, and fancied that he did not feel the weight of the leaden cushion, which dragged his coat all on one side. She was strengthened in this belief when Mr. R——, bowing as usual, said " Good night; " and when, the following morning at breakfast, he did not mention a word about the cushion, Fredrika got frightened, and imagined that there must have been a hole in Mr. R——'s pocket, and that he had lost my mother's pincushion without observing it, in going up-stairs. She did not know what to do to find out the matter, and at last went up to Mr. R——, asking him if he did not see a pincushion somewhere ? " A pincushion ! " said Mr. R——, with great difficulty trying to keep from laughing. " What pincushion ? " It now came to an explanation between him and Fredrika, who confessed what she had done, wondering that he had not felt the weight of the heavy pincushion in his pocket, saying that there surely must be a hole in it. Mr. R—— went to fetch the cushion, which he returned to Fredrika. Many a time afterwards have we been amused when we remembered this trick of Fredrika's, and her anxiety about the lost cushion.

Another time, amongst the many, when " Bonne Amie " was disputing with Mr. R——, after having finished their game at chess, Fredrika broke the cotton with which she was knitting a stocking, took the ball, and fastened the end of the string with a pin to Mr. R——'s coat. When he began walking about the room, the ball was rolling after him ; but Fredrika could not understand why he kept constantly walking in a circle, and always round her, so that he entangled her feet in the cotton. It was a good while before she became aware that Mr. R—— had observed her trick, and wanted to punish her for it in his good-natured and jovial way.

" Bonne Amie " had promised us that at the age of fifteen we should be allowed to read aloud to her some good novels in the evenings, after we had finished our lessons for the day. In order that we both might share this great pleasure, she let Fredrika read with me, although one year younger than myself; and Fredrika was beyond measure happy, when, on my fifteenth birthday, we began "Les Petits Émigrés," by Madame de Genlis. We were not permitted to read more than half an hour each at a time, and for this hour we longed the whole day. After having gone through "Les Petits Émigrés," we read Miss Burney's interesting and cleverly written novels, "Camilla," "Evelina," and "Cecilia," abounding, however, as I afterwards discovered, in romantic adventures.

How little profitable such reading is for young girls, especially at our age, and so entirely without experience as we were then, soon became manifest by all the fancies and imaginations which we got into our heads about ourselves and what might happen to us. We only longed to escape from our convent-like seclusion at Årsta. We did not at all doubt that, when we came out in the world, we should become the heroines of romance, and, like the heroines in novels, find many admirers, and meet with many adventures of which we had not even dreamt previously. Who could answer for it that even now, before we came out in the world, some extraordinary adventure might not happen at Årsta. During the whole autumn, I was listening every evening in the dusk, to hear a ladder raised against the wall under one of the windows of my room; and, although the escape down the high ladder might be a break-neck affair, yet I felt a kind of foreboding that, like the lovely Indiana in "Camilla," I should be carried off, I did not know by whom, — this I could never guess, — but the hero would perhaps afterwards discover and declare himself.

Fredrika had also forebodings of abductions: either she or myself was to be the object; but neither did she know by whom we were to be carried off; she was sure that it was going to happen in broad daylight, on a Sunday, on our way from church, to which we drove, as usual, accompanied by " Bonne Amie," to attend divine service. Fredrika was, therefore, sitting in the carriage, looking with eager attention, first to the right, then to the left, to see whether any horsemen would be rushing out of the forest, commanding the coachman to stop. When, therefore, Sunday after Sunday, we came back to Årsta without any adventure, Fredrika found herself greatly disappointed.

After having been locked up the following winter, as usual, in Stockholm, Fredrika and I felt a greater desire than ever to walk out and take exercise in the fresh air; but how this was to be managed we were at a loss to understand. We discussed the matter together, and it was determined that we should ask my mother's permission to go out occasionally, at all events twice a week. With a palpitating heart I preferred my request. My mother answered that she did not like it, and that it would not look well for young girls to go out alone in the streets; that if we were in want of exercise, we might stand behind a chair, hold on to the back, and jump. When I came back to Fredrika with this answer, she was in despair, but what was to be done? I proposed that we should begin the jumping that same evening, after we had said "Goodnight" to our parents and come into our room. We did so, and that night I made two hundred jumps behind my chair, resting now and then for a moment; but Fredrika had not performed one hundred before she gave in, began to cry, went to bed and fell asleep, glad in sleep to forget every thing. I continued jumping almost every evening, and persuaded Fredrika now and then to try the same, fancying that it did me a great deal of good, which it also might have done her, being deprived as she was of other exercise, but I could seldom induce her to do so. In one thing, however, we agreed, namely, that no novel writers ever would fall upon the idea of letting their heroines jump behind chairs, by way of taking exercise. They would, no doubt have hit upon a more agreeable manner of gaining their object. Meanwhile I found myself thriving very well under this regime of jumping, and continued it this and the following winter. It had the same effect upon me as two cups of elder tea, and I slept excellently.

At the age of sixteen I was preparing for Confirmation. Fredrika was not considered steady enough to take this step, but she read together with me for the Rev. T. Colliander, curate of Adolphus Fredric's church, a man at that time highly esteemed as a clergyman and teacher. He gave us religious instruction in my parents' house. The following year he prepared Fredrika for Confirmation, and I was always present as a listener. He was a good, sincere, honest Christian, and was often moved to tears while explaining to us the doctrine of the Atonement. The sum total of his teaching was this: that one ought blindly to believe what one could not understand, and try to live according to Christ's divine doctrine.

Fredrika and I had, when children, read an excellent book called "Gumal and Lina," written for children with a view of imparting to them the first ideas of religion, by Caspar Friederich Lossius, deacon of Erfurth, and translated by Broocman. The latter died soon after having finished the first volume of this work, and the two last volumes had not been translated into Swedish. We determined to translate them, and we did so during the time that we prepared for our First Communion. Fredrika took upon herself the second and I the third volume. After two years this work, which had interested us in the highest degree, was finished, and the following Christmas presented by us to our father. This touched him so deeply, that he embraced us both with tears, and the following year he had the work printed and published at his own expense.

I had "come out" a year before Fredrika, and I was allowed to go to balls and suppers, at which latter there was then dancing, which afforded me a great deal of pleasure.' Fredrika made her entrance into the world the following year; but she found less pleasure there than I did; she was not always invited to dance, and therefore soon got tired of these gayeties. But she was, on the other hand, very much interested in the many good plays which my parents were kind enough to let us go to see. All this was new to us, for we had not been to the theatre until we had completed our sixteenth year.

In the winter of 1817 a young gentleman, born and settled in France, was introduced into my parents' house. On my birthday in May he gave me a charade to guess. The significant word, full of mighty moment, had a double meaning. The following morning I found a note lying upon my bed. I opened it and read these lines: —

> "All grandeur renounce, choose virtue and worth,
> So taught the wise men of the ages:
> Then let us while choosing our lot on this earth
> Adopt the advice of the sages.
> For grandeur resembles the foam of Champagne,
> It flies as we gaze on its swelling:
> Blest he who renounces Chateaux en Espagne
> For peace in a northern dwelling."

These verses were in Fredrika's handwriting, but signed "J. P. Mallén," the name of an old man at that time known in Stockholm as a writer of occasional poems.

After our Confirmation, my father wished Fredrika and me to go through a regular training in household duties, and to learn the art of cooking. In the beginning we had each our week, when, under the superintendence of the housekeeper, we had to give out to the cook every thing that was required for the various meals, and to see that nothing was wanting at table. Later in the summer a clever superior cook was engaged from Stockholm, and as we were to learn to prepare the most delicate dishes, we had a feast every day. My father, who was very fond of the luxuries of the table, thought this delightful; and we, especially myself, found it very pleasant to prepare the choicest viands. Many times in my life have I gratefully acknowledged my parents' wise idea, to let us learn thoroughly all that belongs to the management of a house and household. A wife, who has learned all this in her youth, becomes quite independent of her servants' ignorance and will have every thing in her house good, but less expensive than if she had no experience in these matters. For two summers the Stockholm cook stayed with us at Årsta, a couple of months each time.

It was now determined in family council that we should study the art of musical composition and thorough-bass, and that I should learn to sing, as I had a good voice. The Italian language being necessary in singing, we had studied it several years under the guidance of an Italian settled in Stockholm, a Signor Cartoni, who had at last advanced so far in his knowledge of languages, that he could not speak any language correctly. We studied thorough-bass under a very eminent musician, Professor Strurve, formerly a physician, who had given up his practice in order to occupy himself exclusively with music, and now we were to try our skill at composition.

Fredrika wrote a theatrical piece in one act, called "The Poet," and I composed the music to it. When my teacher was going to play the overture, he exclaimed, "What a very difficult piece! it is really such a muddle I shall never be able to play it!" He expressed more satisfaction with my music to a couple of romances, with which I was delighted myself. This masterpiece, "The Poet," was to be performed on my father's birthday, the 2d of April, 1818. Several of my parents' friends and acquaintances were invited by my mother to tea. After tea, the company sat down in the dining-room upon chairs placed in rows; the doors to one of the drawing-rooms, which had been fitted up as a theatre, were thrown open, and I was discovered sitting at the piano playing my exceedingly difficult overture. I broke down at least three times, and long before I had finished, I was ready to burst out crying.

Then came the comedy, which has since unfortunately been lost; but the first verse of one of the airs, written between the leaves of the music-book which I have still in my possession, is as follows : —

> "To woman, issuing from All-Father's hand,
> The fruits of glory were denied; this was her duty:
> The soothing balm of comfort to dispense, to stand
> By grief with sympathy, and grace life by her beauty."

My father, as usual at these little entertainments, was touched and delighted, and patted and thanked us children. He was very fond of music, and since Fredrika and I had now, for our age, become very good performers on the piano, he liked us to play to him every day some of his favorite pieces. This we always did with pleasure. But he now also wished to let other people hear how clever his daughters were, and this did them no good. I shone with the overture to "The Caliph of Bagdad;" Fredrika, with "La Bataille de Fleurus," and we both strove to paint the booming of the cannon, the drums, and the trumpet-clangor in "The Battle of Prague," as powerfully as possible. My father enjoyed the praise which was showered upon us; then we had to produce our landscape-drawings and our flowers in crayon. This had no good influence upon us, least of all upon Fredrika, whose innate desire to be praised, to win renown and glory, was stimulated to such a degree, that she often found herself really unhappy when she thought she had no chance of distinguishing herself. I had not the same desire, but began to be fond of admiration, and to entertain a high opinion of myself, partly on account of the praises which I received, partly on account of the greater tenderness which my father always had shown me, as compared with the other children. Fredrika had an instinctive feeling of independence, which manifested itself more and more as she advanced in years.

This jarred upon my father's temper, and became the cause of many unhappy moments for her.

These exhibitions of our talents were always held in town, for nobody was ever invited out to Årsta.

Although Årsta was situated at a distance of only twenty English miles from the metropolis, our family led there, nevertheless, a very solitary life, totally separated from the outer world. If the milk-carriers had not brought out news of what was going on in the neighboring capital, we might have imagined that we were distant from it hundreds of miles, in some very remote province. My father felt embarrassed when receiving visitors in the country, and would therefore never invite any body to see us while we were there. The Rector and Curate of the parish, with their wives, were the only people who once or twice were invited to dinner; my father seemed then to have performed an arduous duty, and these people were the only ones which we saw during the summer. My father, who in his youth had studied at two universities in Germany and afterwards had travelled a great deal in foreign countries, felt occasionally the want of change and diversion. When, therefore, the life at Årsta became too monotonous, he went to town for one or two days; but it happened frequently that, on his arrival there, he never left his rooms, and returned to Årsta without having spoken to a single human being.

When he came back and had saluted us, he always asked for news; but as never any thing happened at Årsta, we had no news to tell. One day, however, we were more fortunate. It was late in the autumn; a number of bullocks had been let out to be watered at a pond, and when they had approached a spot in the "English Park," a kind of inclosure near the mansion where, at that season, the gates were taken away, every bullock, on crossing that spot, was seized with a dancing fit, so that they began jumping, prancing, and kicking their hind legs in the air. This was something very strange, something wonderful, a real *évène-*

ment at Arsta. My father returned the same evening from town. I must at this time have been fifteen or sixteen years old, because we had now removed into the upper storey, and I had got my mother's distinct permission — a permission not given until we should have reached that age — to eat as much as we liked both at breakfast, dinner, and supper.

We had just finished supper, and went as usual into my father's library, to converse until the clock in the old tower had struck ten. I do not remember how it happened that the four elder children did not follow our parents into the library, but only I, who, when my father was seated on the sofa, and, as usual, asked for news, related to him the wonderful occurrence of the day. My father listened attentively to my recital, wondering what could have been the cause. Then in came one of the other children, relating the same story. My father listened, but said nothing. Then came a third, repeating what the others had told; and when at last Fredrika made her appearance, and began with "Do you know, papa, that the bullocks" — my father interrupted her, saying, "Ah! very well; this is the fourth time I have heard that story, and now there must be an end of it." A general silence ensued, and no one had another word to say until the clock struck ten, when my father said "Good night," and we went to our own rooms.

In the long, dark autumn evenings at Årsta, we all assembled in the "yellow drawing-room." At ten minutes to six the footman entered to lay the cloth for tea, and shortly after came the housekeeper, who was to make and pour out tea. Our party consisted always of my mother and father, our governess and my eldest brother's tutor, Fredrika, Hedda, and myself. When they all had had their tea, with the exception of us three sisters, who were mere lookers-on, the housekeeper — fortunate woman! — disappeared, and we sisters remained sitting, with our work, at a table in one corner of the room; my mother sat down in a corner of a sofa, and my father beside a table in the centre of the room, reading aloud until supper-time at nine o'clock. My father, who was only interested in classical literature, chose in preference historical works, which were rather tiresome for his young daughters to listen to, especially as they were written in German and in English, my father's favorite languages, which he read beautifully, but which we did not then understand well enough to follow when he was reading aloud.

After the first ten minutes, my mother fell asleep, and we were often ready to follow her example. Fredrika yawned till the tears rolled down her cheeks; and if my brother's tutor, the good Mr. R——, had not hit upon several tricks to keep us awake, I do not know how we should have fared. But sometimes we were on the point of being found out; for instance, when we were seized with an irresistible youthful desire to laugh, which fortunately my father did not notice, as we were sitting far away from him. Once, however, while we were nodding, half asleeep, Mr. R—— happened to strike his hand so loudly upon the table that my father looked up and said, "What was that?" "It was — it was" — answered Fredrika, quite frightened, "the table that was going to jump." My father looked displeased, but said nothing more, and continued after a time his reading. In this manner we labored through Schiller's "Thirty Years' War," Gibbon's "Decline and Fall of the Roman Empire," and Robertson's "History of America," the two last in English.

After supper we all went into my father's library to converse until ten o'clock. When we came back to our own room Fredrika often sat down to cry, and, dejected as we were ourselves, neither Hedda nor I could offer her any consolation.

The monotonous, joyless, and inactive life which we led was felt by us all, but especially by Fredrika. One year was exactly like the other. We had certainly occupation; we read, drew, embroidered, played scales, sonatas, and themas with variations, and Fredrika wrote both prose and verse, but she wept often and said that nobody understood her. The relation between my father and Fredrika had certainly become much better than formerly; and when, on his or my mother's birthday, she wrote some little play, which was performed by us children, my father was much amused and pleased; and when it was my mother's birthday that was to be celebrated, he copied out the parts himself.

The monotonous resemblance of one year to the other continued until 1820, when Fredrika and our youngest sister Agatha were ordered by our doctor to drink mineral waters. Inexpressibly happy to be allowed to see a little of the world, I had also permission to be of the party. We went with my mother to a Swedish spa, but so late in the season that most of the mineral-water drinkers had already left on our arrival. We led there a quiet, agreeable life during three weeks' time. The country around was very beautiful, and an amiable old married couple, owners of the spa, and residing on their estate in the neighborhood, did all in their power to make our solitary stay there as pleasant and agreeable as possible. This little trip did us all a great deal of good, especially Fredrika, who really stood in need of getting away from home, which to her appeared more dull than to us.

For a couple of years it had been my father's wish to sell Årsta, and to settle in the south of France. During his many travels in foreign parts, he had not seen any country which pleased him more, and every succeeding year his desire to live in a milder climate became stronger and stronger. As, however, he could not obtain the price for Årsta which he had asked for it, it was determined that the whole family should travel a year, and spend a winter in Marseilles.

In the beginning of August, 1821, we all set out upon

this long journey, in two large travelling landaus, each drawn by four horses. After having, on our way to Ystad, visited some relatives at their estates, we sailed from Ystad to Stralsund, in the mail-packet. Leaving Stralsund, we ploughed our way through the sandy deserts of Pomerania and Lüneburg, occasionally with six large horses harnessed to each carriage, and two postilion smoking-pipes to each set of horses. It was nevertheless with great difficulty that we could get along the bottomless roads. Not until we came to Hanover could we proceed along good, firm *chaussées*. In Darmstadt, Fredrika became ill. She had already, in Frankfort on Main, felt unwell; but it being in the height of the "Messe," — the large annual fair, — and the town being full of travellers, and consequently very noisy, my parents determined to push on to Darmstadt, and remain there in case Fredrika should get worse. She became seriously ill. The most skillful doctor in the town, Baron Wedekind, physician in ordinary to the Grand Duke, was called in. He declared that Fredrika's illness was a bilious fever, not dangerous, but which might be lingering. We remained for three weeks quietly in this pretty little town, with its well-built houses surrounded by their gardens and fine, old, shady lime-trees. The good old Baron Wedekind came to see Fredrika every day; and when at last she got so well that she could go out for a drive, he sent her his own equipage daily. We were staying at an excellent hotel, "Die Traube," on one side of a large square, and our landlord and landlady were very kind and attentive, and did all they could to insure quiet and peace to the invalid foreigner. Only one single night was our rest disturbed. We were all roused out of our sleep by the most horrible noises and shouts. The officers of the garrison had been assembled at the "Traube" for some festival, and they finished off by smashing dishes, plates, glasses, and bottles, and even the tables at which they had had their banquet. Noble exploits for the defenders of their country!

Time passed quietly and pleasantly for us at Darmstadt. My father had the kindness to let Hedda and me frequently go to the pretty little theatre, where the famous Madame Schröder-Devrient was then playing. We read many good books, sometimes taken at a circulating library, sometimes sent by Baron Wedekind; we took long walks with my father in the beautiful environs, and visited occasionally the painting-gallery, where we admired the works of the great masters. But it grieved us very much to see Fredrika for some days really so very ill, and that she could not participate in our pleasure.

During the whole of this time, my father had been in an unusually good temper, and it was therefore with trembling that we looked forward to the day when our journey should be continued. Nothing tries so much the temper as travelling, and my father, who could stoically and submissively bear serious misfortunes, could less than many others bear trifling annoyances, — such as, for instance, when my mother, the six children, and his Swedish servant were not quite ready to start at the appointed hour. There was then a scene as if some great calamity had happened; and, although we all tried to be punctual, it occurred nevertheless, frequently, that, amongst so many as we were, some one got into the carriage a minute or two too late. This and similar trifles became, therefore, a serious drawback to the pleasure which we otherwise might have derived from a journey through a beautiful country. As soon as Fredrika had somewhat regained her strength, we proceeded on our journey, but she being still very weak, we were to make only very short stages the first days, and to begin with, not further than to Heppenheim. Before we arrived there, we saw, in passing the fine park of the castle of Auerbach, the summer residence of the Grand Duke, a horseman coming at full gallop towards our carriages. It was Baron Wedekind, who had promised to see us once more, and who, in order to escape the ducal dinner party at Auerbach, had made the Grand Duke believe that my father had written to him to say that Fredrika was worse. "Go, go, by all means!" was the Grand Duke's answer, and now the good old doctor accompanied us to Heppenheim, to assure himself that we should be well lodged in the hotel which he had recommended to us there, after which, with tears in his eyes, he took leave of us.

Our journey now lay through the wealthy, beautiful Baden to Basle, and thence through Switzerland to Geneva, where the news reached us that the yellow fever had broken out in Marseilles. In order to obtain further information, my father determined to remain for some time on the borders of the Lake of Geneva, at all events until there should not be any danger of infection; but, having received positive news that the disease was gaining ground, and that numbers of foreign families were leaving Marseilles, all thoughts of spending the winter there had to be abandoned. After a short excursion to Lausanne and Vevay, and, after having placed my eldest brother Claes in a boarding-school with a professor in Geneva, we crossed the Jura Alps to Dijon, going thence to Paris, where we were to remain over the winter.

My parents having engaged comfortable apartments in the "Hotel de Bruxelles," Rue Richelieu, — "the same suite," said the landlord, as "vôtre compatriote, Monsieur de Lagerbié (Lagerbjelke), Ministre de Suède," had occupied several years, — we sisters had the benefit of excellent teachers, good and expensive, in music, drawing, painting, and singing. At the larger theatres we had an opportunity of seeing and hearing, at least once or twice a week, the famous artists which appeared there at that time, namely, Talma, Mademoiselle Duchesnoix, Mademoiselle Mars, Mademoiselle Georges, Madame Pasta, Madame Mainville, Fodar, and others. None of them enchanted Fredrika and me so much as Mademoiselle Mars, and at no one's great fame were we so astonished as at Talma's.

We both agreed in thinking that in his tragic parts he was devoid of truth; and that on the contrary he exaggerated; and we could not understand why, the more he made his raised arms tremble, the more the audience applauded. We went also during the winter to some grand balls given by families whose acquaintance my parents had made through my father's bankers. Galleries, museums, and collections of works of art. we visited often; and in the spring we made excursions to Versailles, and other remarkable places in the environs of Paris. We returned to Sweden in the month of June, passing through the Netherlands and Germany, and came back to Stockholm without meeting with any adventures, and soon after we were once more installed at our old Årsta.

In the beginning we were very happy to be at home again, and to enjoy the quiet of the country; but when autumn came, our life resumed its former course. We had now, however, much to speak about, and many reminiscences from our travels to fall back upon, during our evening conversations in the library. This always amused and interested my father; but Fredrika sat generally silent, and very rarely took part in the conversation. To her these compulsory conversations and our inactive life were a real torture; she longed to get into the world; longed for something to labor and work for; longed to distinguish herself in any way. The realization of these longings was the aim of all her desires and endeavors, but how it was to be accomplished was still hidden in darkness. She had projected several plans, but she did not venture to propose them either to my father or my mother; and every thing, therefore, remained as it was. After tea, at six o'clock, my father read now Schiller's "Maid of Orleans," "Don Carlos," and others, and Fredrika seemed to derive new life. While listening to these masterpieces, we were deeply interested and often touched, but Fredrika was at times, as it were, dissolved in tears. She, however, felt herself happy during these readings, until the conversations after supper again froze her feelings.

As in many ancient country mansions in Sweden, there was also an old tradition that the manor-house of Årsta was haunted. One evening while our family was assembled round the tea-table in the yellow drawing-room, the steward came in and told my father that he could not prevail upon any of the men to go up to the attic to fetch down some empty bags which were wanted in the morning, on account of their fear of ghosts. He added, that he knew there stood in the attic a wooden chest, in which were lying a cannon-ball and bloody garments, and that there were hanging two swords, of which one was two-edged, and with which somebody had been beheaded. My father gave the steward orders how to act; but we soon heard that he had not succeeded, and that he had to go himself up to the much-dreaded attic and place the bags outside the door, so that the men could fetch them thence in the morning, when it was daylight. It was believed that the gory clothes lying in the chest had belonged to Admiral Bjelkenstjerna, and that the ball was the identical one with which he had been wounded during the Thirty Years' War. Afterwards, it was ascertained that the clothes had belonged to an Admiral Claes Fleming, who was killed during the war with Denmark, in the reign of Queen Christina, on board his ship in the Sound, by a hostile ball, while he was making his morning toilet, and this ball, it was said, was the one lying in the chest.

On the broad, two-edged sword was engraved, that with it John Fleming had been beheaded at the command of Charles IX. The other sword was without any inscription, but unusually long. The old chest and the two swords were on the following day sent to the Bjelkenstjerna Mausoleum, in the church of Öster Hanninge, where they are now preserved.

After our return from our long journey, my parents hired

a beautiful suite of apartments in the Blasseholm Square, in Stockholm, to which we moved in 1822. With mutual pleasure we saw our near and dear relatives again; but most of our acquaintances looked upon us with rather envious eyes, — scrutinized our fashionable and elegant toilet, and thought that we were giving ourselves grand airs. After all, perhaps, they were not far wrong; we were proud of our talents, and considered ourselves rather distinguished. In those days it was a rare occurrence that a Swedish lady had travelled in foreign countries, — and *we* had been travelling so far and seen so much of the world!

Fredrika, who did not like dancing as much I did, often begged to be allowed to stay at home when we were invited out to balls; therefore, Hedda went instead. Fredrika now began painting portraits in miniature under Professor W——, and it was soon evident that she had great natural talent for catching the likeness, but always beautified, and with wonderful expression. There was a great deal of genius in her manner of painting portraits. Under the sense of the heavy atmosphere in our home, she found a great comfort in her painting, and therefore spent many hours every day at her easel. My father was pleased with Fredrika's beautiful works, and admired them exceedingly. Fredrika had not much of a voice, but she sang duets with me, and the charming "Nocturnes" of Signor Blangini, my singing-master in Paris, for the sake of amusing my father. His temper became every year more gloomy and irritable. His return to Sweden and the cold climate had an unfavorable influence upon his temper and his health.

In the summer of 1824 my mother went to Paris with my sister Agatha, in order to place her in an Orthopedic Institution. She had, unfortunately, of late become very crooked, and in those days there was no remedy in Sweden for this disease. Hedda and Claes accompanied them, in order to assist my mother on the journey. After a fortnight's stay in Paris they returned home, having left Agatha at the above-mentioned excellent institution, where, before their departure, she already felt herself improving under the treatment. Two amiable Parisian ladies, acquaintances of my parents, Madame Holterman and Madame Pictet, promised my mother to take the little, lovable Swede under their maternal care; and these good, excellent ladies fulfilled their promise faithfully during a period of two years.

My father went one day, about the end of September, down into the park at Årsta, and took a bath in the bathhouse built there. This had such a bad effect upon his health that he became seriously ill the following day, and he felt his feet becoming almost paralyzed. Our family physician, the eminent Dr. E——m, was sent for, and he declared that my father must be at once removed to town, in order to have proper attendance. The following day my father was placed in a close carriage, and my mother and I went with him to nurse him. My sisters and brother came to town a fortnight later; and now commenced a time of sickness and severe suffering for my father, which returned every winter, but which he bore with admirable patience without ever once complaining. Only the expression of pain in his face betrayed how much he suffered. The disease, which was gout, having now attacked his body, my father was so kind, so little exacting, so satisfied with every thing, and frequently so cheerful, that we felt convinced that the gout had formerly been in his temper, because my father when ill, and my father when in health, were two very different beings. Probably, also, his more cheerful temper was owing to his altered diet.

It was the wish of my mother, and of us all, to make this time of severe trial as pleasant to my father as possible. When his sufferings were not too severe we read aloud to him a great many accounts of travels, which always interested him; and whenever the gout did not attack his hands, we played chess with him all through the long winter evenings. My father was passionately fond of chess, but he did not like to lose the game; whereas he laughed at us when we were checkmate. This vexed and annoyed Fredrika very much, who disliked exceedingly that my father should laugh and chuckle while capturing those of her pieces which she frequently left unguarded. She could, on such occasions, rarely restrain her tears. This displeased my father, who sent her away, and I had to come and finish the game, which, in most cases, stood very unfavorably for her. Sometimes she had only the king and the queen left, and these I had to move about until I became checkmate. I used to take it very coolly, and was glad, although astonished, that my father could find any pleasure in seeing such a wretched end to the game. Hedda did not know how to play chess; it was therefore Fredrika and I who each alternately had to play with him. Poor Fredrika went with an insurmountable aversion to the chess-table. I determined to manage so that I won one or two games every night, in order that my father should not consider himself too clever; but by some wrong moves I always let him win the last game, for otherwise he lost his temper, and that he should be in a good temper was, after all, the main point. I begged of Fredrika to think of this, and to try to overcome her aversion; but she never could calmly submit.

Not until about midsummer did my father so far recover from his illness that he could be moved out to Årsta, and how delightful this was to us sisters I can hardly express. At the dear old Årsta we again breathed freely.

During the summer, no less than five daughters of peasants belonging to the estate applied to us to be dressed as brides, and to be married at Årsta, in the autumn. Almost every autumn, one or more such weddings were celebrated in our large dining-room, with the ceremonies customary in the district. There was something so old-fashioned, so peculiarly mediæval in the costume of the brides, and in the appearance of the bridal-train, that they are well deserving of a more detailed description.

On the evening before the wedding-day, the bride and her two bridemaids came to the manor-house with the " forming," as it was called. The bride was too grand to carry any thing herself, but the bridemaids carried each a gigantic round pewter dish with wheaten bread, biscuits, tarts, pastry, and a variety of cakes, etc., etc.

This " forming " was intended as a present to the Lord and Lady of the manor, but it was always given to the housekeeper, who distributed it amongst the servants. Then the housekeeper and my mother's waiting-maid took charge of the poor bride, who, before going to bed for the night, had to submit her head to the following treatment, in order that she might look splendid on the wedding-day, namely: her hair was parted across the head from ear to ear; the hair on the back of the head was then braided into eighteen narrow plaits; the hair on the front of the head was cut off in such a manner, that what remained of it was barely long enough to be laid in curl-papers, which were afterwards pinched with curling tongs. The French proverb, " Il faut souffrir pour être belle," was verified here; for the wretched bride was always sleepy, and sat nodding, and got the headache from this troublesome and unusual process, long before she was allowed to retire to her bed. If a word of pity was spoken to her, she always answered, " Oh, I shall get used to it by and by."

Late at night the bride went to bed, and the following morning she had to be up early, in order to be dressed in her bridal costume by one o'clock, when the clergyman, after the close of the morning service, was to come to Årsta to perform the marriage ceremony. After having strengthened her nerves with some wine and other refreshments, the toilet commenced. The eighteen plaits were combed out, so that they fell in curls, like a cascade, down her back; the curl-papers were removed, and the whole of the front hair was dressed so that it stood straight up all round the forehead, which was left free. This head-dress was then powdered and adorned with all kinds of tinsel, pieces of cut and colored glass set in brass, — so-called Falu jewels, — gilt leaves, buds of flowers, the more the better. Behind this high head-dress was laid a small cushion, and upon it was fixed the bridal-crown, made of silver-gilt, and very heavy, which, on the morning of the wedding-day, had solemnly been brought to Årsta from the church by the bridegroom, accompanied by two of his *svenner*, or bridegroom's men. On one side of the crown were then fixed three long ostrich-feathers, standing straight up, one of which was white, one blue, and one red. And now the bride's head was dressed! If the bride was good-looking, which sometimes happened to be the case, she then looked very grand in this costume.

Then the bridal robe was put on. It was one of my mother's cast-off black silk dresses, which had lost its original *fraicheur*, and had now been renovated and trimmed all round the bottom with a broad gold band. The sleeves, which in two divisions reached down to the elbows, were trimmed with very smart black lace, exactly as one sees it in old portraits. A berthe or cape of black lace was fastened to the dress round the neck, and a large bouquet of natural flowers from the greenhouse was fastened in the front of the bride's dress. Two or three chains were hung round her neck, and a gold band encircled her waist by way of sash. But now comes the drollest part of the whole costume. To this sash were tied all the bridegroom's presents, consisting of a black silk neckerchief; one or two cotton ditto; a white handkerchief for the head, embroidered with colored cotton thread; one or two pair of gloves, etc., etc. All these things were hanging straight down her dress, so that the body looked like an itinerant clothes-shop; whereas her head looked as if it had belonged to a queen of the Middle Ages.

The Psalm-book, which was also one of the bridegroom's presents, was held in her left hand, together with a white pocket-handkerchief spread out, and so large that it looked like a towel.

When the bride and the bridemaids at last were ready, the latter dressed in white, with enormous bouquets of artificial flowers, not always of the prettiest, but full of gold tinsel, stuck in their bosoms, they were conducted to the upper storey, in order that the bride might admire herself in the pier-glasses in the large drawing-room, and there she wandered about a good while from one glass to the other, and thought that she was " cruelly grand."

There was a popular belief in our parish that the one, of those who were going to be united for life, who first should catch a glimpse of the other before the ceremony, would be the one who should afterwards obtain the sway in the house. We sisters were of course very anxious that the bride should first catch a glimpse of the bridegroom; but nobody was more anxious about this than Fredrika, and she always stood on the lookout, that she might call the bride when she saw the bridegroom with his train riding up.

This train of bridegroom's men, all on horseback, was most amusing to look at. It was headed by two musicians playing the violin, who had the greatest difficulty in the world to manage their horses, which seemed to be the case more or less with all the equestrians, as the horses dashed hither and thither during their calvacade up to the courtyard. When they were assembled there, and the riders had got off their steeds, and the female part of the assemblage had alighted from their vehicles, and they all had entered the large hall, the bride, who a short time before had gone down into the housekeeper's room with her bridemaids, made her appearance, giving her hand to her future husband, curtseying to him at the same time. Two processions were then formed: a fiddler, scraping his vio-

lin, preceded the male procession, which was headed by
the bridegroom, with a large bouquet of artificial flowers
stuck on his breast, and followed by his groomsmen,
all with smaller bouquets, and by a number of other
people; the other fiddler led the female procession,
which was headed by the bride and her bridemaids.
Each procession walked up a separate flight of stairs to
the upper storey, to the accompaniment of music; and the
fine large hall, with its granite columns and double flight
of stairs, all crowded with people, presented a grand appearance. The crowd then entered the dining-room,
where, as soon as the clergyman arrived, my parents and
we children made our entrance, saluting the company.

After the ceremony, my parents, in going up to the
newly-married couple to congratulate them, gave the
signal to all the rest to do the same, and then began a
bowing and scraping and curtseying that seemed as if it
would never come to an end, and was very amusing to behold. Thereupon my parents sent round wine, cakes, and
sweetmeats, for which the guests returned thanks to us by
innumerable bows and curtseys.

Finally, the whole company marched off and went to the
house of the bride's parents to eat, drink, and dance. The
festivities often lasted for a whole week.

One of the brides who was dressed and married at
Årsta this autumn had a complexion dark as a gypsy.
While dressed in her bridal costume, and looking at herself in the pier-glass in the drawing-room, she said: "I
don't know what can be the reason that I am so red in the
face! Sure I am that I have done every thing to get
white. Every time I was washing linen at home, I
scrubbed myself with soap-lye, and then laid myself down
beside the linen on the bleaching-ground in the sunshine;
and I have done it many times besides; but it has been of
no use." I do not remember whether any of us had the
heart to tell her that she and the linen could not be

bleached by one and the same process; the thing was incurable now.

If the wedding was celebrated on the large islet, Gålön, belonging to Årsta, then the bride and bridegroom, each with their train, arrived in boats decorated with foliage; and when the procession returned, the bride sat in the first boat, with her parents and bridemaids and musicians, heading a long line of boats full of people in holiday dress. On a fine day in autumn, such a procession, with its music on the calm waters, was very imposing and pleasant to behold.

We children were always invited to these weddings, but were never allowed to go. The housekeeper and steward always accompanied the bridal-train, and were, together with the clergyman, the guests of honor at the wedding dinner, which usually lasted three or four hours, after which dancing began, which I believe frequently was rather boisterous, when the bridal-crown was to be danced off, as it was called, and when there was a fight for the bride between the married and the unmarried women, which, of course, was to end in such a way that the married ones triumphantly carried her off.

Another autumn was now at the door. Instead of reading aloud after tea, my father proposed that we should play whist, dummy, or chess, on alternate evenings. After we had continued this for some time, Fredrika became more and more melancholy, especially on those evenings when the chess-board was brought out; for, when Fredrika was check-mate, my father wanted to find out how she could have avoided it, and the pieces were again arranged as they stood before the fatal moves were made.

The same was done in my case, so that on these wretched chess evenings it often happened that the clock in the old tower struck both eleven and twelve before we were allowed to go to bed. The gout was again in my father's *temper*, and Fredrika trembled at the thought of the winter. One day, while we were speaking of our trials, Fredrika said that she could not stand such another winter as the last, and that she had made up her mind to write a letter to our parents, and candidly tell them that she could not bear the life which we led at home, and beg of them not to be displeased if she went into one of the hospitals in Stockholm as a nurse. She would tell them how much she suffered from not being able to do any good, and from leading a useless and unprofitable life. I got alarmed at this determination; begged of her not to be too hasty; to remember what a dreadful storm she would raise; that she would not gain her point; that our parents would never give their consent to her proposal; and that her position, after such a refusal, would become much more painful than before. Besides, our parents would look upon her conduct as ungrateful. They had surely no idea of how painful our home was to us; but, as they had given us a good, careful education, regardless of expense, I was of opinion that there remained nothing else for us to do but patiently to submit to what could not be avoided. Fredrika promised to defer writing the letter, and — it never was written.

Ever since our stay in Paris, where Fredrika had seen those excellent "Sœurs de Charité" wander about early and late to nurse and assist the indigent sick, she had longed for such an occupation in the world. Such an institution did not then exist in Stockholm, and our home was so shut up that she had not liberty to go out when she liked. She therefore saw no chance of coming into the much coveted activity except by entering a hospital.

Meanwhile Fredrika continued devising plans for the future, partly in this direction and partly speculating on coming events, which might afford her an opportunity, by some great sacrifice on her part, of becoming famous and spoken of. We had in the country each our own room; and except those hours of the day when we took our walk, or played billiards with my father, we had liberty to occupy ourselves as we pleased. All this time Fredrika was busy writing both prose and verse, which she often read to me. This was to her a pleasure and a pastime, and helped her to forget and escape many heavy hours.

Little did she suspect then that she was laboring to accomplish what one day was to gain for her the desired renown.

Many of the beautiful poems, of which some have already appeared in print, and others will be found in the present work, were composed during this time, and bear the stamp thereof.

This desire, this thirst after fame, had in later years greatly subsided. Now and then, however, it revived again; but in a journal, in which Fredrika occasionally noted down her thoughts, impressions, and inspirations, we find the following sensible and true observations:—

22d November, 1822.—" Practice is the nurse of virtue. Virtue is a child which decays and dies before it reaches maturity, if we neglect to feed it every day and to cultivate its strength. If we rarely find an opportunity for great deeds and sacrifices, still we have every day an opportunity of practicing patience, submission, self-denial, and many simple virtues, which often are the most difficult to practice for certain minds, because these virtues are in themselves so quiet and unobserved."

24th November.—" Why burns within thee the desire to become famous and renowned? When thou art laid low in thy cold grave, dost thou then hear thy name mentioned on earth?"

27th November.—" Life is a journey! Let this thought penetrate thee: that all the daily petty annoyances which meet thee on thy road are as nothing when compared with the beautiful goal that lies before thee."

28th November.—" Father, thy will be done, and not mine! It is an inexpressible happiness to be able to pray this prayer with a fervent heart. It is the outpouring of love to Eternal Love. Father, O my Father! grant that I may always pray to thee thus, with the same devout, blissful feeling."

How characteristic of Fredrika's rich, loving heart and lively soul are the following lines, written a few days later in the same journal!

"Love, and thou shalt be happy; love all mankind; press the whole world to thy heart. Some one will meet thee with equal love; but even if none should thank thee, should love thee in return, — oh! still I must love mankind, or I should be deeply unhappy."

"What a strange thing is often the heart of a young girl! All thoughts, feelings, imaginations are linked together, are blended with reality, round which they sport like a Will-o'-the-wisp. She suffers, enjoys, weeps, smiles, hopes, despairs at one and the same moment, and all this with her thoughts alone, without the influence of outward circumstances. Her soul resembles a magic lantern. The figures gambol past in pleasing or repulsive forms, rarely leaving a lasting impression behind. And yet every atom of her life is full of feeling; every pulsation is a joy or a pain."

4th December. — " Pray often. Accustom thy thoughts to follow thy glance up to the bright firmament. It will give thee a cheerful and heavenly mind."

10th December. — " Eternity! Immortality! Celestial promises! Who can contemplate you without shedding tears of joy!"

9th February, 1823. — " To have suffered pain does always good afterwards. Early discovery of my twenty years' experience!"

On the 1st of March, the same year, Fredrika wrote in her diary : —

"How stagnant, like a muddy pool, is time to youth dragging on a dull and inactive life."

"I am only twenty-two, and yet I am often tired of the

world, and wish I was taken from it. But then, we do lead a very dull life."

18th March. — " Never marry, Fredrika ! Be firm ; thou wilt bitterly, bitterly repent it if thou allowest the weakness of thy heart to induce thee to such a step. Watch, pray, struggle, and hope ! "

13th April. — " In vain, young, enthusiastic girl, in vain does thy fiery heart beat for all that is great and noble ; in vain thy eye looks forth into a world where every thing appears to thee to be great and noble ; where the temples of honor and virtue, raised amongst rocky heights and precipices, appear to thee so easy of access. Poor young girl ! Soon, very soon, shall thy bold step be arrested by opinion and the etiquette of every-day life ; soon shall thy feelings be damped, thy thoughts be lowered to trifles, enthusiasm die away in thy soul, thy heart become debased ; and soon shalt thou find every thing around thee as weak and wretched as thou art thyself."

On the 9th of July, 1823, Fredrika writes : —

" How is it that almost all old people become more and more egotistical with increase of years ? I shall do all I can to guard against this despicable, low feeling. I will remain unmarried, in order not to attach my heart exclusively to those whom I should have to call mine ; but I shall, for the sake of God and of Eternal Love, love all my fellow-men ; help and comfort all, as far as lies in my power, which ought to be so much easier when no domestic cares weigh upon my mind. That must be a beautiful and happy life ! "

In the summer of 1826, the two years which had been fixed for my sister Agatha's stay at the Orthopedic Institution in Paris had expired. She had perfectly recovered her health, and her deformity had been considerably reduced, but it was considered necessary that she should continue the same treatment another year in order to become perfectly well. This could be done in two ways : either by letting Agatha remain another year in Paris, or by purchasing an orthopedic bed, with the necessary machinery, and bringing the same over to Sweden, so that Agatha might here continue the same cure as long as it was expedient. She had in several letters complained of homesickness, and it was therefore determined that my mother, myself, and my brother Claes should go to Paris to fetch her home. My father, who never looked at expense when the welfare of any of his children was in question, gave a considerable sum of money for the journey and purchase of the requisite machinery.

On our arrival in Paris we found Agatha, who, two years previously, had been brought thither ill in health, suffering, and prematurely old, now well, happy, youthful, and full of life. Such a blessed effect had this treatment had upon her. A little elegant French woman amongst a number of merry and lively companions, her friends in the institution, she spoke now only of her joy at returning to Sweden. My joy at our happy meeting was in some degree embittered by the thought of how Agatha would thrive at home; but I trusted in her innate happy and cheerful temper as long as she remained well.

I took lessons for a fortnight of one of the brothers Milly, superintendents of the institution, in order to be able to continue the orthopedic treatment, and at the expiration of that time we returned to Sweden.

After a few happy days spent at home in our family circle, without restraint or machinery, the treatment prescribed for Agatha was again commenced. But the orthopedic bed was found to be so long that it was impossible to find a suitable place for it in our rooms in town. It was therefore decided in the autumn, when our family moved to town, that Agatha should remain over the winter at Årsta. I ought also to have remained there to nurse Agatha, according to the method which I had studied in Paris; but my father would not hear it mentioned that I should not go to town with him.

Nobody was more anxious to remain in the country than Fredrika, partly for the sake of tending Agatha, and partly to avoid the life in town, so painful to her. But this had great difficulties — was almost impossible. Fredrika did not lack good-will to attempt even the impossible, but she wanted physical strength for some of the gymnastic movements, which Agatha had to exercise several times every day, and attentiveness to observe carefully that all the various pieces of machinery belonging to the bed came in due connection with each other when the patient laid down upon it, and this was of the utmost importance. Nobody dared to believe that Fredrika would be able to attend to all this, and our parents therefore made up their minds that Hedda should remain at Årsta with Agatha, and that I should initiate her in every thing that I had learned with regard to the prescribed treatment.

Nothing, of course, was mentioned to Fredrika about any doubt of her being able to understand how to attend upon Agatha, — this would have grieved her deeply, — but only the physical strength, required for the daily gymnastic movements, was put in question; and our good Hedda was the strongest of us all.

Fredrika was much grieved when she heard what had been decided. I spoke to my mother, and begged of her to arrange so that Fredrika also could remain at Årsta over the winter. I spoke also to my father about it. He gave me his hand, saying with emotion, " If I get ill, as usual, you alone will have to nurse me." I spoke of my strength, of my good health, and of Fredrika's ardent wish to be allowed to remain over the winter at Årsta. At last my father gave his consent, and, full of joy, I hastened to bring Fredrika this good news. Permission was given to her and Hedda to assist each other in nursing Agatha.

My mother had the kindness to arrange with an old French lady, Madame Laval, who had been *lectrice* to the Queen Dowager Sophia Magdalena, to come out to Årsta as a *chaperone* for my sisters.

We moved to town. Our family, formerly so numerous when we went to Stockholm for the winter, consisted now of only my father, my mother, and myself. My brothers were absent. Claes was staying with the judge of a district, in order to become in time a judge himself. August was a student at the University of Upsala.

I determined courageously to go through this winter alone, pleased that my sisters were happy and comfortable together; but my strength began to fail. My father sickened already early in the autumn. In the beginning, I and an old faithful servant watched over him alternately every other night. Afterwards I read aloud to him for days together, and often until late at night; and I became at last so weak and worn that Dr. E—— had to tell my parents that it would never do in the long run for me to be shut up in my father's sick-room, but that one of my sisters ought to come to town to assist me in reading aloud, and "mount guard," as he expressed himself.

My father, who had not noticed any change in me, became alarmed, and wanted me to go out to Årsta on the following day; but it was necessary to prepare my sisters for this change, and I remained, therefore, a few days longer in town.

Fredrika had written several times, both to my mother and to me, offering to come to town to assist in nursing my father; but when we asked him which of the sisters he wished to come, he answered, most decidedly, "Hedda."

On a bright, sunny winter's day, toward the end of January, I was seated in my grandmother's little covered sledge, on my way to Årsta, calm, but very depressed. On my arrival in the afternoon I was received with open arms by my three good sisters, who, wrapped up in furs, met me in the court-yard to bid me "welcome." We went up-stairs together, and entered the dining-room, in the centre of which stood a richly laden coffee-table, and a cheerful fire was burning and crackling in the stove. Excited and weak as I was then, I could do nothing but cry in the beginning; but, reproaching myself for this weakness, and fearing that I should disturb my sisters' innocent happiness, I soon plucked up courage, sat down with them at the cosy coffee-table, and before night we had many a hearty laugh together; I forget now at what innocent ideas, words, and remarks. Only one little incident do I remember. In the numerous accounts of travels that I read to my father during the winter, when I occasionally stumbled upon words or sentences which were not exactly fit to be read aloud, I fell upon the idea of saying, " Well, here comes some Latin." Often, when I was sitting up very late reading, and thought that my father had fallen asleep, I stopped, when he suddenly looked up and said, "Is there now Latin again?" He never found out what kind of Latin the book contained.

Our good, kind Hedda was not pleased to leave Årsta, but she made no complaint; she was glad that I could have some rest; and on the following day we wrapped her well up in furs, and she set out for Stockholm.

I resumed my office of nurse to Agatha, and we lived a quiet, cheerful, and cosy life at old Årsta. Agatha, with her French vivacity, merry as a little bird, singing French songs and romances, was happy to feel herself well, and lived in the hope of perfect recovery. Fredrika, delighted at the liberty which she enjoyed in the country, and feeling herself independent of the whole world, read and wrote a great deal, and wandered about alone in glen and forest. She had also begun to practice medicine; made up drugs of her own composition, and made several successful cures. She had a peculiar luck in prescribing medicines which there was reason to suspect would do her patients more harm than good.

An old peasant woman, living some four or five English miles from Årsta, came one day and begged Fredrika to give her some remedy for her eyes, in which she had for some time felt a severe pricking, while she had observed that her eye-sight had become weaker and weaker. Fredrika took her down into the so-called "Dispensary," and gave her a phial, with directions to put every day two or three drops of the contents into her eyes. A couple of hours afterwards another patient came and wanted some drops for toothache; but when Fredrika was going to give her some tincture of cloves for the teeth, she observed that it was this which she had given to the peasant woman for the eyes. Fredrika became alarmed at her mistake, and came to tell me of it; I wanted her to send a message at once to the woman with orders not to use the powerful tincture which had been given to her; but Fredrika said it would be of no use, because, at the distance where the woman lived, our messenger could not possibly reach her until after she had used the tincture twice, and if any harm came of it, it could not now be prevented. I was astonished at seeing Fredrika, always so anxious to render assistance to others, take her mistake and the possibility of some misfortune arising out of it so coolly; but I was still more astonished when, about a month afterwards, while I was again staying with my father in town, I received a letter from Fredrika informing me that the tooth tincture had perfectly cured the diseased eyes, and that the good peasant woman had come on the previous day to Årsta and asked Fredrika for some more of the "blessed drops" which had done her eyes so much good.

I had scarcely been a fortnight at Årsta, when my mother wrote to me to say that my father wished me to return to town, provided I had had sufficient rest; and the following day, when Hedda came back to the country, I went to town. At midsummer we were all again assembled at Årsta.

In the beginning of November, 1827, my cousin and most intimate friend became a widow, after only two years' wedlock, with the hope of soon becoming a mother. Convinced that I was willing to come to her at any moment, she wrote to me, asking at the same time, in a touching letter to my parents, permission for me to spend the following winter with her.

In the beginning my father thought this impossible, and that I could not be spared from home; but after turning the matter over in his mind a few days, being very fond of his niece, — she being a daughter of the sister whom he had loved so much, — and deeply sympathizing with her grief and her wish to have a friend staying with her, he gave his consent at last.

Preparations were at once made for my departure. It gave me great pain to part from my sisters, especially Fredrika. We had hitherto faithfully shared joys and sorrows together, and we promised to write frequently to each other. We kept our word, and the mail had to carry, at least once a week, a heavy letter from the one to the other. These letters from Fredrika, or extracts from them, are now laid before the public, together with the verses and beautiful pieces of poetical prose writings which she composed during this time, and sent to me.

In company with a relation and friend, General H——, I went about the middle of December to his estate in Småland, where, a few days before Christmas, I had the happiness of embracing my two cousins, — his wife and my sorrowing friend, the Countess W——, who had arrived there a short time previously. After the Christmas holidays, spent in quiet and sisterly confidence, we both set out for her home in C——a.

Fully determined not to make any new acquaintances, or go into society, I wished to live only for my friend, and endeavor to make her life as happy and as comfortable as possible. We tried to arrange our mode of living in the most agreeable way. The greater part of the day one of us read aloud to the other the works of good authors. Now and then, gloomy forebodings cast for a moment their shadows over our happiness; but they were entirely dispelled when, towards the close of February, a fine, strong boy was born.

Delighted as she was at the birth of her child, my friend yet suffered deeply at the thought of her departed husband, who on this occasion, to which he had looked forward with so much longing, would have been so happy.

After a lengthened stay of about two years with my friend at her beautiful estates, I——hus and T——ö, I returned home, in compliance with my father's wish, in the autumn of 1829. I was very much touched at his evident delight to have me back again, and I was happy to find Fredrika more calm and cheerful than formerly. Only a short time were we now allowed to enjoy undisturbed our quiet, sisterly life at Årsta. My father was very unexpectedly visited by a slight attack of apoplexy, and hurried preparations for moving to town were therefore made at once.

My father continued to suffer more or less during the whole of the winter, and he bore his heavy sufferings, as usual, with wonderful patience and fortitude.

Fredrika, Hedda, and I watched over and nursed him, and read aloud to him when he had strength enough to listen to us, while my mother, as much as lay in her power, devoted her attentions to him.

My mother had, from the very beginning of this his last illness, taken upon herself the superintendence of the Årsta property, and the management of the other affairs of the family. In order that my father, whose strength was evidently beginning to fail, should be near his doctor, it was determined that we should not go to Årsta in the ensuing summer; instead of which a summer residence — Lilla Ingemarshof, near Stockholm — was taken, to which we went about midsummer. There my father seemed in some measure to recover strength, and he enjoyed indescribably much the pleasure of sitting out in the sunshine during a few warm, splendid days; but he soon got worse again, and on the 23d of July he expired tranquilly, surrounded by his wife, his children, and a near relative, dear to us all.

Soon after this we went out to Årsta, whither my father's body was taken; he was buried in our family vault in Öster-Hanninge church-yard, under the shade of four beautiful lime-trees, where the remains of his daughter, the pretty, charming little Sophie, who died at the age of fourteen, had previously been deposited.

My parents had given their consent to my betrothal with ——; the wedding was to be celebrated in November, after which I was to go to my new home in Christianstad. My good sisters, and not the least Fredrika, were indefatigable in assisting me to provide every thing requisite on such occasions; and on the 7th of November, the day fixed for the wedding, only our nearest relatives and my father's old friend, Bishop Franzén, who was to perform the ceremony, were invited.

Fredrika, so sympathizing in every thing that concerned me, saw in this marriage a store of only joy and happiness for me, and augured, in a prophetic spirit, that it would be one of the few really happy unions on earth.

Shortly after the wedding, my husband and I left Arsta. and, as soon as I had arrived in Christianstad, a very animated correspondence was again opened with Fredrika.

In the summer of the following year, 1831, I had the happiness of embracing Fredrika in my own home. She came to stay with us at least a twelvemonth, to read, study, and write in quietness. Previous to my arrival in Scania,[1] she was already known there and loved as the authoress of "Sketches of Every-day Life," since, at the close of the preceding year, her former *anonyme* had been unveiled. The highest, most intellectual, and elegant society of Christianstad longed to make her acquaintance.

[1] The southernmost province of Sweden, in which the town of Christianstad is situated.

Fredrika had determined not to mix in society or accept any invitations, but to live in retirement at home, and develop herself for what she now considered to be her mission and her vocation, namely, to become an authoress; and, enriched by experience of the world, to devote in a double measure her talents to the comfort and succor of the suffering and the unhappy.

Fredrika found and felt that she required to learn much, and that she stood in need of a firm religious faith, which she had not. The contradictions which she saw in the Bible and in the world had long shaken her faith, and raised doubts in her soul to such a degree that, at times, with her reflecting and searching mind, they seemed to darken her whole life.

The teacher or guide whom Fredrika had so much yearned after, she found in Christianstad. The head-master of the high school there, the Rev. Pehr Böklin, was the man who, by his philosophical education, his clear mind, his profound, truly Christian faith, imparted that faith to Fredrika, and thus gave her peace of mind and strength to proceed on that path in life which she had determined to follow.

Elaborate and elegant biographies may be written, but not often do we through them become intimately acquainted with the inmost mind of the person described therein. Fredrika showed me one day a letter from her teacher and friend, and from it I have copied the following passage:—

"Your mission is a beautiful one, Miss Bremer! Your mission is the noblest in the world. Regardless of our own cares and sorrows in life, to walk with heavenly comfort through earth's cells, so full of agony, is the lot of an angel. May God's finger appear to you and show you the right way! As a brother I will stand by your side, and, praying and meditating, I will impart to you every ray of light that may be vouchsafed to me!"

How clearly, from these simple words, do we not perceive the kind of spirit which lived in and animated the pupil as well as the teacher!

In our house, Fredrika made the acquaintance of many amiable, intelligent, and pleasant persons. They tried to prevail upon her to go out in the little world of Christianstad, that is to say, " La crême de la société " there, but all in vain. Fredrika remained true to her determination to live isolated in order to educate herself for the aim in life which she had in view, nor was she tempted to recommence a social life which had never been to her taste. At home in our house, she liked, however, to meet with people, and she moved with ease and cheerfulness in the little circle which frequently met there. She was liked by all. One lady in this circle formed a passionate friendship for Fredrika. She was talented, witty, handsome, musical, but passionate, frivolous, and exceedingly worldly minded. How a woman with such a character could feel such a violent friendship for Fredrika, who was now so seriously minded and so free from vanity, I could not understand, and it made me a little uneasy. In the beginning, Fredrika felt averse to a more intimate acquaintance with her, and was rather embarrassed by her long, daily visits. Sometimes she came twice in the course of the day, which interfered with Fredrika's studies and work; but soon Fredrika began to return her friendship with equal warmth. I was aware that this lady could not exercise any good influence over Fredrika, but she hoped to be able to exercise a good influence over her. "Nina" became, although somewhat later, the visible result of this acquaintance, — "Nina," which contains so many poetically beautiful sketches, but which does not carry the same impress of purity as all Fredrika's previous charming works.

Early in the summer of 1832 we had a very unexpected visit from my youngest brother August, who had felt unwell for some time, and, by the advice of his physician, was now going to consult the famous Surgeon Gräfe in

Berlin. I had the pleasure of having this much loved brother, the Cornet in "The H—— Family," staying with us for a few days, after which he continued his journey to Berlin, when Fredrika, my husband, and I went to Stockholm, and thence to Årsta.

After a visit of a couple of months, my husband and I were again on our way to Christianstad, but Fredrika remained with my mother, with whom she was to stay until the autumn, when she would come back to us.

Some time after our return home I received a letter informing me that my brother August had become much worse. He expressed an earnest wish that my mother and sisters should spend the winter in Berlin. After the receipt of a second letter from August, in which he said that he was getting worse and worse, my mother determined that she and my three sisters should fulfill his wish, and on their way to Berlin they paid us a visit. I was not allowed to have these dear guests more than two days in my house; they were in a hurry, and I hoped only that they might soon reach my brother.

Shortly after their arrival in Berlin, I received a letter from Fredrika, telling me that my dear brother had ended his days, and that he had died without suspecting that his end was so near. He had for some time before suffered severe pain. Fredrika adds:—

"Pure was his life, warm his heart, and patiently he suffered. He yearned for light and freedom, and he has found both." "Blessed are the pure in heart, for they shall see God."

On the 21st of September, Fredrika wrote from Berlin:—

"Dear Sister,— Under acacias 'im neuen Kirchhoff' our August is now sleeping. On Wednesday morning, between seven and eight, we sisters and August's friend Caspar W——, who has faithfully watched at his bedside, followed him to his last resting-place. Theremin held a funeral oration at the grave.

"It was a beautiful and solemn scene. The morning was so splendid, the sun shone so brightly, the breeze was so fresh and invigorating, that every thing spoke to us more of resurrection than of death. The people who had assembled round the grave showed deep sympathy, and we . . .

"I did not feel it so heavily. Ah! how I longed to have been with August!

"On the plain monument, which will be raised over him, is to be engraved: 'August Bremer, his mother's and sisters' darling. Born, . . . Died, . . .'

"I cannot find words to describe to you our Ambassador's (Braudel) kindness and care of August during his illness.

"More when we meet again! On the 28th we shall probably be in Ystad, and on the 7th of October we shall be with you."

A few days later Fredrika writes: —

"We are all now more composed. This morning we have been to plant some beautiful acacias upon the grave. The cemetery is out of town, and in the style of Père la Chaise, near Paris, full of fine trees and flowers. We leave on Monday. In Ystad we shall have to undergo a long and wearisome quarantine."

On the appointed day my dear relatives arrived in Christianstad. They remained, however, only a few days, it being late in the season, and my mother anxious to be at home before the cold weather set in.

During these days there was a table in our drawing-room always covered with the choicest fruit, — pine-apples, grapes, peaches, apricots, plums, pears, and transparent Astrachan apples, — presents from my good friends and acquaintances, who daily, from their splendid greenhouses and gardens on their estates in the neighborhood, sent me these fruits to offer to my mother and sisters. Such magnificent grapes, in large bunches, as those which I got from Å——p, I have scarcely seen even in the south of Europe. They were sent to me by the amiable Countess W——, formerly Lady F——, daughter of the former owner of Årsta. I always gratefully remember this graceful kindness.

My mother and my two youngest sisters left for Stockholm, but Fredrika remained with us.

Much as I loved to see Fredrika in our house, I yet dreaded the winter, when her friend would return to Christianstad from her estate in another province. But matters were changed. Her friend came back, but seized with a mortal illness, and now Fredrika became her guiding, ministering angel, pointing out to her the road to heaven, to which Fredrika wished to lead all.

In the spring, Fredrika's friend longed to go into the country, and in an almost dying state she was carried out to her beautiful country-seat, distant some miles from Christianstad. Fredrika wished to join her, and I accompanied her thither. Fredrika remained with her friend until about the middle of summer, when she returned to us, deeply affected and mourning her whose eyes she had closed. At her death-bed Fredrika gained a new friend, the Countess S——, a near relative and friend of the departed. Countess S—— invited Fredrika to spend a year with her at her estate, Tomb, in Norway, provided she was not afraid of the complete seclusion from the world in which she lived there.

Fredrika accepted this offer as one of the most desirable which could be made to her. In her then melancholy state of mind, she only longed to get away from people and from society, "the farther away the better," as she said when, in August, 1833, we took leave of each other. I felt happy at seeing her under the protection of the good Countess S——. She remained two years at Tomb. The quiet and perfect retirement which Fredrika enjoyed there was to her a real "elixir of life," as she expressed herself in one of her letters to me. What added to her happiness was, that she was allowed to arrange her mode of life exactly as she pleased; was at liberty to remain in her room those days when she did not wish to see any body; but always was welcome at any moment when she wished to come down to the Countess S——. Generally, Fredrika spent the whole of the forenoon in her own room, reading and writing, and came into the drawing-room in the evening, when the day usually closed with a game at chess, of which the Countess was passionately fond, and of which Fredrika was now no longer afraid. Fredrika paid a visit of a couple of months to Årsta in 1835, but returned in the autumn to Tomb, where she spent the winters of 1836, 1837, 1838, and 1839, visiting in the summer baths and spas, either with the Countess S—— or with my mother and Agatha. When my mother, in the autumn of 1841, went to Nizza with Agatha, in the hope that the milder climate of the south might strengthen Agatha's weak health, Fredrika remained quite alone at Årsta, and enjoyed then her solitude and her perfect freedom. In June, the following year, my mother and Agatha returned to her from Nizza.

While, in 1844, I was using the cold-water cure at Söderköping, I saw again the Countess S——, suffering and very sickly; she was also going to try this cure, "invented for witches," as she called it. We were together almost daily in the intervals between the five baths which we each had to take every day, and Fredrika was frequently the subject of our conversation. "Sincerely as I love Fredrika," the Countess said to me one day, " still I never liked her whim to enter the hospital at Christiana as a nurse. Every year, when Fredrika was staying with me, she wanted to realize this fancy, and it never was so near being realized as in 1835. The day had already been fixed for our journey to Christiana, to install Fredrika in the hospital. My arguments, aided by an expression used by me about the hospital — calling it her Hermitage — caused her to weigh the matter over in her mind once more. She herself proposed immediately to postpone our journey; the plan was given up altogether; we did not again mention it, and glad I was that Fredrika never again alluded to the subject."

Fredrika stayed with this friend and excellent woman again the following year, 1845, and, for the last time, to watch at her sick-bed and close her eyes.

After her return from Norway, Fredrika remained some time at home with my mother. She did not feel happy; she longed for a change in her position in life, and she now began making plans for her voyage to America. She did not, however, communicate these plans either to my mother or to Agatha, fearing that they would meet with strenuous opposition.

Already, before Fredrika had been spoken of and had a name as an authoress, — that is to say, before she had completed her thirtieth year, — she had had three different offers of marriage; but she did not wish to marry.

One of the three persons who more than once tried to persuade her to alter her resolution, was an amiable young man, of good family, for whom Fredrika, in her earliest youth, had felt a kind of childish love; but she would not let herself be persuaded, believing that she was not made for the married state, and that, if ever she were to try the experiment, she would bitterly repent it, find herself unhappy, and lose her dearly loved independence. Once only she hesitated; but it was for one moment only, when an amiable, good, and original elderly gentleman hoped to find in his union with her a compensation for the domestic happiness which he had lost through the death of a beloved wife, and who saw in Fredrika the only one capable of being a comfort and happiness to him during the remainder of his days. After her thirtieth year, and when she had already gained fame, she had several offers; but she remained true to her determination to live *ena* (single), — a good expression, which she had learnt in Norway.

My husband's appointment to another post was the cause of our removal to Stockholm about the latter part of 1847. This made Fredrika, the following year, consider the time propitious for announcing her plans for travelling. She thought that she might now set out, easy in her mind, knowing that my husband and myself would be near my mother and Agatha. We all certainly represented to her the risk of the long voyage, which Fredrika intended to undertake quite alone; but she would not listen to our arguments. Agatha cried and was in despair at these plans. In order to comfort her, Fredrika promised to write to her all her letters from America. I do not deny that it appeared to me really awful, that Fredrika, this delicate little creature, should start quite alone on such a voyage, and I did not understand how she could have the courage to do it; but she never wanted courage; and I remembered her wish, when she was a child, to enter the army and join the Swedish troops in Germany. The only consolatory thought for us at home was, that immediately on Fredrika's arrival in America, she would be met and received by friends, who, although personally unknown to her, had, after reading her works, invited her in the most amiable manner to be a guest in their homes in New York.

In August, 1848, Fredrika left home, paying first a visit to her old friend and teacher, the Rev. P. Böklin, in Scania. The autumn and following winter she spent in Copenhagen, and after several trips to the Danish islands during the ensuing summer, she travelled to New York by way of London.

I shall pause here a few moments in my narrative, in order to give some account of Fredrika's first appearance as an authoress.

It was during the year 1828 that, for the first time, the thought arose in Fredrika's mind of publishing the best of all that she had written the previous years, in order thereby to procure the means of satisfying the dearest wish of her kind heart, namely, to assist the poor. She had hitherto written to give expression to her feelings, and to retain the images of her ever-active fantasy, and for this intended work she now wrote " Axel and Anna ; or, Correspondence between two Stories," and " Letters on the Supper-parties in Stockholm."

Uncertain whether she would succeed, and uncertain, too, whether our parents would allow her to appear publicly as an authoress, Fredrika determined to send her manuscript to Upsala with my brother August, when he went to the University in the autumn of that year.

He found a willing publisher for her little work in Mr. Palmblad, the printer. He was, however, so little certain how far the enterprise might succeed, that he considered that the edition ought not to exceed three hundred volumes, and the price of the copyright was therefore low in proportion, although sufficient to make Fredrika happy and satisfied. The book was published before the end of the year, under the title of " Sketches of Every-day Life," without the name of the author, of which, also, Mr. Palmblad was left in ignorance. It gained the approval of the public and the praises of the reviewers, although not unmixed with a few friendly remarks. In one of the reviews, it was supposed that " a lady, a young lady," was the authoress, and the critic hoped that when her talent had become more matured he might have occasion to give her works more unlimited praise. On a copy of this review Fredrika has written, " Yes, dear critic ; that rests in the hands of God."

This success encouraged Fredrika to proceed on the path which she had chosen as an authoress, and to try to write a novel. She occupied herself with this during the summer of 1829, and the result of this attempt was the first part of " The H—— Family," which, together with some other minor pieces, she had designed for the second volume of the "Sketches." For the publication thereof she caused negotiations to be opened — I do not know for what reason — with a publisher in Stockholm, to whom the manuscript was sent for perusal. He declined the proposal, — so uncertain were people at that time about the value of Fredrika's works. But through the instrumentality of the former publisher, Mr. Palmblad, the second volume was printed and published in 1830. The great applause with which it was received, the sensation which it created, surpassed every thing which Fredrika thought she could have expected. In a newspaper review, Swedish literature was congratulated on the acquisition of such a talent as that of the authoress.

Fredrika's authorship had, from the very beginning, been kept a secret between her and her sisters. She did not wish to reveal it to our parents until she knew whether she would succeed. But now she thought that the time had come to mention it to my mother. Meanwhile the book had become the subject of general conversation in all circles of society in Stockholm. When one day Franzén, while paying us a visit, spoke of it in a highly flattering manner, expressing an ardent wish to raise the veil behind which the authoress concealed herself, my mother and Fredrika thought that, out of consideration for this old friend of the family, the secret ought to be confided to him. Shortly after this, the Swedish Academy awarded its lesser gold medal to Fredrika, as a token of its esteem and approbation. Thus the hitherto preserved secret of the authorship was revealed.

The success which also the third volume of these "Sketches" met with seemed to point out the road on which Fredrika had to find the realization of her mission in life. She obeyed this call, by laboring diligently as an authoress, at shorter or longer intervals, until the end of her life. Most of her works were translated into foreign languages, were read with avidity, and made her name known, loved, and respected abroad.

The fame which they attained called forth, in her native country, a new public distinction. On the anniversary of the Swedish Academy, on the 20th of December, 1844, the president, after having announced which of the writings, handed in during the year for competition, had been rewarded with a prize, said: —

"The academy being of opinion that it would act in accordance with the prescribed rules in following attentively the events in Swedish literature, even beyond the arena which it has opened for competition, has more than once had the satisfaction, in acknowledging distinguished merit, of uniting with the public in paying homage to such merit.

"It is now thirteen years since the academy awarded a prize to a young genius, whose first essays gave signs of a talent of uncommon order, in a branch of literature for which we hitherto have been without a model. The rare union of the qualities of the heart and of the mind, of beauty in delineation and purity of thought which breathe through the pictures of domestic life, beginning with 'Sketches of Every-day Life,' and continued in a series of charming paintings of the interior of social life, often hidden from the eyes of the public, had drawn the attention not only of Sweden, but also of Europe, to the authoress. The Swedish Academy has requested and obtained the sanction of its illustrious patron [1] to award to the authoress, Miss Fredrika Bremer, its large medal in gold, with the motto, '*Genius and Taste*,' not as a reward, for this can-

---

[1] King Gustavus III. founded, on the 20th of March, 1786, an academy, which, under the name of "The Swedish Academy," and with the motto "Genius and Taste," was to consist of eighteen members, whose object it would be to labor for the improvement of the Swedish language, to encourage emulation in eloquence and poetry, and sing the praises of the great men who had either ruled or served or fought for their native country. With the sanction of the king, as patron of the academy, the academy is empowered to distinguish with the large and small medal in gold Swedish authors for meritorious writings, even when such works have not been sent in for the purpose of contending for the annual prizes.

not come in question, but as an acknowledgment of a merit which, according to the words of the founder, 'has raised the fame of Swedish literature in foreign countries.'"

When Fredrika, in 1861, had closed, under the title of "Life in the Old World," the narrative of her travels in Palestine, Greece, and other countries, she does not appear to have been occupied with any larger work. The imperfect outlines of such works, found amongst her papers, which she has left behind, bear the stamp of belonging to a previous period. But her pen was not allowed to have perfect rest. She contributed, together with some other ladies, to the publication of "Writings for Children,"[1] and at Christmas, 1865, the first part of "A Little Pilgrimage" appeared in print. Her intention was, in this little narrative, to make an exposition of the most essential and highest doctrine of the Christian religion, in a manner simple and plain enough to be understood even by children, which *essential* was intended to be shown more clearly in a subsequent number. But, in order to be able to do her best, she considered that she ought first to read again Olshausen's "Commentaries on the New Testament," and Neander's "Leben Jesu." In reference to the latter, she said, in a letter to my husband, that although one might differ in much from the opinions of Neander, still it was impossible not to love his love of truth, the candor with which he had expressed his thoughts, and to learn much from his profoundness and honest research. These studies, and the continuation of the little narrative, were interrupted by Fredrika's death, which took place soon after.

I resume here the thread of my narrative. When Fredrika returned to her native country from America, in the autumn of 1851, she was met by mournful tidings. Our sister Agatha, whose health had long been weak and

---

[1] As a specimen of Fredrika's talent in this kind of literature, I subjoin two tales, *The Ugly Hand and the Beautiful Hand*, and *Christmas Eve and Christmas Matins.*

failing, had, some time previous to Fredrika's return, fallen into a state of hectic decline. Calmly, and apparently without pain, she departed this life. In order that Fredrika should not return to her own home unprepared for this painful loss, and not find Agatha any more there, my mother and I wished to inform her of this sad event. We knew that she was on her way home, but we did not know which route she intended to take. In this uncertainty, letters were despatched to her both to Dalarö and to Gothenburg. The former she received on her arrival in Sweden, and her return to Stockholm and her home was any thing but joyful.

After a few days' rest, Fredrika resumed her old habits and occupations. The forenoons were devoted to reading and writing. During these moments no one was allowed to enter the room, and she received no visitors until one o'clock, when she usually went out to breathe a little fresh air, or to visit some friend. Fredrika was allowed to manage and act as it best suited her convenience, and she therefore now led an independent life at home.

Fredrika had during her career as an authoress, partly in consequence of her own experience in youth and partly from what she had witnessed in the world, made it the aim of her life to labor in the cause of Woman, oppressed, according to her notions; and on her return from America. 't became her favorite idea to work for the entire emancipation of the Swedish woman and her deliverance from the traditional restrictions in her social position, which Fredrika considered to be both injurious and opposed to her natural rights. She wished, therefore, that women should, like men, and together with them, be allowed to study in the elementary schools and at the academies, in order to gain an opportunity of obtaining employments and situations suitable for them, in the service of the state. According to Fredrika's ideas it was a crying injustice to deny women, even those with exceedingly brilliant intellect and great talents, such opportunities. She said she was firmly convinced that they could acquire all kinds of knowledge just as well as men; that they ought to stand on the same level with them, and that they ought to prepare themselves in the public schools and universities to become lecturers, professors, judges, physicians, and functionaries in the service of the state. She predicted that if women were permitted, like men, to acquire knowledge and skill, they would, when their capacity and indispensableness in the labor of society had become more generally acknowledged, be found fit for a variety of occupations, which partly already now existed, and partly would be required in future under a more energetic development of society; and she maintained that Woman ought to have the same right to benefit her native country with her talents as Man.

We had many conversations on this subject before "Hertha" was written. I fully coincided with Fredrika's opinion, that a great injustice was contained in our legislation not to allow Swedish women, as women in other countries, to attain their majority when they arrived at a certain age,—for instance, when they had reached their twenty-fifth year; and consequently to dispose of their future life and their property; but in other respects our opinions differed. I could not see that the management of the business of the state was the province of women, and I begged Fredrika to consider well before writing, even with the best intentions, and encouraging Swedish women to enter upon a path which, according to my view, would lead them to misery instead of happiness. "Let us," I said, "remember the beautiful lines of Pope, which we learned by heart when we were children:—

> "'A woman is born to dignify retreat,
> In shade to flourish, and unseen be great;
> Fearful of fame, unwilling to be known,
> Should seek but Heaven's applauses and her own.'"

Fredrika observed that the noble virtue, modesty, ought

not to be abased in order to veil under it a glaring defectiveness in the education of women. The youth always finds for his education a sure guide in the schools of his native country, and a possibility of choosing a sphere of activity according to his capacity and mental gifts. Such advantages are to the young woman forbidden fruit, and her aspirations to attain them considered derogatory to female modesty.

The sense of Pope's lines, just quoted, I considered to express in general woman's quiet, noble mission, although naturally there are exceptions. But one ought not to regard the exceptions, but only the general rule. I acknowledged that there existed a great diversity of mental gifts, and that Fredrika, with her rare talents and accomplishments, had chosen the path in which as an authoress she could labor, ennobling humanity, and thereby effect an immense deal of good; but how small is not the number of women who have been so gifted, and how dangerous would it not be to encourage young girls, who are generally inclined to entertain a high opinion of themselves and of their capacities, to choose a career, in which, while contending with young men in their studies and in employments under government, they would or could be subject to influences detrimental to true womanhood and modesty. Educated with this aim in view, they would become neither men nor women, and, when older, unfit for domestic life.

As a wife, a mother, or instructress, — only there I saw woman in the place which God had assigned her; and if she rightly understood her exalted and important mission in the world, she might become the educator of the whole human race, and as such be of infinitely greater use to the state and her native country than by holding an employment under government. Woman's influence upon the rising generation — how incalculably great is it not! None stands nearer to the child than a woman; none knows better how to guide it from its earliest age, develop its mind, teach it to think, to hearken to the voice of conscience, and lead it in the fear of God and love of truth and justice.

I entreated, therefore, Fredrika, who had drawn woman so beautifully and truly in her proper sphere of activity, and who had, by her previous writings, drawn forth the motherly element in society, to write her new book in the same spirit, and to teach women to ennoble themselves, to develop themselves into truly Christian, prudent, clever — not learned, but enlightened — educators, able to lay the sure moral foundation on which all education ought to rest, and which now, in general, is wanting. I owned that more ways than hitherto of providing honestly for themselves ought to be made accessible to women with indifferent capacities, and that the question here had reference only to women more highly gifted.

Considering Fredrika's projects impossible to realize, in a physical as well as a moral and economical point of view, I asked her to propose, just for these more gifted women, that they should, several or few of them, unite in establishing educational institutions for girls in the country, in the vicinity of towns, where they could remain until their education was finished, — not in a superficial, frivolous direction, such as now is frequently the case, — but aiming at their immortal soul's development in purity and in Christian spirit, while at the same time they could enjoy every innocent recreation and amusement, learn practical utility, and acquire every useful knowledge in languages, &c., &c.

I proposed that these gifted women should also establish similar institutions for boys of between six and ten years of age, after which time their more learned education begins. During this time the good moral foundation, which so many children cannot obtain in their parental home or in ordinary schools, could be laid by these women, through a guidance which would develop the children into thinking, honest, and conscientious beings, to the improvement and advantage of society, when in a more mature age they began to act, if coming out of the first mentioned institution, as well educated mothers and teachers; or, if out of the latter, as men in the state. And how beneficially would not such an education in the country influence the children's health both of body and mind!

But I was of opinion that these gifted women ought not to be too young; that they should be from thirty to forty years old; that they ought likewise to be distinguished by capacity and experience as well as in a moral point of view. They would then have sufficient time to prepare themselves for their important mission, and I imagined that this preparation could be compassed in a practical way by the experience which they could gain as teachers in private families or in good boarding-schools. In these also unmarried women would have an ample field for a noble and blessed activity, provided they understood the word education in its spiritual and moral sense, and did not confound or consider it equivalent with mere teaching and acquiring knowledge, — which, of course, they would have to impart to the young.

Nobody understood better than Fredrika, as will be seen by her previous writings and by her active life, how to estimate in its full significance woman's mission to be the mother and educator of the human race; but, after her return from America, her predominating thought was how she might be able to secure liberty and an unrestricted sphere of activity for Swedish women. She remarked, that a number of functions belong to human life, which cannot be said to be either fatherly or motherly, but which — as she maintained — the "fatherly" had in all times undividedly taken upon itself. She seemed to understand the reason. Man is superior to woman in physical strength, and as long as people lived for the most part in a kind of savage state, man was woman's natural master, and woman merely a part of the man. But now, Fredrika argued, the ancient tradition about Adam's rib has undergone a considerable modification through Christianity itself. Our life is now more essentially a spiritual life — a spiritual world — in which no one is man or woman with respect to right of inheritance, majority, or the unbounded productiveness of mental gifts. Through Christianity woman is already emancipated, but the force of habit is strong, and strongest in woman. The old, so to speak, natural condition, she has been used to look upon as the most convenient. Fredrika felt herself called upon to give woman a strong reminder of her true, that is her full, mission.

Woman's true mission and sphere of activity in general, appeared to me to have been pointed out to her by her nature, which in all times and amongst all nations, in ordinary cases, is the same, and which in Christianity has received her highest and noblest mission in leading man's immortal soul to God.

Fredrika had frequently requested me to communicate to her any thing which I had found uncommon, — any peculiarity in people, especially in unmarried women, and what afforded them any pleasure here in this world. This I had often done. And now I related to her some beautiful traits in children, in case she should wish to make use of them in her new book, and as illustrations to my project for her eminently gifted women, for whom I was anxious to point out a higher and more important mission, more suitable both for their head and heart, than that of becoming public functionaries.

I was one evening, some years ago, at a concert in Stockholm, with one of my friends and her son, then ten years old. The lad was sitting before us. On the other side of me I had another intimate friend. She noticed in the course of the evening that the boy several times put his hand to his forehead, and she asked him therefore if he had the headache? "No," he answered; "I never have the headache." My friend began then to converse with some acquaintances who were sitting behind her. After a little while the lad became very uneasy, and it seemed as if he wanted to say something to my friend; but she was deep in conversation with her acquaintances. At last he was unable to wait any longer, and he said to her: "I say! I say!" And when she turned round to him, he said: "I told you just now that I *never* had the headache; but it is possible that I have *had* it, although I do not recollect it." It was the word *never* which disturbed the boy's conscience, because he was not sure that it was perfectly true.

One day I paid a visit to one of my friends. On entering the dining-room, I saw two of her sons, of about seven or eight years old, sitting each in a corner of the room. They came forward to greet me, and I asked them the reason why they were sitting so far apart. "Well," said one of them, "mamma has said that when we get angry with one another we are not allowed to fight, but that we must sit down as far as possible from each other, until our anger is over." He had scarcely finished these words when they both ran as fast as possible to sit down, each in their corner, looking fiercely at one another. "Is not your anger over yet?" I asked. "No," they both shouted at once. I went in to my friend, and when, after a quarter of an hour, I came back into the dining-room, I found the little brothers playing together. "Is it over now?" I asked. They answered, quite pleased, "Yes, now it's over." What an excellent method to teach children to conquer their violent passions, to calm themselves, and to think before acting.

One day when I had gone out shopping, a gentleman, one of our acquaintances, saw me, and came into the shop where I was to speak to me. A moment after, a young lad who had seen me also, entered for the same purpose. Mr. de R—— exclaimed: "Ah, voilà mon bon ami George!" adding, while he turned round to me: "Nous nous sommes rencontrés l'autre soir à un bal d'enfans, et nous sommes devenues de si bons amis. N'est ce pas que nous sommes bons amis?" he said, patting the lad, who was twelve years old, on the shoulder. The latter looked a little uneasy, but answered, after a short reflection: "Je crois certainement que nous le deviendrons lorsque nous nous connaîtrons mieux." It was impossible to answer more candidly, and at the same time more politely.

These boys had the invaluable happiness of having mothers who had understood how to lay the best foundation of all education.

"I know no other sphere of activity for your gifted women, none more useful and blessed for the state," I said to Fredrika, "than to educate the youth of the country, and to give them the compass which shows them the right way on their journey through life, and the beneficial influence of which extends over generations."

Fredrika did not say much in reply to my educational projects; she wanted to see woman active in all directions of the world's stage.

My mother and sisters had several years previously founded a school on an estate in the neighborhood of Arsta, also belonging to our family. An elderly widow had been engaged as teacher, after having passed the Normal School for National School-teachers in Stockholm, and her daughter instructed the girls in sewing, knitting, and spinning. My sister Hedda, who warmly and truly appreciated the practical in life, superintended this department of the school, and saw that the girls were taught to mend their stockings, and patch and repair their clothes. Every thing went on excellently in this school. The children were industrious, good, and very anxious to attend regularly. In this manner it was carried on many years, until 1842, when a statute was passed in which more extended knowledge was required as a condition for competent teachers in national schools. These requirements our teacher could not fulfill. A good and clever man was engaged as teacher in the parish, and the old school had to break up for want of a sufficient number of pupils from our estate. But one consequence of this change was, that the instruction in handiworks, so useful and so necessary in female education, ceased; for the school-master was not bound to give such instruction. Fredrika, who was much interested in the school, which she had helped to establish, was exceedingly sorry for this; and when she heard that in the neighboring parish, in which there were some farms belonging to Årsta, a youth of only eighteen years of age had been engaged as teacher, who had neither judgment nor patience with the children, but, on the contrary, taught them what was bad, she was very urgent that only women should be admitted as teachers in national schools.

That such would be the case, both Fredrika and I hoped, because, from what we had seen ourselves, none but a woman could exert a motherly influence over the children, — none better and with more patience correct their faults, make them obedient, orderly, and cleanly, which ought to be the first object in educating children. And how incalculably must the good moral foundation which these female teachers ought to understand how to lay, influence the future conduct of the children! But when this change was to take place we could not guess. As late as 1842, a learned, wise, and witty bishop, with whom Fredrika and I spoke on this subject with all the warmth of conviction, when he one day paid a visit to Årsta, only answered, "They won't do! They won't do! There must be male teachers in the schools!"[1] And how many, both widows and unmarried women, might earn their bread in a position so suitable for them, where they could labor so beneficially for the rising generation!

In the spring of 1853 my mother fell ill, and had to take

[1] Not until many years later, in 1859, a statute appeared, that what had been enacted respecting teachers in schools should apply also to such women whose capability had been tried and approved in the Seminary for Teachers in National Schools.

to her bed. It was therefore out of the question to remove her that summer to Årsta, and consequently Fredrika remained in town in order to keep her company and to nurse her. Her illness, with an occasional temporary improvement, lasted two years, until the 2d of March, 1855, when my mother, after much suffering, borne with Christian resignation, departed to a better life.

Fredrika, who was never slow in rendering assistance, whenever she had it in her power, devoted to the promotion of charitable undertakings of greater extent, both her personal activity and the power which she possessed of deeply touching with her words all human hearts, when she wished to move them to alleviate the distress of the suffering.

When, in the summer of 1853, the cholera broke out in Stockholm, Fredrika joined a society of noble-hearted women, whose president she became, and whose aim it was to take charge of, and procure a home for, those children who had lost their parents by this epidemic, and to render assistance to those poor families in which either the father or the mother had died and left children.

She published in the newspapers an invitation to a subscription for the benefit of these children and families, and had the satisfaction of seeing the money thus collected amount to Rg. 26,000, besides contributions which were promised to be continued for several years. It was arranged for the orphans that the society should take the entire charge of them, until they had been confirmed, and a place had been procured for them.

In the winter of 1855, Fredrika placed herself at the head of a small association of ladies, whose object it was to visit the prisons of the metropolis. This object was exceedingly good, and I hope that, at all events, some of those who had taken the first steps on the path of vice and crime, and now in the cells of the prisons had leisure, in silence and solitude, to meditate on what had been said to them, returned, after undergoing their punishment, to the path of virtue. The greater number of them seemed to be sincerely grateful for the sympathy shown to them, and when one had time to disentangle their notions of right and wrong, they listened with sincere repentance, and joyfully, to the exhortations to confess candidly their crimes, patiently to submit to the punishment inflicted upon them, and then to endeavor to become new beings.

These visits were continued during the following winter, when Fredrika was residing in Stockholm. The hope of having effected some permanent good in this way was, however, more than once disappointed; because several of those for whom much had been done, and for whom, after they had been discharged from prison, good places as servants had been procured, returned again to a life of vice and crime.

Fredrika, together with two other ladies of this society, also visited the large penitentiary for women. Those who were imprisoned there were more hardened and more practiced in crimes; still they were not inaccessible to the endeavors made with gentleness and in a Christian spirit, to awaken their feelings and create in them a wish to repent.

On Fredrika's visit to this prison on New Year's Day, 1856, the following New Year's greeting was presented to her by its inmates: —

> "Now entering on another year,
> E'en with its course our hope grows clear,
> That God the erring keeps in mind,
> Though worldly judgments are unkind.
> With moved and grateful spirit
> Our thanks we send to thee,
> Who God's good pleasure's pathway
> Hast made us clearly see.
> We here before thy feet do humbly lay
> Our New Year's greeting, and we pray
> That thou our words will not despise,
> Though they from captive hearts arise.
> May health and joy and peace in full
> Be with thee until life depart;

> When thy last morning greets thy sight,
> To choirs of angels take thy flight."

Fredrika likewise devoted her pen and her eloquence, during the last years of her life, to call upon society to collect money for the benefit of several charitable institutions; for the erection of dwellings for laborers, for which a considerable sum was gathered; for an asylum for aged females, and for the so-called "Silent School" for deaf and dumb children, and for several other institutions.

After reading Alexandre Vinet's excellent works, Fredrika longed to follow more attentively on the spot the religious movement, which had been called forth in Protestant Switzerland by the "Free Church," of which Vinet was the founder. This occasioned Fredrika's journey to Switzerland in the summer of 1856. She had intended at the same time to visit Greece, and spend a year in Athens. I did all I could to dissuade her from undertaking such a long journey, upon which she proposed to set out, as usual, quite alone. But when Fredrika had once got an idea into her head, it must be realized.

To her desire of knowledge, was now also added a certain restlessness of temper, a longing for change, which, when she had been at home a short time and in quietness, made her fancy that she required to travel. When she left Sweden this time, she had, however, no idea of making such a long journey as it eventually turned out, namely, during five years, through Switzerland, Belgium, France, Italy, Palestine, and Greece. While travelling, a desire awoke within her, and opportunities presented themselves, to visit one country after another. Fredrika returned home in the summer of 1861, and in the following year she again visited Germany. But this was the last journey which she made.

Fredrika was permitted to live to see four important events realized at which her heart, always warm and sympathizing for all progress in a noble and good direction, felt the sincerest joy: the abolition of slavery in the United States of America; a law passed in Sweden, that unmarried women should attain their majority at twenty-five years of age; the organization in Stockholm of a seminary for educating female teachers; and the parliamentary reform in Sweden, carried through in such a dignified manner.

It was more especially after her return from her last journey that Fredrika was constantly importuned, not only by a number of persons who wanted to beg or borrow money of her; by authoresses who came to request her to read through and improve their, for the most part, unimprovable writings; but also by both men and women who wanted her assistance to procure employment for them. She got in this way more and more overrun by all kinds of people. Frequently poor Fredrika felt very unhappy that it was not in her power to assist all the really poor and destitute; but she assured me that she had taught herself to say "No!" with the greatest coolness to persons who were perfect strangers to her, and who wanted to borrow of her both large and small sums of money.

Fredrika, while she was residing during the winters in Stockholm, had been in the habit of giving small evening parties, sometimes twice a week, in her comfortable little home, to which a few friends and more intimate acquaintances were invited. But she had now become tired of these *soirées*, and wished to live henceforth in quiet.

This wish, and the feeling that it would be necessary for her to flee from Stockholm, in order to escape from all those who came to ask for assistance, and almost every day occupied her time, made her determine to remove some miles from Stockholm into the country, and thus the thought and wish arose in her to remove to Årsta, which, since the autumn of 1853, had not belonged to our family. Before making up her mind to stay for any greater length of time, she wanted first to try how she would find herself there under these altered circumstances, and therefore she spent three months of the summer of 1864 at Årsta.

On her return to town, Fredrika was greatly charmed with the patriarchal family who were now the owners of our former paternal estate, and she had vastly enjoyed the peace and quietness in which she had lived there. She therefore determined to remove to Årsta the following summer, to board with the present owners, and she chose the rooms which were to be put in order for her. Besides the hope of the rural peace which she would enjoy there, her kind, generous heart was gladdened when she thought that by this change she would save a considerable portion of her annual income, to give away, compared with what she was able to do formerly, while living in Stockholm.

In the spring of 1865, Fredrika was seized with a severe attack of erysipelas, and until the month of July she had not recovered so far as to be able to remove to Årsta; but there she soon recovered her health and strength. During the visits which Fredrika, later in the summer, paid to my husband and me at our little country-seat, we heard with sincere pleasure that she found herself more happy and contented than she had ever felt before at Årsta. Her mind was also now at ease; all doubts of God's goodness and justice had vanished; all rebellious feelings, which had been awakened in her, when contemplating the unequal lots on earth, were silenced; and when we, especially on her last visit to us, spoke of some unhappy people whom we knew personally, and who in poverty and sickness had for years been suffering great bodily pain, I found Fredrika full of hope, and convinced that their sufferings here below would be requited in a double measure in a better world. In a word, I had never before seen Fredrika so hopeful and so calm.

I cannot better paint the peaceful state of her mind than by quoting her own beautiful words, written, most probably, at the close of her life: —

"No longer against destiny I murmur;
The Providence of God I clearly see;

> It makes itself not known within the world's
> And chance's ever-shifting, changing forms,
> But it reveals itself in hearts of mortals,
> And thus in them expressèd is its spirit:
> 'That sons of earth in greatest earthly need
> May then on " bread of life " from heaven feed;'
> And when I hear them tell how fate ungentle
> Has acted 'gainst some mortal good and noble,
> Fate is to me a darkling cloud no more,
> A cloud which hides the sun of light and beauty;
> Praise be to God! I know now how it is, —
> I know that in the sufferer's meek submission
> Lies strength concealed to feed and nourish gladness;
> I know that in the martyr's crown of thorns,
> When borne with patience, there is not one point,
> Which or in time or in eternity,
> Blooms not into a rose."

Although fully prepared and joyfully looking forward to a better life, Fredrika yet believed that she was destined to remain longer in this world, in which she fancied that a great deal still remained for her to do, while leading a life full of love for mankind and wandering in the paths of our Saviour: to help, solace, and comfort the destitute, the suffering, the unhappy, the abandoned, who from all quarters turned to her for assistance and consolation.

But this belief was not to be realized. Although Fredrika, after having taken up her abode in the country, had regained health and strength, she yet felt a something within her foreboding the great removal, — arising either from the prophetic element in her nature, or from a consciousness of physical decline; probably from both. She communicated her thoughts and feelings on this subject to an old friend in Sweden and to a friend in America; but as she never was in the habit of paying much attention to her bodily ailments or dangers to life or health, she did not attach any particular importance to these forebodings, not suspecting that the solemn hour was so near.

It was in the beginning of September when Fredrika, for the last time, visited us in the country. On the 30th of December we received two letters from Årsta: one, a long letter to my husband, dictated by Fredrika, relating to her worldly affairs, in which she told us that she had caught cold on Christmas Day, after having attended the morning service in church; but that she now felt better, although still very weak. The other letter was from the physician who had been called in, informing us that Fredrika was suffering from inflammation of the lungs, and preparing us for the possibility that she might not have strength enough to go through this serious illness.

My husband and I drove out at once, in a heavy gale of wind and rain, to Årsta. On our arrival, at nine o'clock at night, I asked Fredrika's kind hostess to prepare her cautiously for our arrival. She was exceedingly weak. Alas! I saw at once death in her face. She was glad when we entered her room, and said, in broken accents, "It is so kind of you to come and see me! I have been ill; have suffered much pain; I have never been so ill." — "Do you feel yourself better now?" I asked. "Yes, much better," she answered. After a little while, during which she seemed to have fallen into a short slumber, she looked up, saying, "Have I dreamt that my sister and brother-in-law are here?" We again approached her bedside and took her hand, while we said a few loving words to her. Much talking she could not bear. Again her mind seemed to wander for a short time; when again she looked up, she said to me, "You cannot think how kind and attentive every one here has been to me; they have watched over and tended me in the most kind manner. They are such excellent people!"

It did my heart good that the amiable family at Årsta, who, sorrowing, surrounded her bed, should hear from her own lips these expressions of gratitude.

Shortly after Fredrika had said these words, the last earthly struggle began, — that between life and death, — and, thank God! it was a short one, although painful, lasting about an hour, after which all consciousness seemed to be gone, and Fredrika peacefully drew her last breath, at three o'clock on the morning of the last day of the year, to awake again in heaven.

Happy they who have lived as she had done! they are every moment ready to enter into the mansions of the blessed.

The wind had gone down, the sky had become bright and clear, and the moon lit up the room in which Fredrika was now lying quietly, as one asleep.

She had finished her earthly career, during which she had been permitted to realize the dearest wish of her youth, — to live for the sake of comforting, consoling, and relieving her suffering fellow-men; and this noble, loving heart, which had glowed so warmly and bravely for the light of truth and the weal of humanity, had ceased to beat. Many are they who bless her memory and mourn her loss. The following day we got a detailed account of all the particulars of Fredrika's last illness. Fredrika, whose greatest pleasure it was to give pleasure to others, had, on Christmas Eve, invited thirty children belonging to the families of the farmers and laborers on the estate. After a liberal entertainment, every child got a Christmas-box, and they were then allowed to dance round a beautifully decorated Christmas-tree, radiant with light. Fredrika danced with them, and taught them several games; in a word, she over-exerted herself, and went to bed later than usual. On Christmas Day she drove to church. After the service she stood for some time in the church-yard conversing with several people. The wind was high and piercing, and it is supposed that it was then she caught cold. She was, however, well and cheerful the whole day. During the night she was taken ill, and when Mrs. S——g, her hostess, on the following day, wanted to send for a physician, Fredrika would not allow it, saying, that she knew her own constitution well, and that if she did not get better in the course of the day, she would then take some

of her small homœopathic globules. It was not until the
fourth day, when Fredrika felt herself getting worse, that
she gave permission to send for a physician. When he
arrived and found, on inquiry, that she was suffering from
a severe inflammation of the lungs, she requested that her
relatives might be informed of her illness. She did not
herself imagine that there was any danger; and, notwithstanding increasing pain and difficulty in breathing, she
could not be persuaded to lie down, but walked about even
the very last day of her life, exceedingly restless, moving
from one place to another in her large drawing-room. Her
mind was as usual, always calm and cheerful.

To her young nurse, who assisted her to change her
position, which soothed her pains, she said: "It would be
delightful to die in this way, without pain; but not yet; I
would wish to finish my last work. And you know it is
not my death-year," she added, alluding to a dream which
she had had several years before, and according to which
she ought to have more than a year to live.[1] On the
Friday after, she went, leaning upon the arm of her nurse,
from window to window in the large room; and it seemed
as if she wanted to take leave of the surrounding country
which she loved so much. Then she spoke with a faint,
scarcely audible, voice, broken sentences, repeated often:
" Light, eternal light;" and, while taking her nurse's hands
between her own, she said, with a glorified expression in
her face: "Ah! my child, let us speak of Christ's love, —
the best, the highest love!"

My husband and I returned later in the day to town, in
order to make the necessary arrangements for the funeral.
It took place on the day before Twelfth Night, the 5th of

---

[1] This dream had made such an impression upon Fredrika, that she
really believed, and often mentioned to her most intimate friends, that she
would live to be sixty-six years and two months old; which age, dying
as she did, at a little more than sixty-four years old, she was not permitted to reach.

January, 1866. Besides the Årsta family, the clergyman and his wife, and a few of the neighbors, only our nearest relatives, and two elderly gentlemen, Fredrika's old friends, were invited, with my husband and myself, to accompany her to her last resting-place. Some people from town had also the kindness to join us.

On Fredrika's birthday the previous year, while she was staying at Årsta, her kind hostess, with her daughters, in order to afford her a pleasure, had invited to coffee all the survivors of those who, during my parents' time, had served on the estate. When they had assembled, it was found that these old faithful servants — male and female included — numbered twenty-four in all. Now the male portion of them were invited, and they were to carry Fredrika to the church.

The beautiful coffin was entirely covered with garlands of flowers, sent from friends in Stockholm, and were mixed with those which we and the invited funeral guests had brought out from town. But none of them were so beautiful as the garland sent by the children of the "Silent School;" it was made of dazzling white camellias and the most beautiful feather-like grass.

On one of the plates of the coffin was written: —

"FREDRIKA BREMER:

Born at Tuorla Manor, near Åbo, in Finland, on the 17th August, 1801; Died at Årsta, at three o'clock in the morning, the 31st December, 1865.

Beloved and regretted by all who knew her, she leaves after her only dear and loving memories."

On the other plate was written: —

"Blessed are the pure in heart, for they shall see God."

After having partaken of some luncheon, the procession set out for church, where we were met by a number of young ladies from Stockholm, amongst whom were several of the teachers from the Seminary, who, grateful for the kindness and friendly favors shown them by Fredrika, had wished to follow her to the grave. The coffin was placed upon the catafalque before the altar, covered with flowers. The church was filled with country people, who had come to witness the funeral, and who all seemed to be deeply moved. The organ pealed forth the 461st psalm: "Oh, day of hope, which brightens now," of which the first, fifth, and eighth verses were sung.

Hereupon the clergyman, the Rev. Mr. L——ll, approached the coffin, and held a funeral oration,—dignified, eloquent, true, and delivered with deep and sincere emotion.

After the ceremony, the 452d psalm was sung: "I go towards death where'er I go;" and then, in a chorus of young, fresh voices: "Hosanna, David's Son!"

The old servants then approached, took the coffin, and carried it to the grave, into which it was lowered under a shower of flowers, offered with sincere tears and deep emotion by her young friends.

At the head of the grave, shaded by two lime-trees with luxuriant foliage, stands now a handsome monument of polished granite, with a cross on the top. On the pedestal is engraved in golden letters:—

"HERE SLEEPS

FREDRIKA BREMER,

BORN 17TH AUGUST, 1801; DIED 31ST DECEMBER, 1865;"

and underneath, according to Fredrika's own wish, the following words of Scripture:—

"When I cried unto the Lord, He delivered me out of all my trouble."

AUTOBIOGRAPHY.

THE first word which my infant lips uttered in this sublunary world was "Moon." Eight years later I wrote my first verses, "À la lune." My first juvenile feelings, so far as I can now recollect, were immoderate greediness after sweetmeats, and likewise an immoderate desire to distinguish myself and be spoken of. These were soon succeeded by warmer feelings and nobler desires, which all wore the stamp of passion. My first love was my native country. I loved it as Elizabeth in "Sketches of Every-day Life." In the description which she gives of her youth and her feelings, I have portrayed my own. By degrees, as my intelligence and my mind became developed (both equally warped and chaotic), a spirit of inquiry was also developed within me — a why and wherefore — which none of those who were around me could, or cared to, answer or enlighten. My education was of a very desultory kind. They stuffed my head full of fine precepts against vanity, but they planted vanity itself in my heart. During my endeavors to deaden wild sensations, I went for the first time to the Lord's table. An atmosphere of innocence and purity, emanating from my mother's whole being, breathed round my home, and for a long time kept aloof from the children's souls all knowledge of evil; but the desire for it was, unconscious to me, slumbering in my soul. Modesty, in its widest sense, I knew not. But I had an ardent and enthusiastic feeling for all heroic virtues, a boundless capacity to love and to sacrifice myself with joy, in small things as in great, for the good of those whom I loved; a desire to give, to make happy, and to comfort. Yes, if I could have done it, I would have given to the hungry the flesh of my own body. I loved my mother most tenderly and passionately, and longed, above every thing else in the world, to please her. I failed herein completely. I walked badly, sat badly, stood badly, curtsied badly; and many bitter moments this cost me, because my mother wished that her daughters should be perfect, as the heroines of romance are perfect, by birth and nature. This, of course, we sincerely wished to be, but to me Dame Nature was rather unfriendly, throwing all kinds of difficulties in my way. None of those who surrounded me understood how to guide a character like mine to good. They tried to curb me by severity, or else my thoughts and feelings were ridiculed. I was very unhappy in my early youth, and, violent as I was in every thing, I formed many plans to shorten my life, to put out my eyes, &c., &c., merely for the sake of making my mother repent her severity; but all ended in my standing on the margin of the lake, looking down into the water, or feeling the pricking of the knife in my eyeball. Unhappy at home, because I was a restless, passionate creature, without the least of what one would call tact, my soul clung ardently to the events of the outer world. The war against Napoleon stirred within me all my deepest feelings. I determined to flee from home, to proceed to the theatre of war, which I imagined would be an easy matter, and, dressed in male costume, to become page to the Crown-Prince (afterwards King Charles XIV.), who at that time appeared to me to be little less than a demigod. I entertained these plans more than a year, until they melted away slowly, like snow in water. Gradually my patriotic and warlike feelings were lulled, but only to make room for new ones of another kind. Religious enthusiasm and the most worldly coquetry were struggling within me, with feelings for which I was unable fully to account, but which seemed to burst my young bosom, and which sometimes filled it with a heaven and sometimes with a hell. Like two all-consuming flames, the desire to know and the desire to enjoy were burning in my soul, without being satisfied for many long years. The mere sight of certain words in a book, — words such as Truth, Liberty, Glory, Immortality, — roused within me feelings which vainly I would try to describe. I wanted in some way or other to give vent to and express the same; and I wrote verses, theatrical pieces, and a thousand different kinds of essays; composed music, drew and painted pictures, some of them greater trash than the others. I was brought out into the world, went out visiting, went to evening parties, balls, and concerts, and very rarely enjoyed myself anywhere except at the theatre, and there my soul was thrown into a state of topsy-turvy.

My nose, naturally large, used to become illuminated in hot places, and, I had almost said, become double its ordinary size, darkening my prospects of pleasure and of admirers, which latter it kept at a distance. I have said it: I was a coquette, and I became more and more a coquette when I observed that I found favor with my parents in proportion as I anywhere or in any thing was admired by others. In company I frequently behaved in a ridiculous manner, because it was utterly impossible for me to keep my soul or my body quiet. Thence arose fresh troubles for my mother, and consequently fresh troubles for me. *Du reste*, my vivacity and my *fraicheur*, which, so long as it did not concentrate itself into my nose, was rather pretty, procured me admirers and flatterers, when we happened to be in any place of public entertainment. This was a consolation to us both, namely, to my mother and to myself. A young gentleman, betrothed to the daughter of the oldest friend of my parents, came one day to pay them a visit. He was exceedingly handsome, full of vigor and life. I saw him for a couple of hours and — became enchanted. During a fortnight I felt the arrow sticking in my heart; then it dropped out. Another young gentleman, nowise handsome, but rich, saw me a couple of hours, while I was paying a visit, and — he fell in love with me. With his hand upon his heart, he whispered to me his agony. He tried to get an introduction to our family, but the door was forcibly shut against him by my father, who willingly would have got all his daughters married, but who never could tolerate the face of a suitor in his house. I was then seventeen years old, read Madame Le Prince de Beaumont's works, and determined never to marry. From this time forth there was for me a vacuum of suitors and lovers until 1820, when I was twenty. N. B.—It was fortunate, for the keeping of my word, that during this time no suitor appeared to put my word to the test. Meanwhile I had improved somewhat in my gait, in sitting, in curtseying, and got my person a little more into shape; got the name of being witty; had less love for and more favor with my mother. I understood better how to agree with people, and to suit myself to them. I had, moreover, begun to acquire a certain quantity of every-day wisdom and common sense, which made people entertain some hope respecting my understanding, the doubts and questions of which I tried to stifle as vain fermentations. In 1820 I accompanied my mother and sisters to a watering-place. It was during the third term of the season, and we were therefore alone. A very amiable and chivalrous elderly gentleman and his wife, residing in the neighborhood, did all they could to make our stay as agreeable as possible. They had a son, a young, gay, good, and handsome lieutenant. He began to sigh for me, and I began to warm a little for him. It was a pastoral moment, when once, " in the green fields," I was wiping and scraping some tar off one of my shoes, and when he, with half words and sighs — well, nothing more came of it. We left at last, and he accompanied us to the nearest town. I remember, not without a pleasant sensation, this first silent, friendly harmony of my soul with another's. We parted. I gave him a carnation and a curl-paper, and he gave me a few sprigs of lavender. I cried the whole night after our parting, and for a long time afterwards I sighed his name in my heart, but very calmly.

In order to please my parents, I had labored very hard to get used to household duties. I succeeded, because I had then, as now, a very strong will, although I rarely understood how to give it the proper direction. I also worked and labored hard at my piano, and rose at four in the mornings, merely for the purpose of playing the scales. I wrote theatrical pieces in honor of every birthday in the family; arranged small fêtes, and began to flatter the heads of the family in a delicate manner; in a word, I became a complete courtier, and rose with my parents to the rank of favorite. By means of this favoritism, I wished, however, to get an opportunity of serving my sisters, and I succeeded sometimes, but not often. Nowhere have I seen so many *impossibilities* for every thing, except for very long journeys, as in our house. I wrote during this time some humorous and some tragic pieces, which I believe gave promise of something better; but nobody cared to take the trouble of trying to develop this promise. I had no idea of being able by industry to make something of myself in the way of intellect and knowledge.

All my actions during many years were devoid of plan or order. In 1821 we worked through our continental trip, and journeyed in covered carriages, and "toiled on our weary way" through Germany, Switzerland, France, and the Netherlands. For all the treasures of this world, aye, even for the genius of Tegnér, I would not again make this journey in the same way. I will only speak of the suffering which more particularly fell to my share. The desire for knowledge and the desire for enjoyment were reawakened within me a new, all-consuming fire, at the sight of the masterpieces of Nature and of Art.

I suffered like Tantalus. Within a year we had returned to our quiet home in the north. Then began for us a life, the heaviness and torture of which it would be vain to attempt to paint. Our home became to us a prison, compared with which a real prison would, so it appeared to me, have been a delicious retreat. We saw nobody in our house, and those whom we saw in the houses of others were unkind and unfriendly to us on account of our foreign journey, and on account of the airs which people fancied we wanted to give ourselves. Year after year a heavier and darker cloud lowered itself over my home, and still more over my soul. Gradually all illusions vanished. With a soul infinitely lively and active, I found myself shut out from all activity. If a charitable hand had then pointed out to me the road to light and future usefulness, through cultivation of my intellect and a judicious division of the time to be devoted to this purpose, — oh! then so many years would not have rolled past me like zeroes, and I would have borne better every day's bitterness and pain. But my soul was still, as it were, in its swaddling clothes. I read heaps of novels; they awakened within me a longing for happiness and love, which could not be realized. I read large quantities of sermons, which did not make me a bit better or less unhappy. I played the piano, and occupied myself in one way or other, but more and more listlessly. I waited for a turn in events, in order to enter into activity, but no such events happened. Embroidering an interminable gray neckerchief, I became more and more benumbed, that is to say, in my vital powers, in my desire to live. The sense of pain did not become benumbed; it became, on the contrary, more sharp every day, like the frost in a steadily increasing winter. The flame in my soul was flickering fearfully, and wanted only one thing — to be extinguished forever. My sisters suffered with me; they suffered in me and I in them. During the common sorrows of our continental journey, we had become sincerely and closely united. During the common sufferings of our domestic life, we became still more tenderly united; and under affliction and tears those ties were knit which nothing can make stronger, which nothing can tear asunder, and which are now the chief source of my life's happiness. Years rolled past, and every thing remained in the same state; physical pains, caused by inward pains, seized me; an eruption covered my face; my eyes became yellow. I felt, both in body and soul, a sense of the utmost discomfort, a kind of frost, a sensation as if I was becoming mouldy. I had a fear and horror of people looking at me. My position, with respect to them and to myself, was insupportable. The fate of women in general, and my own in particular, appeared to me to be frightful. I saw assurance and courage in men's looks; heard them express openly their thoughts and feelings, and I — was doomed to silence, to live without life. I was conscious of being born with powerful wings, but I was also conscious of their being clipped, and I fancied that they would always remain so. I saw that I was disagreeable and repugnant in the eyes of others, and I felt that it could not be otherwise, for I was dissatisfied with myself, with my inward and outward being.

But during all this suffering, a certain strength was called into life within me. My glance penetrated deeply into the dark mysteries of human life; I understood every thing called suffering; and in my own name, and in that of all unhappy beings, I raised a painful and rebellious cry to Heaven: —

> My cheek was pale, my eyes were running o'er
>   With bitter tears; my heart, in desolation,
> Saw suffering, like a vast and rankling sore,
>   Prey on the vitals of God's fair creation.
>
> I looked for dawn, — I found but nightly gloom,
>   No hope of happier days, no blessed faith;
> Life turned like some wild meteor on a tomb
>   In my sad heart, — I only prayed for death.

Now I stood in need of faith; now I stood in need of religious comfort. Wildly impatient, I prayed for it; my agony remained the same. Exasperated, I turned away my looks from heaven and asked, with my eyes riveted upon the night of human misery, a shuddering wherefore? No voice, either from heaven or from earth, returned an answer; my faith and my hope were shaken in their deepest foundations. Every thing was tottering; I doubted, I despaired, and now I understood — hell. I suffered so deeply, so dreadfully, but at the same time so quietly, that just thereby I felt a kind of superiority over other people; because, during this suffering, I became so good, so gentle, that I would willingly have suffered still more to save the most insignificant insect a pang. And I knew nobody so good as I. God — may He forgive my weakness this irreverence or blindness — permitted this suffering. Man humbled me, because I was a kind of Lazarus, at any rate in my own imagination; but I overlooked mankind; in my soul raged giant agony. I felt that I could suffer, and that I suffered more than others.

Although at this time I should have found it easy to achieve any great and noble action, even at the sacrifice of my life; yet I must in truth confess, that on the other hand, I have never looked upon crime and vice with so little abhorrence as then, and it is only Him, who rules events and circumstances, to whom I ascribe the innocence of my actions. One thing only afforded me some consolation during this long time of suffering, and this was painting. Seated at my easel, I frequently forgot, for hours together, my agony and the bitterness of my life; and in creating the beautiful with my pencil, I found therein consolation for not being able to re-create myself, for I was ever weak for beauty. In order to find pecuniary means for assuaging affliction which made my heart bleed to hear mentioned, I tried to earn money with my paintings. I painted little portraits of the Crown-Princess, whom I had seen in the theatre; painted that of the King; sold them in secret, and within a year I earned nearly two hundred rix-dollars. To employ this sum, afforded me for the moment a healing balm.

My sister Agatha had finished the orthopedic treatment, which she had gone through in Paris, and returned home in the summer of 1826. She scarcely knew me again, so much had I become altered in two years. It was decided that she, my sister Hedda, and myself should remain in the country, in order to continue Agatha's treatment. We were allowed to remain there alone with an old French lady as a *chaperon*.

My sister Charlotte accompanied my parents to town in the autumn. These sisters were and are good, gentle, patient, and pure beings, — beings, whom nothing in the world could tempt to deviate from what they consider virtuous and right. My life now gained outward peace, but severe bodily suffering, toothache, and rheumatism in the head, together with the chaotic state of my soul, prevented me from enjoying this peace. By degrees there awoke within me an intensely deep desire for improvement of, and for conciliation with, my better self. I did not hope to arrive at light and truth until after death, that dear, longed-for dawn of a better life.

So it appeared to me in my calmer moments. In the country around me, near and far, there were many poor and sick. I became their physician, nurse, and helper, as far as I had it in my power. I felt an intense pleasure in exposing myself to and braving cold, tempests, snow-storms, even hunger; because the food which I took with me on my excursions I gave away. Battling with Nature's roughness, I felt with delight the moral strength of my being. I submitted joyously to the most loathsome medical employments. My bodily feelings were disgust, my mental feelings were delight at suffering in order to soothe and heal. I denied myself all kinds of comforts, in order to give them to others. In a word, I was during two years a Catholic enthusiast, but became, in the mean time, a better, purer, more virtuous being than I had been before. I studied the Bible assiduously. I was often, very often, on my knees; yes, rose in the night to pray for light and peace. A breath of the celestial children's wings fanned now and then my heart. The fruit of such a moment is the passage in "The Solitary One," beginning with "Now is peaceful, blessed rest," &c., &c. I had indeed moments of inexpressible happiness; but my feelings, like billows, rose and fell; I felt no settled calm. A warm feeling of piety filled my soul. My doubts were not solved, but I had faith and hope; I had a measureless love for all sufferers; for all who were in affliction; for all unhappy ones. To exercise this love unwaveringly, during the whole remainder of my life, became my sole wish, and I made the firm determination, that, as soon as I should become my own mistress, I would enter a hospital as a "Sister of Charity," and devote my days to tending the sufferers of the poorer classes, little caring for what the world or my own family would say of it; — so little was at that time the right application of the "principle of usefulness" understood by me. With my soul full of the determination to devote my life to God in this way, I drove one Sunday, a gloomy winter's day, alone to church, in order to consecrate myself, as it were, to a new life by taking the Sacrament. I remember still, with a feeling of pleasing melancholy, how I was sitting alone in my pew, shivering with cold, while, with a calm pleasure in my soul, I contemplated the altar-piece, representing the Resurrection, and heard how the congregation, one by one, with heavy footsteps walked up the aisle and entered the pews. All of a sudden the sun shone out brightly, and threw his life-giving rays upon me. They continued during the whole service to warm me gently, and with blissful tears I felt this as a blessing from Heaven. At the foot of the altar, I laid down the offering of my whole life, but found, during the holy act and after it, my feelings to be less warm than I had wished. However, every thing now became better than it had been previously. I imagined that I had closed my accounts with the world; the desire for its life and enjoyments was extinguished within me. My soul became pure and at the same time true. My incessant activity gave me a delightful consciousness of being here in this world a consoling atom. In consequence of frequent and fatiguing exercise in the open air, my body became invigorated, my blood flowed more freely, my health improved.

One day, about the end of March, I walked across snow-covered fields just as the sun was setting; the tear of gratitude and joy of one, to whom I had just then given comfort, had fallen like balm upon my heart. I had been walking very fast to avoid coming home in the twilight, and I had stopped a moment to recover breath and to inhale the mild, pure air. I stood still, with my eyes turned to where the sun was sinking in a flood of purple and golden glory beneath the western sky. Then came thence towards me, sweeping across the wide expanse of snow, a breath of air delicious and full of a foretaste of spring. I drank in its life-giving freshness with body and soul. I collected my excited feelings to more calmness, looked round, and turned, with full consciousness of the state of my being, my thoughts upon myself, with this question: Would I now wish to die? For the first time during many years, I felt that I could answer, No! Oh, moment of immeasurable delight! Now awoke within me the hope of a resurrection to happiness even on earth, — a hope, which has not been deceived, but which has been beautifully realized.

During this period of my life, a rather unusual circumstance contributed to give my mind a new direction. A noble-hearted and estimable lady, who then learnt to know me in my outward, and partly also in my inward, life, conceived for me a friendship which amounted almost to a real passion.

She was, and is still, one of the few friends whom God has given me, and to whom I can say: "Go," and she goes; "come," and she comes; "do this," and she does it. I felt that it was only through the ennobling of my own being that I had gained this power over her, and I rose accordingly still more in my own estimation. To describe all my own feelings would be impossible. There is something so gigantic and so full of the infinite in every deep feeling which fills my soul, that words cannot express it. A medical treatment, which I prescribed for myself during this time, contributed essentially to restore the equilibrium of my whole being, and to make me find some comfort in myself. I bathed frequently in lukewarm water, which had an inexpressibly beneficial effect upon me; and I was repeatedly bled. This drew from my poor head the quantity of blood which used to rush into it, and which caused all my uneasiness. At last I applied a seton to each arm. They made the eruption in my face disappear, and drew out of my body the humors which had accumulated therein for years. My complexion became clear, and I became bodily like one new-born.

During the last winter which I spent alone in the country, I wrote the first volume of the "Sketches of Everyday Life." It afforded me pleasure; but I felt, while trying to produce something as an authoress, how very chaotic was my whole world of imagination, and I had no idea that within me could lie any talent in that way. The chief motive for having my little book printed, was the hope of getting a little money to assist the poor in the country. When my brother August wrote to me from Upsala that Mr. Palmblad, the publisher, was willing to pay for it one hundred rix dollars, my sisters and I danced with delight.

I now accompanied Agatha to town to spend the winter there. I had determined to go nowhere, and obtained at last permission, although with infinite difficulty, to live quietly.

I had of late read, and was still reading, several good books, which in some measure reconciled me to my sufferings on earth, by showing me their unavoidableness and their aim. Herder's "Ideen"[1] made a deep and soothing impression upon me. When I came to town with my improved complexion and my calmer soul, I found, as a visitor in my parents' house, a distant relative, with arms and crest on his seal, with a major's title, and an estate in the country. Honest soul! I listened patiently to his Laponic French; played to him, "Welcome, O moon, my ancient friend;" and got from him an offer of his heart and hand, his crest, and his estate in the country. My family agreed perfectly with me in giving him a friendly refusal.

I made also the acquaintance of another gentleman, who inspired me with a pure and warm feeling, which, although it was never responded to, yet had a powerful influence upon my development, and which still lives silently and ennobling in my heart.

During the summer of 1829, I wrote, encouraged by an occasional eulogy on my little book, the second volume of my "Sketches."

The better feelings which I had experienced, I expressed to a certain extent in "The Solitary One," and in "The Consoler." That kind of humor which is found in "The H—— Family" was, until then, entirely unknown to me, and the discovery of it in me was quite unexpected. It was first shown in a small sketch written during the previous winter, "Christmas in Sweden."

The following winter my father's long and last illness began. Towards the spring, I offered to H——, the printer in Stockholm, my manuscript of the second volume of my "Sketches." He was at first willing to receive it; but, after having had it some time for perusal, he refused to print it or to pay any thing for it. Then my opinion of

---

[1] Herder's *Ideen zur Philosophie der Geschichte der Menschheit.*

my talent as an authoress received a heavy blow indeed. Nevertheless, I had my manuscript offered to my former publisher, Mr. Palmblad, who at once undertook to print it in the course of the summer. Meanwhile we nursed and watched over my father. It did me good to tend him and to watch over him during his last long suffering, borne with heroic fortitude. He seemed to improve a little, and we went with him to live at a place in the environs of the town. There he enjoyed for a few days the summer air, but soon got worse, and died calmly, with my mother and sisters surrounding his bed. It was a comfort to see him at rest after a troubled life; a comfort to shed tears of reconciliation upon his cold hand and forehead.

Shortly afterwards we removed to Årsta, where we led a quiet, retired life. In October the second volume of my book made its appearance, and I soon reaped a rich harvest of *eulogia* and compliments from all quarters.

Charlotte's wedding was celebrated on the 7th of November. This was one of the happiest days which I have spent in our family.

The presence of Franzén; his verses to me; Charlotte's happy and joyous state of mind, contributed to make this day a bright spot in my life. But the whole of this time was full of happiness and innocent joy in our home. Charlotte's departure caused me much pain.

Soon after, we moved to Stockholm, and I now passed a winter which, in many respects, was rich and full of importance to me. I got a great deal of praise and distinction for my book. The Swedish Academy awarded me a gold medal, accompanied by a very flattering letter. I had now what I had so warmly coveted in my early youth, — distinction; and now it gave me but little pleasure; nay, I felt frequently even cold and indifferent to it all.

But at this time I made the acquaintance of Miss Frances L——, and, through her, of Bentham. She showed me that the more knowledge I could acquire, — the more clearness and perspicuity to which I could train my intellect, — the greater would become my means to labor for the benefit of mankind, and to become happy myself. Bentham gave me, in his "Principles of Utility," a new light, and at the same time I had an opportunity of frequently conversing with distinguished and highly intelligent people. A new world opened within me; I beheld a new sun, and in his light a paradise. My happiness at this new resurrection within me was inexpressible. My old plans, to which I had hitherto adhered, fell to the ground. I soon saw the road which I ought to follow. Oh, delight! Now I would and I could rise higher and higher to light and truth, and every one of my steps would bring with it some fruit for my fellow-men. My soul rejoiced.

Letters arrived about this time; one for my mother and one for me. The young gentleman, who therein offered me his hand and heart, spoke with such warm sincerity, goodness, and real excellence of soul, and with so much candor and openness of himself, that I was deeply touched by it. I felt no aversion for him; but I did not wish to marry. By the refusal which I gave, I considered that I had forever placed a barrier between myself and marriage. I did not fear that the fulfillment of my duties as a wife and a mother would not be my chief aim if I entered into the married state; but it became clear to me that my mission as an authoress would then become totally neglected, because I knew and I felt that one cannot unite these two vocations without failing in both; while by devoting myself exclusively to the latter, — that of an authoress, — I believed that I could make myself as useful as my power admitted.

The third volume of my "Sketches," which I wrote in the winter of 1831, in a hurry-skurry, appeared in print in the following spring, and the success which it met with, together with the advice of several highly estimable persons, determined me to devote myself seriously to the life of an authoress, and to develop my talent as much as possible.

I am now thirty years old, and am working systematically and with earnestness towards a fixed aim. My worldly position is prosperous, and within me is life and peace. If it pleased God, I might become a respectable and useful writer.

For the sake of my sisters, more than for my own sake, I wish to succeed and to gain honor and applause. They live so much in me, and I have so much to thank them for, especially my dear Hedda, who is as good as an angel.

LETTERS.

Årsta, 14th January, 1828.

It is still early morning when I sit down to write to my darling Lotten. I see by your letter, which I received yesterday, that mine had not then reached you. Dearest Charlotte! If you but knew how much good your letter (although far too short) has done me, you would at once abandon needle and thread, piano-forte and music-books, or what else you may be busy with, in order to fabricate another such letter, which shall more vividly and clearly picture to my longing eyes Agatha W——'s and your own every-day life. Thanks be to God that Agatha is so well, so comfortable, so sensible! Thanks be to God that you are beside her! and that, while contributing to render her life more pleasant, you can yourself enjoy the delightful feeling of leading a comfortable and useful existence. Born and qualified, as you are, for an active life, and to devote yourself to others, how must I not rejoice to see you fulfill now *for the first time* your beautiful mission; yourself happy, by making others happy. How delightful your plans for this winter! Music and reading, life's poetry; work, its most enchanting prose; and I feel convinced that its more commonplace yet necessary side, to eat and to sleep, will not be forgotten. But I must have a more detailed sketch of all this. Until then I shall find no leisure myself, either for eating or sleeping.

. And then this little "expected stranger," how he interests me already! How sweet he must be, and how happy!

He shall therefore be the first who again awakens my slumbering vena: —

> * Slumbering cherub,
> Quietly nestling
> Safe in thy mother's
> Fluttering bosom;
> Fondly we greet thee,
> Child fondly longed for,
> Hail to thee, hail!
>
> Life bids thee welcome, —
> Life with its thousand
> Joys that await thee;
> Yet in mysterious
> Darkness reposing,
> Thou love-created,
> Know'st not what shadows
> Brood over life;
> Though life already,
> Warm as the genial
> Breezes of spring-tide,
> Quickens thy breast.
>
> Time bids thee welcome;
> Little thou knowest
> Him, who in wisdom
> Tenderly fosters
> All things created, —
> Time, who will fold thee
> In his embrace.
>
> Earth bids thee welcome;
> There as a merry
> Child shalt thou gambol,
> Rip'ning through youth to
> High-hearted manhood,
> Active and strong.
>
> Suffering and sorrow,
> Darkest of shadows,
> Loom in the valley,
> Yet fear them not.
> Fondly a mother's
> Love never-failing,
> Like a strong buckler,
> Shelters thy wand'rings,
> Shields thee from harm.

Briers, sharp and thorny,
Fierce-stinging nettles,
Spring by the way-side,
Yet fear them not.
Soon shall a tender
Hand be up-raisèd,
Smoothing its roughness,
Strewing with thornless
Roses thy path.

Spirits of evil,
Dark and malignant,
Lurk 'mid the od'rous
Flow'r-laden coverts,
Yet fear them not;
For on love's snow-white
Pinions upspringing,
Guarding thy young brow,
Heavenward hovers
A mother's prayer.

Angels aforetime
Guided the pilgrim
Up to the holy
Hills of the faithful.
Blest was his lot!
Slumbering pilgrim,
Wake from thy dreaming!
Morning already
Glows in the welkin,
Whilst at thy side an
Angel is waiting:
Waiting to lead thee
Up to yon sun-bright
Heights of the blessèd,
Where spring eternal,
With its green palm-branch,
Crowneth the feeble
Though faithful strivings
Of mortal man.

Who is the guardian
Angel that watches
O'er thy young life?
Whose is that fair form
Over thy cradle,
Singing and weeping
Tears of delight?

> Who at her bosom
> Wakes thee to gladness, —
> Gladness and life?
> Pilgrim thrice blessèd!
> Thou who still sleepest
> Peacefully resting
> Close to thy mother's
> Quick-beating heart;
> Babe of our prayers,
> Yearn'd for so fondly,
> Lo, in yon angel,
> Thy mother behold!

Do not read this to Agatha, if you think that it will excite her. You know that every thing which I write is more or less helter-skelter work, and that these poetic effusions are founded upon my blissful ignorance of rules and correctness, so important, however, if one wishes to produce any thing above mediocrity. I shall send you the verses which you have asked for in my next letter. I have no time to-day.

I have nothing more to add to the description, which I gave last, of the life led by the Årsta colony, except that I am painting most industriously for a certain General, who has implored me on his knees for a picture, and — that we consume a great deal of water-gruel.

August fancies himself in heaven with his cornetcy and his uniform. General H—— is very kind to him. He will probably begin [1] to pass his grades for the military service in February. F—— is his oracle, and what "F—— says" and "F—— thinks" is as incontrovertible as the Bible. It is quite delightful to witness his happiness. And fortunate it is that, while life is fresh and we are still young ourselves, Fate shows itself like a complaisant and loving bride, and not like a surly and quarrelsome old woman, who, grumbling, follows our every step, — which often happens to many an honest wanderer.

[1] In order to obtain an accurate acquaintance with the details of military service, an officer has to do duty for some time (in the cavalry from four to six months) as a private, as a corporal, and as a non-commissioned officer. This is termed "passing the degrees," or "going through the grades."

Our father is very weak; Hedda watches over him every other night; and, knowing this, it is with real remorse that at night I lay my head on my pillow.

Our Agatha is thriving excellently well amongst her machinery, such as it has lately been arranged for her. She is merrier than formerly, singing from morning till night her favorite refrain, —

> "Witschly, watschly, witschly, watschly,
> Bump, there goes one!"

My dear little Charlotte! For aught I know I have nothing more to relate to you. Amongst more indifferent acquaintances, I know of nobody who is dying, or who is going to be married. With the exception of these two epochs, there is nothing in their life interesting enough for me to write about.

Farewell, my dearest Charlotte! A long letter I expect and beg from you. Remember how deeply I am interested in all that concerns you, and that nothing so effectually disperses the melancholy which sometimes affects me, as to hear and know that you are enjoying yourself and are happy. Give my love to Agatha. How happy I am, how I rejoice to know, that you are together; but tell me much, much of yourselves. Farewell!

February, 1828.

"Good gracious! Oh, how fortunate that is! Well, how happy I am!"

Do not blot out my joyful effusions, my good, my happy Agatha, my sweet Charlotte, with a contemptuous ejaculation, only because they are not served up with tears or with phosphoric flames.

> You may be very dull,
>   Inditing phrases crude,
> Yet may your heart be full,
>   With richest stores imbued.
> Of feelings warmly glowing
>   You may pour forth whole hoards,

> Both earth and sea o'erflowing
> With flow'ry, flaunting words.
> Yet on the board of common sense,
> A simple dish, without pretense, —
> Say plain potatoes, crisp and dry, —
> Should have a value full as high
> As puddings ever so delicious,
> Served up in gold or silver dishes;
> > Then Agatha, my dear,
> > You must not think it queer,
> > If I in simplest language here
> > Present you my good wishes: —
> " May this dear boy both stout and strong
> In heart and soul and body be.
> And may his lady mother long
> Live in good health right happily!"
>
> Amen.

You will certainly think, my dear Charlotte, that I have nothing else to do than to think and dream of those I love, and, like a turtle-dove, coo out my feelings. All a mistake! A tremendous mistake! I am overrun with people from morning to night; and what do you think they want? Hear only: —

> 'T is either the good mother,
> Or 't is the darling brother,
> Or else the small boy quaking,
> All with the ague shaking!
> Now round the good Mam'selle,
> Who in the house doth dwell,
> They crowd in anxious mood,
> And beg her to supply
> Some sovereign remedy;
> No matter where 't was brewed,
> Or how they gulp it down,
> With many an angry frown;
> If it but make them well,
> From direful ague free,
> 'T will life's elixir be!

And this elixir of life I compose of all kinds of ingredients; such as ale, allspice, Swedish brandy, wormwood, and caraway-seeds, etc., etc. One person I really believed

I had poisoned; but she recovered, and my remedies upon the whole succeed very well.

Your letter made me happy. You are calm, therefore I am so too. It arrived on a Sabbath morning; and, after we had read it, — Agatha and I, — we had our morning service, and prayed fervently and repeatedly: " Charlotte, dear Charlotte! God grant that she may be happy!" Oh, yes! God, the All-good, grant that you may be happy, Charlotte, you and all my sisters, and Agatha W——. I feel that, to complete my earthly happiness, I need you all; and if I only attain this, the saddest circumstances which can surround me in future will not be able to disturb the peace of my soul. Towards that future, to these objects so sorrowful, yet for me so dear, you know, my whole heart and soul yearns, whilst it thanks God for the peace it now enjoys.

> * Morning sun and star of evening,
> All the garish hours of daylight,
> All the silent midnight watches,
> In each throbbing heart discover
> One bright hope, one bitter anguish,
> Still the same unchanging ever,
> And the same deep, fervent prayer.
> In the darksome mine is smouldering
> Fire that preys upon its vitals;
> Sudden as it finds an outlet,
> Lo! its blaze ascends to heaven,
> Like some altar-flame majestic,
> That in clear effulgence glowing
> Rises o'er this earthly sphere.

How busy you must have been for the christening! I picture to myself every thing that is near and about you. How happy we were to hear of Agatha's safe confinement, I cannot describe. It cured *our* Agatha's headache, and I did every thing topsy-turvy the whole morning. Farewell, dear, kind friends. My compliments to the little Count.

1828.

. . . To your grave questions I answer by referring you to my last two letters. It is not now left to my own choice to travel; but rest assured that my choice and my wish is, that it should remain as it is now.

. . . You are right, my dear Charlotte! I should certainly not be able, as you think possible, to bear stoically such trifling discomforts as those which you anticipate. I may in this respect compare your soul to the stout satin, the smooth surface of which can withstand many creases and much wear and tear, in comparison to the soft muslin, which the slightest rough handling spoils, and the likeness of which I recognize in the composition of my own weak and helpless soul. Be not uneasy about me and my disposition. Gay I am not, it is true; but I am often very happy when I contemplate this peaceful life of self-denial, which, I trust in God, may guide me to the goal which I have always deemed the only one worth longing for. Earthly happiness I hope to receive at the hands of my brothers and sisters, especially my sisters, and I know that their happiness will render my own too great almost for this earth. Do not see herein any feature of melancholy. It is, believe me, not melancholy. On the contrary, in these ideas my brightest hopes are clothed; and also the belief (I will not call it a fantastic one) that the fervent and constant prayers which a heart, renouncing all its own claims and devoting itself to God, pours out for those whom it loves above all others, and for their own sake, will not be ineffectual. Do not deprive me of the happiness of hoping that one day I shall be your invisible guardian angel. And if your Fredrika, once so worldly-minded, should seek, under a more serious exterior, for peace and a more spiritual life, it ought not to make you uneasy, dearest Charlotte, you who know that it is necessary, especially for certain characters. My dearest Charlotte, you can never write too much about yourself; for me it will always be too little. You are really very good to write, when I know that letter-writing does not much interest you. But you think of me, — you wish to make me happy, — and you do it.

The painting of the old man with the cap, which was hanging in my bedroom, I have copied in sepia in miniature, on ivory. I intend giving either this or a "Sainte Famille," also miniature in sepia, to the General. My "Napoleon" is indeed very good; and he who wants to have him must pay me seventy-five rix dollars for him.

My vena is very dry; but when it again begins to flow, it shall flow towards you.

The manuscript of the narrative of the "War with the Barbarians" has chanced to be made an *auto-da-fé* of, together with some other contraband; and our father has got the newspaper. As you want it, I shall ask Hedda to copy and send it to you.

Embrace Agatha for me, and say to her every thing that is loving.

ACCOUNT OF THE WAR WITH THE BARBARIANS.[1]

Extract of a Letter from Årsta, dated 20th of March, 1827.

"This neighborhood has lately witnessed terrible scenes; and even if time were to throw its thickest veil over the heroic deeds which they engendered, still History would be able to read, without spectacles, the letters shining like flames through night's darkness, and record the eternal characters upon her tables. But I will not keep you any longer upon the rack of curiosity.

"Innumerable hordes of Barbarians overran our peaceful neighborhood; their fearful shouts and grunting filled,

---

[1] When my sister Agatha, while undergoing the orthopedic treatment at Årsta, and still using crutches, and wearing round her head an instrument or machine resembling a helmet, and called "Minerva," was one day going to take a walk, together with Fredrika and Hedda, they were surrounded in the court-yard by a herd of pigs. Their terror and confusion was much increased when all the dogs began barking at and chasing these animals, until my sisters were at last saved by the man-servant, Lindberg, who came to their rescue. Fredrika wrote the same night an account of this incident, heading it the *Årsta Gazette*, which she wrote in printed characters, to imitate a newspaper, and sent to town in order to amuse my father on his birthday.

even at a distance, the hearts of the inhabitants with terror, and dreadful was the havoc committed by them wherever their sharp swords encountered any resistance. The earth shook under the thunder of their war-engines; the danger was pressing; while, with noble self-sacrifice, Brigadier-General Hedda di Bravura made a sortie from the fortress of Årsta, at the head of the regiment 'Fredrika,' so renowned for its bravery, but now reduced, in consequence of heavy losses, to a small corps. In another direction was seen hastening to the attack, in double-quick time, and with loud war-cries of 'Bow-wow!' the heroic volunteers Terrible, Vainqueur, Diana, Camilla, the youthful hero Arrow, the undaunted Hunter, led on by the *Général-en-chef* of the jumping infantry, the incomparable Agatha della Poltronna. Their plan was to surround the enemy. The attack of our generals from two opposite sides was made with the greatest valor; and notwithstanding the triple superiority of the Barbarians in numerical strength, their war-cry becoming louder and louder every moment, they began to show that disorder and terror was spreading through their ranks; when all at once, in consequence of the too great ardor of the curveting volunteers, a momentary confusion arose among our troops; friend and foe were fighting in one entangled mass, scarcely able to recognize each other; every thing was in a hurly-burly, and terror and confusion reached its height, when, in the very brunt of the battle, General Hedda di Bravura, while performing deeds of marvelous gallantry, fell, as there is every reason to suspect, more in consequence of the incautious onset of the curveting volunteers, than in consequence of the cuffs of the Barbarians. The regiment 'Fredrika,' seeing with despair its undaunted leader down, took to flight with inconceivable celerity; while the youthful Della Poltronna stood alone and unconquered, in the midst of the combatants, animating by voice and example his volunteers, already flagging from over-exertion, to a renewed attack. It seemed as if

Minerva herself was hovering over his head, and by a well-timed application of certain war-engines, called crutches, he succeeded, as by a miracle, to turn the scale in our favor. He became, however, soon aware of the necessity of a speedy retreat; and he was just weighing in his mind how this could be effected with honor, and without too serious a loss, when suddenly a helping angel, sent from above, came like a whirlwind to the rescue. It is Alexander! It is Bucephalus! In a word, it was Lindberg! He runs, he gallops, he flies; he is everywhere. The enemy was, after a few minutes, dispersed in a headlong flight in all directions; he was pursued with unflinching energy by Lindberg, flaming like the Aurora Borealis; and before night had thrown its mantle over the scene, innumerable prisoners were made. Scarcely had the battle-field been cleared of the hostile army, when, to the amazement of every body, General Hedda di Bravura, who was thought to be amongst the fallen, got up, and, staring at the field of honor with tearful eyes, struck up with a loud voice a thundering song of victory; after which, with glowing countenance, he turned towards the fortress, where the regiment 'Fredrika' was lying in ambush, ready to open, if necessary, a brisk fire through the windows, and shouted with all his might these words: 'Veni, vidi, vici!' which were answered by the said gallant regiment with loud huzzas! 'Long live our General, Hedda di Bravura!' With triumphal music and huzzas the conquerors held their entry into the fortress, where General Hedda di Bravura, under careful tending, will recover from his wounds, which were found to consist in merely a severe contusion.

"There are strong reasons (and I mention it with great indignation) to suspect the commander of the fortress, Chevalier C. B——, of being in secret understanding with the Barbarians. The inefficient measures taken, and the want of energy displayed by him during their daring inroad, would alone have been sufficient to inspire this belief, even had he not himself confirmed the same one day at dinner, when roast pork was put upon the table, by openly proposing a toast for the Barbarians. It is even whispered that a colony of these brutes, founded in a neighboring allied state, is in a very flourishing condition, owing to his secret agency."

1828.

The latter part of your letter, my dear Charlotte, has effaced the painful impression which its other contents made upon me. That you are well is to me a necessity, and this knowledge throws a light upon my path, like a friendly little star, so that complete darkness never surrounds me. Do not reply to this by any thanks: it is not of my own free will that it is so; it is necessity, it is fate. And if I had a choice, I might perhaps not have submitted to it, because my beloved banner, Independence, will therefore always be in danger. Meanwhile, I am tolerably reconciled to my fate. On you alone rests the responsibility and duty to take care, above all, of your own happiness for the sake of mine. Remember well what I am now going to write, my dear sister. I feel convinced that it depends only upon yourself to remain where you are as long as you like. Our father is exceedingly pleased that you and Agatha, whom he really loves, are together, and he says "that he cannot now understand how he could ever have made any difficulties about it." We all, and I especially, wish that you would remain there; every thing seems to promise you an agreeable life, and more useful activity than could have fallen to your lot at old Årsta. I——hus and T——ö, so it seems to me, will in their shades harbor my little Charlotte so pleasantly and so comfortably, and no doubt soften every thought of regret at not wandering among our hazel-woods and gooseberry-bushes. Sincerely happy as I should be to see you again, and conscious, as I am, that my longing will increase in proportion as the days grow shorter, still I shall enjoy this summer in a double measure, provided I can be sure that *you* do the same; a thing which you have not done for many years. Consider this well, dearest Charlotte, and then follow the dictates of your own free will. A letter from Agatha, who writes so well and so engagingly, and one from yourself, will surely cause a prolongation of your stay.

I do not share the apprehension which you express, as long as you always remain what you were created to be, — artless, good, and obliging. It is not a new, but a true, thought, that every body ought to endeavor thoroughly to know the intrinsic worth of his own character, and, like a skillful sculptor, to form, work, and polish it until the rough cast made by Nature stands out in its harmonious and original beauty; that every thing foreign — every angle — may disappear. This is the work of at least half a lifetime. For the remaining other half one stands, in the most fortunate case, like Psyche in Sergel's studio. The master who carries the ideal in his soul, is never perfectly satisfied with his workmanship; the small alterations and embellishments which he makes, are most frequently visible only to his own artist eye.

Your expression " that I have returned to life," amuses me. I am still the same that I was when, by some chance, I became so painfully depressed; perhaps even more calm, more submissive, more meek, and therefore less in danger of being again exposed to any thing similar. Gay I am not, and not merry, except in my letters; and shall perhaps not be so again; nor do I even wish it after the bent which my feelings and my thoughts have taken. But I am so calm that I often feel happy, and am ready to derive enjoyment and pleasure from even the least of the good things of life. A flower, a book, a fine day, gives me pleasure now as much as when I was a child; and above all, my painting, upon which I build great speculations.

With respect to my grand project of travelling, I see plainly that nothing can now be done. I must wait. In my present position, — especially my pecuniary position, — patience is the best wisdom. God's will be done! Meanwhile I intend to be more active in all that surrounds me. Be it said with due permission, I am thoroughly healthy and strong. But who will believe my words?

Farewell, my dear Charlotte; write more about yourself; read "Grandison," and be not more reserved than this model of perfection, and his Miss Byron.

ÅRSTA, 13th June, 1828.

Our letters cross each other, my dear Charlotte! By your last, addressed to us all, I see with sincere delight that you seem to thrive well and to amuse yourself occasionally. When next you write, tell me more particularly how you feel, and of the state of your mind, etc., etc. It interests me more than any thing else. Ah! how exceedingly delightful it will be to see you again, and yet I wish that it may not be so soon. Our family atmosphere is heavy, and I know that if I should see it depress you, I should again lose the strength which I have recovered in the course of these two pleasant, but solitary winters at Årsta. I am a poor child, dearest Charlotte, sensitive in the extreme both for myself and for others; and amongst these others, you are nearest to my heart. Do not, however, believe that I am sad; far from it; I enjoy very gratefully and contentedly the many peaceful days which I now have; and the glances which I cast into the future, although half shy and by stealth, reveal to me always what I wish for my sisters and for myself. I occupy myself as usual, and more I might do if I would meddle in the internal state affairs of this place. Now and then a peasant or a peasant woman come to solicit my intercession and my protection in one thing or another; but I, poor thing, who have less influence than the dishclout of a Prime Minister's cook, am obliged to put them off with fair words and slender hope.

Agatha W—— has written an amiable and eloquent letter (according to her wont) to our mother, in which she asks that you may stay over the summer with her. How happy I am that you are so dear to Agatha!

I am not going to the L——séns for many reasons, the most weighty of which is, that I want to be all I can to our dear Agatha, especially now when she requires care and assistance. We are now busy getting up her wardrobe. I sew, turn the wrong way, as usual, and have to rip open and sew over again; but I get through, after all. The day when August makes his appearance here in full regimentals, I intend dressing my darling in dazzling white and rose color. I shall give you a full and detailed account of this meeting, which I heartily rejoice in.

Now, farewell, my darling; remain well, sleep well, sing well, and enjoy yourself well.

Agatha embraces you with a volume of Madame de Genlis' "Memoirs" in her hand.

Årsta, 16th September.

Having now been alone a whole week, I have with all my heart and soul enjoyed repose. Solitude is my greatest happiness; why or how I do not understand, when sisters, good as angels, are my daily companions. But so it is. Only when I am quite alone, do I feel happy.

Our mother has gone to town to meet our father, from whom we have not had any letter for three weeks. Two have now arrived which our mother sent out to us yesterday. Our father is feasted, caressed, and made a great deal of by friends and relatives, who drink our healths and hold banquets to celebrate his arrival in Finland. You, my dear Charlotte, who are so very fond of all relatives, ought to have been with him on this journey, which, to judge from his and Claes' letters, must have been very pleasant. Agatha is now up, often half the day; is stronger, and very charming. Hedda is weaving down-stairs in the corner room, and I — I preserve fruit, write novels and write letters, paint, spin, go and come, in and out, and when evening comes I look to see whither the morning flew so fast.

My sisters stretch out hands, unsoiled by ink, to embrace you.

Årsta, 20th October, 1828.

Yesterday we received the Holy Communion, Agatha and I. I returned thanks for two years of rest, and prayed for strength; prayed for strength humbly to receive all future dispensations; prayed for the happiness and peace of all those who belong to me, and also most fervently for her who now, for the first time after several years, went to the Lord's table. Agatha was deeply and sincerely moved, and this impression upon her did me an infinite deal of good. Ah! may she be happy; may she be good! May in her the former effect the latter. The path of sorrow is so bitter and embitters so much! I am a little sad to-night, and I ought, perhaps, not to write to you.

I long very much to hear that you are enjoying yourself. The winter will, I hope, be a pleasant one for us, and if Agatha has any pleasure, it will give pleasure also to me. But the anticipation of the town air gives me the horrors. To-morrow we expect our mother and Claes here, and then the day for our moving will be fixed.

27th October.

Bishop T——s arrived here to-day. I liked him very much. Energetic and wise — a real bishop. He led the conversation to Wallin's sermon on Annunciation Day, which last year caused me so much racking of the brain.[1]

---

[1] The subject of Bishop Wallin's sermon on Annunciation Day, 1827, was "Woman's noble and humble mission," for the faithful fulfillment of which the Bishop urged, by examples taken out of the Virgin Mary's life, the ne-

It was excellent, thought the Bishop. We argued the point for a little while, when he allowed that Wallin, in one

cessity of the following qualities: "Pure and sincere piety; unassuming and unaffected modesty; wise and gentle meekness; tender and delicate attention; all-sacrificing and all-submissive love." In accordance herewith it was argued, "that the domestic sphere was woman's proper world;" it was further said, "that what especially belonged to her mission was, that she ought humbly to step back when sudden angry passions vent themselves upon her; that there is no circumstance in life where a contrary conduct could be excused; that, in order to triumph, she ought carefully to watch her own temper and submit unconstrainedly to that of others; have respect for the opinion of others, without any prepossession in favor of her own; and that even where her own opinion should in reality be the right one, she ought patiently to wait her time to make it valid. Without pure and sincere piety, woman's virtue was nothing but vanity; her liberal education nothing but surface; her life nothing but a volatile play, and her whole existence nothing else but an endless contradiction. But a *man*, even if he does not always see the heavenly truths with the same quickness, or if he appears sometimes to doubt them, or think less of, or live less in them, would still, provided his words or actions do not otherwise stamp him as blasphemous or godless, in most cases merit only pity, and his unfortunate state of mind could be, if not exactly excused, still often accounted for, by saying that no pious mother had formerly given his mind a better tendency, or that in later years no pious wife had turned his dim and confused thoughts from earthly to heavenly matters. But a woman who does not feel that religion is the soul of her soul, is an inexplicable and odious deviation from the celestial order of things," etc., etc.

The incongruities which Fredrika Bremer imagined with sorrow that she had found in the social position of woman, appeared to her to have been, as it were, systematized and advocated in this sermon. It made a most painful impression upon her; and on coming home from church, she gave vent to her feelings in an essay, held in a satirical tone, on the superiority of man and the inferiority of woman, finishing with this dialogue:—Man, with head erect, striking his breast proudly with his hand: "*I !*" Woman : "Thou!" Man: "*I will !*" Woman: "Oh, very well !" Man: "*Go.*" Woman goes. Man: "*Come back.*" She comes back. Man: "*Be merry.*" Woman dies. After her death heaven was opened to receive her; but when afterwards the man also tried to get admittance, it was denied to him by the porter at heaven's gates, who referred him to Bishop Wallin, under whose surplice he hastened to conceal himself.

On the following day, Fredrika Bremer wrote and sent an anonymous letter to the Bishop, in which she requested that woman, to her noble and peaceful mission, might have a counterpart in a delineation of the *man*, such as he *ought* to be in his domestic relations, and drawn with the same severity and power, in order that the first picture might have a companion, and in order, also, that men may in the former sermon not find an excuse or two places, had not been quite sincere. "Meanwhile," said he, "Wallin is perfectly right in advocating religiosity amongst women; for if it is not found amongst *them*, then all is lost. A man returns always to his wife and children from the world, from his errors, from noise and bustle; but if he does not find religion amongst *them*, he remains forever a stranger to it."

On Friday, the 31st, we are move to town. Oh, my beloved, my beautiful country!

As you, my dear Charlotte, and also Agatha W——, are so very indulgent regarding my poetry, I shall trumpet forth a piece, which I composed last night in bed.

The incident which I sing is true, and its unfortunate little hero is to come to me to-morrow:—

THE SON OF MISERY.

A desolate cottage stands by the wood's verge;
  Within it is dismal, and wretched and dreary;
  Deep sighs issue forth as from hearts that are weary,
And outside the owl hoots a funeral dirge.

A girl so defenseless and needy and lone,
  On pallet of straw in the cottage was lying;
  But none came to comfort or care for the dying,
Till kindly Death took her and made her his own.

for their indifference in religious matters; that the despotic nature of a great many amongst them may not, on the strength of the same, try to prove that the duty of woman is to be man's most humble servant, and to bear patiently all the heart-gnawing sorrows which, through his faults and his conduct, he might every day cause her, and still be entitled to demand of her love and all love's sacrifices; and if he (the Bishop) would soon deliver a religious lecture or sermon, similar to the one addressed to woman, by which the conscience of all destroyers of domestic peace might be awakened, woman would then have to thank the Bishop for increased happiness; and the grateful hearts of many women would call down blessings on him who had insured this happiness to them, by convincing men, in his stirring and powerful language, how essentially their conduct would contribute to the comfort of home, to the wife's happiness, and thus enable her more willingly to fulfill her duties.

This request was never responded to.

Then hushed was the heart that uneasily beat,
  A heart fond and loving, though erring and failing;
  And silenced the voice that 'mid anguish was wailing
To Jesus to pardon her lover's deceit.

The offspring of frailty and misery drear
  Alone in the hut by the death-bed was playing;
  O'er stiffening limbs his fond fingers were straying,
Caressing the mother who 'd held him so dear.

His look was bewildered, and pale was his cheek;
  No word did he utter, though hungry and chilly;
  A dog could have begged, but he, stricken and silly,
Though sorely in want, was unable to speak.

I looked in his face, and methought I saw there
  Expression, though faintly for life it was striving;
  A spark from the Author celestial, surviving,
Might yet burn brightly in life-giving air.

Now toll the church-bells, and the dead on a bier
  To silence is borne in humble procession;
  And wanting that noble, that precious possession, —
His reason, — the orphan walks carelessly near.

Oh, God! he ne'er dreameth that he has no more
  A tender and motherly heart to watch o'er him;
  That now from him taken has gone on before him
The one who in sorrow to sorrow him bore.

The coffin is raised from the black-covered bier;
  Already deep down in the earth it is sinking:
  Ah! none at this grave, of the lonely one thinking,
Will offer a flower, will weep but a tear.

The grave is soon filled, the cross stands in its place,
  A sign which to perishing sinners proclaimeth
  And showeth that God, who this sinner reclaimeth,
Is full of compassion, and mercy, and grace.

His pale cheek he leaneth against the church wall,
  Neglected, forgotten; he now has no keeper;
  While psalms for the last time are raised for the sleeper,
And slowly on breezes of evening they fall.

The sun has gone down while he rambles around,
  But kind stars protectingly over him brighten,

And home to a cottage his tired soul they lighten, —
His mother's — ah! there will no mother be found.

But gladly the boy sees his wanderings end,
  And now towards the hut so deserted he presses,
  Expecting fond motherly cares and caresses:
The mother has gone to the penitent's Friend.

Alone in the cottage, so patient and mild,
  The orphan is waiting, and while the day beameth,
  In mercy deceived, his poor fancy still dreameth
That soon — soon the mother will come to her child.

When day-time and evening to darkness have rolled,
  A painful disquiet the little one haunteth;
  He wandereth round, seeking that which he wanteth,
As restlessly seeketh the miser his gold.

He looks in the bed where his mother has lain,
  And where she sat spinning, in all her old places;
  Her longs for her loving, her tender embraces,
He stretches out fond little arms, but in vain.

The clothing she wore in the cottage still lies,
  He toucheth it, thinking 't is hers, and he crieth,
  And faintly a stammering "mammy" he sigheth,
But never — but never the mother replies.

M. R. W.

30th October.

I did intend to have taken a sketch to-day of the poor little boy, whom an old grandmother, aged 70, living in the hut "Bakom," takes care of. Agatha took a lively interest in him, and wished very much to see him. I must confess that I looked a little awkward when I beheld a little stout and chubby boy, with a face radiant with happiness. He is six years old. He cannot articulate any words, but he produces a variety of sounds. He was otherwise highly, although idiotically, comical, making the sweetest, smiling grimaces; and only when now and then he called out, "Aja" (his mother's name was Maja), the expression of his face and the tone of his voice became very sad. For the little sketch of the "Son of Misery" in my album, I therefore took only his eyes, and all the rest out of my own head.

STOCKHOLM, 3d November.

Here we are, my dearest Charlotte! And while writing this I can scarcely refrain from tears. On Friday we left for town. The weather was in the beginning rough and unpleasant, but the nearer we came to town, the more the sky began to brighten before us, until we approached the outskirts of the metropolis, when it became perfectly blue and brilliant. I mention this because it made me think. in the beginning it will be heavy and dull, then better, and ultimately well. When one has doubts and fears, one easily becomes a little superstitious.

In the evening I received your letter. How happy I am to see that you are thriving so well! F—— came a little later to see us, gay and lively. I went early to bed, with an autumnal night in my heart and in my soul. Saturday was to me an indescribably sad day, and I wept bitter, bitter tears; a tribute to past moments, against the heavy and gnawing return of which no seraph's wings can protect us; and, as so often before, I only sighed, "Alas, die, die!" In the evening I got a little better; I read a good book, prayed to God, became calmer, and vowed to bear up against it.

4th November.

I shall say only a little more of ourselves. We are very comfortably lodged; our drawing-room is elegantly furnished and very cosy. But I miss what I value more than every thing else,—a private room all to myself, if ever so small. We are very quiet here, and are allowed to be much by ourselves down-stairs. Our father's good and gentle temper is gone; as yet it is not difficult to manage, but may at any moment become so. Our mother is cheerful and kind; Hedda calm and quiet, but not gay; Agatha joyous and full of hope (as long as it lasts), and I — alas, my dearest Charlotte! I fight against oppressive feelings;

I say to myself, "I *will* be cheerful," and I weep. "But it will be better when the worst is over." Do not moralize, dearest Charlotte! I know how well you mean it; but it is all in vain. Born to feel every thing deeply and vividly, philosophy and reasoning can, only to a certain and very insufficient degree, avail, until submission to God's will can have time to fill my heart with peace and repose; but before that, my poor heart must have become faint from its own pulsations. Meanwhile I have hope, and that is much. In my next letter I shall be able to tell you that I am better. *A propos*, write more about yourself and less about us, my dear Charlotte. How much good it does me to know that you are so happy!

I send you now the verses which you asked for: —

* THE MOURNER'S LULLABY.

Cease thy weary beating,
 Heart with care opprest!
Life's deep canker, Sorrow!
 Taste the balm of rest.

Close, ye heavy eyelids,
 O'er each burning tear!
Eve, with starry mantle,
 Waves her poppies near.

Slumber, gentle slumber,
 Soon o'er earth shall reign;
Airy dreams are flitting
 Lightly in her train.

Soft as mists of evening
 Spread their downy wings,
In the silent midnight,
 Peace and rest she brings.

Lo, the day is ended,
 Day both long and drear!
On my pillow falling,
 Drops the silent tear.

Tears are friends in sorrow;
 Soft as dew they flow

On the fire that burneth
  In our day of woe.

O'er the troubled spirit
  Peace is stealing now,
When sleep, like an angel,
  Kisses this sad brow.

Hush! oh let me slumber;
  Let me dream of bliss;
Cease, fond heart, thy throbbing
  Grudge not rest like this!

Oh, my silent pillow,
  Friend so true, so dear!
Where, in dreams Elysian,
  Joy still hovers near.

Fancy's star above me
  Beams with lustre bland;
Hope's fair daughter, smiling,
  Takes my willing hand.

Then the weary captive
  Bursts his fetters sore,
Sings a song of triumph
  On a fairer shore.

Sees, as in a mirror,
  Future ages gleam;
Faith, with bark unswerving,
  Stems the surging stream.

Feels all pangs departing,
  Sees the heavens grow bright,
Sees the journey ended,
  Sees the Lord of Light.

And a voice melodious
  Whispers, He is thine!
Holy hymns shall praise Thee,
  Father of all — and mine!

Fain of such glad tidings
  I would yet dream on;
Of all pangs forgetful,
  Thanking God alone!

M. R. W.

STOCKHOLM, 22d December, 1828.

I steal away from my Christmas-boxes and all bustle, in order to write to you a few lines. If I had not had so much to paint at daylight and also at candle-light, I would have written a great deal.

August, the dear boy, came home on the 11th instant, full of life, in good health and high spirits. His examination testimonials are the best that have been given during the last twenty years for a civil service examination. He got two "cum laude," and two "laudatur." This examination has really created quite a sensation. I have never seen our father so touched and overjoyed; he pressed August to his heart, and wept for joy. One ought to acknowledge that it is very praiseworthy in a youth, just turned eighteen, to have passed the grades, and, after three months' study, to deserve such testimonials. Agatha, who, with our mother, has been to the opera to see "La Dame Blanche," was the whole evening very much enchanted with the White Lady and the studious cornet. August is tall, thin, very plain, but looks very nice nevertheless.

God bless you, and consequently also me, with a happy and good New Year!

STOCKHOLM, 18th February, 1829.

This time I shall not send you any formal letter. For a while I have been too lazy to write. Neither has any thing happened worth writing about. See here, however, what is most remarkable. Yesterday evening, after my mother and sisters had gone to pay some visits, I went up-stairs to our father, who sat reading his newspapers at the tea-table. He asked me whether I wanted some tea. I answered with a gentle "No, thank you." I then asked him if he wished me to read the newspapers to him. He answered with a gentle "No," but said that he had something for *me* to read, and went into the next room and returned with a letter, which he gave me; the handwriting was unknown to me. I went into the drawing-room and read, to my astonishment, a very well-written offer of marriage in due form for my *chétive* person from ——, who probably had waited for his promotion to a higher office before making a final attempt, which rather astonished me after all that I had told him. The letter is otherwise very good, and I was really sorry for the man, that he should have addressed the wrong person. Having read the letter, I returned it to my father, who asked me what he was to answer. Without the slightest hesitation, as you may well imagine, I begged of him to say, "No, I thank you most humbly!" And there was an end of it for that evening. This morning my father sent for me, read me his answer, and asked me whether it was according to my wish. It contained many good things, but others which might have been left out. But it would never have done for me to make any remark. Afterwards I agreed with my mother and sisters, that, in order to enjoy life's mediocre happiness, which, perhaps, is all one can expect, one would do wiser to take a ——, than many another one with great external gifts and large estates,— provided, *nota bene*, one intends to enter into the holy state of matrimony, which I pray, together with all the tortures mentioned in the Litany, to be spared from. I confess, however, that I would rather wish to be able to exclaim, with one of Sir Walter Scott's personages, "Mon mari, épargnez notre ennemi," than "Généreux ennemis, épargnez mon mari;" which latter, no doubt, ——'s wife will have to learn by heart.

You ask me whether I would like to stay with Agatha W——? I should like it, at least for some time, for a winter or so. One of my reasons is, that I should like to write and try my wings as an authoress. Here in town this is impossible. All my energy, my wit, my ideas become mouldy. Besides, I have a great longing to breathe a little fresh air, and would wish at the same time to be, if I could, of some comfort to Agatha W——. For my sisters I can do so very little, because my mind is not happy. I believe that my letters, far more than my conversation, would amuse them. Our father feels now sometimes a feverish longing to have you at home, and we shall see whether I cannot obtain permission to be absent for some time. It is strange with what a heavy hand time has led us through our years of youth. We — you and I — are approaching thirty years, and what enjoyments have we yet had, although we are both, I venture to say it, made to enjoy and to give enjoyment to others. How little have we not been able to do, although both gifted with so much energy and desire for useful and beneficent activity. However, I will not complain of those two last years, which I have spent in the country. I have during that time been useful, and frequently happy. Rarely a day went past when I had not an opportunity of alleviating some sorrow and giving some happiness. Besides, I had liberty, this precious elixir of life and health, and I drank of it, and of the fresh country air, in full draughts. My health, both of body and of soul, improved, and I enjoyed a life free from pain, especially as it was not a useless one for others. I often remembered your frequently expressed wish, that you might have beside you some mouths into which you could put the food which you thought superfluous for yourself. This pleasure I have had almost daily, often at the expense of my own enjoyment, and this little voluntary low diet did me a great deal of good. But all this is past. I am now a zero in liberty and in power. It is, however, not with any bitter or dissatisfied feelings that I have to-day thrown a sad glance over the past years of our youth. I believe that a wiser will than our own has guided our destinies, and I trust that the remaining part of our life may with more reason be called *the better part*, as being more useful, more active, and therefore more happy. I say, I hope so, because the prospects are as much, and perhaps more, limited than they have ever been. All the happiness, all the joy which I now ask is, to be allowed to be a silent witness to that of yourself and of our sisters. Alas! when shall it be so? Our family frigate either sails too much by the head, or lies becalmed, or is rolling in a ground-swell, and since she was launched she never has had a fair wind. Blow, winds, blow!

I send you herewith the verses which I wrote the other day.

As regards my authorship, I intend continuing "Sketches of Every-day Life," and also novels with this title. I have several such in my head, and have begun one, which I fancy will be interesting and useful. But these poor butterflies want fresh air and warmth to enable them to take wing. I do not intend devoting myself to composition. I hope, if it pleases God, to do something better in this world for myself and others. It is a mere pastime for the present.

*THE EARLY CHRISTMAS SERVICE.

Hark! the chimes in mellow cadence fall:
   See, the church is decked in festive state;
Fain her children round her she would call;
Peace and joy she would pour forth on all,
   And to God earth's children consecrate.

Winter's icy hand o'er hill and bower
   Spreads his shroud of snow in northern clime;
Yet on earth we hail the sacred hour
When a bud, become Life's glorious flower,
   Thorn-encircled sprang from depths of time.

Silver stars still twinkle in the sky,
   Fires of joy are kindled o'er the earth;
While the angels tune their songs on high,
Jubilant the ransomed bands reply
   In the house of God with solemn mirth.

Say why far and near, through darksome night,
   Gleam those countless lights, with flickering ray?
Hark! a heaven-born strain replies with might,
O'er the mists of yore has dawn'd a light,
   Let us sing, "A child is born to-day!"

May each infant heart in hut or hall
    Beat with joy, as dawns this happy day;
On their knees may pious mothers fall, —
Teach their babes with lisping voice to call
    On that Child in lowly crib that lay;

Tell how child-like hearts to Him are dear;
    How the pure, the meek, He loving sought;
And, as runes in bark cut deep and clear,
On their infant minds impress whate'er
    Jesus did on earth and what He taught.

Haste, ye nations, to His courts with song;
    Praise in tuneful strains His name most blest;
Children, pure in heart! the young, the strong;
Ye aged! that slowly creep along,
    Hasten, in your Brother's arms to rest!

He hath lit a star in darkest night,
    Through the mists of life it sheds its ray;
Heav'n-born Hope its name, that maiden bright,
Who the pilgrim guides to realms of light,
    Where all mysteries shall be clear as day.

Dark the midnight hour that's passed away, —
    Dark as death; but once, when time shall cease,
Dawns the morning of eternal day,
That with countless lights of purest ray,
    Hails the reign of endless grace and peace.

STOCKHOLM, 12th April, 1829.

I am so eager to write to you, that I really believe that the mail will have to carry every post-day the extra weight of a letter from me. My first thought when I awake in the morning is " Charlotte." And this thought is now so cheering, that I fancy we have got sunshine and spring weather, until I look out of the window and see that winter and snow-storms have not left us yet, in the midst of April. How I long for a letter from you! I am sure I wish —— every success. "Brilliant match!" God save us from it! I can never couple with it the idea of *happy marriage*. I believe that with —— you will enjoy real, true, domestic happiness. Of his character and qualities you will soon be able to judge best yourself. I am only afraid that you expect too much. I learn to value more highly every day in a man, goodness and justice. But I have such a sincere and joyful hope that these rare household gods shall change my Charlotte's earthly home into a heaven. By the by, *notre futur beau-frère* is, I suppose, now in C——a? The other morning we had an immense deal to do to remember his physiognomy. Hedda knew it a little better; but you must be so amiable as to come to our assistance, especially in what regards the shape of his nose, which has entirely escaped our memory. And, once more, my dear Charlotte, I must ask you to write about every thing; the greatest trifle is now of interest. I shall now try to speak of something else.

Last Monday I was at the Baroness F——'s *pour toute la journée*, together with the L——s; it was very agreeable, not to speak of the pleasure (of which I feel very little nowadays) of being warmly complimented by the assembled company upon my paintings, of which only two were there, namely, that of Countess B—— in sepia, which always hangs behind Lady F——'s chair; and that of L—— in colors, which latter I had just finished, and which has afforded me a great deal of pleasure, by the pleasure which it gives his wife.

1829.

After dispatching my letter to you last Friday, we three sisters here at home sat down together on the sofa to read your letter over again; made again our commentaries on the same; and gave free vent to our cheerful hopes in (I may well say so) the innocence of our hearts, and in our affection for you. The imagination of girls, like young fiery colts, is sometimes disposed to bolt, and ours cleared with a few bounds all the five-barred gates of time, while we thought of how to furnish the house and how to do all the needle-work for you. Hedda had seen charming curtains made with patchwork, which she wished to take as models. Agatha thought of pocket-handkerchiefs and lots of embroidery. I declared that I had not courage to venture upon this kind of artistic needle-work, but offered to do all sorts of hemming, stitching, and felling, which might be required. We all agreed in being perfectly satisfied with the exterior of the person in question, and in our fervent hope, or rather belief, in his being excellent and good. Inform our mother soon of all. By doing so, you do not in any case bind yourself to any thing against your own inclination, because without inclination you ought certainly not to unite yourself to him; but remember this good and true passage: —

"The happiness of human life is at best comparative. The utmost we should hope for here is such a situation as, with a *self-approving mind*, will carry us best through the present scene of trial; such a situation as, all circumstances considered, is, upon the whole, most eligible for us, though some of its circumstances may be disagreeable."

In another place in "Grandison," where Lady D—— tries to persuade Harriet to marry her son, she says, with equal truth: —

"You are pious, dutiful, benevolent. Cannot you, if you are unable to entertain for the man who now with so much ardor addresses you, were you married to him, the passion called love, regard him as gratitude would oblige you to prefer any other man who is assiduous to do you service or pleasure? Cannot you show him as much good will as you could any other man whom it was in your power to make happy? Would you esteem him less than a person absolutely a stranger to you? The exertion of your native benevolence, of your natural obligingness, of your common gratitude, of your pity, is all that is asked of you. The exertion will make him happy; and if you retain that delight which you have hitherto taken in promoting the happiness of others, who are not undeserving, you will be yourself not unhappy."

This might at all events be said to you, unless, as I believe, —— soon manages so that all persuasion will be superfluous. May this be so!

I might have all sorts of trifling and funny things to tell you, but I have now neither thoughts, ink, nor pen for any other than the one subject. Why has not the mail wings? Write soon and about every thing.

The other night, at the Franzéns, my mother heard my little book spoken of. It was very much liked, and many surmises were made as to who the author could be.

STOCKHOLM, 30th June, 1829.

Lost in the infinite, an obscure Atom bewailed his nothingness: "Why was I created," he complained, "if, amongst all that lives, moves, and acts, I alone should feel the pain of my insignificance? Oh! that I were only a dew-drop, fallen from the clouds to refresh earth's flowers. Oh! that I were only a particle of the fountain's crystal water, so salutary to earth's noblest son, man; or a breath of air, which, at the Creator's will, cools the weary pilgrim's throbbing temples; or a flower's fragrant exhalation, which, life-giving and lovely, loses itself in the air which it enriches. Oh! that I were for only one moment of my obscure life, a comfort to some one, — then would I bless my existence!" Thus moaned the Atom.

Brightly the sun shone upon earth, giving life to all and blessed by all. The rippling waves caressed the shores where flowers gratefully bent over the refreshing stream, on whose bosom their smiling images were mirrored. Freshly and merrily the wind played amongst flowers and foliage. Evening came. The dew fell upon the earth, which gratefully sent up endless fragrance to benign Heaven. Nature in silence scattered her favors. Nobody and nothing either wanted or missed the Atom. He felt it, and in a dim void, he thought that his life was slowly ending or sinking like twilight into night. And night rested upon the Atom; but he felt his own darker night. Then upon

Aurora's rays came the Angel of Consolation, a bright seraph, who, with inexhaustible treasures of celestial balm, soared forth over the earth; and wherever a martyr suffers for truth, wherever a down-trod ant feels a pang, there he halts, gives life, enjoyment, comfort, forgetfulness, or — death. The seraph saw the suffering Atom, and heard his silent complaint.

"Rejoice, suffering Atom!" said his friendly voice. "Thy wish has been heard by an ever-listening ear. A tear of compassion and consolation, thou shalt glisten in my wreath, and fall, a drop of balm, upon Affliction's burning pain."

He spoke, and already the Atom glittered, transformed, blissful, and bright, like a smiling tear, upon a beautiful poppy in the seraph's wreath. "Oh!" whispered he, with humble joy, "I am but a drop; but, beautiful seraph, if sanctified by thee, it gives to me the power to comfort a sufferer, then will I praise my glorious destiny, — then will I bless thee and my eternal origin."

Who is the Atom, dearest Charlotte, — who else but your poor Fredrique, who hopes and strives to become this soothing drop of balm? My second volume of the "Sketches of Every-day Life" will contain several smaller pieces, in which, from my own experience, I intend sketching, under the form of real occurrences, several misfortunes and sufferings, and also eventual comfort and balm for the same. I am just now busy composing these. The little piece, which stands here above, is intended to express, at the conclusion of the book, the fervent wishes and humble hopes of the "Atom." I wrote also the other day another piece, called "The Home of Prayer," which I now send you, as I suppose it will give you pleasure to read it.

We have some relatives in town, my dearest little clan-loving sister, and it was a pity that you were not present at a little dinner-party which our parents gave in honor of them. In the evening I sketched and colored Hélène Franzén's portrait, and wrote underneath it: —

> " Voyez ici Hélène,
> Non pas l'Hélène de Troie;
> Elle est bien mieux, ma foi,
> Elle est fille de Franzén.''

She is very handsome, and her parents were exceedingly delighted with the portrait, which really represented a young, beautiful Greek maiden, and besides, it was very like her.

Shall I have no letter from you to-day?

THE HOME OF PRAYER.

Billows, bitter as Affliction's tears, were beating wildly and with monotonous sound against a rock, on the dull gray surface of which not even the tiniest shrub had taken root, and whereon no little bird ever perched chirping, to search for a seed or a grain, carried thither by the winds of heaven. The thunder of malediction seemed to have swept over that dreary rock. Dark, cold clouds crowned its top. Yonder, on that awful height, a solitary being was sitting — a woman. Known she is to many a child of mortality. Deadly pale was her face; but her paleness was that of sorrow. Calm she sat and quiet, like one devoid of hope. Eternal tears coursed each other, drop by drop, down her cheeks slowly, as, for her, time's endless minutes vanished. Closed were her ashy lips; but the expression which played over her features, like a dark genius, seemed distinctly to say these words: "I suffer, I suffer!" In her sunken, yet flaming, eye; on her forehead, from which waves of gray hair were floating on the icy blast, while she was bent low, not by age, but by suffering, — stood written that her heart was cankered. Happy art thou, who, in the bright heaven of thy heart, never sawest even the shadow of this picture! Happy art thou, oh favorite of angels, who canst say: "I know her not!"

Alas! *I* have known her. Already, in my childhood's heaven, I saw the lightning of her bloodshot eye, and many, many know her well; her life is suffering; her name — Affliction.

Radiant in the light of beatitude, the genius of heavenly love soared one morning through space. A glance from his bright eye lighted, like a ray of the sun, upon the cloud-capped height upon which Affliction hopelessly wept.

He beheld her, and he loved her; for she suffered; and his mission was to scatter happiness around him.

He bore her away into his beautiful Eden, tended her, loved her, and comforted her, and tried, but in vain, to teach her to hope.

She bore him a daughter, a wondrously beautiful child, on whose angelic face the father's bright smile and the mother's tears were blended in sweetest harmony. They called her *Prayer*. Clasped were her hands, half-open her lips, like a rose-bud; and her beautiful eyes, in which tears were trembling, were raised on high.

At the sight of this beautiful being, Affliction's torn bosom vibrated for the first time with joy; for the first time she gave a look full of tender hope to her heavenly consort, whose eye, overflowing with happiness and love, rested upon her. She pressed to her heart her first-born darling, sighed, smiled, and looked forward into the future with confidence. But in Affliction's soul joy lingered only for a moment. Longing for her dark home, she returned to it; but with one comfort, — that she had given birth to Prayer; and with one hope, — that she one day should cease to exist.

Under her father's care, the beautiful daughter grew up amongst heaven's flowers, disporting with heaven's angels. But the more she became developed, the more she felt a dim, half-understood presentiment that *there* was not her right home. She had tears; and these strangers in the abodes of light were unknown to heaven's children. The eternal and unchanging beauty of things on high were in disharmony with her inner being — her soul. Longing, she cast her eyes downwards, and saw in foreboding dreams a lower world, not far separated from her mother's home, where dusky clouds often darkened the sun; where vapors curled over rose-gardens, and where heaven itself shed tears over a green-clad world. And her heart beat, and she sighed, " Thither, oh, thither ! "

The genius of heavenly love, marked with loving looks his daughter's silent sadness. And when the time had arrived, the hour which Jehovah had appointed, he took her hand, and soared with her through creation's endless space. They approached a star, called Earth, where the seraph's eye with melancholy joy found again images congenial to her heart and soul. Bright tears glittered in the bells of flowers. The sun burst through heavy clouds. Summer days and winter nights rested alternately on the shadowy vales, and gloomy fogs rolled over its loveliest landscapes.

" Here let us linger, — here let us rest ! " whispered she, beseechingly. They lowered their flight and alighted upon a hill, from which wide-spreading cedars threw their lengthening evening shadows. Sweetly smiling, the seraph looked round, looked towards heaven, over whose face bright clouds were wafted by gentle winds, and then at her heavenly guide, saying : " Here it is good to remain ; here is my home ; here let me stay ! "

" Daughter of my love," replied her father, " yes, here thou shalt stay, — here *is* thy home ; Jehovah wills it so ; here is the cradle of immortal beings — man's native land. Here, under suffering, are born eternal joys. But, in order that man shall not miss his goal, thou shalt be near him, a link between me and my eternal home, which shall be his also one day. Thou shalt teach him to pray — that is, to trust and hope. Thou shalt watch at his cradle and at his grave. Thou shalt teach him, in all changes, to look upwards, that a ray of the Eternal's brightness may throw light into his soul. *Consolation* shall be thy name; thy mission, a woman's, to comfort and support."

So saying, he spread his dazzling pinions, and, slowly soaring upwards, fixed a look full of measureless love upon the daughter, who, kneeling, with clasped hands and smiling in her tears, prayed: "Oh! let it be so; oh, my father, my happiness is to do thy will. Morning and evening, in the bright hours of day, in the silent watches of night, I will direct man's looks and man's heart to thee. But, that I may be always full of hope, full of comfort and joy; that my smile may always beam triumphant over my tears, oh! therefore, be ever near me, abandon me never, my father!"

The genius of heavenly love vanished behind a veil of clouds out of the supplicant's sight; but a breath full of heavenly sweetness fanned her fair curls and gently kissed her forehead, cheek, and eyelids; and she felt conscious of a father's blessing. Tremblingly rustled the cedar-branches, and "Never!" softly whispered with a sound as if out of eternity, reached her ear. She felt that he was ever near her.

Earth became Prayer's home. Prayer became man's good angel. She watched at his cradle, watched over his youth, comforted him in every period of his life, cheered his old age; and, amongst the foliage of the trees which overshadowed his mortal resting-place, she was still heard to breathe peace and joy,— whispering that now she had borne him home, and there he did not need her aid any longer.

Consolation she was called. She taught man to smile in tears — to hope.

And we, my brethren and sisters, we, whom she longed to comfort and make happy, let us not misunderstand the sweet seraph; let us follow her teaching. Let us pray with childhood's stammering lips, in our youth, in manhood, in old age, in temptation, in joy and in sorrow, in our last hour, in the hour of strife, and in the hour of victory — let us pray, let us pray!

Årsta, 19th November, 1830.

Heaven be praised! the weather is fine, bright, and mild. You have, I hope, a pleasant journey. We speak of you continually; make remarks on the weather every other minute, and, for the first time in my life, I find this to be one of the most interesting topics. My dearest Charlotte! Since we parted from one another I have been like sour, unripe fruit. I was tolerably calm when you left; but the agony began soon after. Yesterday, all the afternoon and evening, I felt a dreadful longing to see you once more; to embrace you, weep, and bless you, and to pray you to forgive every little unkindness of which I may have been guilty towards you. My tears are flowing while I am writing this. Charlotte, my dearest Charlotte! will you perhaps one day forget how warmly, how long, how sincerely we have been united? Will the novel scenes and new relations into which you enter, the novel sensations which gradually will fill your soul, ever let old memories wane? I dread it sometimes. But, above all, may you be happy — feel yourself happy. *That* is all I want.

I have no heart for brothers-in-law; I feel that they take from me what I hold dearest — my sisters. But —— may perhaps one day be able to convert me. If he makes his wife happy, he shall in me find an affectionate and *grateful* sister.

Now for a sketch of every-day life. In rain, wind, and in darkness, Hedda and I drove to Årsta, while you and your husband drove in another direction under the same celestial signs. We got soaked, shaken, and fatigued, but were concerned only about you. In Egyptian darkness we came to old Castle Blow-hard, where we found our mother and Agatha cheerful, comfortable, and well, longing to chat about you and yours: we have hitherto done this most indefatigably. It is an inexhaustible well. Our mother's thoughts are stalking about everywhere, building castles in the air here and there. " L'étoffe a pris son pli."

We are busy setting up our little dumb pensioner. It is not yet decided where to dispose of him.

I must now finish, dear Charlotte, because I have both headache and heart-ache. Thank God, you have such beautiful weather for travelling! Our mother's best love to you and to your husband, in which Hedda joins. It is pleasant here and quiet; nevertheless, I am peevish, and could make sour faces at ——; but, after all, that would be silly.

Farewell, my dear Charlotte! Half of my heart, farewell!
        Your
          FREDRIQUE.

Årsta, 30th November, 1830.

What a delightful little letter you wrote to me from Djula. We had just finished our tea and our potatoes when it arrived. In fact, I had already gone to bed, fatigued and tired of the world. Your letter was brought to me; my mother and sisters all assembled round my bedside. I read it aloud; but when I came to where you say, "—— has few who can be compared with him; I am happy!" I could read no more. I wept for joy, and sympathetic tears stood in the eyes of the smiling listeners. Also in August's eyes tears were seen to tremble, when the following evening this passage was read to him. You see, my dearest Charlotte, how beloved you are by all! Remember, my dear sister, that when you are happy, you thereby add to the happiness of others. I wrote my first letter to you under very melancholy feelings. May —— pardon my lamentations and my doubts. I sincerely believe that, with a husband like him, it depends only upon yourself to be happy, and therefore I ought to be tranquil. The description of your journey hitherto sounds very pleasant. God be praised for every happy day you have!

I ought now to speak a little of ourselves. To-morrow by this time we shall probably be in town. I cannot say that this prospect delights me; but, of course, every thing can be done. We sisters in the beginning have to occupy our old rooms, and that pleases me. Our mother pictures to herself this winter as a little "partie de plaisir;" but I expect to find it very dull. She intends to receive visits, to issue invitations, etc., etc.

May Agatha remain as well as she is now! As to myself, I intend this winter to read, to write, to paint a great deal. I hear from all quarters much that is gratifying and flattering about my "Sketches," but it makes very little impression upon me: and then how far is it not to the stars; and to him who strives upwards, what are these exhalations floating upon and dispersed by the winds? Meanwhile I long to write, and may perhaps in the course of the winter publish, the third volume of the "Sketches." Since you left, I have written a little lively piece for this volume, which I have entitled, "Spring in the North." Perhaps you would like to read it. Here you have it.

* SPRING IN THE NORTH.

Lo! the Queen of Spring one day,
Angrily her pinions folding,
Gave her son, young May, a scolding:
"The first of May!
Alack the day!
Art not ashamed, thou wicked boy?
Weeping still,
Damp and chill,
Dost thou come
Looking glum,
Marring all our hope and joy."

"Thou hadst orders
O'er our borders
Flowers to spread, and azure skies;
To deck the woods

With fragrant buds,
Sporting like the butterflies.
Words of mirth,
In our North,
Thou should'st speak to every soul:
'Lo! I bring
Lovely Spring;
Fill with wine the sparkling bowl!'

"What a shame
To take that name
Given you in the almanac;
'Month of flowers,'
Gracious powers!
Say how dare you thus to mock?
Pouting? — Ha!
Mind, mamma
All such tempers soon will settle;
If you dare,
I declare —
I'll whip you with my first young nettle!"

"Mother, why,"
Cried the boy,
"Do you take me thus to task?
Brother April scold, I pray, —
He was lazy, would not ask
The sun to melt the snow away;
Let it lie on lake and plain;
Left old Boreas free to reign;
And when I at length came forth
On my merry birthday morn,
Hailed with joy by all the North,
Fain would I this earth adorn:
But 't was still so cold and nipping,
That I quaked with aguish fears,
With my garments wet and dripping,
And my face all blurred with tears."

Quoth April then,
With angry mien,
"Who such wretched falsehood utters?
Have n't I washed and cleaned the gutters?
Have n't I broken up the ice,
Swept the roofs quite clean and nice?
On my honor I declare,
Your demands are most unfair!

Surely, if the truth you'd search,
I've battled hard with brother March;
With all kinds of wind and weather
That I e'er could bring together,
I have tried to force my way
Through his serried, firm array
Of some twenty odd degrees
Of cold, enough your blood to freeze.
I have sought through shield and spear,
By fair means a path to clear,
Where I might on flying wing
Plant the banner of the Spring.
Vain my prayers. 'Avaunt!' quoth he.
Thus the fault lies not with me."

With a pout,
March cried out:
"Must I all these burdens carry?
Sure I'm bound to sweep the tomb
Of old uncle February;
Filling all the North with gloom,
With a mountain's weight it lay,
Held o'er earth its icy sway.
Nought remained for me the while,
Save drive my plough [1] across the soil,
On the snow without delay,
Till the drifts were cleared away.
Thus I did my best, you see,
In frost-nipped humility!"

So said March. The Queen of Spring
Stood awhile, considering
Which of all the urchins three
Most deserved severity.
Each threw blame upon his brother;
But the wise and prudent mother
Bit her lips with action grave,
Thought a moment, and then gave,
With a rod of nettles bound,
To each one a whipping sound.
How the wretched boys did squall!
How they promised, one and all,
To amend their evil ways,
To call forth the sun's warm rays,
Scattering flowers o'er hill and plain,
Till the earth should smile again!

---

[1] The *snow*-plough, used in Sweden to clear away the snow-drifts.

To-day we have boarded and lodged our little "Son of Misery" with "*good*" Mr. Gardener, at any rate for the first six months. The kind Christine has promised to take most tender care of the poor little child; perhaps he may be able to learn to think and articulate. He left us well and amply provided for with every thing. When I this morning marked his linen, I stamped it, without thinking of it, with a small cross, in shape like those which are here put upon graves. I wonder whether there was any thing prophetic in it for the child. Our mother and I did celebrate the day of Jubilee in church. H—— bawled dreadfully about our forefathers being all in utter darkness and the shadow of death. The sun — this beautiful image of intellectual light — broke through heavy clouds, and throwing now and then his brilliant rays into the church, was the best part of the whole service.

Farewell, dearest sister; millions of greetings from all at home; also to your husband.

STOCKHOLM, 7th December.

You are a dear, kind, darling one for writing so often and so fully. You cannot imagine how greedy we are for your letters; how we all gather round every one of them, when they arrive, like so many flies round the cream; and how we taste and taste, again and again, and chat, and wonder, and are delighted with you and your journey. I received this morning your letter from Hellinge, but I am most anxious to hear something of you from Christianstad. I believe you will arrive there to-day. Oh, if I were there to welcome you! I shall now say something about ourselves. My dearest Charlotte, do not get frightened, when, for the sake of truth, I must confess that I have not had courage to write to you sooner from Stockholm, because every thing here has appeared to me so heavy, so cold, and even intolerable; but, thank God! it looks considerably brighter now, and will no doubt become still brighter.

Hedda has also been very low-spirited. Agatha alone has kept up her courage. However, we are now all in good spirits. The first discomfort was not to be avoided. To-day especially we are all very animated on account of the occurrences of the day, — Brinckman's letter, Franzén's, Wallin's, and others' overwhelming eulogia. What a wonderfully fine letter! — and this I am to reply to in writing? In what way? That I do not know yet, but I will tell you next time I write to you. Reuterborg has been here. He said, "Go where you will, you hear nothing spoken of but a *Lady* Bremer, or *Miss* Bremer, who has written, etc., etc., and to whom verses have been dedicated." Farewell, my dear sister. Our mother is kind and cheerful. Possibly things may become better at home. I shall write more by next mail. Kind remembrances to your husband.

Hedda insists upon copying Brinckman's letter, "in order," as she says, "that you may get it quite fresh." Fresh! That may be, but sugared over and spiced beyond measure. I inclose it herewith: —

"STOCKHOLM, 6th December, 1830.

"Not without fear of being considered like an *uninvited guest*, too bold and intruding, do I now seize the pen in order to pay homage to an amiable and charming Muse, who cannot condescend to a personal acquaintance with *all* those whom her genius has filled with respect and admiration.

"But I have hitherto not gone beyond the wish that, by some well-known friend, I might be introduced to the illustrious *Unknown*, and my noble friend Franzén has promised to undertake this kindly office, 'as soon as circumstances permit it.' But in what most nearly concerns genius and the heart, one can rarely rely except upon oneself; deign therefore to pardon my warm, perhaps too impatient, longing to express personally to you my gratitude for the greatest and holiest enjoyments, which the polite literature of my native country has for a long time afforded me.

"Franzén's sensitive Muse first drew my attention to the 'Sketches of Every-day Life,' of which the very superficial review in the periodical 'Heimdal' did not give me any more favorable or higher ideas than of many other ephemeral, pretty, poetical effusions, of which that periodical has issued baptismal certificates. But how shall I be able to describe to you the deep impression of true delight and warm interest which the first perusal of your work made upon me, whilst reading it in a single night. Full of this impression, I hastened on the following day to Franzén, anxious to express to him the gratitude which I felt for the veracious testimony which he had given to the younger sister of his Muse, and telling him that I would willingly make a pilgrimage of many, many miles with naked feet, in order to behold the features and listen to the voice of her who, in a manner so living, so tender, so witty, and so affecting, takes us by storm in every line of her splendid poetry.

"'Unglaublich! Wie! Ein solches Mädchen hatte mein hand und *ich*, und *ich* erfahr' es heute zum ersten Mal?'

"So exclaimed Don Carlos, and still he found himself deceived! I know, however, for certain, whom I can trust. An artful, coquettish beauty, such as Eboli, may perhaps, during a few moments of conversation, *act* a character foreign to herself; but a poetess, such as she who has written these 'Sketches,' is '*herself alone;*' she is, whether in the playfulness or in the earnestness of her genius, and in all other circumstances of life, genuine, innocent, and true to her soul's inspirations.

"See here, my noble benefactress! my candid confession of faith. I am proud that our literature can boast of such an authoress; but it is humiliating to our critics, that the first volume of your work should have vegetated amongst them in silence for more than two years, and that not one amongst them all should have discovered the high lineage and innate wealth of the modest stranger. But then you have restricted yourself to 'every-day life,' and it is not there where these gentlemen try to discover the realms of poetry, but rather among the stately palaces of the great. I am acquainted with the choicest literature of most countries, but I defy them all to produce, in the *genre* which you have chosen, more beautiful or truer pictures, not only of reality, but also of the ideal world which lives and breathes within us. Nobody in our country, either man or woman, has, as far as I am aware, hitherto understood living events more thoroughly, with the penetrating eye of genius, nor drawn with a more masterly hand their varied forms, and the miniatures of domestic life. And all this with such genuine, unmistakable *womanliness!* I have heard some silly maidens say, ' She must surely have been assisted by some *man*, some scholar.' Pardon them; they know not what they say. It was therefore with unfeigned delight that I heard the most appropriate opinion of your work expressed by a noble-hearted and highly intelligent Countess, who is not unworthy to be ranked amongst the congenials of your own soul. She pointed out to me many passages which she had marked. ' Look there,' she said, ' my friend, what none of you *others* would have found out; you may thank Heaven if you can feel and appreciate the peculiar excellence of such holy revelations of female genius!'

" But I did not intend to produce an improved edition of the certificate of ' Heimdal.' I only wanted to signify my longing, and remind Franzén of his promise that, if ever you should come to Stockholm, he would ask permission to introduce his friend to our mutual enchantress. I hand this letter over to him. May he speak more eloquently in my favor than I am able to do it. Be gracious and merciful, and do not say ' No!'

" A stranger's greeting, deep respect, and sincere devotion.

"V. B."

STOCKHOLM, 12th December, 1830.

It is absurd, absurd, absurd! I believe that some kind fairy has pronounced some hocus-pocus on me and my little book. The sensation which it creates is quite ridiculous. It is now the *ton* to read it, especially in the fashionable world. It is spoken of everywhere, and so is its authoress, who cannot now any longer hope to remain anonymous. I am obliged to listen to so many fine things, that I am only astonished that they do not make me quite giddy (which, after all, they do not). " Medborgaren " (the newspaper) has also reviewed the work, and in a most flattering manner it speaks of the unusual talent of the authoress; and " The H—— Family," especially, gets the most splendid encomiums. Palmblad has written to G——ström that the book meets with such a rapid sale, that he must provide a second edition thereof.

Last night we were very animated at home. Franzén came with Brinckman, who was almost half crazy. He actually courted me. I was fairly overwhelmed with flattering compliments. Brinckman quoted my book continually, saying, " that I had not *read it* properly myself." Franzén also was full of kindness and praises. Anxious to make his *protégé* shine as much as possible, he asked to be allowed to see my paintings. They went through them all; and when Brinckman heard that I also was *musicienne,* he exclaimed, " Indeed, I begin to get quite tired now." The conversation was exceedingly animated. Mrs. De R—— and some other friends also came to see us. Then I got some more rosemary. Mrs. De R—— had the previous night been to two large parties. She told me that there was nothing else spoken of except my " Sketches." Brinckman finished by going down on his knees to me, when, after a three hours' visit, he took leave. Your husband would have been very much amused if he had seen Hedda and Brinckman together. He made her his *confidente,* continually whispering in her ear all sorts of things about my book, giving her now and then little " pats," in order to awaken her attention, which " pats " Hedda seemed inclined to pay back. She expressed herself to him, once or twice, in such honest and plain terms, that they formed a ludicrous contrast to his sugared compliments. B——an, who was here the evening before last, asked me whether we were not overrun by all sorts of people coming to look at me, such a sensation has my talent as an authoress created. In a word, my dear Charlotte, it is absurd, absurd, absurd! I do not think that all this would amuse me much if our sisters were not so delighted with it. In fact, Agatha jumped about like a fish out of water. But I must say good-by to the anonymous. *Vogue la galère!* Blow, winds, blow! I say, and by that I mean a prayer to my Muse, who also seems willing to hear my prayer. I am working at the continuation of " The H—— Family."

Franzén says that people expect to see the blind one acting a part. She shall do so.

Sunday, the 13th.

The day before yesterday all was brilliant; last night every thing was flat and dull. So changeable is the wind! August was not at all well; to-day he is seriously ill. Agatha has had an attack of her old rheumatic complaint, and is not well yet; but she has good courage, and then all is well.

STOCKHOLM, 23d January, 1831.

Yesterday I received your letter of the 16th. I was very much touched by it, and it made me very happy, because the state of your mind, which it shows, is so beautiful, so noble, so amiable, that, as surely as the spring brings flowers in its train, so surely must it bring with it happiness and all its joyous flowers. I feel convinced that in another respect also you will feel yourself more and more happy, when, as you say yourself, the memory of a gloomy life begins to fade from your view, and at last dies altogether. Yes, a good and noble husband is the chief good in married life; such a husband throws over all circumstances in life thousands of comforts and charms, of which formerly one could have no idea. God bless ——! When you get quite settled in your new home, you will surely find yourself still more comfortable. Write to me, dearest Charlotte, especially about your state of mind.

Not every thing at home is quite as it ought to be. Our little Agatha, with whose health and spirits we have been so pleased, has for the last fortnight been rather on the decadence in both. The other evening, when, in spite of her ill health, she was out, we had a brilliant *soirée* at the " Singing Union." The Royal Family was there, and had a few words to say to every body. We sang choruses from " Guillaume Tell," which succeeded famously, and made a splendid effect. That evening ended in a brilliant way for me. Acquaintances and strangers of the fashionable world flocked round me, and showered eulogia and thanks upon the little authoress, who curtsied and thanked and thanked again. Baron Å—— requested to be introduced to me. Our mother was sitting the whole evening, hearing how the Countess Sp——, a whole row of the ladies of the court, and a great number of gentlemen, had been discussing my " Sketches," and the merits thereof. The sensation which the little book is creating is indeed ridiculous. It is the regular *souper-conversation* all over the town (which, be it said in parenthesis, does not mean much), and not a day goes past without my hearing what has been said of it here and there, and always in praise of it. In the booksellers' shops, all the copies have been sold. Palmblad wrote a few days ago, to say that he must print a second edition as quickly as possible, and that for that purpose he must employ three compositors, because there is a desperate run upon his agent in Stockholm, by all the booksellers, for more copies. I wonder how long this will last? It has become, I am afraid, a mere matter of fashion — *mais n'importe!* — but upon this matter of fashion I shall this year earn three hundred thirty rix dollars, which is delightful! Perhaps I shall in future reap as much severe criticism as eulogy now. May it find me equally calm, or, rather, indifferent; but of *that* I am not quite sure.

Next winter, my dearest Charlotte, Agatha and I are going to visit you. We intend taking the two rooms on the ground floor, and we wish to board with you. May we not do so? How pleasant it would be! But " l'homme propose et Dieu dispose! "

Our little dumb boy has now closed his eyes. He died after about a month's decline. Peace be with him!

You have probably seen by the newspapers that the Swedish Academy has awarded me a gold medal on account of my authorship. It would, perhaps, have been possible to have warded off this honor, if the " Aftonbladet " had not trumpeted forth the news all over town, before Franzén had spoken of it with my mother.

If you should happen to see any remarkable personages, any real originals, please describe them to me. I want to make use of them in my "Sketches." But pray, dearest, mention this, or whatever else I write to you about my authorship, to nobody. People are in general very frightened of being described in books, and in our country an authoress is often looked upon as a regular scarecrow. If I should come to Christianstad, I wish to be known there merely as the sister of Mrs. ——, which I am sure will be the best letter of introduction for me.

CHRISTIANSTAD, October 25th, 1831.

MY DEAREST MOTHER, — Ah! what a joy it is to be able to turn in full confidence to the one whom we have to thank for our existence. I say thank; for life seems now to be of value to me. Formerly it was not so. My youth has not been happy; on the contrary, it has been a time of suffering, and its days, to a great extent (this is indeed truth), have passed away in a continual wish to die. But now it is otherwise. As a compensation for that long time of suffering and compulsory inactivity, another has succeeded, which gives me the means of usefulness, and therefore also of new life and gladness. We hope, we desire, my sisters and I, nothing else than to be able to do some little good, whilst we are wandering here on earth, and according to the power that is given to us, to work for the good of others, and live ourselves in peace and harmony; and perhaps our joyless youth, if it has deprived us of some of the enjoyments of life, may in some measure have led our minds to higher aspirations, and to a stronger desire for real usefulness.

At this moment my plan for the future is the following: to spend as little as possible of my own fortune upon myself, so that I may be able as much as possible to devote my life to acquiring all the means that may be of service to me in the development of my mission as an authoress.

Never have I felt so much that I have been created for this aim as now; never have I felt my intellectual being, as it were, grow, strengthen, gain stability and clearness, as now; knowing what it is to desire to live and learn, and never to have had the joyful hope (to speak in the language of St. Paul) " to be a vessel formed to honor." The desire and the hope that I become to you and to my sisters a subject of rejoicing, is to me — how shall I express it? — a spur of roses.

Yes, dearest mother! what I have often felt, what I have often wanted to say to my beloved ones at home is, I am happy. Never has any one enjoyed their life more fully than I do at this moment. The brightening thoughts within me, which promise such sweet harmony for my soul in future, contribute much to this: and then my own little quiet room. Oh! dear mother, if I should be at home next winter, do you think I could get a little garret in Mr. Bruhn's house? It is more important for me than any one can believe, to have a little quiet nest of my own, where I can be quite undisturbed. In the suite of apartments in our house this would be impossible; but in the garret it would be delightful, if it only can be managed.

Томв, 30th August, 1835.

In my last letter, my dear mother, I told you such a miserable story, that I feel a need of coming to you with something more cheerful, and of such subjects there is no lack. I begin with what touches me most. I must therefore tell you, that my good and excellent friend has returned from Alingsås. She is so delighted and happy to be here again. I cannot imagine how such a warm-hearted and lively creature could have resigned herself to live for eight years alone at this solitary Tomb; but no one can excel her in the power of quietly fixing a purpose and then pursuing it. This she calls her "fool-hardiness." I count myself happy to be able to be something for her; we suit each other admirably. The solitary life which she leads is delightful to me. Here in this quietude, in a new neighborhood, surrounded by new objects, there awaken within me many dormant feelings, many interests that I knew nothing of. I am going through a spiritual "mineral-water cure," which will strengthen me in body and mind; and they both needed strengthening.

Norway's history, ancient and modern, its literature, nature, and relationship to Sweden, interests me greatly.

I inquire into, I think of, many things which never before gave me a thought or an interest. Plans for new "Sketches" are in progress; thoughts stream forth, and I feel that both the time and the place are important for my development. The spring air which I breathe, being continually beside the Countess S——, and the influence of her heart, her character, and her temper, certainly does me good; but what is even more to me than all this, is that I am allowed to be so perfectly in peace. You cannot think how delightful it is, my dear mother, to be so far away from all *acquaintances*, to have no visits to pay and none to receive. This kind of unsociableness is a real disease, but is at present unconquerable. My nervous system has been weakened. I trust that in the course of time, living in retirement, and with prudent care of my health, I may get stronger, and get rid of that most painful feeling; but until then, it is so good for me not to have that feeling tried. When I am alone in my quiet room, the blue sky peeping in, and with my books and papers around me, then I think the whole world is mine, especially if a dear letter lies before me, bringing good news from those who belong to me, and telling me that they love me. Then my heart beats gratefully to the Great Father of all, and full of hope to be able to do some good for my fellow-creatures; then I am as happy as any one can be; then I love mankind best and live best for them.

On Sunday the Countess had invited a small party to an

oyster-dinner. After dinner, I kept the young people at the piano, and they sang Norwegian songs both grand and simple. Between whiles ——, who is said to be a bookworm, and I, who am the same, taught each other a number of pieces out of Lord Byron's works, whilst I in secret admired our perseverance in keeping up a mutual instruction of which we both knew equally much, or equally little. After this lesson, I was obliged to go out, overpowered by my *migraine*, which the music had kept back, but which the conversation about Lord Byron had brought on again. At last I was obliged to go to bed.

Nearly all with whom I have come in contact here appear to me to have the universal characteristic of kindness, cheerfulness, and enjoyment of life, together with a homeliness which is almost too *naïve;* but from the last I must except the Countess W——, who in any society would be distinguished for her natural wit and elegant taste.

Life here is absorbed in domestic occupations, and from people with cultivated minds, or longing after cultivation, one often hears painful lamentations that they stand alone, have no one to speak to, and that the duties of their daily life entirely exhaust and kill their *Aand* (soul). In general, I think the Norwegian mothers of families are to be pitied, for they must be housekeepers to a degree which we in Sweden have no idea of. It is true, they read here with pleasure all the modern authors, and young ladies discuss Bulwer, "tout comme chez nous," and we have even in Moss our masquerades with Greek and Swiss girls, and great hospitality, and kindness, and good-will meets one everywhere. I have had a good share of this, which I hold in grateful memory; but by the culture among the country people, I have been very little edified. I saw with astonishment last Sunday, when the people wended their way to a chapel in the neighborhood of this estate, peasants and small farmers in dress-coats and fashionable hats, regular "dandies;" their wives and servant-maids and others in bonnets with gauze ribbons of various colors, with shawls, caps, gigot-sleeves, and curls, quite like the better tradesmen's wives in Stockholm. I went into the church and waited to see if the service accorded with their progress in fashion; but, oh dear! oh dear! quite the reverse. The music was absolutely barbarous, and the sermon so stupid and dull that one could have wept over it. The clergyman, a young man of respectable appearance, was smartly dressed, and looked very well in his broad frill *à la Henri Quatre*, which belongs to the priests' canonicals here. The service was different from the Swedish; but, in my opinion, not to the Norwegians' advantage.

I am glad that you liked the easy-chair which I bought out of the profits of my book. "Nina" just owed her kind patroness this proof of her gratitude. That you, my dear mother, from the beginning have liked her so much, has been a great comfort and pleasure to me. It seems now as if others would follow your example. From east and west I have flattering notices of her being taken into favor and honor. Yet she has many faults, and above all there is one which I would give much to be able to take away, and that is in reference to Edla. "The Neighbors" also has many faults, and I sincerely acknowledge them and all my great short-comings and imperfections; but still I have good hopes for future "Sketches."

TOMB, Easter Eve, 1837.

What shall I give you, dearest Charlotte, for all the good and pleasant things which your letter contained. My life is so quiet and monotonous outwardly, that the description of one day would do for them all. Inwardly it is certainly living and stirring enough; and during three fourths of the day, while alone in my room, I feel how foolish it would have been of me if I had married, because I see with pain how short and insufficient are the days and years for all that I wish and require to learn, and to make clear to myself. More than ever do I work, in order to improve and perfect what gifts I possess, so that next time I may appear before the public less unfinished. But I shall yet wait awhile. It does me an immense deal of good to be alone, to see so few people, to live undisturbed for my calling. Besides, I have a kind of nervousness which makes me unfit for, and also disagreeable to people. This is at times very painful to me; but I feel with gratitude that it brings with it some more positive good. I will, therefore, devote myself more exclusively to my calling. Amongst certain people I find myself, however, more at ease, and to them I feel a kind of gratitude. You, my dearest Charlotte, are one of them, and I remember this with delight from the town where I was with you last. Beside *you* I always felt repose and comfort. So also I do beside my splendid Lady Stina. Her's is a bright, energetic, and artless nature, and in her society one gets refreshed in body and soul. And then she is so good and amiable! I love her most sincerely.

You have heard of Hedda's strange complaint. It makes me exceedingly uneasy. I cannot help fearing that it will prove dangerous, and God save us from the grief that Hedda should ——. I dare not write it, I dare not think it. I do not know what then would become of us all. May God protect our dear Hedda! I long to see her again, and intend going home this summer for a few weeks. I shall then return to this place. It is best so for us all.

You are right, dear Charlotte! "I have not been able to make Bruno [1] fall deeply enough" with respect to *deeds*, for only then true love could reveal its power and sublimity. Ah! when the guilty to the eyes of the indifferent spectator disappears in the depths of his dark abyss, when he has forfeited every body's sympathy and interest, and when the pure and the good turn away from him with horror, then it is that true love triumphantly feels its power,

[1] In *The Neighbors*.

stoops down to the forsaken one, seizes hold of him, and does not rest until it has raised him out of the slough. I know that it is so, and that this picture is true. But it would have been truer and better, if I had chosen for Bruno another kind of criminality. A murder would have been more in accordance with his character; but there is something so horrible in a murder. On the other hand, a participation to a certain degree in the slave-trade may be imagined without the participator necessarily being a hardened villain, especially when his active share in such a trade is soon given up, which his confession seems to imply. It would, therefore, have been better if I had more clearly defined Bruno's share in the misdeed. Some persons have reproached me for having made Bruno finally happy. But to these I can only reply, he never can be happy, whatever he may appear to be in the eyes of others (as for instance, in the eyes of the Rosenvik people). He says so himself in his confession, and one feels that he speaks the truth. The thunderbolt, which grazes his forehead, lightens also in his soul, and shall there lighten reproachfully till the end of his life. Conscience and memory are his tormentors. But he has stepped into the courts of atonement. Celestial melodies will occasionally find an echo in his soul, and the angel who has gained the ascendency over his heart, will guide him to the goal.

STOCKHOLM, 29th September, 1837.[1]

Dearest sister Charlotte and ———, you who have tended our Hedda, you who have loved her so much, who have

[1] While my husband and I were staying at a watering-place in Germany, our mother communicated to us her wish that we should accompany my sister Hedda to Paris, to consult the physicians there about her illness. We hastened accordingly to meet her and my youngest sister, Agatha, in Hamburg. Having found no relief, she returned after a short time in a hopeless state. My husband and I were obliged to take a painful leave of her in Ystad, and she died a few days after her arrival in Stockholm.

witnessed her sufferings and watched her incurable disease, — you will feel resigned and thankful to God, as I am, when I now inform you that she has found peace; that God has taken her away from us. When I wrote to you last Tuesday, she was still happy; found enjoyment in her home and in the society of her family, in conversing with them. Towards evening the same day her pains increased. The remedies which were given to her to alleviate her pain gave her no relief. The same was the case the following morning; and now began, oh, merciful God! such horrible agonies. The doctor arrived about noon. The medicine which he prescribed gave her relief for a time, for which we thanked God. But her strength began suddenly to give way, and the pains began again. Hands and feet became cold, and I felt that her Redeemer was approaching. She suffered a great deal during the night. In the early part of it, Hedda, although continually lying in bed, was constantly on the point of swooning. At last she fell asleep, and when she awoke she felt a heavenly joy. She said repeatedly how happy she was, how free from pain; she praised God, embraced us all; her eyes shone with a loving, glorified lustre, and her frequent, deep-drawn sighs seemed to announce her approaching dissolution. It came at last; but she had still moments of great suffering; they passed away, and she fell asleep peacefully and quietly like a child. She died at a quarter past ten this morning. Agatha has patiently and unceasingly sat like a comforting angel beside her bed. Poor, dear Agatha! Nobody loses in the departed one so much as she does. Hedda is now lying there so peacefully and quietly, and all her sufferings are ended. F——, who has shared with us the anguish of these last days, like a son and a brother; K——, and Frances, and several more, have to-day been sitting round her bed, wept over her, and said how good, how amiable she was. Yes, during these days she has been like an angel in human shape. What she said was so full of love, of purity, of patience, and so void of all selfishness! Her looks, her words, her tears, her submissiveness and her gratitude to God, her bitter sufferings, have made an indelible impression upon me; and her cold, clammy hand, which in her agony so often stroked my forehead, has not rested there in vain. God be praised! I say it from my very heart, when I think that now she has peace. But now comes the consciousness of the heavy loss, and then — oh! it seems so very hard that *she* should have suffered so much; and bitter, bitter tears must I weep over this. And my dear Agatha: how will it be for her? I shall endeavor to be to her and to our mother all I can; but I can never be the same to them as Hedda. Dear sister and brother, you have done much for Hedda; this memory must be dear to you. Farewell for this time. It looks dark in more ways than one. Think with love of your

FREDRIKA.

STOCKHOLM, 4th October, 1837.

My dearest Charlotte! Another heavy day has passed, and every thing I hope will now become better and more serene. Agatha even feels it so. She bears her heavy loss bravely; she is so good, so strong, both in mind and in body. You remember that our Hedda always wished to be buried in Solna church-yard. We have chosen a place for her there. But she could not be taken out there at once. A great many preparations were required, and meanwhile her coffin has been placed in a vault in St. James' Church. This was done the day before yesterday, and yet a day so mournful made the most soothing impression which such a day ever can make. F—— had set apart a room in our suite of apartments, and, with white cloth, had arranged a kind of funeral chapel there. The door opened to the dining-room, where the funeral guests were assembled. In this inner room, Hedda's last bed stood. There she was lying beautifully shrouded, like one sleeping, so peaceful, so saint-like her whole appearance. She had scarcely changed at all, and the light of the lamp, which hung down from the top of the little vault, prevented our seeing the first traces of decay, which were noticeable by daylight. In her hand she held her crown of myrtles; bouquets of myrtles and heart's-ease were laid in the coffin round her feet. The *castrum doloris* was richly decorated with beautiful flowers, and the floor strewn with myrtle and many flowers. It was a beautiful death-bed. It was like Hedda's memory. All said that they had never seen death in a more pleasing form. Tears of sincere regret were wept over her. Brinckman, strange to say, wept most bitterly. On the plate at her feet was written, "Blessed are the peaceful, for they shall be called the children of God;" and on the plate at her head, "Hedda Bremer, her mother's and sisters' darling. Born ——; died ——."

After the funeral, to which only the most intimate acquaintances and our relations were invited, F—— and the K——s remained with us all the evening, and it was not a sad evening. *She* was free from pain, liberated, and saved in the bosom of her Heavenly Father! Oh, what a comfort it was to know this! I cannot tell you how much comfort I especially feel at this deliverance! Her suffering was to me a chalice full of bitterness. I dreaded it, I revolted against it. Her death was to me, as well as to her, an opiate. Our mother's grief is deep, but she is so resigned and tolerably composed. To-morrow we leave for the country, but return to town next week, to accompany Hedda to her last resting-place. I trust that Agatha's health and the tender love of her friends will enable her to keep up her courage.

F—— has been all to us during the whole of this time. Tenderly as a brother he has wept for Hedda, at whose death-bed he was present; and ever since he has been like a son to our mother, like a brother to us. May you and your husband reap much benefit from a journey, one half of which has been so full of uneasiness, but which, through you and Agatha, became so beneficial to Hedda. I have done the least of us all for her; but I have loved her truly, and the influence she has had upon me shall never be forgotten.

STOCKHOLM, 21st December, 1837.

Now, my dear Charlotte! I will sit down and write a tolerably long letter to you, and at the same time thank you sincerely for yours. Thank God, that you and your husband are in good health, and have good courage to encounter all the evening parties which you will have to go through! I should be terrified if I were you. But I would gladly taste your delicious suppers. I declared myself decidedly in favor of "Zampa;" our mother was in favor of the roasted blackcocks; and Agatha, the little greedy one, declared her desire to have a taste of every thing.

I have had the pleasure of seeing Geijer several times of late. It is indeed a great pleasure to me, and I must tell you all about a little *fête* which we had arranged for him last week. I had written a little play, which was to be acted by Frances, Agatha, and myself. I had procured some beautiful flowers; a few friends were invited to tea, and amongst them "le héros de la fête," Geijer, who came kind and cheerful, very different from what he is said to be generally in society. When the company had assembled, and we had conversed a little while, the folding-doors to the dining-room were thrown open, and there the little *scène* was acted, of which I am now going to give you a sketch. A good, but somewhat old-fashioned aunt finds her nieces reading, the one Geijer's "History of the Swedes," the other, his "Poems." She gives them a scolding for it; condemns ladies' reading history and poetry; abuses Geijer, and so on. The nieces defend him and his writings; show the influence of both upon the mind and upon life; many witty and many grave things are said; and ultimately the aunt allows herself to be convinced, gives her nieces per-

mission to read all that Geijer has written, and promises to
invite him, in order to have a chat with him over a cup of
tea. She goes away, and the nieces continue their conversation for a while; get into ecstasies at Geijer's words
about the aim of education, which words I recite; they
wish to thank him for so much good; get suddenly the
sublime idea of presenting him with the wreath which they
had bound in the morning, and I exclaim, " Let us imagine that he is now sitting here before us." We go to him
with the wreath, and say to him (here we went up to him,
and I recited the following verses) : —

> Oh, dear to every Swedish heart,
>   Thou who didst thy " Memorials" write
>   In every spirit pure and bright;
> What wisdom do thy lips impart!
> Laurels thou hast for all true worth,
>   For every pain sweet melody,
>   For dissonances, harmony
> From some far brighter home than earth.
>
> On Swedish annals thou hast thrown
>   Fresh lustre; fame on thee she showers;
>   Thou deck'st her homes with fairest flowers,
> Accept from us this floral crown.
>
> When History on her varied pages
>   Has graven deep thy honored name,
>   When centuries have borne its fame
> To the dim shores of future ages,
> E'en then thy strains melodious sung
>   In peaceful homes, shall charm the ear,
>   Thy songs call forth full many a tear,
> Thy name be blest by many a tongue.

With a trembling voice I repeated the last lines. I was
moved, and so was Geijer; so were we, in fact, all of us.
When I had finished, he put his hands upon my head and
kissed my forehead; so he did also with Agatha. How
amiable and how full of life he was afterwards! He played
some exquisitely beautiful *capricios* on the piano, with so
much fire, with so much genius, and then accompanied

Frances to some of his own charming songs. Frances and her brother sang some of their beautiful Irish melodies. At supper, anecdotes were told, and loud and merry rang the laughter. All were happy and pleased except myself. I do not know what sadness had come over me this evening; and although every body was kind and pleasant, and I had succeeded so well, yet I could not warm either my cheek or my heart. Frances had been very nervous about her part in the *scène*, and K—— was in great fear about his wife. When the little play was over, he was therefore radiant with joy. And Frances had really acted her part wonderfully well. She preached and moralized in such a serious and anxious tone of voice, that one could scarcely believe that it was mere acting. Geijer came the day before yesterday to say good-by. There is such a grand and vigorous heartiness in this man! I really love him. Yesterday I heard him speak in the Swedish Academy, where he presided as president, and where he addressed Baron Berzelius, who appeared there for the first time after his election as a member of the academy. His address to Berzelius created a general feeling of delight. Unfortunately I sat too far away to be able to follow him properly, especially as he occasionally lowered his voice. Some of his expressions I shall try to quote, such as I understood them. He spoke of the influence which Sweden has exercised upon the rest of the world, not only by warlike, but also by peaceful deeds. "The names of the Swedish kings," said he, "had gone far; Linné's had gone farther." Turning to Berzelius, he said, "The whole intellectual world considers your name coupled with Sweden's glory." When Geijer had finished speaking, Berzelius held his inauguration speech, which was intended to be a eulogy on the late Archbishop. This subject was rather a dry one, and the speaker's eloquence not very great. Berzelius did like a sensible man; he cut the matter as short as possible. I did not hear well, because he has rather a weak voice. All

I can remember was his saying that "the study of Nature does not constitute so great a part of the education of youth as it ought to do," and on this occasion he gave a cut at Upsala University. Berzelius' entrance in the hall created a universal sensation of delight. Finally a young clergyman was honored with a prize for a poem on Luther and his friend Alexis, which our new Archbishop (Wallin) recited with his fine, melodious voice. It was beautiful; but, according to my taste, the plain recital of true events has far more savor and poetry in it, than verses written on the subject. Exaggeration spoils truth; and where truth wanes, beauty also wanes. The Queen and the Crown-Prince and Crown-Princess were present; the hall was crowded. The greatest enjoyment I had was from Geijer,— from his dignified manner and his powerful language. My soul has this autumn been like a gloomy day. Geijer has passed across it like a ray of the sun; for many years, nobody has made such an impression upon me as he has done. I am happy to know that I shall see him again in March.

TOMB, 2d March, 1839.

My dear Charlotte! Your description of the state of the young girl has touched my heart; for her own sake, and for the sake of those who speak for her, I shall with the greatest pleasure do what I can. See here what I am thinking of: My book, "The Home," is still in hand, and not even ready to be written clean, and notwithstanding I have already borrowed three hundred rix dollars on account of the expected profit on the same, in order to contribute to save a respectable man, father of a family. Until autumn the book cannot possibly be ready for the press, and until then I have no means at my disposal. But I think I can already now, without hesitation, promise you three hundred rix dollars about that time, for the cure of the poor girl, if required. Most willingly will they be given. May it please God that some cure might be found for the poor sufferer. Thanks, dearest Charlotte, for having applied to me in this matter. May your kind exertions on her behalf be crowned with success!

We are all very happy to hear that your husband is now so well again. It is so pleasant to be able to number you amongst the happy couples in this world. I number myself amongst the happy odd ones; I am satisfied with, and grateful for, my position, my solitariness, which gives me peace in my dear occupations, and for a friend so good, so amiable, so gifted in point of heart and head, and perfectly harmonizing with me. I am proceeding slowly with my book. My anxious desire for completeness and perfection induces me to do so. How much kindness have I not met with on my path as an authoress! The only way of proving my gratitude is to produce a better work. We shall see how I succeed. Do you know, dearest Charlotte, any elderly ladies, not married, kind and happy? If so, would you tell me something of them, and of what affords them the greatest pleasure in this world. I have to provide a few such characters in my book; and it is good to seize upon some touches of nature here and there. If my book should be launched in autumn, I intend to let some minor works succeed it in the course of winter.

Årsta, 15th June, 1841.

Now, my dear Charlotte, I intended executing what I have so long contemplated, namely, the great achievement of writing a long letter to you, in which I shall make friends and acquaintances appear higgledy-piggledy; but the fact is, ever since yesterday morning, a terrible woman has been sitting here, who incessantly repeats: "Goethe says," "Byron says," "Börne says," "Schiller says," etc., etc., etc. And then follow such trite and commonplace sayings, that every good sort of man or woman, with a little common sense, could say just the same things. And then she comes down upon one with quotations from

"Euphrosine," Grafström, Böttiger, and other poets. All this has fatigued me very much. In order to refresh myself a little, I sit down to write to you, and shall begin with thanking you very much for your letter of the 4th of June. Ever since Whitsuntide, I have led a very active and stirring life amongst a great many people, whom I shall here introduce to you. First, then, comes the Baroness Knorring, *née* Zelow, who spent the Whitsun holidays here. She is an exceedingly animated and very witty lady; but she is also, what is better than this, more cordial and amiable than the majority of people, although this is not observed until after a more intimate acquaintance with her. She resembles in this respect her own face, in which there is not, strictly speaking, any thing very agreeable, when the expression is listless, but in which the prettiest looks, full of life and grace, are, as it were, budding out, when, in the course of conversation, she becomes animated with speaking or relating; and this latter is her most brilliant part. The days which she spent here with her daughter made in many respects a mutually bright and cheerful impression. The weather and Nature were wonderfully charming, so that one felt inclined to accept the old popular belief that God's angels, at this time of the season, soar up and down between heaven and earth, in order to impart to the latter some of the glories of the former.

On the Monday after Whitsun week, our mother and I went to town. There I again spent much of my time with the Baroness Knorring, and I had the pleasure of introducing to her several literary notabilities, such as Franzén, Geijer, Brinckman, Grafström, which was very pleasant, and afforded her great delight. Brinckman became very animated on account of this new acquaintance. He invited us to tea, together with several others; and he will certainly not fail to hover round the witty Baroness during her mineral-water drinking in Stockholm. Brinckman and I have, after a three years' silence, commenced some fire-works together. But they turn out only ashes in the end. Not so my intercourse with Geijer. You, who have seen him only a short time, cannot imagine what a wealth of goodness, of fresh, bracing, noble life there is in this man. His influence is in the highest degree invigorating and ennobling; I do not know sometimes in what way. His mere presence brings this with it. Like the billows of the ocean, he is tossed, or *seems* to be tossed, about by impulses; but they are directed by a wind from heaven, so pure, so fresh. I am very fond of him, and will therefore not say any thing more of him, because I cannot speak of him highly enough to please myself. But, thank God, that I have made Geijer's acquaintance! The Baroness Knorring was very much charmed with him; he less with her, although he was exceedingly friendly, and did not do what Brinckman and Franzén could not leave off doing, — tease her about her supposed authorship. Franzén has got very old, and it seems as if he could not long tarry here on earth. But he decays in a noble way, like the temples of antiquity; he looks well in his pallor, with the poetical expression of his face, and with his gentle, patriarchal manner. To me he is exceedingly kind. But, now to lesser notabilities in the world of mankind, who, nevertheless, in God's world may stand equally high as the more prominent ones. Who ought not then to stand here on the top of the ladder, but thou, honest, good R——, so firm in friendship, so faithful in the fulfilment of all good deeds and of your duty; although a little intolerable when you repeat the same thing over and over, making the same indifferent remarks, till from very weariness one ceases to argue a point on which it is impossible to coincide with you; but a little harmless tediousness is permitted to nag as much as it pleases: the heart is nevertheless in the right place, and so is the head. R—— is in good health this year, and in good humor; he carries always about with him in his pocket Franzén's lines on "Strife and Peace," and a German criticism on the "Sketches," and reads them out aloud wherever he finds an opportunity. I am afraid, however, that it is not always *à propos;* but I am grateful for his kindness, and for the lively interest which he takes in them.

It is said to be decided now that Jenny Lind is to go to France in July. Her singing and acting in "Norma" has raised her reputation still more. I attended, in company with L——, the first representation of "Norma," and we were very much delighted with Miss Lind. Her acting was so pure, so artistical throughout, with the exception of two or three movements, which I think might have been more impressive if they had been properly interpreted. L—— informed me that this was Jenny Lind's first rehearsal of "Norma," as far as regarded the acting. She can never act during the usual rehearsal, but leaves this until the moment when she appears before the public, when she often gets the most beautiful sudden inspirations. L—— was really a little anxious on her account, because she felt an aversion for this character, and did not know what to make of it. He was, therefore, the more delighted with her beautiful, powerful acting.

ÅRSTA, 11th February, 1842.

After about a month's stay in town, I have now been allowed to return to my dear peaceful country. Amongst remarkable things which happened during my stay in town, I can tell you about a conflagration, which fortunately was extinguished after having consumed the roof and the garret of the house. I was that evening visiting some friends, not far from where the fire was. It was a splendid sight. The inhabitants of the house on fire took it very coolly. Relying on the solid fire-proof flooring of the attic, a gentleman was quietly sitting in a room next below the burning roof, reading, with two burning candles beside him, and holding a pitcher of water in his hand, having got a promise from the chief of the fire-brigade to let him know in case the fire should choose to come down to him. But the fire did not come down to him; and the gentleman was left in peace with his book, his candles, and his pitcher of water.

STOCKHOLM, 12th October, 1846.

From your letter to Agatha, my dear Charlotte, I see that you want some detailed accounts of the last illness and death of the Countess S——; and being now at home, after my melancholy watching at her bedside, I will give you all the information which you have asked for. I had intended to write to you under all circumstances about her, as you liked each other, and as her welfare or her sorrows could not be indifferent to you. You know already that her mineral-water cure was succeeded by a wonderful change for the better. Both herself and I, who immediately on my arrival in her house had almost daily both thought and spoken of death, and had prepared every thing to receive this guest, — a guest always expected with solemn feelings, although without fear, — began now, with real surprise, to believe that he would not arrive, but that instead life and health would be restored. She said several times, "I begin now myself to think that I shall continue to live;" and she was happy in this thought, because her mind was lively and strong, and took a warm interest in every thing, — the same as in her healthy days. This was still the case when her relations arrived at Tomb. The meeting with them was like a joyful festival. Lady Stina had been very active in all the preparations for their reception, and she felt herself very happy. This lasted three days. On the fourth day there was an end to it. After dinner she got a violent attack of illness, and pains soon began, which brought on violent delirium; and I was nearly in despair. Her last moments were, however, free from pain, and she fell asleep. During this last illness, we often read psalms to her, and her dearest thoughts were her reunion with the beloved ones who had gone before. Love and hope never left her heart. Thank God, that I was permitted to come and be near her during this time. I would not barter the bitterness thereof for much that is sweet and delightful. Above her grave heaven's vault expands itself, full of bright promises of glittering lights. The day of her funeral was very fine, and all went off beautifully and well. She would have been pleased with it herself. I left Tomb a few days after the funeral, and on my arrival at Årsta I had the pleasure of finding our mother and Agatha well and in good spirits, and our home peaceful and happy as usual.

TOMB, 26th November, 1835.

Dearest Frances! The thanks which so long have been on my lips for your friendly lines, must at last leave them and take wing. Let them also tell you, that it makes me so very happy that you think of me, and that you find pleasure in my epistles.

Many, many times have I intended writing to you, and to speak with you about the real and the ideal, about religion, about morals, etc., etc. I wished to tell you my views on these subjects, in exchange for yours; but of these I have always remembered something since last winter. Do you remember how we then read together some passages out of Miss Martineau's pleasant little novel, "Briery Creek?" do you remember when — strangely enough for such an intelligent person — she expresses the idea that *knowledge* is the highest aim of man and of civilization, and that virtue is to be considered only as a means to that end; how we both were unanimous in saying, "No! virtue is the aim; knowledge only the means of attaining that aim?" But if we agree in this point, I have been thinking, — What in the world do we then dispute about?

And it appears to me that it is quite unnecessary to wage any war with each other, when we agree on the main point. For I know that we hold the same opinions, not only about the intrinsic worth of virtue, but also with respect to its eternal origin, the source from whence the veins of truth and strength well forth. We agree that virtue is the highest, and that we ought to practice it, each in her own path in life. Your life seems to be like an endless kiss, a tender embrace, in which you give your own self for the good of beloved beings; my life does perhaps span a more extensive sphere, but it is also less warm, less tender, perchance less good. Indeed, yours appears to me to be more beautiful; and I think often of Byron's words:—

> "Many are poets who have never penn'd
> Their inspiration, and perchance the best:
> They felt, they loved, and died, but would not lend
> Their thoughts to meaner beings; they compress'd
> The god within them, and rejoin'd the stars
> Unlaurel'd upon earth, but far more blest
> Than those who are degraded by their jars
> Of passions, and their frailties link'd to fame," etc., etc.

Many times, when thus I have thought and felt, have I been tempted to abandon a path on which selfishness, ambition, and many weaknesses so easily steal into the heart, and to choose instead a new one, which would lead to a purification of the soul, and would fill the heart with love and patience. But an irresistible voice has lured me onward, has put pen and paper in my hand, and has whispered to me, "Proceed!" I have determined to go onward; but I have invited *Earnestness and Love* to be my travelling companions, to guide, to support, and to enlighten me. To you will I also confess that the life which now lies before me gives me pleasure; that the perfect freedom which I enjoy to devote myself to my beloved occupations, is to me like fresh, pure air, in which one joyously breathes and lives. I believe that my real working-time shall now begin. Much have I yet to learn, and great is my thirst for knowledge. *Man* is the subject of which, before all others, I shall treat. It is therefore man whom I must study more closely. And I hope that Philosophy and History will lend me the key: Philosophy, by explaining to me more in general his powers, his elements, his affinity with heaven and with nature; and History, by showing me the concrete man in his doings, in all his various stages of civilization, in different climates, in all the changing scenes of life. By these means alone I hope that I shall be able to judge rightly of man, such as he is at present, with reference both to the general tendency of the age, and to his own individuality. Man and the State are surely not children born to-day. Neither have they been created out of nothing. Their inner organism has its root far back in antiquity; their life derives its origin from a life which is beyond all time and beyond all change. It is only by contemplating them in their connection with an historical *past* and a spiritual eternity, that one can rightly understand them; that is to say, understand their heart, their inmost, intrinsic, real life, and that, as a moralist, one can hope to effect any good for them. I should wish to tell you much about all this, if I could come to you, or could transport you hither, and place you on my sofa beside me; we would then, if you did not get tired of me, have a long, long chat about all this. A chat by correspondence about these subjects is for me too heavy and too tedious; therefore, now to something else.

You have been in Norway, my dear Frances. You have crossed the Swine Sound. You have there seen how the hills, after having long followed you on the Swedish side in bleak and barren undulations, suddenly rise on the borders into mountains, both on the Swedish and on the Norwegian frontier, their tops crowned with "evergreen," which they wave, as it were, in mutual salutations, until at last they sink quietly their brows into the sound, whose waters part, and at the same time unite, the two countries. When I walked up the mountain on the Norwegian side, I read on some red and white painted sign-posts on the road-side the word *Sorgenfri* (free from cares). I took this word gratefully as an omen, and did not allow some cackling geese, which met me with hostile intentions, to disturb my contemplations. And this word has hitherto proved itself a true prophet; for not only has my own life been as free from cares and as pleasant as one could wish to have it here on earth, but I fancy also that the life of the inhabitants here is more free from cares and more fresh than in Sweden. I have not seen much of it myself; but I have heard a great deal, partly through the Countess S——, whose delicate tact rarely leads her into any mistakes, and partly from the inhabitants themselves. See here what, amongst other things, I have noticed: greater simplicity than in Sweden, more naturalness in the social order of things and in social life. Education is more generally diffused, and consequently there exists scarcely any difference of rank. *Huusjomfruen* (the housekeeper) prepares the dinner and other meals, and then goes with *la Comtesse* to pay visits and to balls. She says "thou" to the daughters of the house, and nothing happens in the family with which she is not as well acquainted as every member of the household, and her voice and opinion is listened to in all matters. The steward at Tomb goes to dine with Baron W——, without being invited; he occupies, as a guest, the seat of honor at table; the host converses with him as with one equal to him in rank. They show him the young ladies' embroidery; they chat with him and he dances with them, when there is an opportunity. The Counts' as well as the peasants' daughters say "thou" to their parents. The clergyman's daughter is *fröken* (lady); whereas the daughter of a rich landed proprietor, unless her father is a high military or civil officer, is simply Miss, or *jomfrü*. Beside this humane spirit of equality, there is amongst the good Norwegians a strong sentiment of

national pride, which frequently degenerates into personal
rudeness and *dorskhed* (clumsiness), which they themselves
turn into caricature by calling it *Norskhed* (Norwegianism);
and they seem ever ready to say, "Get out of my way,
thou! nobody in the world is as good as I am!" The
inhabitants of Trondhjem distinguish themselves above all
others by this spirit, and consider the name, a *Trönder*, the
highest in the world. Beyond Trondhjem, in towns separated from each other by a distance of one hundred and
fifty to two hundred English miles, and obscured the
greater part of the year by a veil of darkness and cold,
there prevails, I understand, a higher degree of civilization
than in the more southern parts of Norway. "What is
the reason of this?" I asked the steward here, who was
born in the north. "Because," said he, "people in the
north have so very few amusements, and they are, therefore, thrown more upon their intellectual resources; to
these they must look for what makes life valuable and
beautiful." — "But," I said, "the labor for daily bread, to
procure the means of existence, must be very heavy there,
and cannot allow much time for a more refined education?"
"No, their requirements are easily satisfied. Their extensive fisheries, which constitute their most lucrative branch
of trade, enable them to procure with facility all they want,
and their material wants are few. The majority of the
inhabitants are in good circumstances, and find themselves
happy and comfortable."

My dear Frances, does not this sound delightful?" I
wonder whether the people up there in the dismal north
do not, after all, live a more buoyant, a better, a more humanly beautiful life, than most of the inhabitants of turbulent Paris, and of the great workshop London, the mighty
centres of art and of the civilization of the present century? Thank God! little is required to live a life humanly pure and happy.

With respect to Sweden, the temper of the Norwegians

is a little *aigre doux*. Norway regards the union with Sweden with rather sour looks. Many complaints have been made that Norway is not allowed to have her own flag, and that in the Swedish flag, which they are obliged to use, Norway is represented as a province subject to Sweden.[1] But if the Norwegians are not yet quite satisfied with Sweden, they are, nevertheless, far more pleased at being united with the Swedes than with the Danes, which latter they look down on. They are, however, most satisfied with themselves, although the more enlightened amongst them look upon this self-satisfaction rather as a fault. History shows the Norwegians to be a brave, but a turbulent and always grumbling people. Possibly the philosophical — and with it also the humanistic — education, which begins to be spread here more and more, may alter this and produce more peaceable feelings between neighbor families, as well as for the neighbor country. I can say nothing but good of the Norwegians, as far as my own experience of them goes. To me they have always been most friendly. The Norwegian women especially appear to me very agreeable, on account of their pleasant, lively, and *naïve* manners. One feels perfectly comfortable and at home in their society.

Farewell, dearest Frances, and be happy!

Tomb, 18th April, 1830.

My sincerest thanks, dearest Frances, for two letters, and especially for the last one, so kind, so like yourself, which might awaken in me a desire to write a whole volume in answer to it. Let me first congratulate you on having revisited your native country, your relatives, and your friends, and let me express my sincere wish and my hope that this journey may give you strength and reëstablish your health.

Yes, it is true that body and soul are in close connection

---

[1] This matter has, since the above was written, been satisfactorily arranged.

with each other. The former influences the latter, and so *vice versa*. I have never mistaken this reciprocal influence; but under certain circumstances it is good and perhaps even necessary that the body should suffer, in order that the soul may take a higher flight. Childhood and youth ought to be carefully tended and corporeally developed; but the adult, the man, who is too careful of his body, his sleep, his meals, in a word of his health, will never become a *great* man. In order to become such a one, waking, working exertions of all kinds are required. Theory and experience prove this. And if I must succumb, I will much rather do it for the sake of my soul than for the sake of my body. In most cases, however, this alternative is not required; and if only the foremost word in life is *soul*, then the second may, gladly for me, be *body*, namely, in mature age. *My* disease has had, as it were, its seat between body and soul; but the real life of the latter it has not touched. Even when I felt its influence most; when I felt that I was a bore to myself and to others; when I was obliged to shun those dearest and nearest to me, even then I could, like Gregoire (in Victor Hugo's novel, "Notre Dame de Paris"), to whom somebody said, "Vous êtes donc bien misérable et malheureux," answer, "Misérable, oui; malheureux, non." In truth, I know only one thing which could now make me perfectly unhappy, always supposing that I do not lose my reason. Do you know what would turn my spring into winter; make all happiness a misery; change all interest in life to dust and ashes; make my body mouldy and dried up, and make life a burden to me? If I were to lose my belief in all-loving God and Ruler of the Universe, and in his perfect revelation in Jesus Christ. Then would I go forth amongst the miserable and destitute in this world, and say to them, "Brethren, let us die; life's greatest treasure is mere vanity, and beyond that every thing is only corruption!" and I would lie down and starve myself to death. But I have no need of saying this, for another voice has made itself heard, and has lighted life's darkest riddle; the stone has been removed from the grave. Since I have gained certainty in this, and my belief has been firmly established, I am calm. It is this certainty, dearest Frances, which causes me now to contemplate the world "couleur de rose," and makes my cheeks easily borrow that color. When my soul's sanctuary is not encumbered by doubts, my body bears buoyantly up against every thing. And it has done so. I am quite well again; at any rate much better. It is true that Selters-water, repose, and my leaving off tea has essentially contributed hereto; but that which, more than every thing else, has contributed to it, is that I have for months drank living mineral-waters; and this well, out of which I have been drinking, is called Countess S——. I will not attempt to describe her to you; you have *guessed* her, dear Frances; but one must know her, to be able to understand what she can be to those whom she loves. We have thought, talked, wept, and laughed together, and I have recovered my health. Repose, solitude, country air, a friend, serious and dear occupations,

—— " and mirth,
That humblest harmonist of cares on earth: "

how should I not get well with all these!

Certain it is, my dearest Frances, that, with different natural qualities, different dispositions and characters follow different degrees of activity and happiness. But there is one name that comprises all that life has most powerful and most gentle, most sublime and most holy; a name that has its origin in a moment of struggle between life and death; a name which God himself once did pronounce in love and in agony, and that name is — *mother*. O Frances! no other attribute and no other name can bestow what this name, this attribute develops in the human heart of love, of virtue, of pure self-denial, of true beauty. And therefore I have prized your lot in life higher than mine.

But do not therefore believe that I underrate mine. No, I thank God for it, and I will endeavor to guard against the egotism and meanness which so frequently sully an author, by that earnestness which grasps life in its profundity, and by thinking only one thing is of importance — to do good. In my walk in life I shall also try to labor for the good. Should I not succeed, I shall then rejoice if others succeed better. That God's will be done and the welfare of mankind be promoted, that is the essential, the beautiful, and the good of life.

I thank you most sincerely for your remarks about "Nina." If you will let me hear some more of them, I should be still more grateful to you. Your words are always delightful to me, and afford me many subjects for reflection. You are right in saying that I ought not to shrink from the severest criticism, as long as it is profound, true, and enlightening. But a criticism, like that of Mr. A——n's, which is full of arrogance, superficial, bitter, hasty, full of contradictions, neither sensible nor true, can only provoke indignation. But do not fancy that my indignation was either bitter or of long duration. It was like April snow, or like the crackling of burning pine wood. This unwise criticism defeats its own end, and truth is indeed not a gainer thereby. It is no easy task to be a good critic. It requires a knowledge and a profundity of thought, of which common critics have no idea. Fortunate it is that an author has other sources than these, to which he can look for light and power. The opinion of highly educated women is of the greatest value to me. In feeling and in judgment they have a *correctness* which is incontrovertible, when man and what relates to him is in question. Women have been my best critics, and if I could have followed their advice more I should have avoided many faults. Yes, many and great faults have I made in my calling; nobody can feel this more acutely than I, and nobody can be so dissatisfied with "Nina" as I am. Mr. A——n was quite welcome to exclaim "Woe! woe!" if he had only done so in a reasonable way. But I cannot be angry with him; he meant well, and every body has his own way of doing a thing. But smile I must, when I see how the critics think that they can make "la pluie et le beau temps" for the authoress. That which gives light to thought and power to the heart does indeed not come from them.

Yes, my dearest Frances, there exists a source of happiness and of goodness, — for the soul becomes good by drinking of it, — a source which makes us independent of our own fortune or misfortune, and that is — philosophy; the contemplation of life, of man, of God and His works. The more we therein attain coherence and clearness, the more the great and the little, the past, the present, and the future gain consistency in a higher light, the calmer and the happier our mind becomes. Oh! there is happiness, devotion, bliss in this path, which only he feels who, with a warm heart, has wandered along it. Malebranche's "Vision en Dieu" is, rightly understood, I believe, the result of true philosophy, and therefore it makes me so happy. Those who imagine that I here mean a fantastic sight, or what we in every-day language call a vision, understand me very little. But you, Frances, will not misunderstand me.

Certainly, dearest friend, I would wish to go to England. I would wish to become acquainted with the people, whom you know, and whose active philanthropy has made them so lovable; I would wish to learn more to value the important questions, the useful and practical sciences, which your native country, *par excellence*, works out for the benefit of mankind. (When I say *value*, I do not employ the right word. I can value them, because I know their tendency; but I should wish to *understand* them better.) But perhaps this would not be of any importance for my real development. In order to be able to work out something good, one ought to perfect oneself in some special branch of knowledge and ability. To do this, one must, above all, learn to know one's real powers. I believe that I have found out mine, and I am of opinion that my literary activity ought to confine itself to the delineation of family life, which is the nurse of the State, of eternal life, and of the individual man. To portray that which makes the family tie delightful and secure; which, in all changes of life, makes the individual man safe and good; this, and the delineation of original characters and of peculiar events and circumstances, I consider to be my task, — that in which I ought to try to improve myself. Solitude, reflection, and good books will, I believe, guide me to the goal, although certainly conversations with enlightened people, and a more extensive knowledge of the world, would be of immense value to me; but one cannot have every thing at once, and for my present purpose the first-mentioned means are the most important.

I may perchance not be able to see you again for many years, and I wish therefore that you, who have been so kind to me, and whom I value so highly and so sincerely, should rightly understand me. Take, therefore, here this hasty sketch of the plan of a work which, above all others, I have in view; one to which all my other works are mere preludes; one which is never out of my thoughts, and for which I wish to mature and to labor for several years to come. It is closely connected with my views of life. But remember, that I do not here propound any axioms for others, but merely state my own opinion.

To man, his religious views are of paramount importance. Consciously or unconsciously, he regulates his life, his morality, in accordance with them. Man's happiness and virtue depend entirely upon the idea which he forms of God, of His will and His Providence, of His relation to mankind, man's own mission in the world, and his belief in a future life. The best police regulations cannot supply what is wanting in society, when this life-giving longing for all that is good, for the knowledge of God and love of His will, is gone. An impenetrable veil hides the truths of the gospel from most people's eyes. Philosophy in our days has partially removed this veil. But this philosophy is any thing but popular. My sincerest wish, my earnest labor shall be to make it popular. This labor shall be my last will and testament. What philosophy has taught me, I shall teach others, in simple language, which the learned do not like, perchance cannot employ. It is mainly this: philosophy has taught me to understand the connection between the kingdoms of life; has taught me to conceive how the same mighty power is working throughout the universe, although in different degrees. Above all, the philosophy of history has taught me to comprehend that the voice which pervades all mankind, — this: "See! I tell you a secret," — which in all religions has preached to man of a higher Being, of a life after this, of punishments and rewards, has spoken purest and clearest through Christ; that Christianity is the only pure ore of all religions; and that Brahma, Buddha, Odin, and others, in their best doctrines have said, only imperfectly and partially, what has been so beautifully revealed in Christianity. And this revelation, contemplated in connection with other religious doctrines, and with reference to man's nature, I intend to unfold, such as I have comprehended it. But this would require a whole book; for a letter it is too much. May I one day be able fully and clearly to explain all this! Then I shall die happy.

5th April, 1837.

Only a moment ago all was as gloomy, as silent, as if no spring, no song existed in the world; but, on a sudden, came a little wind, which soon dispersed the clouds, and a lark rose singing toward heaven. I listened to her song, and I thought of you, dearest Frances, and saw in the lark an image of your buoyant soul, which for a moment can be oppressed by a gloomy day, but soon again soars on high full of life and joys of spring. And the breath, the light which calls it into life — oh! I know whence that emanates. Be it love, be it the spring sun, or a secret, unutterable hope of life and trust in the eternal goodness, still all comes from Him, who fills creation with His life and His power, and who awakens here on earth love, hope, life, that He may one day perfect them all. Believing this, as I do, with my whole heart and soul, I think, full of sympathy, of you and your departed darling, your only daughter; although, while reading your letter, I wept bitterly for you both. Silently to mourn for a beloved being, who has been taken from us, is indeed a comfort to our feelings, and makes us beforehand feel familiar with another world; it seems to us as if it were the beginning of our own impending removal. " Where your treasure is, there will your heart be also." Agatha had in her early youth a painful dread of death; but this vanished when she saw her beloved brother August die. The thought that he was expecting her in another world dispelled to her the darkness of the grave. I have never feared death, on the contrary; but no thought can so much sweeten my last hour as this, — that I shall then be again united with the friend whom I have so sincerely loved; who has been lost to me for this terrestrial life, but who always lives in my heart, so good, so amiable, such — as the world never knew her!

ÅRSTA, 23d June, 1838.

You have been ill, my dearest Frances! I will now imagine that you are lying on your couch, and that I steal into your room with the wish to divert you by all kinds of prattle. To begin with, then, a word about your brother, whom we saw before we left town after our return from Upsala. He was delighted: he was charmed; not by Ole Bull, whom we heard play the evening before, — oh dear, no! he could at most be called " an ingenious charlatan, a fallen angel;" not by the oranges which were offered to him, — no, indeed, he never liked to eat oranges, especially not this time; not by the lilies of the valley, which he was allowed to smell, — oh, no! they also were to him fallen angels, having now lost their original beauty; no, but he was delighted, he was enchanted at having got completely drenched in a heavy shower of rain, — a pleasure which certainly not many envied him. Otherwise, he was agreeable, kind, and interesting, as he can be when he likes.

That the Emperor Nicholas came down in the midst of us like a bomb-shell, you know already long since, and you have probably also heard some of the thousands of anecdotes which group themselves round this "lion," which all have heard, and yet every body tells every body else. The general opinion of him can be best expressed in your brother's words: "He is really a man with a thoroughly imperial exterior." In him one saw the personified ruling majesty. But it was more the majesty of Power than the majesty of Mercy. But even the former has its beauty. How rich is creation! Of all its forms, of all its revealed thoughts, there is not one which does not possess its own peculiar beauty. Creation is a diamond, all the facets of which can be turned towards the light, reflecting its pure and glittering rays. Every age, every stage of development, every nation, every condition of mankind, every individual man carries within him this celestial ray, although it is not always placed so as to be visible. Affliction — cannot even that call forth a peculiar beauty; beauty, beside which all the splendor of happiness, of health, and of the world becomes pale? The purest, the brightest ray of heavenly light which I have seen, shone out of an expiring eye; on a face wasted by bitter sufferings, and already darkening under death's lengthening shadows, have I seen celestial bliss reflected. Like a solitary, steadily burning light, this vision will follow me through life down to my grave, and throw its light upon it.

But I have wandered far away from Nicholas. No matter! Agatha does not much like that we speak of him;

she prefers speaking of Upsala, and the people there who she thinks are "such real human beings." I will not say No to this, because it was pleasant to see so many people of distinct *species* inwardly and outwardly, and these both pleasant and amiable, each in their way and in their contact with others. Such a merry and free social life I have nowhere met with. Much kindness and hospitality was shown us by every body; we exchanged "*thou*" with whole battalions of ladies, — with girls of seventeen up to matrons of seventy, — and we felt besides quite "*thou-ish*" with professors and with students. "Brother" Törnros, "Brother" Atterbom, "Brother" Fahlcrantz, "Brother" Bergfalk rose spontaneously to our lips. Beautiful songs we heard both day and night, and enjoyed conversation and curiosities, more almost than we could digest. I cannot say that I have picked up many gold nuggets of wisdom in that learned city; neither is my mind much bent upon them at present. I would rather hear a story of quiet, private life, with its joys and its sorrows, than listen to abstract reflections upon times and customs and manners, history, arts, and so on.

You have been in Upsala, and I cannot, therefore, tell you any thing new of what is interesting there. But I suppose you have not seen the fresco-paintings of Sandberg in Gustavus Vasa's chapel in the cathedral. They are very beautiful, but most of them are, as it seems to me, not expressive of deep thought. The chief personage, Gustavus Vasa, has, in nearly all of them, not succeeded well. I like him most in the painting in which he is represented as saying his last farewell to the assembled estates of the realm. You see here the old, but still vigorous king, his face pale with age and cares, but with eye full of fire, feeling death's approach, and bidding a last farewell to the people over whom he has ruled with force and with kindness, whom he has loved and made great. You fancy you hear the words which he said on this solemn occasion:

"If I have done any good, give God the honor; what I have failed in, from human weakness and error, overlook and forgive it for Christ's sake. Many have called me a hard king; yet a time will come when Sweden's children would gladly pluck me out of the earth if they could!" These words are in golden letters on blue ground engraved under the painting. It is a fine idea to let this gallery of paintings round the tomb upon which the marble image of the great king is lying dumb, speak of his achievements and remind us of his life, his toils, and his undaunted energy. Do you remember Skytte's tomb — that prayer in marble; that devout eye; those clasped hands, which thus have watched and prayed for centuries? Were I a great man, I would then like to be so represented after death, or not at all. Did you see Linné, where he is sitting absorbed in the study of Nature's book, enraptured at the wisdom and the deep meaning which he reads in a tiny flower? But I must not leave the cathedral without making my "reverence" to the splendid, lofty cupola. That is also, as it were, a prayer, a bold, fervent approach to the Most High; a gently rising heaven under heaven. Fahlcrantz said to me, "When I become peevish and irritable, which happens occasionally during my toils of every-day life, I know no feeling so elevating and cheering as that which fills my soul when I wander under this dome." And so I say farewell to the old cathedral! Of all the remarkable objects of interest, which I have seen in our little trip, this is the only one which has made a grand and lasting impression upon me.

Årsta, 11th September, 1838.

I thank you most sincerely, my dearest Frances, for the pleasure which your letter has given me. You say, "I am happy." No words have a more pleasant sound in my ear. It does me so much good to hear this from your own lips, and to fancy that I see your eye beaming with happiness. I feel with regret that I have not been to you what I ought.

to have been. It is much my own fault, arising from want of calmness and clearness in expressing myself; but much is also owing to circumstances. Last winter I went often to see you, my soul overflowing with words, which I thought would have been full of comfort to you after the loss of your daughter; for I know there was consolation and light in them, — light which streams forth out of the treasures of the *Word*, but which the human soul is not always capable of receiving with equal life and clearness. I longed to communicate with you, but you were never alone, and it is impossible for me to speak on serious subjects in the presence of a third person, a mere listener. We shall meet again, if it pleases God, and then, I trust, in a brighter and more hopeful frame of mind. Yes, oh yes! we shall again rejoice in the light which the gospel sheds over the gloomiest portion of our life, of our fate. Next year I shall devote almost exclusively to the study of the Bible. In much I hope to gain more clearness, more coherence; but I know that many of the details will remain dark and incomprehensible to me. But during this study, I shall steadily adhere to one opinion; and that is, that the Bible, like all writings, has its body and its soul. The body may change, may grow old, may become deformed; yet the soul will remain the same in all its main features. The written word is the body; the spirit is the soul. By rightly becoming acquainted with the latter, we shall learn to interpret the meaning truly and best, even where it has become less clear from bodily defects. But I know that what is dark and incomprehensible will not disturb me any more. The knowledge of the wants of mankind, and a devout acquaintance with Christ's individuality, give to his existence, life, and teachings a reality, and give also a firmness to our belief (namely, to a sensible, rational belief) in Him, which no obscurity of occasional passages and no fit of doubt can shake. And these difficulties, doubts, disquietudes, and sufferings, which formerly so often have assailed me, have now, like questions humbly waiting for reply, fallen at the Redeemer's feet, patiently waiting for the hour when it shall please Him to remove the veil.

Tomb, 9th March, 1839.

Your letter, my dearest Frances, has made me both sad and happy; sad, because I have so little deserved it, and at the receipt thereof, I could not but reproach myself very deeply for not having earlier congratulated you on the birth of your little son; happy, on account of your hearty and loving words. I have often longed to speak with you about life's fullness and beauty, and to share with you your happiness in the future, which probably is in store for your children. Love and purity in the home, harmony between the parents: this is a blessing to the children; it opens at an early age their eyes and hearts to all that is good and noble in life. Ah! well may we rejoice at having been born in this world, although here is much of evil, much of suffering, if we only would see that our life is an education, leading to perfection, under the guidance of an all-good and Almighty Father; if we would but see that it is a progress upwards to a heavenly home. You know that affliction has to me been a heavy burden in this world, both to my heart and to my mind; yes, it has dimmed for me all the beauty of this world of ours; but the happiness which, during these latter years, I have deeply felt, has opened my eyes, while the Crucified One has reconciled me to the sufferings on earth, or has chased away its darkness and bitterness, through the light which He has shed beyond the grave, beyond all earthly darkness, sorrow, and affliction. There is a last and highest court to which mankind can appeal for the solution of all life's enigmas; a Judge to whom we can refer those cases on which no earthly tribunals can give a verdict. But that One is all sufficient. With our eyes steadily fixed on Him, we can confidently wander through life, rejoice at the good, and, each in our way, add our mite thereto. Pleasing in the highest degree, indeed, is the ferment of the times in which we live: the development of the state into a constitutional society; a development founded upon the spirit of Christianity, of liberty, and equality, and which makes every individual, every talent, every power valuable and useful in the whole. Christ is the first originator of true liberalism. He made religion popular, and with it and through it also every other good teaching and wisdom; for if all human beings are in reality the children of the same Father and equal before Him, then they also have all an equal right to enjoy the blessings which the genius of man can create. Is it not *this knowledge* which, after and through many long and sanguinary conflicts, permeates the age and reorganizes society; erects schools; instructs the children of the poor; spreads amongst all classes the results of scientific researches; resounds in the chords of poetry's lyre (the whole of the modern literature of romance is but a lay, a development of the moral truths, which flow out of this one great truth); draws nearer to each other master and man; unites more closely parents and children; eradicates hateful prejudices and humanizes the world? Long life, therefore, to printing-presses, steamboats, and all such inventions, for they are the heralds of *ideas;* and, above all, long life to the ideas themselves, — the great, the noble, I mean; to their organs, mankind; and, above all, praise to the Great and the Good, who sends them! This was a wide embrace, my dear Frances; but such a one is sometimes wanted, to be able heartily to embrace also what is little within our own little world and sphere of activity. In contemplating this great institution, the world, we can better understand our own place there, our mission and our children's, be they human beings or books.

For my next work I want a vignette, representing a butterfly fluttering over its chrysalis. The world-life in all its forms, has no truer image of its reality, its essence.

The chrysalis — this body of earth's dust, which envelops and fetters Psyche's wings — *that* it is which binds, which impedes, which burdens you and me and most people. The chrysalides of home are the household cares with all their concomitant difficulties and hardships. I know many married women, who, like yourself, endure and manage these against their inclination, from a mere sense of duty and necessity; but to you, as well as to them, the thought must be very encouraging and consolatory under all the moments devoted, to all appearance uselessly, to speculations about eating and other household duties, that it is only under this chrysalis that *home's* Psyche can develop herself. But I hope meanwhile that in future this machinery of life may be simplified and made more easy. This would be especially desirable for our mothers of families here in the North. Be this as it may, our soul becomes materialized from too much occupation with the material.

18th May, 1839.

True it is that a mother, a housewife in Sweden, is obliged, more than in southern countries, to devote herself to practical life in her house and in her home — provided she wishes to fulfill her duties — and that she must deny herself, comparatively, many of the enjoyments of intellectual life and of the fine arts. And if human worth consisted in these, or if they essentially contributed to the development of our *eternal* nature, then it would be a hard fate to be a wife and a mother in Sweden. But it is not so. That which really constitutes human worth is moral virtue and an exalted mind; it is only this which unites man with God; which gives the rank of citizen in His kingdom here on earth and in heaven. Oh! my dear Frances, this was always a delightful thought to me, and this doctrine of Christianity, which equalizes all ranks on earth, which weakens the power of all external contingencies, *this* it was that from my earliest youth drew me to the gospel, already before I understood all the depth, all the happiness, contained in its "joyful message." You see, dearest friend, that it is *this* which makes the poor fisherman, the simple peasant's wife, quell what is evil in their propensities and in their nature, in order to follow Christ's teachings, and thus stand nearer God than the greatest philosopher and the most distinguished scientific man in the intellectual circles of London or Paris, if these do not also overcome their sinful nature, their pride, or other evil passions which may possess them. If now we contemplate woman's position in our Swedish homes, we shall find it brightening more and more, when we consider that the practical life in the same, the relation between parents, children and servants and others, tends more to develop people's moral virtues than books and all the intellectual education in the world. From this, however, I except Christian knowledge, which comprises the wisest doctrines of the past and present times relating to God and man, and which knowledge we stand in need of in order to live as we ought to do. This knowledge we all gain, in the civilized world, directly or indirectly through the gospel; for all the state, society, literature, etc., etc., is now founded upon Christianity, and almost all of us know what we *ought* to do. But these moral duties are not easy to fulfill; moral goodness and nobleness is difficult to attain, surrounded as we are by sinful fellow-creatures, and in our contest with them and with our own faults and weaknesses. How deeply have I not felt and do I not feel this in my own weak and restless soul! It is only Christianity's doctrine of God; of His love to us; of what He has done for us and intends doing with us; it is only the love for Him, which is a result thereof in our hearts; only prayer, through which we approach Him and experience the affinity of His spirit with ours;— it is this only, which can strengthen our desire to practice what is really pure and good; which can create within us the harmonious frame of mind, from which emanates meekness, tolerance, patience — in a word all the virtues of Christian love, which give peace to our own heart; make our home pleasant; our nearest and dearest happy; and which opens for us, after this life, the heavenly home, where harmonies resound, more beautiful than those with which Mozart's Genii in the "Magic Flute" enchant our ear, as a foretaste of the eternal harmonies. The songs of the Genii in the "Magic Flute!" Yes, if any thing can give us an idea of Paradise, it is that music. How well I understand the feeling that has been awakened in your soul; such sensations I have myself often experienced during the preludes of the organ in our churches, before the hymn was sung. There is something so sweet and earnest in these melodies, quite separate from earthly joys, but which tells me of the joys of the blessed in heaven.

26th August, 1839.

Well now, my lazy hand! take up the pen, for I must tell my dear Frances what I have been busy writing to her every day in my thoughts. Yes, — what was it all about? Indeed, I can now only remember your own words in your last letter: "What a happiness it is to love!" for these words have haunted me continually during all this time of sorrow as well as happiness. Yes! to love — that is happiness, that is bliss, that is life's summer. How well do I not feel the truth of St. Theresa's words about the wicked: "The unhappy! they do not love." Could we but always love — first God and then our fellow-men. Yes, then life would not be weary. Oh, Frances! He who revealed God, our Creator, as Love, and who ordained that love for Him and for our fellow-men should be the law of our life, should be the condition for gaining eternal life, eternal bliss and fullness, — has He not at the same time given us the surest guide to attain eternal bliss. Indeed! He is the best teacher how to gain happiness. How have

I not felt Him to be so, not only in my heart, but also in my home. But I ought to *speak*, not to *write* about this. About this: "What a happiness it is to love," I said the other day in a few words to the good, honest Ågren. You would have embraced him if you had seen the indescribable expression of love which spread over his honest face, while tears rolled down his cheeks, when he said, "that to love certainly gave happiness, but that it also caused so much pain, so much suffering, that it is quite dreadful." Alas! it may be so; but also this suffering has its sweets. It does not embitter, it ennobles. Our soul does not become mouldy under it; it becomes invigorated and soars heavenward.

And now let me speak of what has called forth this paraphrase of your words. Agatha has been very ill. Our mother and I have been exceedingly uneasy on her account, and yet, in the midst of our distress and our anxiety, we felt peace, aye, had even many happy moments, because we loved one another and felt it then so warmly. Now, when our Agatha, after nearly three weeks' painful illness, is again restored, we feel so happy, and cannot say gratefully enough: "God be thanked!" and she is now more than ever every body's in the family "little lady;" is lauded to the skies for every morsel which she eats; is protected against every puff of wind, and is fondled and petted in every way. Yet, I have never found her to be a more earnest and amiable creature than just now.

9th September, 1839.

Only a few words to-day, my dearest Frances, to thank you most sincerely for your letter of the 30th of last month, and to tell you, that those who here love you so warmly sympathize with you in the loss of your friend, and long to see you well and happy again. Happy! yes certainly, for the departed one was, as you say yourself, *prepared*, and thus she lives and will love you in the better world which

God has prepared for those who are His own. The death of a good person, has to me something beautiful in it, because I look upon death in the light of Christianity; as a transition from this to another life — for those who are good to a higher existence. I do not wonder, dearest Frances, that the doctrine of the atonement is still so often obscure to you, for I know from my own experience how deeply rooted in our mind are the notions which we have been imbued with in childhood and in youth, and how difficult it is to divest ourselves of them, notwithstanding that they so often appear unsatisfactory and dark. I wish that I could express my thoughts so that they found an echo in your heart. I shall endeavor to do so, if you wish it, when I have more leisure and peace. I shall now only remark, with regard to the 6th chapter of the Gospel of St. John, that Jesus himself divests his words of all material interpretation, when in the 63d verse He says: "*It is the spirit that quickeneth; the flesh profiteth nothing; the words that I speak unto you, they are spirit and they are life.*" *Blood*, in the Hebrew, and in many languages, is equivalent to *life*; bread signifies *doctrine*. Jesus represents Himself here as the *bread of life*, by His life as well as by His *doctrine*. With *everlasting life* is here and everywhere in the Scriptures not meant eternal life, with reference to space of time (for even the wicked have thus eternal life), but the real, full, blissful life; in a word, God's, the *Eternal life*. Our Saviour says in this chapter: "The bread (manna) which feedeth the body is not heavenly food, and saves neither from spiritual nor from bodily death" (the hardened sinner is said to be spiritually dead), "but I, my life (blood,) my doctrine (bread,) am the true bread which cometh down from heaven and giveth life." This new life (God's life, eternal life) by which man gains strength to overcome his evil passions, to become purer and more loving, Jesus has grafted on the world ("I am the vine and ye are the branches") by His life, and His doctrine of His revelation of God's heart and will, and our relation to Him and to the next world. By grafting that life on the world, upon us, He has reconciled the world and us with God, or, according to the words of St. Paul: "God was in Christ, reconciling the world unto Himself." When He makes us good, He takes away our sins. Christ's *justification* consists therein, that He makes *us justified*. All moments in the life of Christ, His temptation and His transfiguration on Mount Tabor, His death and his resurrection, are moments of this great work of atonement, because they all affect beneficently different moments of our life.

I have frequently been astonished at the innumerable different ways of understanding and of explaining the doctrine of the Atonement, ever since the introduction of Christianity until this day, and at the great number of sects, each explaining their belief in a different way, and still all calling themselves Christians, and I have come to the conviction *that this must be so*. These disparities are a consequence of people's different intellectual capacities and different experiences in life. There must, in consequence of Nature's manifold creative powers, be found turnips and apple-trees, lichens and cedars, in the world of mankind, as well as in the world of Nature. If only each species tries to gain the benefit of light, so that its fruits can ripen and become good, then also is each species good. But there are plants and herbs of lower and of higher degree; and there is also a profound as well as a superficial way of explaining Christianity. But Christianity has also this resemblance to the sun, that the little as well as the great drink life out of it. Nobody can sound the depths of Christianity without having first dived into the depths of life; but even the most superficial thinker, the most shallow natures, can from some one of its rays gain light and strength enough for life. It is the river "through which the lion can swim and the lamb walk."

Pardon this rhapsody. I shall be able to write better another time. Oh! that I could clearly enough express the truths which I acknowledge; I am then sure that your heart and your reason would find peace therein. Man's wants also in this respect are different. May each one find what he needs, and may every body (for this is the most essential) follow the doctrine of Christ, and he will then come to His "*eternal life*." I have lately heard Mr. T——'s and Agren's confessions of religious faith. What contrasts! and yet how they agree as followers of Christ. They shall therefore be left in peace by me, although I find the former's views of God and His revelation so deplorable, and the latter's so unsatisfactory. But may I be found worthy one day to meet them in the mansion of our Father.

Årsta, 2d October, 1840.

Dearest Frances! After having read your letter, which I received last Wednesday evening, I thought to myself, now I will at once sit down to write, because it would be a great shame if a solitary dweller in the country, who has nobody else to take care of but herself; nothing to look at but fields and phlegmatic oxen; nothing to manage but her goose-quill, — I say it would be a great shame if she could not find time to write a pertinent letter, when the wife of the chief of a government office (a government office *chiefess?*), residing in the capital, who has to cut a figure in the world; give grand dinner and evening parties; be wife to her husband; keep a watchful eye upon four boys; upon the debates in the House of Nobles; upon erring fellow-men; and upon the improvement of the world, etc., etc., and having all this to attend to, still can find time to delight her friends with her letters.

Now, my dearest Frances, attention! I shall now come with a really fine and polite Swedish phrase: "How delighted I am not to be in *your* clothes," — which means, how pleased I am not to have your responsibilities in the vortex of the world, because I should find myself utterly unfit for it and lost. But do not think that I pity you. No such thing! I might perhaps say to you, when you are fatigued in body and soul: "Oh! how sorry I am for you, my dearest Frances;" but I do not pity you on account of the life which you are leading. It is really so ordained in this world, that in every direction, and in every position in life, one can improve one's self, and develop a peculiar beauty and excellence. And she who lives in the great world, active in all domestic duties, gains thereby strength, assurance, *aplomb*, and ability, which the solitary one never attains, even if she could get into her head all the books which she collects round her in her silent and quiet little home. She can also develop herself, and work good in her own way and in her retirement; but she would miss much of what is gained in a more stirring, outwardly more practical, life. It makes me happy to feel how every one can go onwards in his own path. All depends upon going forward in the right direction. The retired study has its dangers, its temptations, as well as the *salons* of the great. One can become dried up in the former, whilst in the latter one evaporates. All roads have their by-roads. It is therefore necessary that we should take with us the proper guide. My sincerest thanks for your encouraging words about my "children." I wish only that I could properly execute what I intend and ought to do. But it is with books as with deeds. We know what is right, but we are not able to achieve it. Frequently, when I have finished some book, I feel with anxiety and a kind of pain how much of it I could have done better. In order to console myself, I look forward to the future and to new works. I wonder whether I shall be more pleased with *them?*

What you say of our Swedish Psalm-book delights me. Its compiler has well deserved Tegnér's eulogy: —

> "The merits of Wallin sure we may all discuss, —
> He 's yet a psalm-book in advance of us."

Do you know the psalm, No. 201 : " Create in me, O God, a heart, which holy is and good and pure ? " It is my favorite morning-psalm; and the splendid invocation, No. 131 : " Holy Spirit, Spirit of Truth," — I know no words which flow more naturally from heart and lips in solitary and agitated moments. Besides, I think that psalms ought to be an outpouring of the heart, either imploring or praising; but not long self-meditations, which so many of our psalms really are. For such, prose is more suitable. Psalms are prayer's efflorescence; and prayer is the soul's flight upwards to bloom in heaven. Prayer is the conductor by which we put ourselves in connection with eternal life's current of light, which thereby being drawn to us, elevates and animates (electrifies) us. Therefore prayer is of such great importance, and so strongly commended in our Christian religion, and without it — namely, prayer in the spirit of Christianity — no thorough improvement is possible. It is a true and beautiful saying of one of the fathers of the Church : " Prayer will either make us abandon sin, or sin will make us abandon prayer." . . .

ÅRSTA, 12th January, 1841.

For a long time I have been writing to you in my thoughts, my dearest Frances. When I was last in town, we had never an opportunity of saying all that we had to say to each other. Sometimes one is not in the vein, and then there is no help for it. I was also, I know not why, morally shut up. The soul and the mind have their winter as well as their spring; and it is sad that increasing age often spreads a benumbing snow-covering over the mind. In youth we are often on the point of melting from mere feeling; in old age we are often in danger of congealing to ice; and the last danger is greater than the first. We find a remedy against it in the gospel, in the sun, and in good, noble-minded people. Warmed by such spirits of spring, we again begin to thaw. What a delightful sensation it is to thaw under silent tears of love, under happiness, or gentle sorrow. It is like the sweetest music.

Why do we, in all descriptive sketches of heaven and of the realms of bliss, always find something resembling music? Because music only can interpret the unspeakably deep and sweet in human feeling, the melting harmony, the transition of the soul, or rather its glorification, in an element of the purest love and beatitude. Surely you and your husband will one day sing the song of the blessed together in harmony's perfect world.

When I was last with you, you did not then sing in concert together; each of you had your own part; but they were somewhat discordant in a question respecting *anger*, and whether this feeling was blamable and ignoble or not. I remember that we have sometimes spoken on this subject; and I will now make a fair copy, of which I then made a rough one.

I believe that anger, like any other affection or impulse of the soul, has its truth and its good. It is the violent protest of the sense of right and justice against what is wrong and unworthy. Such is anger in its purity — in God. In its impurity it is a violent outbreak of the mind against every thing which wounds its opinions and will, be this what it may. And when you, my dearest Frances, said, "I do not think that I am sinning when I get angry," I side with you, provided your anger is just, — that is to say, directed against what is wicked and bad. But when your husband says: "We never act so prudently when we are angry, as when we are calm and collected; we are generally carried away from what is reasonable, and let, in our passion, the guiltless suffer with the guilty;" then I place myself beside him, humbly giving him right; and thereupon I place myself between you two, and wish to decide the question thus: —

There is a noble and an ignoble anger. There are

moments and situations in life when one requires a burst of anger, to be able to grapple powerfully and lend justice a strong helping-hand. But such moments come seldom; and the danger of falling, in the annoyances and little vexations of every-day life, from a noble into an ignoble anger, is so great, that we ought to do all we can to govern and conquer this emotion and its eruptions. When our Saviour, in noble wrath, thundered his anathema against the hypocritical Pharisees, *He knew what He did.* But we, weak, narrow-minded beings, often know not what we are doing when our feelings are agitated. A noble, high-minded character ought, therefore, not to *quell* any of the feelings which the Creator has interwoven with his nature; but he ought so to rule and direct them, that, like the waves in a river, they fertilize its banks without inundating them.

And now to something more trivial. Whilst you, Frances, are waging a war here and there in the world, we spin out life here in quiet and peace. I begin now firmly to believe that, for Agatha's sake, we could not have come to a better determination than to remain at Årsta over the winter. I did not believe this last autumn; but in all transitions from one condition to another, there arises usually some suspense, something wavering; in a word, something uncomfortable. So it is in the autumn, within as well as out of doors, when we have to pass from summer into winter. When we are tacking, the sails hang shivering uneasily until they are again caught and swelled out by the wind. Thus it was with us last autumn. We have now tacked about; our sails are again caught and filled, if not by a strong, at all events by a steady and gentle breeze. We are bounding along, and ever and anon we call out, "All's well!" During day-time I am left much alone; but in the evenings I read aloud to our mother and Agatha, until we take our little "tea-supper," and soon after bid one another good-night. Agatha and I then chat together until, very quietly, we fall asleep. It is a great pleasure to me to converse with Agatha, about any thing. "Vivent les gens d'esprit!" It is refreshing to live with somebody who can understand every thing, and who is always ready prepared with sense and wit, especially when this is joined to real goodness. With the truly good and the truly sensible we inhale fresh air, and if even now and then we should come upon small stumbling-blocks, we do not run against or stick fast upon them.

You are on a sailing-excursion very unlike ours (Heaven knows how I have managed to get out to sea, from whence it seems as if I could not come back). Yours is more exciting, but also more unquiet. Your four boys occasion many contrary winds, and you sail amongst reefs and sunken rocks. But while love and good sense are at the helm, you have a prosperous voyage, and I am sure that after a heavy day, you exclaim in the silent hours of night, gratefully, "All's well!" and then I would join with you in a "Thank God!" for it is His spirit in the heart of man which leads them victoriously through dangers and difficulties.

But I must now make for port with my epistle. I embrace you in thought and beg you to remember me kindly to your husband.

Årsta, 13th July, 1841.

. . . .

"You say, my dearest Frances, that you feel yourself getting older, and feel the consequences thereof. I also have for some years (and I am a couple of years older than you are) distinctly felt within me this transition to an advanced season in life. I have welcomed and blessed it. It does me so much good to feel the cooling evening breeze fan my temples and my heart; to feel how it gains more and more peace and calmness, and I thus look at life with a clearer eye. This autumn of life is dear to me. Its sun is less scorching and often brighter than summer's sun, which is sometimes dimmed by hot exhalations. If friends have departed this world, they have taken our heart with them to a better home; if many an enjoyment has withered away, other and new enjoyments have come in their stead, and many, many sufferings have ceased. Thus at all events have I found it. Yes, the autumn of life can be a genial, a rich age; one must only guard against fros.. *That* is the danger in this season, and earth's best flower — our heart — is then in as great a danger of being frost-bitten as are earth's more humble and more material children. But for a mother and happy wife this danger is not very great. Round her beat hearts in loving unison with her's, and her's cannot then be chilled. Greater is the danger to her who stands comparatively alone. The only remedy is love. And this feeling can inspire every heart which longs for it, because a heart forever warm beats in the cèntre of the universe, with which we all can have communion.

Årsta, 28th September, 1841.

Oh! if my dream should be realized, my dearest Frances, your little boy would then be in a fair way of recovery. I dreamt that he upset me in one of his lively gambols. I long so much to hear how he is, and I hope the best for your and your husband's sake, for otherwise I do not grieve when people are dying. I have always looked upon the coming of death as a deliverance from one evil or another, so that in my mind death is deeply connected with my idea of something desirable and tranquilizing. I know, however, that it is not always so, and I have to-day had an instance of its bitterness. A young woman here has lost her husband, with whom she lived most happily. It was very touching to hear her subdued and deep wailing: "Alas! that he should go away from me in my youth! Many bitter tears do I weep every night, when the others" (the wives of the other laborers on the estate) "meet their husbands coming home; but no husband comes to me. And how happy we were when he came home in the evening from his work! He was the best of husbands; we lived so happily together. Indeed, it could happen, as it does sometimes happen between husband and wife, that we did not quite agree, and sometimes he would take a glass of brandy; but — never was I afraid when he opened the door!" This last sentence touched my heart. I found it so characteristic of the relation in married life, and I remembered what you told me, and what you feel when you hear your husband's steps at your threshold, and how I have seen less happy wives turn pale and look frightened, when they have heard their husband's footfall near the door, and heard their hand touch the handle of the lock. I wept with the poor bereaved one, whose door will not again be opened by the loved one's hand; whose threshold will not again be touched by the foot of him who was the light of her heart and the prop and stay of her life. And then the three little children, who always asked when their "daddy" is coming home again!

But the same woman, who so deeply bewailed her husband, had but a moderate love for her children. Once last summer she declared openly her conviction that her youngest boy — a fine little fellow — had brought misfortune over her, "because when he was born, her pig died." I moralized her a little for seeing things in this light, and told her that she ought to look upon the boy as a compensation for the pig; but I doubt much that I succeeded in altering her view of the case.

Årsta, 4th, October, 1841.

I have heard through F——, my dearest Frances, that God has taken away your little boy, and I hasten to town to-morrow, to be with you and your husband, and to tell you what I feel for you in my heart. Alas! there is only one word of comfort; as for every thing sorrowful in this world there is only one great consolation — the conviction that over us all, and for us all, rules a good and loving Father, almighty and all-good. With Him is your son, and there you shall one day see him again.

To-morrow I shall be with you.

1841.

Dearest Frances! It made me very unhappy on reading your letter, to find you grieving so painfully. You do not feel in these hours of anguish and bitterness the secret blessing which invisibly rests upon you, like a Father's loving hand placed upon your down bent head; but in your calmer moments you must see it. Your own words bear witness to the holy power of the hours of suffering. Let me quote them out of your last agitated letter: "My dearest occupation now is to read about religious subjects, and to contemplate the same. They so absorb my thoughts that, for the moment, I forget my grief at the loss of our boy, in the happiness which I feel in trying to look up to him."

This and your hopeful words of belief and trust, do they not tell your soul that which must assuage its grief; which must let you see that you are under the guidance of a higher power, under the care of an earnest but loving Father. Alas! it must be so for you, for me, for all of us, that when the bitter cup is held to our lips, we must drain it, even with tears — drain it submissively, and must say in our deepest anguish: "Father! if it is not possible that this cup be removed from me, without I drink it, Thy will be done!" While I am writing this, my tears are flowing and make my words dim. I remember only too well, how in my hours of temptation, I could not say these words, on account of the bitterness of my rebellious heart. *Now*, I think, I could do it. *I know* that when the victory has been gained, come the angels — heavenly messengers, heavenly powers — to administer to man; and I know well from my own experience the developing and beneficial power of suffering. I know that "much bread is growing in the winter's night," and one day also you will verify this.

15th October, 1841.

I do not know whether, at this moment, you are inclined for any deeper meditations. A suffering mind is often more pained than soothed by contemplating abstract subjects. But I will lay before you only one reflection, which I think is full of consolation. You spoke last of the "natural religion," and of your intention to adhere to it, as the true one. But tell me, dearest Frances, what comfort could you derive from it in the present case? What answer could it give you to your questions about your little child? Would it not answer: God is great and wise. He has in his wisdom ordained, that a certain number of individuals shall be born and that a certain number shall die every year amongst the species inhabiting the earth, be they sparrows or human beings; because for the maintenance and improvement of the species the individuals of each must be sacrificed; for the benefit of the whole the individual must give way. God is great!

Hear now revealed religion in the words of Christ: —

God is great and good. His eternal laws of order govern the world in the great as in the little; in the general as in the minute. While generations are continued upon earth, the individuals disappear from it, but *not from the kingdom of God's love.* " No sparrow falls to the ground without your Father's will and knowledge. And man is of more value than many sparrows. But the very hairs of your head are all numbered. Fear ye not therefore misery or death, for God is love." Oh! my dear Frances, is not this a more consolatory doctrine and more worthy our higher notions of God? So also is every thing in revealed religion, which is the fulfillment and perfection of the natural religion.

7th November.

Suffering and anguish have long appeared to me as the

dark genii of life. Not so now. I have seen that they *can* be life's good genii. They become so to us, if with deep and energetic confidence, we cling to the power, to the Father, " who smites and who heals, and who out of the very wounds creates minds open to receive Him." I shall never forget an expression, which I heard more than fifteen years ago, at a time when, in consequence of my own state of mind, I sympathized, with a painful feeling, with every suffering in the world, even with that of the innocent brute creation. Of the injustice of this latter, I said something during a conversation which I had with a man, who used to converse with me on the commonest every-day topics. I cannot describe the expression of his calm, blue eye, and the tone of voice in which he answered: " I should not wish that any created being should be exempt from the capability of suffering." He did not say any thing more on the subject, for I did not understand him. Since then I have learnt to comprehend the meaning of these words; comprehended it from my own experience, and am now inclined to think, that suffering is a prerogative in life. Without penetrating into the depths of suffering, into its bitter " Gethsemane," we cannot climb bright and blissful heights. He who cannot suffer, cannot enjoy. But all depends upon, that we should let suffering purify and ennoble the soul. This cannot come in question with respect to the sufferings of animals, but their suffering is distantly connected with a final atonement, concerning which I cannot now unfold my ideas. I will merely add, that according to the spirit of Christianity, it is through hope, and not through despair, that suffering works upon man.

If only I could be tranquil in my mind with respect to our mother and Agatha in Nizza, I could be so happy here in my solitude. It has always a beneficial, as well as an exalting effect upon me. When I cannot communicate with any body, I seem to expand, like a balloon, with thoughts and feeling, and life appears then so full.

1841.

Thank God! my dear Frances, that we shall one day get rid of this material body. I think that is a glorious thing; for I feel often deeply the truth of what is written in the Book of wisdom: " The mortal body burdens the soul, and the earthly body makes heavy the mind;" and I feel that we shall be able to love more warmly and to think better, when we are set free from the chrysalis, which again and again throws its folds round the spirit longing for liberty. I feel it also now, when a lingering cloud of *migraine* in my head presses down my thoughts and words, which fain would reach you, and infolds the mind so that it feels itself fettered. Ah! it will be indeed delightful one day to get rid of this heavy and infirm load. A body (form, organs,) we shall get, for it is the antitype and indispensable expression of the soul. The resurrection of Christ, is the real manifestation hereof. St. Paul explains this in his splendid Epistle to the Corinthians (1 Cor. xv. 35-57) wherein he says: " It is sown a natural body; it is raised a spiritual body.". . . " It is sown in dishonor; it is raised in glory," etc., etc. Raised in glory, in power! Yes, but on condition that we, here in mortality, develop the life, which beyond the grave shall be thus raised also in outward glory. Is there on earth a nourishment, a food which can strengthen and develop man to become heavenly, to become a citizen in the kingdom of glory? Is there on earth a heavenly *bread*, a heavenly *wine*? You long to reach heaven. Look up to the symbol thereof, which arches itself over our heads. Does not all light come from thence? Light, the cheerful, the warm, the vivifying, which gives to all beings, to all conditions development and beauty; in which all attain their glorification, and which, reflected in millions of rays, gives itself to all beings, gives to all a part of its life. Thus there is in every thing from which our soul derives nourishment, a secret, divine power, a heavenly bread and wine given to us for the development and glorification of our being. It is found in the life of love; in the work of scientific research; in the beauty of art; in the splendor of Nature; it is found in joy, in sorrow, in suffering, in every thing; aye, even in the bustle of every one's business; in the food which we enjoy corporeally. But we must understand this; we must understand the heavenly, which is hidden in the earthly; we must in us receive the eternal, which lives and develops itself in finite (transitive) temporal circumstances. Only in this way do we prepare our real transformation, and make, already here, the wings grow, which shall be made perfect when the earthly shell breaks.

"I am the living bread, which came down from heaven," says Jesus; and He says further: "Except ye eat the flesh of the son of man, and drink his blood, ye have no life in you;" and again, in the same chapter (St. John vi. 63,) "It is the spirit that quickeneth; the flesh profiteth nothing; the words which I speak unto you, they are spirit, and they are life." And at the last supper He says: "Take, eat, this is my body; drink, for this is my blood," etc., etc. Deep is this doctrine, but any thing but dark and mystical. Here Christ says: "I am the life of the world; for I am in the Father, and the Father in me; we two are one." "Even as I gave myself for you, so will God give himself to you in eternity" (for Christ is the manifestation upon earth of what God is in eternity). "As I call you to communion with me, so does God call you in eternity to that heavenly feast, to impart to you His life, for your soul's and your body's glorification. Abide in me; feed upon my life (blood), upon my body (doctrine), then shall you also live through me, and all that you shall do and work, shall be to your own gain; for a sanctified soul will in all things seek for sanctifying food. Be one with me, that I may dwell in you, so that at the resurrection you may be like unto me, for because I live, ye shall also live, and be with me where I am."

In a word: in the last supper is pronounced the profound doctrine of God's relation to mankind (He feeds us with His life and communicates it to us), and the doctrine of affinity between the spiritual and the corporeal teaches us "such as the spirit is, so shall the body be also; the outward as the inward."

Oh! Frances, how feebly does not my tongue stammer forth the profundity of eternal wisdom. Yes, I know it is only in *part;* but in these parts of an inexpressible whole, in these single letters of the eternal word, the soul finds light and joy. So has mine done; therefore it unfolds itself to yours.

Only one word more on this subject. The world is full of weak and also of bad food, in a spiritual point of view. We should deteriorate and go to ruin by it, if we were not strengthened and elevated by a heavenly (eternal) bread — food, and wine — drink. . This goes forth concretely in the holy communion. It is the doctrine of the atonement, expressed in deed; the heavenly synthesis, in which all life's antitheses are annulled (as such) and united and reconciled in a higher *oneness.*

As regards the sufferings of your little children, as an atonement, I can only say, that the suffering which can have a saving quality or one reconciling with God, must be a suffering which develops something good within us, and which thereby can make us active for others. But your departed children work beneficially for you, I can clearly see, from the direction which your mind has taken towards the invisible home, to which God has called them. But whether their suffering (I mean from their disease, for any other suffering these little, happy children could not know) has contributed to this, I do not know. If we can assume that this suffering has had a developing effect upon their innocent souls (and this may be probable), they have thereby attained to a higher capacity. Not your sins, but the sins and the fallen state of all mankind, acted upon them, and acts upon every individual member thereof who is born in this world. He partakes of the *evil* in the world, but through the virtues and truth of mankind — and yours also — he also partakes of its *good;* and in proportion as he develops himself in the latter, he becomes, in his way, a saviour of his race from the former; for no human being stands isolated. What he develops within him of good or bad, works far and wide, although often invisibly.

I know so well from my own experience how difficult it is to understand the doctrine of the atonement, notwithstanding its clearness and simplicity if it is rightly explained; and the reason is, that ever since our childhood it has been so distorted to our understanding. But gradually we seize upon certain main points, and by these the others are by degrees lighted up.

I am writing this with a continually increasing headache; but I do not mention it for the sake of complaining, but in order that you may excuse, in case the cloud in my head should have thrown some darkness over the paper.

ÅRSTA, 21st December, 1841.

Dearest Frances! Not being able to come to you personally during the approaching Christmas holidays, I shall pay you a visit in spirit. I know that during these days a sorrowful memory is awakened in your heart, and I should much wish — not to chase it away; no, no; such memories are sacred guests, — but to contribute to make it calm and bright. Let me now converse with you a short while. If I speak badly, you need not listen to me; if I speak well, then — why — then it *is* well.

It is a general national belief that children, who are taken from us at a tender age, are happy, because they are saved from all life's dangers and sufferings, and are playing as innocent angels in light and bliss round the throne of the Almighty. One may consider this belief as having a reasonable foundation or not; still it is in itself a beautiful, innocent angel beside the death-bed of little children, giving peace to many a mother's and father's bleeding heart. It is always interesting to hear the ideas of distinguished persons on this subject, and I have read some of these during the last days. You have, no doubt, heard something of a celebrated Swedish scholar, the visionary Swedenborg. He is still a problem and a marvel to our philosophers; many have endeavored to explain his visions, but have finished by declaring them to be — inexplicable. All, however, agree that Swedenborg was a man of almost gigantic learning, and his life and character of the highest moral beauty. His visions and his intercourse with spirits did not disturb the equanimity of his soul, and he reached a very advanced age in the happiest and most amiable frame of mind. What I have read of his visions and revelations from the world of spirits, has not struck me as being more *profound* revelations, but often as very ingenious *intuitions*, although absurd and extravagant. But in general his doctrine distinguishes itself by its moral nobleness and beauty. Nobody speaks more beautifully than Swedenborg of, for instance, conjugal love, and his visions concerning the state of married couples in another world are indeed heavenly. He speaks of these visions and revelations with remarkable simplicity. He never proves any thing; he merely says, "I saw it;" or, "it is so and so." With respect to the state of children after death, he has such a beautiful idea, or, as he considers it, revelation, that I believe your maternal eye would rest upon it with delight. I shall begin by quoting his words relating to the parents: —

"When the husband has been taught by the wife to experience love for the children, he shares with her this kind of love, which, in the strength of its disinterestedness and its sacrifices, in which it finds the greatest enjoyment, is, of all human love, nearest the divine love. We see hereby clearly how great and beneficial must be the influences of the love for children in parents, who indeed are life of each other's life, or have 'become one flesh' in the full and sacred sense of the word. And it requires no explanation to show what a delight it is to them, when they are permitted to keep their children with them alive, until, surrounded by them, they close their own eyes forever. But even *that* is a blessing, to have, as one expresses it, lost children by death in their tender age. For these, who in heaven are educated by angels especially appointed for that purpose, until they themselves have become qualified to be such angels, continue to be connected with their parents remaining on earth, by love's immortal, sympathetic ties. These ties are the root of their being, and hence it follows that these ties, by the development of the consciousness of these children, themselves become developed into a constantly higher love; and this makes that from the third or highest heaven, which is the heaven of innocence and of children, they constantly visit the parents through soothing and purifying influences.

"All children who, in their tenderest age, are taken away from earth, are in the beginning brought up in that circle of heaven which has been mentioned first. For this purpose female angels are employed whose distinguishing characteristic during their mortal life has been sincere piety, and great love of children. Thereafter their education is continued by male angels in that branch of celestial knowledge and wisdom to which their disposition directs them. During this latter education, or while growing up, they are removed to other celestial spheres. It then depends upon themselves whether they can again be received into the third celestial sphere. Fully grown up and educated are they, when the innocence of childhood in them is transformed into the innocence of *wisdom;* for just thereby, but not before, are they real angels. In general, this transformation is the common fundamental condition of all heavenly life, although different grades are possible. It is this fundamental condition which is expressed in the words of our Saviour: 'Whosoever shall not receive the kingdom of God as a little child, shall in no wise enter therein.' When full grown, and when their education has been finished, those who have thus been prepared for a celestial social life, receive those angel-spouses which from eternity have been destined for them. But in form and features they remain forever youth and maiden.

"The more thousands of years the angels live, the more beautifully and blissfully do they bloom; and so in all eternity. To grow old in heaven, is to grow younger."

So says Swedenborg, and while he has been speaking, evening has come on, and it is now too late for me to write more. Swedenborg was a most devout Christian, who worshiped God in Christ. One may share his intuitions or not, in part or in the whole; yet, in the most important and essential, one cannot but devoutly side with him, namely: that if in Christ we see the revelation of God's heart, being, and will, we can then confidently and joyously leave ourselves and our beloved ones in His hands, certain that He will order every thing with endless love to the best.

And now I kiss you and say, farewell and be happy!

Årsta, 3d October, 1842.

It is one of the tenets of my good, dear friend, the Countess S——, that when we do not hear any thing from our friends, we may be sure that they are perfectly well and lead a merry life; and I hope, my dear Frances, that this holds good with respect to you, our dear friends, during the long silence between you and us Arsta people. As to ourselves, we have not had quite such pleasant cause for our silence. We have already for some time had a visitor in the house, called Illness, and his conduct has been any thing but pleasant or agreeable to witness. But now, thank God! he is preparing to leave us, together with all his odious train, and Health is returning with her companions, appetite, happy faces, and joyous hearts. Charlotte is still confined to her bed, but the fountain of laughter which is in her is again beginning to burst forth, murmuring duets with Agatha's, which is constantly flowing. Our mother likes this, and is always ready to accompany them. I, who am less inclined for this merriment, must, however, "follow my leaders," — it cannot be helped. It would be difficult to find any place where, while health predominates, there is so much laughter as here. At what? — it would be difficult to tell: at childishness, at nonsense, — in fact, at nothing. Such merriment belongs to the family mysteries, and by no means to the worst amongst them. It often springs out of a number of trifling peculiarities of the family members, which, perhaps, would have become rude and harsh, unless they had in time been partly trimmed and polished by love, and partly been softened by good temper. You and your countrymen understand this better than others. Therein lies, I believe, the source of what you call "humor," of which they have so much.

I am now making the acquaintance of the ancient Finnish national poesy, and I am very much struck by its originality and life. But I am not so enchanted now, after studying the same, as I was in the anticipation. It is a savage beauty, like that of our old, grand pine-forests, with their gloomy recesses, their fresh, wonderfully pleasant fragrance; their wild, mysterious rustling; but which do not afford any food for our imagination and our feeling. It is a magical life of Nature, full of witchcraft, and full of strife between the energetic, prudent spirit of man and Nature's fierce powers, which are conquered and bound by the former, by means of "elementary spells" and the power of music. This latter has frequently great natural beauty, but we miss all moral life and a higher flight. The soul, after wandering about in these regions, longs as much for more solid food as the body after a long, fatiguing walk through heath and forest.

There is a Finnish proverb, which speaks to my soul with indescribable grace: —

> "Listen to the fir-tree's rustling,
> At whose root thy nest is made."

These words are full of deep meaning; they awaken in me refreshing and delicious thoughts.

Simultaneously with this study, I am busy with another

one of a very different description, which ought to afford the soul that food which is denied to it in the Finnish national poem "Kalevala." It is Lord Brougham's "Eminent Statesmen." I wonder whether it is a deficiency in me that I find these delineations below my expectation? I longed to see *characters*, distinguished men, and I see before me only — *orators*. Lord Brougham appears to me to be so preoccupied by the *speeches* of his statesmen, and their talents in that line, that he almost overlooks their actions as moral people; or, at any rate, looks upon *that* character as a secondary consideration, alluding to it only in passing. Lord North is the personage amongst them which I imagine that I know and see; not from Lord Brougham's biography, but from his daughter's, Lady Lindsay, because she seizes just upon those moments in which the character stands out naturally and completely. In order to be able to know man, one must see him in the hours of success and of adversity; one must see him love; see his angry passions roused; see him suffer, and see him — die. I longed to have seen in Lord Brougham's work man stand forth out of the moral *elementary life* (out of which the majority of mankind scarcely ever steps forth), and reveal himself in a form energetic in good or in evil, in life and in death. But I did not find there what I looked for. Lord Brougham's moral feeling, so it seems to me, is of English nature: pure, and noble, and strong. But I miss "la scentilla celesta" in his expressions either of blame or of praise; I miss vigor in spirit and in words.

Well, there you have quite unexpectedly got a whole criticism. Tell me, my dearest Frances, whether it is just or unjust.

Årsta, 1842.

My dear, sweet Frances! I went through your letter from beginning to end, only stumbling over, or stopping at, a few words, of which some still figure as stones and stumps on my road; but they do not now impede me;

for when I walk round them my path lies before me, quite distinctly, with flowers edging its graceful windings. Thanks, my dearest Frances! You come like a good, valued friend, who has gathered the best fruits and flowers which she has found on her way, to gladden the friend whom she goes to see. It is this spirit of kindness and love in a friend, which makes her warnings, her corrections, and serious advice so pleasant to receive, so pleasant to follow. In that pure mirror one will willingly see the spot in one's own soul; by *that* gentle hand, gratefully kissing it, one willingly allows the "beam" to be removed from one's eye. We do not know the best of a sincere friendship until we have experienced it in ourselves. Do you know, dearest Frances, what I fancy that Hedda at this moment would have said to you, whom, next to her own sisters, she held most dear in her heart and in her thoughts, and of whom she spoke so much in her last moments? I fancy I hear her saying: —

"My dear Frances! you have been wandering a long and toilsome road, and you are weary. Sit down beneath this tree; rest yourself, and let it spread its shady branches over you; lean your head against its stem, and let the summer's breeze — that summer's breeze which is the breath of God's love — caress your cheeks and eyelids, and think that all will be well one day. Rest so awhile, until you have gathered strength to begin your walk again; you will reach the goal one day, and then you will see that all is well."

And the tree, under which she tells you to rest, — it is the same under which she herself did rest, and which gave peace and shelter to her life; the tree under which you now so often are standing.

You ask me what I felt in going out to Årsta?

I read lately in a "Gazette of Fashions," that we ought to keep our happiness secret and not speak of it to others, because they cannot "tolerate it." But this is a piece of the Rochefoucauld wisdom, which I hate like the plague, because it sucks all its juice, or rather its venom, out of mankind's plague-blister, *egotism*, which it mistakes for the true, sound nature of man. My faith in the latter is firmly rooted as a rock, and I know its loveableness and its power to feel sympathy; "to weep with them that weep, and rejoice with them that are happy;" and I am, therefore, by no means afraid of telling you what I felt in going out to Årsta, little as it is to speak of.

It was a splendid winter's day. The sun was shining so brightly on the new-fallen snow, and the pine forests smelt so fresh. The rocks were clothed in draperies of snow; the mosses and lichen — my best friends amongst plants — shone so fresh and many-colored from the moisture which they drank out of the melting snow. They are the kind, the pious folks in the vegetable kingdom; there is no nakedness, no poverty, no ugliness which they scorn to hide with their beautiful living carpets, and, through these, to unite with the regions of beauty and light. It is only the really rotten and putrid which they abandon to the parasitical mushrooms. Across the frozen lakes were gliding long lines of peasants' sleighs, and my own covered sledge, with its clear, tinkling bells, flew so merrily along over lake and through forest. It was a winter's day in its most beautiful garb, and to me as charming as summer in all its splendor. Beside me sat my good Marie, with her warm heart and her keen sense of Nature's beauties; ready, at the slightest hint, to melt from mere ecstasy. When, after my pleasant and easy drive, I came out here to these good, benevolent people; to these quiet, large, and lofty rooms, in which many flowers were blooming; when at night I beheld, through a transparent, silvery frost-vapor, the red lights from the windows in the work-people's homes, in which I knew that the households of the laborers on the estate were living comfortably and decently; when I then saw my beloved constellations — Orion and the Northern Crown — slowly mounting the wide, clear heavens, and saw before me a time of solitude and liberty, oh! then all appeared so beautiful and life so blessed! I had received a letter informing me that our mother's and Agatha's health was very much improving at Nizza; all the friends in whose society I lately had enjoyed my life, appeared to be near me, so pleasant, so living. My heart beat warmly for them.

Ah, my dear Frances! in such moments of our life, when every thing in us and around us is so well, we ought to fear one thing: to forget, in our own consciousness of well-being, that the world is full of misery and suffering. But we weak mortals are only too prone to forget this. If all in this world were beautiful, all good, there would be no need of a transformation, an amendment, which we call redemption or atonement. We should, in beautiful harmony, develop ourselves "from one brightness to another." If all were evil, — yes, then no such improvement would be possible, nor a loving God either. Now there is both good and evil. Nature brings forth thistles and thorns (as it is symbolically said in Genesis iii. 18), but she brings forth also roses and lilies. In man there is sin and disease; but also love, truth, and health. A true contemplation of the world owns both and must; man and his world having an organic coherence, apply to this world Tegnér's beautiful words on Nature: —

> "The features of the fallen one transparent
> Shew noble signs of origin celestial,
> And Daphne's heart beneath the bark is throbbing."

With respect to your question, whether I would have the "Morning Watches" translated, I can only answer — that I cannot answer any thing; for, you see, I am a party in this matter. On a more critical examination of the book, I beg you not to forget what it is called, namely, "Morning Watches;" that is, the first faint streaks of light between night and a new day. These leave of course a number of objects only partly lit up, and many still in darkness; they light up only the heights, only the general outlines of the landscape. They forebode and bring with them a more complete light, and this will, if it pleases God, also come in due time. Your impression of this book delights me, and that is all that I dare at present wish. You have rightly understood its leading idea: the right idea of God, as shown in Christ's manifestation, creates in man a higher and nobler life, and saves him from anxiety and darkness. We learn here to know God as *a loving Father*, and we, and those dear to us, repose on His heart and in His care.

I read here for the first time Madame de Sévigné's "Letters." I am delighted with their liveliness and wit, and astonished to see how pleasantly at that time people enjoyed each other's society. Those were other "parties" and other sensations than those of Messrs. N. N. and Company of our own time. But very afraid were they of old age and of death. Rather than encounter these, the charming Sévigné would have renounced the life which she had lived, and wished to have died in the arms of her nurse. The ever-sparkling champagne in her letters could not keep up the interest, unless this thema of ardent, living love, "Ma fille! ma fille!" was not constantly heard in this impetuous, burning heart and mind of the loving and amiable mother.

TO BISHOP TEGNÉR.

Årsta, 7th April, 1842.

A pigeon had one day flown out of the dove-cote and set out upon a journey to foreign countries. Some sportsmen caught sight of her and exclaimed, "What kind of bird is this; whence comes it? We must catch it and pluck it!" And forthwith they began firing at her; but, how they managed, they hit only one or two of her feathers. The pigeon continued her gyrations on high, and the sportsmen, when they had fired at her for some time, became tired and soon lost sight of her.

An eagle — a real golden eagle — had meanwhile from his eyrie watched the ignoble sport. His heart revolted; he spread his mighty pinions and flew to the pigeon, saying, " Fear not; innocence is on your side, and I will shelter you under my wings." But when the sportsmen beheld the royal bird spreading his wings over the pigeon, and heard him deride their attempts, they became exceedingly excited, and cried, " Look here, — the eagle with the pigeon under his wing!" and now began a more furious firing, and the poor pigeon was worse off than before, for the last danger was greater than the first.

In this fable you see, my dear, my kind, for me sympathizing Tegnér, my idea of how matters stand with my " Morning Watches," and with their radical reviewers, and how it would be, if you, in the criticism which you had in view, were to undertake the defense of my work. You say yourself, " Defiled we get, but that we are used to." True! and the eagle need not mind what is thrown at him; he has already soared too high to be reached by the low-minded, and he perches in peace upon his Alpine height. But the pigeon, — the pigeon, which is still on the wing, which does not soar so high, she can be reached and hit, and even if this does not much impede her flight, her joy on the journey which she has begun, still, she cannot with indifference behold her wings soiled by impure hands. Oh, no, Tegnér! she must be glad the sooner the persecution ends, and she may forget it while she is bathing her plumage in some clear, purifying Bethesda water. And has not this been offered to me? Oh, yes! I find this Bethesda is my own conscience, in my joy at having acknowledged the Holy One before the children of men; I find it in the public and private acknowledgment of many an honest and noble soul; in the certainty that in my work, imperfect as it is, I have yet spoken words and thoughts which shall not have been spoken in vain; which shall, like the " dandelion" plant, grow all the stronger for being trampled upon. All this comforts me. And, therefore, peace, peace, dear, good Tegnér! peace and not strife with the world; at all events, not for my sake. I beseech you, peace!

Although in your review and in the verses which you dedicate to me, there are things, which, both for the sake of my own self-love, as well as for the truth and beauty of the thoughts, I would wish to see given to the public; still the publication of them cannot now call forth the acknowledgment which they deserve; because they are too nearly connected with things, which; especially at this moment, would hide them from the eyes of the multitude. *Later on*, when people's minds have become more calm, this review will be gratefully felt and greeted with pleasure.

You have asked for my sincere opinion, and I have given it according to my best and earnest convictions.

TO MR ——.

I am afraid that in our last conversation I have expressed myself on some important points imperfectly, or in a manner easily misunderstood. Do not therefore feel displeased, if in a few words I attempt better to explain my meaning. I spoke of going to work only to pull down. I did not here, however, wish to speak of religion and its spirit. This, I believe, can as little be pulled down or attacked successfully, as the heart can be pulled out of a man's breast, if he shall continue to exist. No, I believe that as long as it beats, as long as a human eye exists here below to contemplate the wonders of the world and of the heavens, so long will the religious truths, which in all times have been dimly felt and have attained full consciousness in Christianity, live and work in mankind. But the forms, in which the human imagination has conceived them, can vary with it. Therefore I spoke of distinguishing between religion and the dogmas or doctrines in which these truths are embodied and have assumed a form. Not that the inner and the outer, the truth and the form, differ in principle. The dogmas of the Church can contain the purest, fullest truths, although many of them have become fixed in a manner and in phrases which no longer suit the more extended knowledge of mankind. This belongs to the nature of the shell, and to throw away with it the kernel, would be the same as throwing away the baby together with the water in which it has been bathing. Within the shell the fruit was fostered for a certain period, and when the shell bursts, it is in order that the fruit may appear in a more complete and purer form; in a form more adequate to its life and truth. The most Christian and learned priests in the Evangelical Church — amongst them the noble Neander in Berlin — acknowledge openly the want of such a regeneration of the Church. But they demand, and they are right, that one ought not to misunderstand, nor let the solid tenor of the dogmas volatilize, and that before creating new ones, one ought thoroughly and rightly to fathom the sense and essence of the Christian revelation. How strange the world would look, if one or the other dogma, one or the other article of our creed, was to be taken away: the experiment is not a new one in the world. During the French Revolution this was done thoroughly, by declaring all the Christian articles of faith invalid, and the soil, on which this was done, became incarnadined with blood. The noble Condorcet, who, amongst all the French Naturalists, urged this doctrine to the uttermost, and endeavored to establish the hope of the perfectibility of mankind upon earth by means of arts and sciences, etc. etc., finished his career by suicide. But this anarchy in the realms of reason could not be of any long duration. The instant a calm moment set in, Robespierre decreed that "there exists a God." And soon again the old doctrines asserted their right, as indestructible foundations of the nature of man and of the stability of society, purified in much from the old dross, but still in many points impure and dark. And why? Probably because the process of purification had, to a great extent, taken the character of demolition, instead of caution. It is tolerably well acknowledged, that the cause hereof was lying quite as much in a faulty conception of the defenders of the old, as of the advocates of the new, doctrine.

But now — is it necessary that this experiment should be tried again? Surely you believe this as little as I do. What then was done, is done. New times and new means have come into the world. The regeneration which formerly was effected by violent means, can now, ought now to be effected by peaceful means; by the power of enlightenment, of conviction, and of truth. For to these the minds of the people are open, and the press is a mighty engine to work upon, hearts and brains. But all its labor for the rights of man and for the regeneration of society, in that Christian sense which equalizes the conditions of men, and makes mankind brothers and sisters, will remain imperfect and lame, if it is torn away from the eternal principles upon which Christianity itself has based its doctrine of freedom and love; and this, because these alone go to the bottom of the thing, and contain and exhaust the whole truth; for they alone comprise "the laws and words of eternal life." What man of sense would plant branches in dry sand, instead of grafting them upon a living tree, where they can grow and live; or who would erect a building without giving it a safe foundation? But they appear to me to do this, who preach the moral and political doctrines of Christianity, while at the same time they contradict the principles out of which these emanate.

But to plead for the former in the name of the latter, would be a task worthy a great reformer, and our times require to see such a one appear. A sense of the greatest want of mankind, a search into its *inmost* history and into its relation to the Christian revelation — these will probably be the most essential conditions for the success of his mission. But blessed be every one who paves the way for him in this spirit. And what subject can be more worthy of the attention of the acute thinker? Nowadays one hastens to point telescopes at every social phenomenon which occupies any tolerably broad historical base: upon the progress of journalism as well as upon that of communism and of others. And a phenomenon (I speak of the religious doctrines) which manifests itself wheresoever society is formed, all over the earth, amongst all nations in all times — what a subject for thought and for contemplation!

TO THE SAME.

In taking the liberty of sending you herewith my little book, "Two Leaves from the Borders of the Rhine," I wish you to receive it as it is meant: the expression of a sincere and friendly disposition of mind. Besides, I wish you to peruse my trip to the Rhine, and that, in reference to the same, you would afford me an opportunity of saying a few words. It seemed to me as if you had only cursorily glanced at the manuscript, and that you had imagined to detect in it some polemical allusion to the political opinions which you entertain. Believe me, I have not had an idea of any such thing. I could not have dreamt of it, as I myself embrace these opinions, in as far as they refer to the ever increasing advancement of liberty, of the people's more extensive share in legislation, and in other matters. My little pamphlet aims, besides an account of the Diaconess Institution of Kaiserswerth, at nothing but a faithful sketch of real circumstances and situations, such as they have been viewed — I venture to say it — by an honest and unprejudiced mind. I have in my pamphlet merely changed names and accessories, as much as it was necessary, in order that some of the characters mentioned therein, might not be recognized. That in the pamphlet the Republican has been allowed to act a part not very advantageous to society, is nothing but a fact; and in relating it I have not intended any political allusion. But if such a one should nevertheless be inferred, I am even willing to admit it in so far as I always consider the man of the extreme left, the ultra-Republican, to be dangerous to be followed, as a leader, by the people. My young friend at Marienberg did not belong to the moderate party, and you would yourself have been one of the foremost to endeavor to bring him to political reason. The position which I occupy in this little pamphlet, is no other than that which I have held in "Sister-life," and in my other writings, and which I should wish to improve more and more. It is a position *above* the parties; one from which I will contemplate and acknowledge the humanly good and pure in the ultra-Republican, as well as in the ultra-Conservative; amongst the Protestants, even if he were an adherent of Bruno Bauer's atheism and communism, as well as amongst the Catholics, even if he were the most obdurate worshiper of the coat in Frier; and I would besides let opinions be valued at what they are worth, even if I should be obliged, in consequence of the imperative force of thought, to join one of them in preference. You have surely, more than many others, felt within you this imperative force of thought, and that is enough to know that others also must feel the same in the direction which they have taken. My meaning, however, is not that all these others are right in their views; but they have a right to adhere to their belief and conviction, even if these are one-sided, until they are convinced of their one-sidedness, and can rise to a more liberal and more perfect conviction. That this can be the case, I believe, for I believe in an eternal right, an eternal reason, and in man's capacity to understand this, and in consequence to coincide in, and to settle, if not *all* controversies, at any rate, all *bitter* controversies. But nothing could contribute more effectually to attain the aim which we covet, than to keep this position above all parties, and to acknowledge willingly the rights and motives of others, wherever it can be done, while, with the whole energy of our mind, we endeavor to throw light upon the subjects under contention, and thus, by the inherent power of truth and light, compel the antagonist to be converted, and amend his views when they are wrong. I do not know whether a writer who is the leader of a certain party, can absolutely hold this point of view in which he acknowledges the good in an opponent and sees the wrong in the ultra, even if he belonged to his own party — the impartial, the Christian point of view; but I feel sure that he would infinitely promote the cause of a higher civilization and the interests for which he works, if he occupies this position (because the acrimony of the opposition would thereby become softened), while, with all the power of political penetration, tact, etc., which are at his command, and which he ought preëminently to possess, he would throw light upon the political arena. He would become irresistible, unconquerable, if in his political phalanx he were to enroll this higher system of politics — aye, made it the commander-in-chief of his army.

Listen to me one moment, as you have done once before on serious subjects. Surely your own sister could not approach you in a more sincere and friendly spirit than I do at this moment. It is therefore that I request you to grant me a moment's hearing, and also — I confess it — because I feel that I have something to tell you, which ought not to be rejected. See herein only a proof of the confidence which I have in you; of the weight and the value which I attach to your activity for our beloved native country, for letter-writing is not my weakness, least of all when it requires any great exertion of thought. I would rather be silent, if it were not that now and then something within me compels me to speak out, at all events to persons in whose head and heart I feel confidence.

In my little pamphlet upon Marienberg and Kaiserswerth, I have shown the contrast between two convictions:

the one, which, disengaged from its eternal foundation, believes in nothing beyond this life and hopes nothing after death; the other, that which believes, hopes, loves, and lives in Christ. I have shown this, because I saw and found it so in the places and amongst the people of whom I speak; and I have also done it because this opinion is rooted in my inmost conviction. And I would rather allow my right hand to be cut off, than cease, directly or indirectly, to point out to man the only true road to happiness, and to show him the darkness and danger which he will have to encounter on the contrary road.

We observe the latter in the national agitations of the present day. These, in themselves, are not for evil. No, they are for good; they are necessary; they are the rising of the oppressed million to civil rights, to the participation in all the privileges and obligations which make man a responsible being, a citizen, and which belong to him in his quality of man; this is the entrance of Christianity upon the political territory. But the barbarity, the bloodshed, and the confusion, by which the ideas, manifested in such agitations, assert themselves, are certainly not the acts of Christianity. The unwise and irritating opposition has much to answer for in this; but an equally great responsibility rests with the unwise demagogues; they, who, like Bruno Bauer, Grün, and others, try to establish the principle that, in order to solve satisfactorily the world's enigma, one need only " Gott ganz wegzustreichen ; " who thereby exempt man from all higher responsibility, making him the sport of his own passions, or giving him up to the leaders, who understand, cleverly enough, how to avail themselves of them. Mügge has therefore very logically said: " Das Volk ist die todte Masse; die grossen Geister sind die, welche es regieren." What this would ultimately lead to, ought to be easily seen by every person, with a good and clear head, who would take the trouble thoroughly to sift the matter. But history has in our days taken upon herself to record this in letters of blood. Laborers and artisans, who believe in God, in his providence and in his retributive laws, will not drench the cities in blood. Christian people will not torture their victims, and call down upon their own heads and upon their country a sanguinary reaction and civil war. They will insist upon the claims to political rights which have been awakened in their breast, and they will also, if necessity should compel them, fight for them; but they will also know how to pray, and how to wield the sword of intellect, instead of that of force. Compelled by the nature of my own mind, which wants to see things in their inmost necessity, I have asked myself: Is it not necessary that atheists, such as Helvetius, Thomas Paine, Strauss, Bruno Bauer, and others like them, should exist? Is it not ordained by the eternal laws and plans of Providence, that they should exist and speak? And I have been obliged to answer — *Yes!* Yes, it lies in the nature of thought that it should develop itself, even to the utmost extremes. Only thereby can they be combated and vanquished. The thinking atheist serves God as much as he who acknowledges Him, although in a different way; the former, as the negation over which affirmation must advance, in order to gain corroboration; and the latter, as this affirmation itself. The former might therefore be looked upon as the martyr of the idea, and of the thought, if he were not deficient in that which constitutes the greatness of the martyr, namely: temporarily to perish, while the eternal truth, for which which he fought, shines in greater glory, watered by his blood, blessing mankind, which will ultimately acknowledge in the martyr their hero and benefactor. But the demagogues of the extreme left, in point of religion as well as of politics, of whom I have spoken, shall perish — many of them probably in the earthquake which they have called forth — without being able to say: "I fall in defense of the highest truths, as the servant of God and of mankind, and my work shall remain as a blessing to the world when I have left the arena." They shall not be able to say this; for the goblet of liberty which they offered to the nations, contained — poison. Perhaps they knew it not; they may be morally irresponsible, but unhappy and unwise I must call them.

I have said that they *must* exist as actors in that life, and those ideas which develop themselves in history. But why should I then speak and fight against them? I do it in the conviction that this moment may be more transitory and more easily overcome, in proportion as its representatives become fewer in number and more insignificant. Certain it is, that the more life's central powers become strengthened (I mean here those which place earthly development in immediate connection with the eternal idea which is its foundation), the more quietly will the development of society progress towards liberty and happiness; the more will the extremes of "right" and "left" be weakened, and become more harmless and vanishing accidents.

One acknowledges pretty generally in the camp of the liberals, that the development of liberty and universal citizenship, which now causes society to ferment, has its foundation in the doctrine, revealed by Christianity, of men's equality before God. It has been said that this is Christianity's origin in political life, and that Christianity ought to become political. I grant this with all my heart. But how does it become so? Why, by grafting the lower, the earthly politics, upon the higher (the branch upon the tree), and by proving its foundation to lie in the eternal, immortal idea, whose doctrine we call Christianity. Only thereby can it grow in strength and freshness, and escape the fate of those branches which are planted in loose sand, and which, though fresh in the beginning, soon become withered.

Richert and Geyer — and also Torsten Rudensköld in his way — have in our country shown how this lower and higher policy can be connected; how the former cannot be consistently imagined without the latter; and the greatest thinker of our day, Hegel, has proved in his work, "Die Philosophie der Religion," how all the powerful thoughts, which now are uttered, claiming as a right national liberty, equity, justice to all, have their foundation and definition only in God, as manifested in Christ. But from this follows also, that every development of liberty, which is not conscious of this its foundation, or which is reactionary against the same, must miss the aim which it strives for, or bring forth weeds amongst the wheat to such an extent as easily to destroy it all.

I once heard you express the fear, that Sweden was destined, as a nation, to sink under, or merge into, the larger continental powers. I believe that this might come to pass, if it were possible to extinguish in the breasts of the people that belief in God, in His eternal laws, in the personal responsibility of the individual — in a word, that belief in a heaven, which is earth's greatest strength, and which hitherto has made the little, the poor Sweden's greatness and power. If it holds fast to this root of its life and its will, it must continue to exist, although it may stand behind in much of the industrial development which constitutes the wealth of other countries. But I do not think that this belief in God can be eradicated in Sweden. But it can be weakened or strengthened, and it may depend upon this, whether the social development, towards which we are now progressing, will be egotistical and sanguinary, or will be founded upon love's free and liberty-giving life.

TO BARON VON BRINCKMAN.

I thank you very much, my dear Baron, for having afforded me an opportunity of trying to explain my views on *the Fine Arts as a part of life*. You have yourself made the remark, that it is the "writing laziness," which is the cause why we so often rest contented with our half-thoughts without knowing their incompleteness. This incompleteness is not discovered until our thoughts are to be ranged in rank and file, and not until then can they be placed in regular order. And in now going to march up my recruits, I must request the experienced general — experienced on the field of fine arts — whenever it is required, to give the words of command: halt! right! left!

If yesterday my words should have made you believe, my dear Baron, that I do not understand how to appreciate the happiness of the collector of works of art, I should be very sorry, because they must then have been more stupid than myself. I only wanted to express a way of feeling, individual to myself, and with reference only to my own life. The indescribable enjoyment which I derive from works of art, the higher life which I feel while wandering about in your museum, must be the best interpreters of what I think of the influence of the fine arts upon happiness, and of the life of the collector. That, notwithstanding this, I shall never be a collector of works of art, nor, like you, surround myself with visible productions of art, is owing to reasons which I do not wish to explain. I will only say this much, that any thing having money value will not long remain in my possession — not even a medal awarded by the Swedish Academy. Offer me fifty rix dollars for any thing, except for a warm cloak, and it is yours at once. Nevertheless, my dear Baron, I adore art, and walk through life — allow me to say it with humble joy — as a novice in art. Of every thing which I experience in life; which I enjoy and suffer; and which I perceive in man, in nature, in my own soul — of all this I endeavor with love to comprehend the meaning and essence, according to my best understanding, and to form out of it a clearer and more perfect image of life with its power, that is to say, a group, in which God, man, and things, live together in harmony. This I would wish to call, the art of life. This seems to me to belong to every intelligent person, and without this art I do not understand life, neither here on earth nor beyond it. It is my sincere belief, that the Eternal Architect of the universe has auditories and laboratories enough, and models also, to prevent the divine exercise of this culture from ever dying out amongst the thinking and feeling spirits. Artists, in the sense now alluded to, I would call not only him who creates æsthetic works of art, but also the honest man who lives according to strict and pure principles, and the good man whose life is devoted to pure sacrifices of love. He creates his world out of the genius of the heart. These are human artists, as well as Shakespeare, Goethe, and Schiller.

I have mentioned Goethe, and this name calls up before my imagination the world of art, *par excellence;* reality embodied in beautiful forms, comprehensible to our outward senses in its reality, in its truth. I have never been able to understand the contrast, which so many — and amongst others Schiller — speak of, in reality and poetry. It is this innermost reality of life, of existence, of things, which to me appear the romance of poetry, and this poetry — but how to express the unfathomable — has seemed to me to be a sound, a power, a spiritual essence; something eternal, living, life-giving; something of God; something which reveals Him within as well as without us. Ah! it is in *such* meetings, when the lyre of the poet resounds involuntarily; when the Eros-image is born within the poet's joy-inspired bosom; when even the Paul's power stands speechless, only to be born anew, glorified, because he has beheld God. The artist does not then invent, he only conceives in a certain form the eternally living, eternally existing. Life, in its highest moments, is called "inspiration." In these moments the image of a God is born; it is inspiration; it is *inborn.*

Goethe's life appears to me to be one of the richest, most perfect artist-lives. Up to his last moments his Genius stood beside him. His making signs with his finger in the air, when his tongue had refused to speak, — this last attempt of the earthly organ to create, — is beautifully touching. These signs appear to me as a sacred signature to his closed career, so near the confines of a new one. Oh! he has not finished yet, — the glorious one. Art is eternal!

The artist's different tasks — faithfully to copy reality in its every-day dress; to reveal it in its ideal form; to copy its details; to form a whole out of many parts — have often been the subject of my thoughts. It has appeared to me that no work of art can be beautiful in the highest sense of the word, unless the beautiful form is based upon an eternal, divine truth. Then shall Milton's "Paradise Lost" stand higher than all the works of Byron; "La Madonna di San Sisto" be worth more than the Laocoön group; Fogelberg's "Oden" — the personification of power and wisdom — more than Hogarth's paintings. For the beautiful, as well as for the good, I would wish to have a Jacob's ladder with an endless number of steps reaching from earth up to heaven; but the lower ones ought to be prized as well as the highest. To value all, enjoy all, do justice to all therein, I see the greatest happiness and an enviable faculty.

I have not yet told you what I think of the life of a collector of works of art. But I have said that it is a happy life. It is a social life in its noblest form: he associates with what life has most noble and most valuable, were it only not in *things!* You see, my dear Baron, herein lies one of the reasons which makes me incapable of becoming a collector, and which has determined my taste for a life *à la Diogène.* With every trifling toy we forge another little chain, which fetters us to earth.

But I will not tire you any longer. I am a beginner, although old in years, and my endeavors to unriddle myself cannot be pleasant to others.

TO MR. GEORGE A——,

Stockholm, 29th March, 1844.

Dear Sir, — The doubts which you have imparted to me, in consequence of the public appeal made by me to the women of Sweden to labor for the establishment of a Refuge for neglected children, gives me an opportunity of discussing thoroughly with you a subject so much deserving of consideration, and so dear to my heart. I thank you for this, and while I look upon it as an agreeable duty to reply to your objections, I shall endeavor, where I cannot satisfactorily solve your doubts, to take a road on which we both, perhaps, with our united efforts, may find an exit out of the labyrinth; a point of rest for our inquiring, hesitating spirits.

That you should have seen in my appeal something else and something more than merely an inducement to a collection, an activity for some special purpose — for this, your way of seeing and understanding things in general, and your letter to me, are a sufficient warrant. My more immediate object has been to call forth or to rouse the consciousness of social life and worth in woman's life and sphere of activity, considered in a Christian and social point of view; I wanted to infuse a fresher life into the public spirit in this sphere, and to do it with a breath of Christianity's holy spirit. The invitation, which some ladies, with whom I am personally unacquainted, have addressed to me, to apply to the women of Sweden in favor of a "Refuge and Reformatory," I at once availed myself of as a welcome opportunity for expressing thoughts, the inmost aim of which goes beyond the immediate visible and stated purpose, and the seed of which I hope will strike root and grow like the grain hidden in the earth. It is not now my intention to speak of these more extensive views. I have appealed to the *motherly* element in society to feel, think, labor more largely, and above all, to take care of the destitute children; to save them, and, at the same time, to insure the future of our native country, in as far as this is dependent upon them. It is this more immediate, practical purpose, which here and there calls forth agitations and echoes, which I also would have wished to have seen revealed in another way. But they may perhaps be allowed without inconvenience to resound, and as far as their power goes, to strike the chords — or expire.

The superfluous will adjust itself, and from under the perishable flowers a really fresh, life-giving stream of spring water may gush forth.

The before mentioned purpose, warmly advocated by many, has, however, amongst several earnest people of both sexes, raised some scruples, which I also find stated in your letter. Let us therefore speak of the rescue of the destitute children, and of the " Refuge and Reformatory " as a means to this end. Some of your objections against the same, especially with respect to the depraved children, and their seclusion in a separate Institution, may be best met by a little historical sketch of the origin of the " Reformatory " in Stockholm.

In the year 1813, when Major Venus was Superintendent of the House of Correction here in Stockholm, several boys from twelve to sixteen years of age, were imprisoned in it for various crimes committed by them. The authorities were uncertain what to do with them, as it was considered dangerous to let them remain at large, with their evil propensities, in a world where they found no more protection or guidance than the birds in the air. In the course of his conversation with these boys, the Superintendent began to perceive that their misfortune might have been prevented, if they, instead of being driven out of their homes, in consequence of the vices or misfortunes of their parents, had been early taken care of by the charity of society, and properly trained; and that they might still be saved from utter ruin, if placed under parental care in a separate Institution, where they could be made, as it were, new beings. Major Venus accordingly appealed to the public, through the "Dagligt Allehanda" newspaper, for the establishment of such an Institution. The Bishop Wallin, and Mr. Wannquist, the Chief of the Police in Stockholm, examined and approved of the plan; but it was not until several years afterwards, or until the birth of Prince Carl in 1826, that these two gentlemen came forward and placed themselves at the head of the enterprise, and this so successfully, that the "Reformatory" soon was established, and opened for a great many unfortunate children, whose number in the capital had increased year after year. In the beginning, both *neglected* and *depraved* children (or children publicly known as vicious, and punished as such) were placed together in one and the same Institution. But soon it became apparent that their separation would be necessary. The *depraved* children, comparatively few in number, stood branded amongst those who were only *neglected*, and had always to hear or to feel from their thoughtless little comrades the reproach, "This you have done." Besides, the Cain's mark was only too distinctly stamped upon their forehead. They were also, after having undergone their punishment, and when they were handed over by the police to the Institution, found to be so depraved, that they not only corrupted the innocent ones, but also became highly dangerous to the "Reformatory," in which a stop was put to their idleness and vices, which roused their revengeful spirit, and their desire — cost what it would — to free themselves from the discipline of the Institution, in order to continue their former dissolute life. It was therefore found necessary to establish a separate "Reformatory" for these boys, which in its exterior became a kind of prison, but which in its interior was organized so as to afford them all the advantages of a home, and of a moral and religious education. Of ten boys who have gone out of this "Reformatory," nine have hitherto remained good; several of them are in correspondence with their former teacher and friend, and only one has again fallen into evil courses.

In large cities it is necessity which compels the establishment of a "Refuge and Reformatory." A fact presents itself there, which cannot be ignored: there exists a fallen race, whose numerous offspring grows up to become a plague-sore to society. Ought we to let them grow up thus? I say "No!" Instead of the fallen race, we ought to foster a better and a more healthy one. Or, how is the evil to be attacked at the root? The number of wicked people's unfortunate offspring is increased by children who are too many in the home of honest but poor parents, or who by death have lost their natural protectors and support, and are consequently thrown upon the world to shift for themselves.

There are, therefore, and with an increasing population, there will probably always be found destitute children in sufficient numbers to make such a Refuge necessary in its *first* form. Possibly its later division may be gradually dispensed with through the efficacy of the former.

I shall now proceed to the second point in your letter:

"Let us grant the necessity and the use of separate Reformatory Institutions — may we perhaps not get too many of them? Have we considered in all its parts *what* such an Institution really is, and *what* children ought to be its objects? Have we formed a distinct idea of the difference between a Reformatory and a Boarding School?" . . . . These questions require to be more thoroughly weighed, and they will no doubt be so now, when the attention of the public has been directed to the chief object, and the public mind is alive to it.

The indispensableness of a Refuge and Reformatory seems to be a settled thing. The number of these Institutions, the locality *where*, and the manner *how*, they are to be established, must depend upon the want thereof, and upon local circumstances, which may be different in each province of the country. The knowledge hereof, and a clear idea of the meaning with, and the purpose of, such an Institution, must decide the question.

One may also imagine this establishment to be at work where no Refuge, properly so called, does exist. It then forms a part of the invisible church, and can, like the visible church, be found in every congregation.

There, where the Refuge stands forth as an independent Institution, having its own government, its nearer relation to society and to the other establishments for relief and education becomes a matter of importance to decide, and the question then touches in the first instance the inner organization, system of working, and the object of the Institution.

With reference to *older depraved* children, it appears to me that one cannot hesitate. For them the Reformatory must have, above all, a moral tendency. It must then be an educational institution. It becomes to the young person every thing or nothing. The State must here, for the sake of its own good and for its own security, meet the prodigal son, as did the father in the gospel. Mercy must there go before Justice.

The case is different with regard to merely neglected or younger children. The security of the State and the good of the children do not require unconditionally that in the House of Refuge they should receive a complete moral and physical education; because, even without it, they can be saved, and become good and useful members of society. Therefore we ought here to consider the important question, concerning the moral injustice which would be done in society, if the children of bad parents, by being admitted into the House of Refuge, were to be better provided for, and if better prospects for the future were to be opened for them, than for the children of honest but poor parents. This question is of the greatest importance, and I beg of you to consider it with me, and try to discover the point at which the influence of the House of Refuge would become combined with the moral justice which is the foundation of virtue and of society, and which ordains that man shall be responsible for his actions, — that "as he sows so shall he reap."

The House of Refuge for *neglected* children in Stockholm is, at the same time, an educational institution. More than one hundred children are educated there at present, and provided for from their eighth year until, when they have been confirmed, they enter into service, which the Directors of the Institution procure for them.

They very easily find employment, because these unusually clever and well-taught children are much in request. All this is well and good; but the greater number of these have come out of the abodes of vice and neglect. Here appears the moral injustice, and this seems to me so dangerous in its consequences in general, that, having been led by thinking people seriously to weigh this matter in my mind, I have taken the liberty to submit to the Directors, whether the House of Refuge ought not properly to be considered as a central depot for these children, into which they should be received and taken care of during the earliest part of their misery, which often is so great, that, being previously nearly starved, they can in the beginning, only with difficulty bear food; and from which depot they may afterwards, as soon as convenient, be transplanted into the country amongst peasants and small farmers, against some moderate remuneration, by which means not only the child would cost scarcely half of what it now costs the Institution; but the Institution would be enabled to admit a much greater number of children; besides which the still more important advantage would be gained, that the children would be placed in the same condition of life, would become inured to the same toil, and would have the same prospects for the future as poor people's children in general in Sweden.

The moral injustice would in this way be, to a great extent, counteracted. Besides, one would avoid the danger of getting, as it is the case now, a superfluity of artisans and mechanics, whereas the healthy and useful class of country people and agriculturists would increase, which in our country is considered to be very advantageous. I have been answered: "Your project is very judicious; but in that case the House of Refuge ceases to be a moral House of Refuge — it is then placed on the same footing as the Orphan Asylum; it becomes merely an extension of the same; and see what is the fate of those children who are taken out of it and placed with other people. Do not a great number of them become utterly lost in the hands of their greedy foster-parents, who do not care for them? Nor does any body know how they are trained morally. Therefore, first to admit the children and then to plant them out, would not be to save them."

Notwithstanding these objections, I cannot help thinking that this method would be the best and the right one; if we consider the matter at large. The dangerous consequences, which you allude to, might be guarded against to a great extent by a strict surveillance. This surveillance could best be kept up by the clergy in the respective congregations; but I allow that the thing has its difficulties.[1]

Some part of the moral injustice of which we have spoken, may be avoided by means of the principles which are followed in selecting the children which are to be admitted into the House of Refuge. In Stockholm this has been actually done in this way: that the Directors in the

---

[1] The plan suggested as above, was a few years ago adopted by the Directors of the House of Refuge, who, after having purchased an island of considerable extent, situated at a distance of about five and twenty English miles from Stockholm, entered into a contract with the peasants and farmers living on the same, according to which they engaged themselves, on the payment of a fixed sum, each to receive, educate, and to instruct in agriculture, one or more children of the House of Refuge, under the supervision of the manager of the principal estate on the island. This arrangement has proved very beneficial to the children. — EDITOR'S REMARK.

first instance admit orphans, destitute in every respect, and *then* children of honest, industrious people, when these have fallen into misery and are prevented by illness from providing for all their children. In general, these parents can only with the greatest difficulty be prevailed upon to give up their children. In most instances they prefer to starve and to suffer any thing, rather than to part with their children.

Meanwhile, there is no doubt that the greatest number of the children in the House of Refuge come from the abodes of vice and recklessness. An important question remains therefore always to be put to the House of Refuge (in whatever way it may arrange with regard to the children and their future), namely: does it not encourage recklessness and indolence?

In reply it may be asked: would there be less recklessness and indolence if the House of Refuge did not exist? I do not believe this. If the former had not been so prevalent throughout society, the latter would not have been wanted or been established. But this question has roots lying far deeper. What else is the House of Refuge than a branch of the universal tree of charity, which has grown out of Christianity? At every new contrivance for the assistance or the saving of mankind, we have heard the warning repeated to us: "The more you assist, the more you call forth distress; the more zeal you manifest to save, the more you encourage recklessness, and weaken the power and the desire of people to help themselves. Why should the sinner be more cared for than the just? By this lax love you make sin abound." All this seems to be true; the dangers pointed at, seem to be a natural consequence. The warners, who thus complain, we find represented in the gospel in the brother of the prodigal son, at whose return the father prepares a feast; and also in the first hour's laborers in the vineyard, who complain that the workers of the eleventh hour receive equal wages with those "which have borne the burden and heat of the day." I confess that this complaint always troubles my heart, because it appears to me to be so reasonable, but the answer which they receive, to be less so.

Well now: either Christ is wrong, and all those are in the wrong who, inspired by His spirit, have preached through the world with words and deeds His helping and saving gospel, or the matter has a much deeper meaning, and under the seeming *injustice* a deeper *justice* is hidden. If it is so, this *justice* must also develop itself to a higher good, to a more perfect order, founded upon the *highest justice*.

And what we see now, can be compared to the perturbations which Newton discovered with anxiety in the solar system, but which was in reality only a transition to that order, where every thing is again restored to its proper orbit and place.

If we contemplate the nature of the world-evolution, which Christianity has caused, we shall find that it consists in a sinking down of the higher to the lower, which the higher attracts, after having filled it with its power, its life, — that it consists in the extension of the participation of all mankind in all the gifts of heaven and of earth; the participation of *all* in the same bread and the same wine. Thus the phenomenon of the regeneration of the world manifests itself, even in our days, in the stir of the political life of the free, living nations, amongst which we with pride can number our own. Here the question is of a deeper justice than the outward, more common one; here the question is of a justice founded upon a great love. This love wishes, in the first instance, to neutralize every injustice and ruggedness of chance, — to remedy all that prevents mankind to stand one day before his Creator as *one* perfect man, created after His image, and in whom all individuals are like brothers and sisters, like children of one father. This love of mankind, inspired by a grand idea, goes therefore forth upon its divine mission, often setting aside ordinary systems of justice, regardless of its contingent irregularities, which seem to be the consequences of its activity; for this love knows and feels within itself that *it alone* is able, in accomplishing its orbit, to adjust all in a higher order; that *it alone* can ultimately "stop the evil on earth."

The labors of love manifest themselves herein in two directions. The one has for aim to lighten pain; to atone for errors, to obviate the consequences or to help to bear them: the other aims at enlightening the understanding; to strengthen knowledge, and to encourage by conferring a share in noble privileges and duties. Both unite in taking an active part in ennobling and making others happy. When the more favored ones on earth thus lower themselves to the destitute, or the fallen, they must necessarily eventually communicate to them the mind and the power which they possess themselves, and in thus lowering themselves, they can raise their fallen brothers to the step of moral worth upon which they themselves are standing, and become their saviours and the saviours of society. The remedy against the momentary disorder, therefore, lies in accomplishing the evolution, not in restraining it.

If now all this should be so, and I believe it *is* so, then do not let us fear the movements which originate in warm feelings, in devout faith. They have in all times been life's prophets; they hold in their hand the divining-rod, which points out life's hidden springs. Let them become free; but let the methodical thought follow them faithfully, light them on their way, and give them the watchword to their presentiments. Let wisdom guide the loving will, and point out the way, prudently to promote the good cause.

My letter has unconsciously swelled into a treatise. It would frighten me, did I not hope that my kind reader would also herein see my earnest wish to answer his questions and doubts to the best of my ability.

TO MR. S. H――.

STOCKHOLM, 16th December, 1853.

I cannot let the old year close without sending you, my young friend in ..... my thanks for your letter of the 15th of October, together with my warmest congratulations on your betrothal to an amiable young lady, and through it to your near connection with a gentleman so estimable and so esteemed as ――. I had certainly heard this betrothal already mentioned by report, but the confirmation thereof reached me only through your letter. It gave me sincere pleasure to hear that report had spoken the truth, for nothing is so beneficial, nothing so develops a good, noble-minded young man and contributes to settle him, as his union with a young woman of genuine female worth.

In a profound and divine manner two such natures perfect themselves in their dependence on each other, while they in love reflect in each other the profound and the good which they individually possess, revealing treasures hitherto hidden to themselves, and a new spiritual life through the union of their souls, creating a reality and fullness of life of which before they had only a dim presentiment, but which they never had felt. I speak here only of the perfect union between two souls in love or in friendship, for these two come very near each other. May you in your wedlock find a happiness which I have also learnt to feel in happy and sincere friendship, but of which now — only the memory is left. Those whom I have thus loved, and by whom I was thus loved myself — are all dead. But to have thus loved, to have thus lived, is an unspeakable blessing. We know then what heaven is, and we believe then in its eternal reality. There lives then in our heart, in our inmost soul, a spot perpetually green, where fountains well forth, where roses are blooming — a peaceful oasis, where an eternal summer is reigning, and to which we can fly in darker moments as to our proper home. For if we have once found such a home in another's soul, then every thing discordant which chanced to come between us, was a mere fleeting cloud in a bright sky; if we once have felt such a deep union with another being that nothing in the world could shake its sincerity; if we have felt that we belonged to one another eternally from a deep, divine necessity, then we can let much in this life come and go as it will; can lose much, suffer much, and yet be tranquil, still have enough, and still thank God for immeasurable wealth in the confidence of our heart.

May it be thus with you! . . . . .

I might be willing to accede to your views, relating to a new legislation with respect to matrimony,[1] if you could convince me that the children's fate would thereby become in a measure as much secured, or that it would not be more exposed to chance and to neglect than is now the case. If we contemplate man, such as he is in general on earth and in society, we find clearly that it is not good to trust to his inspirations.

Caprice and passion play too prominent a part therein; they frequently overrule his better conscience, and would probably do this effectually, if he had not in the higher conscience of *humanity*, and in the laws which pronounce and represent the same, a friendly monitor and a judge, who prevent him from becoming the slave of the tyranny of selfish passions. It is no doubt clear that the judicial ties in matrimony are the means at the disposal of society for protecting the life and the future of the weak and helpless (the wife and children) against the husband's or the parent's neglect, or their disregard of their duties. And the interposition of the clergyman, in the name of the church or of religion, in order to unite man or woman, is merely the visible expression of the inward truth and aim which alone can make the union between man and woman

---

[1] These views appear to have referred to the so-called civil marriage, without the coöperation of the clergy for its legal institution.

something really noble and sacred. It was a sacred union previous to the act performed by the clergyman; but people would either not consider this, or forget it, if the Church did not give to the inward law a form and a word which express its sacredness, and become a tie only because they represent what most ought to unite man and wife. Geijer said once: "Love wants to be backed by duty;" and another time: "One speaks of love as something stagnant, and yet no love can be imagined without metamorphoses." Look round in the world, and ask yourself how many men would continue to be a faithful husband and father, if, during the fluctuations of his love, he had not a support in duty and in public moral opinion (the offspring of duty); if, during the metamorphoses of his life of love, a sacred law did not lead to a normal development.

The Society of Friends, who have rejected all outward laws, and appeal to the inward law, the inner voice, as the only rule of conduct, have yet presupposed that this inner law must be valid for all, and upon it they found their unions. Thus, for instance, in weddings, the contracting parties declare before the congregation that they purport living together as husband and wife, and this is sufficient to consecrate the marriage. But the discipline of feelings, of thoughts, and of the whole course of life, is so severe from early childhood amongst the Society of Friends, that public opinion is more binding for them than are the forms of law and of the Church for us, and they lead with them to the same end. That persons before they bring children into the world ought well to weigh the importance of such a step, and of the duties which belong to it, this, one would think, is the claim of sound morality and of experience. Therefore also it is that one gives the name of *illegitimate* to the union which disregards this higher aim of marriage. That the children should suffer for this as *illegitimate* is unjust as far as *they* are concerned, but how can this be avoided? It is the fault of the parents, and the sins of the parents must always, to a certain degree, be visited upon the children. Society cannot relinquish its idea of pure morality. But charity, which is the crown of society, adheres less severely to this idea, and takes therefore the wronged ones in its supporting arms. This is done every day, partly through private charities and partly by public wise institutions.

How often, in the present time, when after the ravages of the cholera, inquiries have been made into the condition of the children of the poorer classes, have not fathers been found, who have shaken off every care of their offspring, and who have succeeded herein, as they could not be bound to it by any certificate of lawful marriage. Several of these abandoned little ones have been taken care of by our "Ladies' Association." But you will one day, perhaps, be yourself a father, and although I am fully aware that your heart is to you a power more binding than all outward legal forms, still, in looking at your children, you may probably feel yourself, in your character of father, also in the position of society; and you will then, in the name of the parental society, demand the assistance both of the laws and of the clergyman in order to secure the moral and economical guardianship over the rising generation. If this guardianship could be extended so as to protect also the innocent so-called illegitimate little ones, it would be still better.

But I have too long detained you on this subject. I agree fully and most heartily with you in regard to the question of woman's majority, and I see the only safe guarantee for a better future of the rising generation, in woman's moral and social elevation amongst all classes. My remaining days shall be devoted to labor for this end, as far as in my power lies. In the second and third volume of my work, "The Homes in the New World," you will see my opinions and my thoughts on this subject.

Christmas is at the door with its darkness, and will soon come with all its lights. The Stockholm "Ladies' Association" intends during this festive time to let every home, in which misery and death have been guests during the epidemic, shine, in the name of the great Physician, joyously and more richly than ever before. This Association intends likewise to distribute books for children, by native authors, and will try to edit a special Swedish child's literature. Perhaps I shall be able to send you next Christmas a budget of this kind of literature for children, for a little son or a little daughter in your house.

Hearty wishes of joy and happiness, and all good this year and — every year from your old friend,

FREDRIKA BREMER.

TO THE SAME.

STOCKHOLM, 7th February, 1854.

It is high time that I should thank you with a few words for your friendly letter, and especially for the sincere and warm sympathy which you manifest for the condition of my sex. You say that many an unmarried, middle-aged woman would have a fresher and purer mind if she had a child which could be the object of her heart's tender care. I must, however, dissent from your opinion, as if this were the *sine qua non* for her soul's purity and health, and I beg you will now believe a true womanly nature who could have loved husband and child devotedly, and yet voluntarily renounced the same, and who has since *without them* enjoyed the fullness and richness of her existence, aye, enjoys them at this moment, with a freedom, a joy, which not always falls to the lot of every wife and mother.

But if this happiness were egotistical, I would not speak of it. "He, who does not love, knows not God." The life of the unmarried or childless woman has its own temptations and sorrows, but many of these arise (at any rate in regard to their power over her) from the one-sided and false direction of her education and of the literature which she feeds upon, and which refers her almost exclusively, in order to gain happiness and position, to the married state and to the dignity of mother.

Besides, the slavery under which the unmarried woman labors, in consequence of public opinion and the law, is, to a great extent, the cause of her want of moral and physical health, her want of ability and happiness. And may God bless you with a beautiful and lovable daughter for "couching your lance" in defense of the cause of the enchained!

But look, even at the present time, at an unmarried woman, past the first bloom of youth, with some degree of liberty and a little property of her own, with a good heart and a good head. I should like to show you some such women amongst our towns-women, active on behalf of the poor, and you would find a freshness and aptitude, a joyous life, bearing witness of a far happier existence than that of many a married woman with a quarrelsome or careless husband and with perhaps several children, which she has to provide for under anxieties and cares. Yes, if women really knew, previous to their marriage, all the troubles and all the anxiety which the children often cause, then many a one would think twice before she attempted such a venture. At any rate they would, more than now too often is the case, be careful to give their heart and hand only to a man who could be a support and assistance to them in life's more serious situations.

There is also a higher aspiration which does not unfrequently arise, when a young woman does not give way to an inclination so natural at her age, of concluding a matrimonial alliance, which aspiration in Catholic countries finds a more beautiful sphere of activity and life than in our country. The warm feeling, turned away from seeking response and fullness in earthly, turns frequently to heavenly objects, and finds in its communion with and in its life in them a perfection, which every-day life could never so have given. Believe me: there are delights, ecstasies, unspeakable happiness in lonely hearts, shedding brightness over existence, over earthly and heavenly things, over the present and the future, making the heart burn with love and praise. But of these joys, the purest, warmest moments of love, of loving hearts — moments when tears drop upon smiling lips, and one desires nothing more than to sacrifice one's self in order to prove one's faith and love — give an idea. But these blooming moments in man's life become shorter and shorter with advancing years. Something worldly adheres to them, dragging them down to earth or arresting their pinions. Like the Sylphide, in the ballet of the same name, the wings fall off and they die smothered in reality's cold embrace. What of this human Psyche can liberate itself from this embrace, gains new life with immortal wings and with rays which are not extinguished; it belongs not to a natural, but to a supernatural love. Happy they who in wedlock are able to develop and to preserve this latter. Then love is "born of God." If you wish to see what woman's life of love can be, you must read " Les Confessions de St. Thérèse " and then ask yourself how many happy lovers in their earthly circumstances can speak of such joys in such terms. And those joys —*they* are not dependent on contingencies; they are full of hope and promise, and presentiment of eternal life; they do not wane, but become rather more intense with advancing age.

What our unmarried women, both young and old in Sweden, are still much in need of in general, is freedom, and full consciousness of its value, and of their own capability of turning the same to practical account. A noble independence, self-reliance, and trust in God, constitute the first condition for all higher development and happiness.

In every thing which I have written, I have labored for this; but I hope that before I die my labor shall leave a more complete result. Henceforth I shall more concentrate my powers; more exclusively live for this aim.

Thanks for the little beautiful sketch of your home-life at S———o! How glad I am for your sake, at your alliance with this family, which assuredly will give your pure and good heart just what it wanted, to live rightly and actively in your home as well as in society.

. . . .

My favorite study now is the works of the Swiss, A. Vinet. He is a christian Emerson, high-minded like him in the worship of truth and spiritual liberty, but greater in his induction; and in his deduction, greater in humility, more perfect in every way, and to me he is one of the most valuable acquaintances amongst the literature of later days.

Your friend,
FREDRIKA BREMER.

TO THE COUNTESS LOTTEN VON R———.

ÅRSTA, 4th September, 1864.

I write to you to-day from my ancestral hall and home, where I have not resided since about ten years ago, when it passed into the hands of another owner. Previous to that time, I had with the exception of the several years I spent in Norway, Denmark, and America, passed the greater part of my life here, rarely satisfied, never happy, except at those times when I was permitted to stay here alone; in my youth longing to get away from here, out into the great stirring, ever-changing world; away from the monastic solitude of Årsta, where my whole life was spent in my inner dream-world, and in the gleams of light which books and the restless workings of my brain occasionally shed over the same; but never receiving any satisfactory answers to my heaven-storming questions. It has appeared strange to me, now in my old age (I have lately completed my sixty-third year), to be again for a few quiet weeks in this house, and to look back from my observatory in the large, secluded rooms of the upper story, upon my path in life, and upon what I have gained and found in it.

You, who like to contemplate human life in the light of God's love, you will hear with pleasure that these weeks have been to me a continual ·feast of thanksgiving; a rejoicing at the belief with which my own course of life has inspired me, in an all-guiding, loving Providence, although for the greater number of human beings it is not revealed during this mortal life; a thanksgiving for the days of suffering and strife in the dark, which absorbed my soul and gave to its chaotic powers unity in their direction; thanksgiving for the grace, which when the time had arrived, let the caterpillar's life change, and the butterfly burst its fettering chrysalis, or, to speak without allegory — let me find *God in Christ*, and in Him an answer to all my questions; comfort in my afflictions; hope for all who were seeking and suffering, for all who were sighing and struggling; and then to see earth, its nations and generations in the light of this glorifying, paternal Providence, this Redeemer and Accomplisher. How often, during this time, have I not in grateful joy repeated those words of Scripture, which I wish to have one day written on my grave, thence to speak to all mankind: "When I called upon the Lord, He delivered me out of all my trouble."

Something in the state of my body and soul tells me that my actual working-days are over, that I now may have rest, at any rate comparatively, and that my labor henceforth must be more inward than outward. And also this is a pleasant feeling. The amiable patriarchal family, to whom my former home now belongs, and which lets me feel as if it still were mine, enables me here to find the quiet of my old age, a peaceful home after life's restless journey. In about a week's time I return to Stockholm to spend the winter. There I hope to receive a few lines from you, my dear Lotten.

STOCKHOLM, 13th October, 1864.

God's gifts to us, and His ways with us, are various. Me He has led, by the unconquerable longing and desire of thought, to coherence and harmony; to an insight into His manifestation in Christ, and its all-explaining light. Through doubt and through struggles He has led me to certainty and peace, and from one light on to another.

That, while striving to find the precious pearl, of which our Saviour speaks, much of its shell, which to many is identical with the pearl itself, should have assumed another signification than strict orthodoxy admits — and that many of the dogmas of the Church should have taken another meaning than the strictly literal one — this I could not help. Without it I should not have discovered the treasure, the pearl — the word of eternal life in Christ; nor should I, without it, in the midst of the conflict which is now going on in the world, and which is carried on in newspapers and in innumerable periodicals, against the more profound Christianity and its most substantial and consolatory doctrines, have felt so happy, so confident, so certain, that out of the ruins of the antiquated Church, a new one, more real in spirit and in truth, shall arise; when also I shall be prepared to bear witness in her favor, and show that the most profound Christianity is the highest reason, yes, is the most undeviable right of reason as well as of sense and of conscience. Man, nowadays, is not helped with devout confessions, unless these, at the same time, contain light for the thinking spirit.

The religious fermentation of the present day is nothing else than the struggle of reason and thought to penetrate to God. When they have arrived there, they shall worship and sing praises to the Lord, and then the first commandment shall be fulfilled, that which tells man: "Thou shalt love the Lord, thy God, with all thy heart and with all thy soul and with all thy mind," that is, with all thy power.

My remaining days shall be devoted to praising the Lord

with all the strength which He has given me in this struggle, for which he has prepared me. His Spirit will show me the manner and the time.

With child-like love and confidence I shall follow His guidance. The peace and happiness which I have enjoyed during the past summer, spent in the home of my childhood and youth, are deeply connected with and have their roots in, the presentiment that here, where my life developed its first buds in happiness and in affliction, it will produce its last, and I hope with God's help, its ripest fruit,

Årsta, 20th September, 1865.

Well may the devout who rest upon the heart of Christ, "thank God that they do not feel the desire to inquire into those things which God has hidden from us, and which shall never be made clear to us on this side of the grave;" for they rest safely in His love; but they whom God has called to combat with the weapons of thought *for* light, and against darkness and shadows; to distinguish between what is *divine* and what is *human;* they who believe with St. Paul, that "the spirit searcheth all things, yea, the deep things of God," and that man can and shall, step by step, be brought to love and praise God" with all his heart, with all his soul and with all his mind" (or thoughts), *with all his powers*, and therefore also with all the strength of the intellect and reason with which He has endowed him; also they can *thank* Him that they have got a talent to devote to His service and to His glorification.

SKETCHES.

MY DREAM.

I HAD last night a strange dream. I fancied that I was in Stockholm. It was evening. I was expecting visitors: I was just going to dress to receive them, and I went for this purpose through the dining-room, when the door opened, and my good old friend Eric Reuterborg entered, elegantly dressed, his hair speckled with gray, curled in a *toupet* on the forehead exactly as when he was alive. I became alarmed, for I was well aware that he had been dead three years. But I was pleased, nevertheless, for the thought suddenly crossed my brain — think if he is not really dead! and doubtful and astonished, I went to meet him, asking: "Is it possible! Are you not — " "Reuterborg?" he answered in a friendly and cheerful tone; "yes, it is."

An indescribable feeling of awe seized me, while we went into the drawing-room together. I remembered having seen him in his coffin; remembered the cold, sad expression in his face which had succeeded that of kindness and open-heartedness; remembered how I had placed flowers at his feet, and put hyacinths in his cold, bluish hand, which drooped their heads upon his breast; and afterwards I had planted flowers upon his grave. Yes, he was indeed dead, and that which I now beheld was his ghost. While these memories passed before me, I stared at the form which now stood beside me, and I drew timidly back while I said: "But how — how is it possible?"

At the same moment his face, until now so friendly and calm, became troubled, looked disturbed, and he also drew back, became shadowy and dim. Then the fear seized me that he would in this way leave me. I summoned up my courage; approached him again; called him by endearing names; begged him to be heartily welcome, and expressed my great delight at seeing him again. He now grew brighter; came closer up to me, and looked more and more friendly and radiant, yet not in a supernatural manner. It seemed to me that we were both playing a part with each other; that he wanted to make me believe that he was not dead; just as I did not wish him to observe that I looked upon him as having come from the other world. Meanwhile I felt an indescribable longing to ask him how it was there, and whether he was happy; but I was prevented by I do not know what kind of fear. He looked heartily pleased and friendly. I said: —

"You will stay with me this evening, my dear Reuterborg?"

I said this, as if to try him.

"No," he replied, "I must go to some place and read the newspapers."

Half jocularly I then said: —

"Well, well, you read the newspapers beside God himself. That is surely a good place, and there you can learn much."

He only smiled, and I could not help thinking that it was rather cunning of him to want to make himself so living and worldly.

"But," I went on to say, "as you will not stay with me, then tell me, Reuterborg, when shall I come to you in your home? How old shall I be on earth?"

He looked upwards for a moment, and then said meditatingly, but very decidedly: —

"You shall be sixty-six years and two months old."

"So old?" I said, "I must then live still a long time here on earth; but God's will be done."

At this moment I awoke, with a vivid consciousness of having learnt the time of my death. I am now forty-five years old. Consequently twenty-one years more. May God in me accomplish the work which may have been given me to execute.

Årsta, 23d March, 1847.

A VISION.

I saw a throne standing in a bright shining light, and from the face of Him who sat upon the throne, there emanated a radiance which filled and glorified all things. Hosts of seraphs and cherubs surrounded Him, turning their faces alternately to Him and towards infinite space before them, which resembled a boundless ocean of clouds. It seemed as if they were expecting something.

"What is it that is going to happen?" I asked an angel who stood near me.

"Dost thou not know," he answered, "that the *Lord* to-day will try the spirit of the peoples of the earth? They shall be called before Him and receive their reward or punishment, according to how they have fulfilled their charge."

And now I heard a voice, mighty as thunder, exclaim:—

"Arise, thou the oldest amongst the Northern nations! Arise before thy Lord!"

And out of the boundless ocean of clouds I saw a shape rise like a woman's, with noble, earnest features, with a clear, frank eye. A plain white robe, white as snow, fell in soft folds around her strong, but classical figure; on her forehead the Northern star shone with mild lustre, and as she approached nearer the throne, her face looked younger and more beautiful in the light which was streaming from it. I heard a chorus of innumerable voices sing thus:—

"Struggling with want, she has nursed her children; but honestly has she combated. Her liberty she has defended with her strong arm, and at the sound of the eternal Redeemer's voice she banished thralldom from her free soil. Herself free, she drew her good sword and shed her blood for the cause of the oppressed. Therefore her faults shall be forgiven her, and strength shall be given to her to combat her evil spirits, and power to proclaim the gospel of liberty in the name of eternal laws. Fear not, thou little nation! it is thy Lord's will to exalt thee above many wealthy and great nations. Approach to receive thy Father's blessing!"

Adoring, she bowed before the Eternal. Golden clouds enveloped her, and harps resounded. I covered my dazzled eyes; but they shed tears of bliss, for the blessed one, — she was my mother.

When I again looked up, I beheld once more the heavenly legions in endless space, and another form rose resplendent out of the ocean of clouds. Stately was she, and beautiful as a queen; her raiment shone with gold, but the traces of dark passions had marked her features and overshadowed her forehead. But still her glance was steady and open, as if conscious of something great. She looked calmly up to the throne, adoring whilst she approached it.

The heavenly chorus sang: —

"Great have been her sins, but she has abjured them at the feet of the Holy One. She has raised the banner of Him who proceeded out of the bosom of Divinity, to say to earth's children: 'Ye are all brethren, and God is your father!" She has burst the chains of her prisoners, and works of love have effaced the traces of cruelty. Therefore shall her sins be forgiven her, and she shall live to see many glorious days, and proceed from one brightness to another!"

And whilst they thus sang and she advanced towards the throne, her face became glorified by the brightness which she was approaching, and the furrows on her forehead became like streaks of light.

After a while I heard again the voice crying aloud: —

"Thou, the youngest of the great nations of earth; thou messenger of the Lord's latest, last word to humanity! arise! come before thy Judge."

And I beheld something like a green mount rise out of the ocean of clouds, and on it stood a figure — oh, how glorious! Youth and beauty and strength marked her whole being; the rosy morn of hope glowed upon her cheeks and in her beautiful and joyous glance. On her fresh lips the words of life seemed to lie. Rich and splendid raiments infolded the youthful and vigorous form. On her head she wore a diadem of twenty-six stars, glittering with various light. With her right hand she raised a banner which the wind unfurled, and on which stood written: "*Liberty.*"

She was so beautiful that I felt spell-bound before her, and I called her in my heart, Earth's hope. And the heavenly hosts and the spirits of Earth's nations turned eagerly their eyes upon her.

The celestial voices sang sweetly: —

"Step before thy Creator, thou young, thou highly gifted, thou, the youngest and most beautiful of His daughters!"

And she advanced, not straight forward, but in an oblique direction, seemingly not aware of it herself. She stumbled now and then, and her face wore an expression of uneasiness and embarrassment. Surprised, I looked at her attentively, and beheld her ankle encircled by a golden chain, the other end of which was bound on to the arm of a negro, who walked a few steps behind her and who seemed to be her servant.

Also, *he* moved along, but half asleep and listlessly. He was unconsciously approaching the edge of a frightful precipice, at the foot of which, dragons, snakes, and slime-covered monsters of the deep, with horrible shapes, were crawling about.

His beautiful mistress followed, apparently without knowing whither her slave was dragging her, and I saw the moment approaching when both were to be hurled over the precipice. I shuddered, and was on the point of crying out aloud, when I heard the heavenly chorus sound like thunder through space: —

"Awake! unhappy one, awake! see thy thralldom, thy danger. Give liberty and be thyself free. Let the word whose banner thou carriest, become a truth. Else thou shalt perish in thy falsehood!"

The light vanished from heaven, and clouds, like floods of tears, lowered before the throne.

And the heavenly chorus sang: —

"When He turns away His face, then darkness comes over the nations of the earth. When He takes His spirit away, then they perish and return again to dust!"

Then all was silent, so silent and hushed as when the breath is held back in anxious expectation of what is going to happen.

My heart trembled. It asked: "Will she be saved and rise? or will she fall in the sight of the Eternal?" Inquiringly my looks were turned towards space, seeking her, but then — my vision vanished.

A VIOLET.

FOUND IN STOCKHOLM IN 1827.

"Who could ever have expected to find so much virtue, walking between two milk-pails!" exclaimed my friend, Dr. S——, on entering my room one warm August evening; and, sitting down almost exhausted, he wiped the perspiration from his forehead. I asked for an explanation of these words, which appeared to me rather extraordinary, when he related the following story: —

"You must know, my friend, that I have made acquaintance with a person in a house nearly opposite mine — yes, a nice acquaintance with an old woman, who for more than ten years has served me with milk and cream twice a week. During all this time she has come and gone, quietly, neatly dressed, and honest, with a deep curtsey, a 'good morning!' and 'many thanks,' without my ever thinking of looking upon her otherwise than as an old regular piece of clock-work, which strikes the hours at certain intervals of time, or as one of those kind of people who live, they do not know precisely why; who walk through life without knowing wherefore; and who yet from morning till noon, from noon until night, after all, manage better than those who know infinitely more. Last week, during two milk-days, for the first time she did not make her appearance. I began to wonder whether my good old clock-work had stopped for ever, and was just going to see what was the matter with it, when this morning a boy about ten years old called upon me, and with tears in his eyes besought me to come and see his 'dear Nanna,' who was very ill. I accompanied the boy across the street to the house where my milk-woman lived, and was shown into a clean, but poor-looking room, where I found my old acquaintance lying on a straw pallet, and to all appearance in a bad state. A well-dressed lady, between twenty and thirty years of age, with pleasant, but extremely delicate features, was sitting beside her, holding the old woman's hand in hers. A young girl was lying weeping upon her knees before her. She seemed to be of nearly the same age as the boy, who was her brother. I was a little astonished at what I saw, but as I do not like superfluous questions, I merely inquired into the old woman's state of health. She had not much strength herself to speak, but the lady tried, evidently with deep emotion, to describe her malady. I prescribed something; spoke, according to my habit, not many words, and took, in going through the door, a pinch of snuff, much doubting in my own mind the efficacy of the medicines in a creature whom old age, poverty, and disease, were hurrying to the grave. 'And if,' I thought to myself, 'I should even be able to save her this time, it would, after all, perhaps be of little benefit to her. To walk about with faltering steps a few years longer, borne down by care, in order to earn a miserable crust of dry bread, and then to die upon a straw pallet, is surely not worth a rhubarb-powder. To the old and destitute death is a solacing angel in whose way we doctors ought not to stand. Our physic serves frequently nothing else than to make the poor patient again taste, what to him is more bitter than any medicine — life.' During this soliloquy, I stood still on the landing, pulling down a spider's web with my walking-stick, and liberating two agonized flies that showed their gratitude by buzzing round my nose for nearly half an hour.

"I now observed that the lady had followed me. 'My dear doctor,' she said with a quivering voice, clasping her hands together, ' excuse me — but — if you knew what a life is in jeopardy — you would exert all your skill; you would do every thing in your power to save it.' 'A human life, madam,' I answered, ' is always valuable ; my science is not omnipotent, but my exertions are the same for all.' She looked as if she did not quite believe me, and in truth I felt some small stings of conscience ; I muttered a few words that it would interest me to hear something more concerning the invalid. The lady opened a door on the opposite side, saying in a steadier voice : ' Please to walk in a moment, you will not repent it; I will make you acquainted with your patient's character, and you will then, perhaps, think of some other treatment.'

" She led me into a small, well-furnished room, and thence into another one, where even a certain elegance was prevailing. 'Look around you, Doctor,' she said, ' these rooms, every thing that is in them, every chair, every cushion, yes, my own and my two children's clothes, are presents from the poor old woman, who you but now saw lying upon straw.' Tears glittered in the lady's eyes. Roused out of my phlegmatic trance, I asked her anxiously for some further information. We sat down, and in a voice which often vainly strove to be firm, she continued: 'My old good Nanna was a servant in my parents' house, and entered into my service when I married. My husband and myself possessed but little, but it was enough. He allowed himself to be persuaded to become security for one of his friends, was deceived, and we lost our all. Broken down with grief, after two years' illness, he died, leaving me in deep affliction, with two very young children, and with debts which I found it impossible to discharge. In consequence of grief and want of sleep, I had became very sickly, and should certainly have perished in misery with my children, if it had not been for my Nanna. Already during my husband's last illness, when she saw that the little which we had left did not by far suffice for our housekeeping, and for the extra expenses which his state of health made indispensable, she undertook, without our knowledge, to sell milk, and what she earnt in that way, she employed for our benefit. After the death of my good husband, when I was incapacitated from illness to do any thing, she entirely provided for me and for my poor children. She worked like a slave all day long, and often in my sleepless nights I heard the whirring of her spinning-wheel in the next room, or I saw, through a chink in the door, the light of her candle at which she sat working for my little ones and their poor mother. Her indefatigable industry procured for us by degrees better food, better clothing, and good lodgings; her milk-trade gradually became more lucrative as she became more known; but all, all was spent upon us. She lived as if she had no existence for herself; her bed was straw, her food what we had left over, and never could our prayers prevail upon her to share equally with us, even in trifles. Always friendly and merry, although taciturn, we could always read in her looks the words which she often used to say in order to comfort us: "Dearest lady! all will be well again one day." Yes, dear Nanna, you have made it well;

night and day did you work for me, and would not have thanks for it. When I got so well, that I was able to work again, I wanted her to allow herself some rest, of which she was the more in need as her health was much impaired, and she was evidently becoming weaker every day; but all in vain. She continued carrying out milk until last week, when she fell ill. She wishes to live merely for the sake of being of use to me and my children. About herself she is perfectly indifferent, as for one already dead; I have not been able to persuade her to allow herself to be carried into a more comfortable room and to have a softer bed. 'I am used to it,' she says, 'it is good enough for me.' Oh! if you knew, Sir, how, only a short time ago, I rejoiced in the hope of working for her who has so long worked for me; to see her old age made peaceful and happy through our tender care and grateful love, you would also be able to understand how bitterly I must feel it to see her fall a sacrifice to her heroic devotion, just at a moment when she might be able, through me and my children, to enjoy a reward, earned by the self-denial of half a life-time. If it is in your power, try to save her, — do it for her sake; she may still see happy days here on earth, — do it for my sake; for I do not think that I could bear the idea that I should have been the cause of the death of this angelic woman; do it for my children's sake, who love her dearly, and who would lose in her a daily example of the noblest virtues. Oh! save her — and my gratitude —' I rose, asking her not to mention gratitude. 'I consider myself sufficiently rewarded, if I succeed in saving such a life,' I said, and returned to the sick-bed. I confess that I now contemplated her with very different eyes, and I comforted the lady and her children with the assurance, that, unless the thread of her life had not entirely run out, my excellent medicine would add fresh elasticity to the springs and set the pendulum going again as regularly as before.

" Well, what do you think of her?" added the Doctor —

"was I not right in saying, Who would have expected to find so much virtue walking between two milk-pails?"

I agreed with him that such self-sacrificing virtue was exceedingly rare. Still, I believe that if we would take the trouble to look for it, we should far more frequently find instances of it amongst the classes commonly called the uneducated, than in the atmosphere of the so-called refined classes. The nobility of the soul, the qualities of the heart, resemble those sweet juices of honey which the humblest flowers of the fields conceal in their bosom; whereas often the choicest and most wonderful plants of the flower-beds and of the hot-houses contain venom amongst their brilliant leaves. Art rarely *educates* without, at the same time, *miseducating*, and one generally loses in inner worth what one gains in outward appearance.

It is doubtful whether we ought to ascribe to Doctor S——'s wonderful medicines the recovery of the old woman; or whether her own constitution and the tender care of her mistress were not chiefly instrumental herein; but, suffice it to say, she recovered her health completely. My friend allows her a small annuity, which she devotes entirely to the use of her now happy mistress and her amiable children. She carries twice a week the milk to my friend, the Doctor, and all that she consents to accept of him for her own account, is the cup of coffee with sugar and biscuits, which he always has ready for her every morning when she calls. But in return she insists upon deducting six stiver for every can of milk which he buys of her. How they have ultimately settled this important point, I do not know.

AT FORTY YEARS OF AGE.

The age of fifteen has been celebrated in song as life's rosy period, and it has been allowed to bloom up to twenty, aye, even up to twenty-five; the age of sixty or seventy has been honored as being the years of wisdom and of mature virtues: I will sing the praise of the age of forty — the present century's and my own age. I know a lady, who, when twenty-eight years old, gave herself out to be thirty — " for," said she, " what is the use of sticking to those two years ? " Perhaps I also follow a little her footsteps, for, I think with her: thirty-eight, thirty-nine, forty, why, it comes to almost the same thing. The wisdom-teeth and the wrinkles have already come.

Forty years! do not you feel something "set" in those words? At forty one has generally settled down in life. This is why one can quietly walk about and contemplate the world, and — there *is* much to contemplate in this world. Our century has also settled down, but it has settled down in Parliament and meditates upon the State, and therefore it looks neither merry nor uneasy, but thoughtful. So also is woman at forty. The heart does not then any longer beat uneasily before a ball, or still more uneasily after one; nor do we then stand here in life as a poor candidate for *any thing*, a prey to wishes, hopes, uncertainties, contrarieties, happiness, and misery, neither does the frame of our mind, like a chameleon, take the impression of every new object, changing from rose-color to black, from green to gray, in the course of only a few hours; nor do you see in every one whom you meet some important personage in the romance of your life, nor in every uttered nonsense a monster which you are to rush upon and attack, like Don Quixote battling with the windmill; you need not then dance when you want to sit still, nor walk according to the will of others, when you have your own will — in a word, you are above a great deal of anxiety and trouble. Many a rosy light has, it is true, perchance waned, but also many mists have rolled away and brightened. You see your way clearer, you walk along more steadily; not swayed hither and thither by the wind, as in youth; not leaning with faltering steps upon the crutches of old age; you walk sturdily on your own legs, and look round in the world without coming to fisticuffs with it. Forty years is the age of contemplation, of practical thought. Long life be to them!

I was yesterday in town. A large town is after all a strange thing. We feel this most when we have been living a long time in the country. The country! I wish that everybody could live there, and become well acquainted with all its peaceful objects.

How beneficial is it not for sore eyes (sore from contemplating the world and humanity) to rest upon the " Eyes-delight " with which Sweden's Flora has so richly studded our verdant fields; to see in old forests the " *Yellow-bird's-head*," juicy and odoriferous, shoot out of the poorest soil at the roots of the firs; to see and hear the waves beat upon the shore; to rest near the murmuring brook, when the " *Money-wort* " and the "*Purple-specked loosestrife* " shine amongst the bushes upon its bank; to listen to the country-people's songs in the evening, while they are piling the fragrant hay-cocks; to see the cows graze upon the lately-mown fields, and the sheep — pictures all of repose and innocence, bringing peace and refreshing coolness to our soul. It makes you more pious, more healthy. Yes, everybody ought to live in the country, but nevertheless visit the town now and then. This was just what I did yesterday.

Stockholm is not a very large, nor is it a very populous town. London is much larger. But still Stockholm is a real *capital*. I think it is splendid.

Born of a wedding and of a murder,[1] a child of love and revenge, the soil inaugurated by mead and royal blood, the former *Agnefit*, the present Stockholm, rose from out the waters, both salt and fresh. Even to this day, as then, the sea and the lake mingle their floods round its base, and in it thrives and moans in wonderful union, love and hatred, virtue and crime, the great and the little, beauty and ugliness, the bitter and the sweet.

[1] See tales of Swedish history, how King Agne of the Ynglinga dynasty, after having conquered a Finnish king and made his daughter prisoner, and when on his way home, their wedding being celebrated, became intoxicated, and was hanged on a tree at her instigation.

The sun, the high and pure, shone over that chaotic world on an August evening as I went forth for a walk to view the town. Every object around me stood out in bold relief.

The House of Nobles! — hem — what have I to do there? There the legislators of the country discuss the weal of society, and I belong — God help me! (or thank God!) — to the minors in the State, who, as the wise-acres say, ought, for the good of the State, always to remain so (in a political sense).

Two things I believe in, and the third I take to be certain: —

1st. That the wiseacres are right.

2d. That not compulsion, as now, but free choice, free conviction (which must be preceded by a complete emancipation), ought, and one day shall, decide woman's social position.

3d. That I shall not live to see the day when such an emancipation takes place; to see all the madness and the stupidity walk about in open daylight, which are now sitting quietly at home spinning. "For certain it is" (said my youngest sister just now, laughing), "that all the mad ones want to rule, and that would be a disgrace to the whole corps!"

However, I leave the House of Nobles to itself. Gustavus Vasa stands in the square of the House of Nobles. I always loiter some time before that figure. When I turn away from the human faces in the street (mine own amongst them), and look up to *that* face, I fancy there must be some truth in the Indian myth, that some people have emanated out of the head of the Creator, and others out of his feet. It is not, therefore, necessary to arrange them in Indian castes. No Pariahs! Look round on Nature. Do here not grow beside each other moss and holly, turnips and astrakhan apple-trees, anemone and rose-tree? They drink the same dew, and develop and bloom in the light of the same sun. But let us return to the hero's statue. *So* a king and a hero ought to look! So free, so firm, so quiet, so cheerful. It is at the word of command of *such* a king that nations arise and march onward. Gustavus Vasa's last word was "Yes!" so was his life: strongly confirmatory. A truly *royal life!*

While I stood contemplating the splendid head, I saw a large spider spinning its web between the sceptre and his laurel crown. What did *it* want there?

Close by rise the royal sepulchres. Sceptres and crowns have fallen there. Heads and hands that have worn them rest there in darkness, in dust. Happy it is that a bold spire again is raised over them, pointing to the hope beyond the tomb! Happy it is that the temple arches itself over the dead, under whose vault was preached — Immortality.

All round the "Riddarholm" stand fine large edifices, which formerly were private palaces, but now are government offices. A sign of the times!

In a straight line from the king's statue, near the water, there sit a long line of "Queens," every one in her own realm. True it is that market-women always have appeared to me to have a certain resemblance to queens. But there *is* a difference — a great one! There, however, they sat, all the market-queens, powerful and important, each one at the head of a long table, her realm, over whose provinces they kept a sharp and watchful eye. What beautiful provinces! Here vegetables of all kinds; there the produce of the orchard; here again berries of all colors and kinds, and there flowers in pots — and brooms, too.

Housewives and their cooks wander about amongst them to admire, inquire, choose, bargain, purchase. An elderly gentleman — who looks as if he had a well-filled purse — contemplates all the various treasures, but makes wry faces. Surely he must have a bad digestion. Yonder ragged urchin has certainly not many farthings, but oh! see how greedily he eats out of the paper bag which he has got filled with berries. Which of the two is most to be envied? Old-fashioned, silly question! Save us from an answer.

"Storkyrkobrinken!" Book-sellers' shops — book-sellers' shops — book-sellers' shops!

"Roasted pigeons do not fly into our mouths," says an old proverb. Oh! it is far better than that nowadays, my dear Proverb! For what is needed now to imbibe knowledge of all sorts? Only to open your mouth. Happy times!

Along "Norrbro," what a variety of professions and faces! What a variety, what a stir there is around the old palace, standing there in silent majesty, staring out of hundreds of windows, like Argus-eyes, out over the waters and the town, delighting the eye of the wanderer with its grand proportions. Amusing to see people go in and out of the elegant shops in the Bazaar, buying costly stuffs, books, music, "Madame Bishop," "the Archbishop," cigars, and Heaven knows what all; pleasant to see people have plenty of money! I shall not go there, to-day; I prefer looking at the people outside. There a young and charming lady, dressed in the height of fashion, in gauze and muslin, sails past the steps on which a beggar-woman, scarcely covered with rags, is sitting, chewing a mouldy crust of bread! There — but here a young gentleman came across my thoughts.

He came from the "Helgeands-holm." Handsome face, but what traces of dissipation! His dark curls in wild disorder round his forehead, the disorder in his looks wilder still; the hat too small for his face, and much battered; his clothes torn! With hasty steps he sped along the bridge, in the beautiful sunshine, through the motley crowd. A young girl with rosy cheeks and dress stared at him, and — laughed. The silly one! A stout gentleman, with a pompous appearance, looked at him also, and started.

Fancy a large, substantial, ruddy face, in which nose,

mouth, eyes, in a word, every thing, was pointing strongly upwards, and put upon this an expression of utter astonishment, and you will, I hope, pardon me for smiling. The unhappy youth walked along through the crowd. As he walked on, all turned round to look at him, and then quietly turned away again. He walked on the brink of destruction, I fancied; he disappeared. The human stream closed noisily in his wake; the dark-green current surged and boiled through the arches of the bridge. It is here where the salt and fresh waters meet, and struggle, and mingle. Boats, full of people, were rowed backwards and forwards on both sides of the bridge. Fishermen, in their small canoes floating calmly on the river, were angling. Seagulls were making their airy gyrations, screaming and plunging. On the "Ström-parterre" the silver poplars were waving their slender forms. Down below in the garden pretty children ran about playing, guarded by watchful mothers seated on the benches under the trees. Round small tables, small parties were eating ices, laughing, and chatting. Gentlemen smoked cigars and read newspapers. "Necken" shot foaming and smoking through the clear water, and laid to at the parterre, inviting you to a trip to "Djurgården."

Merry folks accepted the invitation, stepped on board, and quickly the "Necken" darted off with them across the blue waters. Cares, gloomy looks and faces — where were they? Not here.

Horses, carts, cabs, and riders, high and low, are unpleasant things in a town. Their riding and driving hither and thither always prevent me walking across Gustavus Adolphus Square quietly and collectedly, and therefore I cannot tell you any thing about my thoughts at the base of the statue of "the Great Gustaf Adolf;" not a word of his generals, nor of the Royal Opera, nor for whom it was that the sentinel just now called the guard "under arms!"

There reigns more quiet under the lime-trees in the

square a little further on. The old "King's Garden" is still a peaceful place, where children can run about undisturbed; where old people can sit down to rest quietly, and where philosophical pedestrians can walk up and down, contemplating, from under the shade of large, wide-spreading, leafy trees, the busy world round about them, the estuary, and the palace. The August evening was very sultry, the town air hung heavily over the garden, but the lime-trees were blooming and their fresh fragrance broke now and then through the oppressive air. Carriages and vehicles of all kinds were rattling out to the Djurgården, and gentlemen were galloping along on fine horses. In the avenues of the garden all was silent. *One* couple was there walking, whom I followed with my eyes for a good while. *He* was tall, middle-aged (about the golden forty), with a noble, manly countenance; vigor and gentleness united. *She* was shorter, a slender figure, a beautiful, youthful face.

They walked slowly, conversing with one another, and when he looked down at her, and she up to him, there was something in their faces and in their manner which made me think, "*So* it is right, *so* it is beautiful!" They walked arm in arm in the shade, close beside each other, full of confidence, united in pure love, and happy.

A little further on, sat on a bench one of the wealthiest and first men in the country. A splendid figure! He was sitting alone and thoughtful, leaning his hands upon his walking-stick.

On the next bench was sitting a wretch, whose rags scarcely covered his body. *He* also sat thoughtful, leaning upon his staff. Over both, the lime-trees waved their fragrant crowns. The bells pealed from the church-steeples. Sounds of music were heard from the water.

My road led me afterwards far out to the outskirts of the town.

Here the houses decrease in size, creeping at last in the

shape of huts and cottages up the sides of the hills or downwards to the common; every thing becomes smaller, narrower, poorer; the town is absorbed by the country, and the street by the turnpike road. Here the poor people live. It is the world of the cryptogamia of town life. Still the student loves to point his spy-glass at them, to try to discover the great, the important, in the seemingly insignificant.

Here, far out upon the outskirts, is a narrow street, and in that street stands a small house, and in that house dwells an old couple. Young, blooming bride! can you think it possible that the woman there was fifty-seven years old when she was married to her equally old husband; and would you believe it, that the little god, who flies from so many young and handsome couples in those fine houses in town, has taken up his abode with the old couple, there in the small cottage in that narrow street? Yet so it is. Husband and wife love one another with all their heart, and surprise each other often with small improvements in their home. The old woman showed me her kitchen stove. It had formerly been low and inconvenient. The old man could not bear to see how the wife was obliged to bend her back when employed at it. He once watched the opportunity when she was absent for a couple of days, and had it altered and raised a foot. Now it was "the best kitchen stove in the world," and cheerfully must the fire dance on the hearth and shine in the little room. I do not think that I would look at the ruins of the Coliseum in Rome with so much pleasure as at that kitchen-stove. The old woman boasted also of a small bit of a garden with *one* tree in it, and a "real bower" of half-naked lilac-tree branches covered with spider-webs. "Swedish poverty!" I thought, and remembered what is expressed in these two words: to find one's self rich with little, with almost nothing.

I peeped accidentally into a dark closet; a shadowy form in it made a curtsey to me. It was a woman seventy years old, not married, who lived there in poverty and contentment, earning her bread with the labor of her hands, and who had never received or asked assistance from anybody. "She bakes a kind of small cakes, which she sells to hucksters at four stivers apiece. Well,—I would'nt eat them," said, with a significant grin, the well-to-do old woman who told me this (the owner of the kitchen stove, the tree, and the spider-web bower), "but boys and such like buy them, I believe, and thus she manages to pay her rent and her food. And as to clothes—poor old body!—she has no others than those she stands and walks in; but content she is with them, and then she is so kind, and always merry."

But would you believe it, that this poor old woman had *her* pride? And in what did this pride, concealed under that only garment, and in that dark, solitary room, consist? —"I have never been a burden to anybody, and nobody shall ever be able to say that I have been a burden to the State either!" said the old maid, and her pale seventy-years' old eyes sparkled at these words with a noble self-consciousness, also a kind of patriotism as good as any other!

Are you tired of my wanderings? I was by this time fatigued myself, and therefore I returned home. From it I wish you farewell! May God grant you clear eyes, the wish, the time, and liberty to look about you in the world, and somebody at home to whom you can relate what you have seen, who smiles at your conceits, sheds a tear at your sorrows, and takes an interest in your impressions,— somebody to love,—and you will see how pleasant, how blissful life can be at forty years!

WINDOW PICTURES.
MY WINDOW, 1825.
THE VISITOR.

WHAT a pity it is that the whole world should know so well what a window is! Otherwise an account of one might have afforded me a subject for very curious descriptions. I will therefore now merely notice, what the whole world has not so very carefully observed, namely, all the advantages which this valuable contrivance, *the Window*, presents to man, and more especially to us towns-people in the winter season, when, in order not to perish from cold, we are doomed, like the bear, to spend most of our time in our warm lair. In grateful remembrance hereof, I have drawn up the following memorial relating to these advantages, namely:—

1st. A prospect of the earth.
2d. A view of the sky.
3d. A survey of our own and other people's business.
4th. An insight into daily life.
5th. An inducement to meditation.
6th. Light during day.
7th. Air whenever we wish for it.
8th. A place of refuge from the hydra of civilized every-day life; that hydra, which causes the Frenchman to commit "sottises," the Englishman to hang himself, the German to write narcotic books, the Swede to drink or play at cards, and the whole world to yawn; which fastens lead to Time's wings and makes minutes eternal; that hydra, at whose door one may well lay half of all the evil which is practiced in the world, which almost everybody knows and everybody dreads - in a word — ennui.

How gladly would I we not turn it out of the house, throw it out of the window, also, annihilate it. But it is immortal here upon earth, like enjoyment and **pain**, and makes its appearance in their absence like a tiresome "dame de compagnie," unless we make an alliance against it with some friend who is more trustworthy and powerful than it.

Personally I am not much acquainted with ennui; but I have known it a little in former days, when in order to fly from it I retreated to my window, and there found a cure for it. I remember particularly one day, or rather one evening! I was at that time young, and carried in my bosom a heart palpitating with a longing for life's richness, for that fullness of existence which I had heard of and read of, and which I had deeply felt that I could enjoy, imparting and receiving, but which I had not then ever tasted. For my home was rich enough in silks and finery and French engravings and parties and equipages; but my life was nevertheless poor, and my soul hungered. This happens to many.

I resided in the capital. All those who belonged to me, my father, mother, and sisters, were at the New Year's ball, given by the Burgesses to the Royal Family, but I had to stay at home, in order to nurse the remainder of a slight cold, and to keep my old paternal grandmother company. (N. B., — I had entertained some little suspicion that the remainder of my cold was magnified somewhat by my good parents, for the sake of the old grandmother, and that she might have company, which suspicion did not much improve my temper.) But — I secretly wiped away a tear; was glad that my eldest sister looked so handsome in her new ball-dress, and that she might possibly have a dance with the Crown-Prince; was delighted with my brother's new uniform, in which he looked so stately, and determined to amuse myself as well as possible in my solitude with reading, music, and — myself. Old grandmother was not a very cheering companion. She was a little deaf, and spent her evenings by telling fortunes in cards to herself, until the hour for going to bed at ten o'clock when, after having looked at her watch, she invariably took her bedroom candle, saying: "No, now we must proceed to the latter part!" or, "No, now we must think of the eider-downs!" which generally was a signal for the whole house to go to bed, but frequently not to any rest for *me;* for restless feelings and thoughts made the "eider-downs" to me any thing but the peaceful downs of forgetfulness and pleasant dreams.

This evening, especially, after recovering from my feverishness, the pulses of life seemed to rise with renewed vigor, and to beat with double strokes. I was walking about through all the deserted rooms longing for something pleasant, something animating. Hitherto I had had very little pleasure in the world, and yet I felt that I could enjoy much. I was alone, had nothing to do, nothing to work for, nothing I fancied to live for. The old interminable "frill" at which I was working while I was sitting at the window in the day, I did not care even to look at. In fact, I detested embroidery. To play the piano was more pleasant, but then — somebody ought to listen to me and find pleasure in my music; but I was now alone and my old grandmother was deaf and was sitting at her cards in the boudoir, muttering in a half-suppressed voice over the Queen of hearts and the King of spades, and about deaths and marriages and presents, and all kinds of adventures; but I was used to this, and used to her prophecies never being fulfilled; for never did any adventures or events, any thing unusual or wonderful, happen in our family, which I thought was exceedingly tiresome, and I therefore sketched one day in my album a figure yawning awfully, and with outstretched arms sighing forth —.

> The worst of all destinies
> Is to have no destiny at all.

I feared that I was doomed to this fate and to live in an eternal calm. Alas! like a bird in its cage, flapping its wings against the imprisoning bars and beating itself to death rather than live in it, such was at this time my poor heart. This evening, at all events, it beat so; it was besides, New Year's Day, and I was so full of life and youth and strength; the New Year had come. Would it not bring a new year for my life, for my soul? Images, forms, presages, mirages of coming events floated over the future: but they were still far distant and indistinct. I did not yet quite know what I was seeking, what I wanted. Some shapes now approached nearer. There was amongst them one figure, dressed in a man's costume, who had shown me a great deal of politeness, — even a little more than that. I did not exactly feel any inclination towards him, but this evening he appeared to me more amiable than usual; this evening I fancied that I could almost love him.

Just then I heard grandmother say over her cards, —

"Somebody is coming to pay us a visit to-night!" Ah! if only somebody *would* come, I thought to myself, and for the first time I ascribed a power of a higher nature to my grandmother's gift of divination. She had pronounced my soul's secret wish. Piano-forte, books, engravings, inanimate objects could not satisfy the cravings of my soul. I wanted a *living* soul, an equal, a friend. And now grandmother promised me a visitor. If he came, surely he came for *my* sake, and not for grandmamma's, and I would have the conversation all to myself, and my grandmamma would have to look on. And that figure — if he came, why, then surely there would be a very interesting conversation between him and me; nobody could tell what it would lead to; yes, when I thought of it, I became almost a little afraid. For there was another figure, also in man's costume, to whom I was far more partial, aye, whose footsteps and voice made my heart palpitate, although he felt no inclination towards me. But this evening — oh! if he should come it might be different; *this* evening I felt that I could charm his heart to me, and there might then be New Year for him as well as for me in this life. And there was a third figure — a friend from childhood — who loved me still, although I have refused his addresses; oh! if *he* would come, I would be so friendly to him, tell him so many beautiful exalted things, that they would make him happy, and we would form a league of friendship for eternity. And then there was a friend, whose very shadow on the wall was dear to me; oh! if she should come, and I could embrace her, open my heart to her, show her my love, make her rich with the wealth of my feelings! True she was some hundred miles distant at her estate, but who knows whether she might not come for all that, as a New Year's surprise; whether my longing could not draw her towards me with magic power. Every thing seemed to me possible this evening. And there was one person, who had done me some wrong; oh! that he would come; I would do him good in return; I would give him a treasure of love and confidence forever.

There was above all, a man, a great man, a genius whom I worshipped and loved almost to idolatry; oh! if he would come! what happiness to see him, to converse with him, to listen to his exalted thoughts; pour out wine for him; wait upon him at the tea-table, and if he should ask a favor of me, my purse or my life, what happiness to give it to him, to live or to die for him! No, that would be too great happiness! He won't come. But there are in this world so many interesting people, so many extraordinary circumstances. If only some of them would come and claim my attention or my activity; my love or my bravery; yes, if nobody else would come, then, at any rate, thieves and robbers; I would perform some desperate act of valor, save my grandmother's life, kill a man, perhaps two, with a log of wood or with the poker, be spoken of, become famous; — perhaps suspected, be imprisoned, appear as a witness before the police courts, which seemed to me to be much more pleasant and interesting than to be or do — nothing. I left the hall-door unlocked, in order to receive the expected visitors, friends or foes. I felt as if I could have governed the whole world. But the world seemed to take care of itself and not to care for me. The minutes fled; nobody came. But was not somebody to come?

Grandmother was sitting in the boudoir telling fortunes out of her cards; I wandered about with noiseless steps upon the carpet in the large drawing-room next to it. The candle in the chandelier threw a romantic twilight over the room, and the hyacinths in the window filled it with summer fragrance. I glanced now and then at the large pier-glass, and thought that I looked very well, and that some one might like, or even fall in love with a girl who looked so. Occasionally, also, I peeped through the window, spying for the expected visitor.

Our house was situated in a square, so that I had an open prospect. Opposite to me, in the corner of the street, a lamp was burning, and almost straight under it was hanging a large, red wooden hand, with the fore-finger stretched out; a dyer's sign. The finger pointed at every person that passed under the lamp; that is to say, when it did not move, for every now and then it was swung backwards and forwards by the wind. It was snowing, and the snow-flakes were falling round about the red hand in the lamplight. There now, it is still, and the large finger is pointing at a figure. I fancy it is a little like that figure which I first thought of. I wonder whether he will come here? No, he turns off to the left. I dare say it was not he. I continue to walk up and down the room. "After all life flies so quickly; it is best to make a person happy, if we can do so, and be happy through his happiness. The perfect is not man's lot, and least of all woman's. They have so little choice, and so little liberty. It is best to take moderate happiness when it is offered to us, and"—again I look through the window. The snow falls. The lamplight is flickering. The hand swings to the wind; now it is still again, pointing at a figure, surely the second one! How my heart is beating! He walks straight up to our house. How could I think of the first one? May he never come! The second one, the right one, is coming. Him, him alone, can I love. He comes; he enters the gate; ascends the staircase; soon he will be in the hall! "Dear grandmother, we shall have a visitor! Shall we not receive him?" "Yes, of course; have I not seen it in the cards? Who is he?"

"I think it is ——; I am not quite sure, though." Strange that he should take such a long time in walking up-stairs. His steps are otherwise so lively; so is also his manner of grasping the door-handle. I know it well. Now — no, it was the wind. Minute after minute glides away. Nobody comes. I must have made a mistake in the person. *That* visit was not intended for my home.

There is a covered sledge, with tinkling bells, driving right up to our house. Oh! if it were she! I open the gates of my heart; she shall drive into it. And were she covered with snow, and congealed to ice, she shall there be welcome and warm. The sledge stops! No, it drives past our door. It was not she!

The minutes fly; now the clock strikes a quarter to nine. It begins to get late for ordinary visitors. But some extraordinary visitor might yet come. The genius, for instance; he measures neither time nor hours. *He* is extraordinary. See there! Does not the red hand point at a figure in a cloak, just like his cloak? It is him; my friend, the genius; the immortal man; and I shall see him, and feel my heart beat for immortal feelings and thoughts. How grand! how splendid life can be! Yes, but how narrow, poor, and empty also. It must not have been he, the genius, my friend. He could not have passed by my home, as that cloak has done.

It strikes nine. The footman enters with the supper for grandmamma and me. Grandmamma sips her milk-posset, and I my tea. We eat and drink in silence. My heart does not now beat so loudly. It is not probable that my friend will call now; and an enemy, or a thief, or a robber — that would be moderately pleasant, comparatively at least.

The supper is carried out. Grandmamma is again at her

cards. I stand again at the window. A white frost-mist fills the air all around, hiding all objects, also the red hand, and the lamp which throws out a faint, sickly light. I can no longer see whether any figures are passing under it; but this is now indifferent to me, for nobody will come now who can make my heart beat, or to whom I can afford a New Year's pleasure. I wander again up and down in the romantic twilight and flower-fragrance of the drawing-room. The clock strikes ten. Grandmamma rises from her seat, takes her candle, and says: " No, my dear Fanny, now we must think of the latter part! Good night, my heart's delight!" Heart's delight kisses grandmamma, sees her to her bedroom and then returns to the drawing-room.

I am now quite alone. When I look through the window again, the mist has fallen lower, and covered the street and its world with an impenetrable veil; but behold! high above it the starry heavens are unveiled, and shine forth with indescribable lustre.

A magnificent constellation rises over my head. What is its name? I had just begun studying a little astronomy, and I hastened to get out my charts and books. Soon I was with my whole soul and life up amongst the stars; gave them names; made the acquaintance of new ones, and learnt about them what astronomical books teach us. This so absorbed my whole attention that I was highly astonished when I heard the clock strike twelve. I could scarcely believe my own ears. But so it was, the first day of the New Year had closed, and neither thieves nor robbers had availed themselves of the unlocked hall-door to pay me a New Year's visit, and really I was not sorry for it now; aye, I was not sad in any way now; I felt wonderfully cheerful, and peaceful at the same time. Heaven's starry vault was, as it were, glittering within me, and as I passed the pier-glass, I fancied that my eyes were sparkling brightly like stars.

How is this? What has happened? I asked myself, while I sat down upon the sofa in the boudoir to rest a little, under the impression that really something had happened to me.

A feeling of exaltation, of inward independence, filled my soul, as if some truth, some light, rich with the future, had arisen in it. Something great had come over me; had made me forget time, solitude, myself, and my petty, selfish wishes, and inspired me with new thoughts; a fresh interest; and when I asked its name, I was answered, "The Glory of God!" For "God's shadow wanders through Nature."[1]

Grandmother had predicted truly. A visitor had actually come; not through the door, but from above — through the window.

MY WINDOW, 1855.
NEW PROSPECTS.
THE BEGGAR-WOMAN.

Now it is autumn; late in the autumn; November. Winter is at the door.

Somebody has made the remark, that after the lapse of ten years the causes of man's happiness or misery in life are very different from those previous to these ten years. How much more applicable is not this to a period of thirty years?

It lies in our nature that, at certain periods of time, we look back upon the road which we have travelled, to measure it from the point which we have reached and the goal which lies before us. We place ourselves, as it were. in the window of our inner room in the world, to survey our life, its forms, its efforts, and its aim, and try to get a clear and distinct view of it.

"The development of individual life progresses from

[1] Linné.

condition to condition," says the modern Simon Stylites, *Aabye Kjerkegaard*, sitting upon his solitary pillar, staring at the sky, and now and then spitting at the people round about him on earth. Upon the direction of this movement depends the condition in which we ultimately remain, or rather to which we arrive, for stop we cannot, unless we become spiritually petrified.

"As we do not," says the Danish prophet just mentioned, "rise from the Christian, the unsophisticated, to become eventually interesting, witty, an artist, philosopher, statesman, etc., etc.; but as on the contrary, out of all these through reflection we become in all more and more a humble Christian," in the same manner also the true aim of life ought to let our petty passions, our love for such and such a one, for this or that, and above all our self-love, fall away, or rather be absorbed, lost, or glorified in our love for — *Love* itself, the only lovable, ever yielding, ever fulfilling spirit. Absorbed in that spirit, man turns again towards the world of humanity, not like the Danish Simon Stylites, but with a new love, more general, but therefore not the less warm; no, fiery and pure, like that of the highest Being whose child it is. That is thy aim, loving heart! Blessed art thou who reachest it!

Thus much about life's "condition." I return to my window. Both window and condition are not any longer the same as those in the picture thirty years ago. All is changed. Only some pieces of the old furniture remind me of the old home. Those people who in it constituted the delight or the misery of my life, are all gone, dead, or away. There is much besides death, which separates people. The heart which then — but hush, hush, or it will bleed, from the memory of the life, the faith, the love, of which it then was capable. It still beats warmly, although for other objects. Thirty years of a life, rich in important events and changes, more rich than all the tropically brilliant and warm dreams of youth, have flown past, but not vainly. They have changed much. There is now snow on my locks, the hot winds have become cool, I feel the fanning of another spring-air from other regions, and I thank God for it.

My window looks again out upon a square, but a different one to that of thirty years ago. I see less of the street and more of the sky. I am living one story higher up. Again I am alone, quite alone in my home, but yet less lonely than ever, and my desire for activity that was so intense thirty years ago has been more than fulfilled, for I have more to do than I can really manage. I expect no visitor, and long for none. But there are visitors which are still dear to me, and heartily welcome. Amongst these is the sun, which about noon usually peeps into my window. In the evening I have his last ray, for my room lies towards that point where he sets. Across a great number of housetops I look forth upon fir-crowned hills on the horizon, and see in the green valleys between them small white rural cottages, and on the heights seven windmills, swinging round their wings and grinding a great deal of corn. When I open my window, I feel coming from those hills a fresh country air, as delightful as if it had not crossed the town and square to reach me. This is a great enjoyment indeed.

I love to stand in my window morning and evening for a short time; in the morning to contemplate the wondrous beauty of the changing colors of early dawn; to behold the sun's first, brilliant rays falling upon the windows of the cottages amongst the hills; to see the active life of the market-place under my windows awake and become astir; in the evening, to see it die away and cease, and to catch the last farewell looks of the sun sinking behind the hills. Occasionally also during the day I amuse myself by looking at the market-place and its bustle and trade.

But that which is the object of my contemplation, what I enjoy, what I receive within me as a bright image, or a perception, I maintain to be *my property* quite as much and even more than if I had acquired it by any legal purchase. What I thus obtain through God's mercy, that I take, I have, and I keep, and nobody can deprive me of it; it is actually and indisputably *mine*. I consider myself, therefore, fully entitled to say not only *my* window, but also *my* prospect, *my* hills, *my* windmills, *my* market-place, *my* market-women, tables, vegetables, etc., etc. — in a word, *my* large household, *my* pantry in the market-place; it is all, all *my* individual property, the same as the large magnificent cupola above it in which the sun and the stars are shining.

My market-place is a comfortable market-place; it has no sanguinary memories, like most of the other market-places in Stockholm. Peaceful industry and peaceful trades have there set out their tables, loaded with inland produce.

You may every day witness the silent, pleasant bustle of buyers and sellers surrounding the tables, covered with every thing necessary for the requirements of the body. But what you cannot see as well as he who lives at the market-place, is how its life begins, how it moves and stirs from morning till night; and it is not uninteresting to contemplate it now and then.

The first groups that make their appearance at early dawn, are the breakfast-groups; the first tables that are laid out are the coffee-tables. There are two or three right in the centre of the square. Comfortably dressed sales-women present themselves with gigantic coffee-urns, carried in enormous baskets, wrapped in linen cloth. Workpeople gather round them from all sides, each paying their half-penny, for which they receive in exchange a cup of the steaming beverage with cream and a piece of sugar. Bread must be bought separately. The breakfast in the open air looks very comfortable. Some Dalecarlian peasant girls and "Madams," *i. e.* women wearing bonnets, make their appearance at the upper end of the square. Then tables are laid out, and are covered with vegetables and fruit.

You may count about twenty such tables in each row, and even he who has seen the vegetable markets in other, more wealthy countries, has very little reason to find fault with the good quality and the variety of the articles exposed for sale. Better cabbage-heads are decidedly not found on the other side of the Atlantic; nowhere are the carrots more beautiful, more sweet, and nowhere can you find better potatoes.

The vegetables do good to our eyes, they look so fresh and so crisp. The tables belonging to the fruit-women are not so well furnished, and we see turnips and other plebeian round-heads intruding amongst the apple, pear, and bergamot baskets, in order to fill up the vacant places on the tables. These vegetable venders evidently consider themselves to be the aristocracy of the market. They wear bonnets and style themselves "Mistress." Their group occupies the upper part of the square. Next after the vegetable-sellers come the potato-groups in small families of sacks and measures. In the centre thereof "Mother" is seated upon a chair, sometimes upon a sack filled with potatoes, quietly waiting for her admirers, who never fail to arrive, carrying away one sack after another. The "Mother" of the potato-family does not wear a bonnet but a hood. In the third row the fish-women are seated, each in a wooden tub with a high back to lean against, and before them large pails and tables full of fish in season, from the Baltic as well as from the Mälar Lake.

In the fourth row stand the tables and bins filled with all the various kinds of Swedish bread, of which I will only mention brown, sour bread (here called anchor-stocks), rye-biscuits, rye and wheaten cakes, buns, penny rolls, aniseed-bread, French bread, almond-bread, saffron-cakes, rusks, and twists of all kinds. A little pale but sharp-looking girl of eleven years is sitting at one of these tables, as shrewd and clever at her business as any "Madam" of forty; but it is not a good school. The bread-tables look inviting at a distance, but afford, upon closer inspection, subjects for less agreeable thoughts; the six-stiver cake has a hole in the centre as large as a small tea-cup and the four-stiver wheaten bread is so small and gray, and looks so miserable, that if I or my friend were obliged to eat it I believe that I would first have to moisten it with — a few tears. " Hard times for the poor," people say, and go past. Next in order come the flour-stands, — small boxes on wheels, beside which floury " Madams," sometimes men, covered with meal, weigh out the produce of the mills. Here in the vicinity are also seen pease, beans, groats, etc., etc. Nearly in a line with these come the booths with canvas-roofs, where a variety of smaller articles of dress, from woolen socks up to gauze caps, toys for children, ribbons, and all kinds of wares, are sold cheap. Between these stand small tables with bread, sugar-candy, fruit, etc. Lower down, in a line with all these lines, we see the beef and pork sellers at their tables, and those who sell butter, and eggs, and salt-salmon in large tubs. In this neighborhood every thing is more higgledy-piggledy; sweetmeats jostling eggs, and brooms poked in amongst the butter; window ornaments, made of the beautiful reindeer lichen, mixed with green moss and red barberries, are thrust in between turkeys and smoked goose-breasts. Ragged women are seen trudging in from the forests, carrying fresh spruce-fir branches and fragrant juniper twigs.

This division of the market-place, commencing at the Bazaar — I must apologize to its " Madams " for not having mentioned them earlier — where all kinds of nice stone-wares are exposed in groups for sale, is bounded by a line of one-horse milk-carts, where Dalecarlian and rosy cheeked milk-maids, with pink checked handkerchiefs on their heads, are enthroned on their vehicles, retailing the beautiful white beverage, which, alas ! is said to be mixed sometimes with a little water. These milk-carts all turn their backs towards the lane dividing the market-place into two equal parts. On the other side of this lane, you may, especially on certain market days, see the country-people with large wagon-loads of hay, grain, meat, wooden utensils, and other produce, as well as cattle. Here is a stir and a life as in an ant-hill. At the upper end of the square, along the houses, women and girls sit busy weaving wreaths of flowers and moss and red whortleberries to lay upon graves, offering you the fragrant produce of the forests.

Here amongst the country people you may admire one or more tall, fine figures, in their provincial dress, and the little Swedish peasant horses, with short-cut, comb-like manes, small hoofs and heads, looking as if they were not capable of long journeys and heavy work, but which the Arctic traveller, Sir John Ross, avouched to be the horses best suited for an expedition to the North Pole. The commerce in this part of the market-place is most lively between the hours of ten and twelve. After that time the place begins to get empty. Business is carried on much longer in the other part. About noon the market-women take their humble dinner, each at her table; in rainy weather, under large umbrellas. After dinner they drink their coffee. This is all very comfortable in fine weather, but in rain and wind — ugh!

We cannot, in contemplating the arrangements here and comparing them to those which are made for similar purposes abroad, help admiring with what few comforts and small resources we here in Sweden understand how to work our way. And yet here, more than in many other countries, some consideration and care ought to be shown those who are every day exposed to the rigor of the climate.

One cannot help wishing that these poor market-women, wives and girls, should have the advantage of wooden flooring and a roof over their head. When we see them sitting all day long with their feet upon the cold, wet ground, their head not sheltered against snow or rain, or at best only by an old ragged umbrella, while their goods are not sheltered at all, we ought not to wonder that in the course of time they become bad-tempered, gouty, morose, quarrelsome, and — which is the case with several of them — ultimately take to the brandy bottle, to help them to keep up their spirits, and keep themselves warm. Discomfort is the mother of vice. Not exactly that the market-women here should necessarily be driven to it. An energetic and God-fearing soul can keep the body in spirits and dry, even in the worst weather. There is, for instance, amongst the market-women, one whom I wish you could know — yonder substantial, good-looking woman, looking so stately in her butcher's stall. She said one day to a young wife, who was crying for the loss of her husband, who had died and left her alone with five children totally unprovided for: —

"Hearken to me, my good Mistress H——. Do not go about in this manner, lamenting and crying, but go home; take off your cloak and put on a proper working dress; get a table, come here, and sell some article. So I did five and twenty years ago, when my husband deserted me. All I then possessed in the world was three children and three shillings. But some kind people advanced me the money to buy a pig. I carried it home myself, cut it up, and came here the next day to sell it. And here I stood until I could afford to get my own stall. I have now portioned off and married my three children; I have three servants, and am the owner of a stone-house in the north part of the town, and the Lord's hand is over me all my days. Do as I did, exert yourself to the utmost, work and trust in God, and all will go well. I shall myself give you the first handsel!"

She to whom this advice was given, did follow it; she is now standing in the market every day, in high spirits, at her pork-table, and has already verified the words of her counselor.

But in order to be able to withstand the rough weather and discomfort of a market life, it requires not only a soul firm as a rock, but also iron health. Our market-women have generally neither the one nor the other.

They who in the course of the day first make their exit from the market-place after the milk-women, are the fish-women and the potato families; then the vegetable, and lastly the meat-women. A few meat and vegetable stalls remain, however, until the evening. Those who sell fruit and bread remain the longest. In the afternoon a number of men with brooms, and large flocks of sparrows, come regularly to sweep away and feast upon the remains of the day's sale. A dog amuses himself now and then with hunting the winged scavengers, and when he sees a flock of them he makes a desperate rush at them; but they are off like lightning, and he stands still, disconcerted, until he espies another flock, at which he again makes a rush, with the same result. The place becomes gradually more and more empty and desolate; there a blind fiddler is led about by a boy, to play outside the various public houses; the brooms and the sparrows are at last masters of the field; only on Saturday nights the sales-women remain until a late hour, and we see the light of their small lanterns glimmer through the darkness in which the whole scene is shrouded.

On Sundays the square is totally deserted, but thousands of sparrows appear to hold an animated and spirited commerce, while the dogs amuse themselves with sparrow-hunting.

As regards the buying population of the market-place, it offers to the beholder little that is characteristic: it resembles the market-place customers of all other Swedish towns. The neat servant-maids, with woolen shawls and black silk handkerchiefs on their heads, and a basket on their arm; the homely housewife with cloak and bonnet, carefully examining the various goods before buying them; the old gentleman, who wants a tidbit for his own and his family's dinner, and who carries off a bird and some vegetables; the servant-maid, who walks home with a large sucking-pig in her arms; the little girl, who buys a half measure of potatoes, an onion and three turnips, a pennyworth of parsley and rusks, a skein of cotton thread, a piece of gingerbread and a Danish lollipop, and stows it all away in her little bag, or "pirate," of plaited straw;. the urchin, who thumbs all the apples before he buys one — you know all these figures, and can see them every day in every market here in town. But what you do not see every day nor everywhere, is a little man, walking upon four legs, and accompanied by three large dogs. Him I saw just now crossing the market-place upon two wooden legs and two legs of flesh and bone paralyzed. It is the horse-butcher, or rather *horse-friend* and poet, Ekeblad, an original; and it would be well if we had many such in this town and in the world, not only for the sake of the poor horses, but also for the sake of those people who suffer pain by seeing them treated with cruelty.

For it was his love for the brute creation, and his sympathy with that noble animal, the horse, which first induced Mr. Ekeblad to wander through our streets and market-places like a missionary, to preach amongst cabmen and other horse-tormentors, kindness to animals. They shut their ears to him and abused him. The horse-friend then began lecturing to the better classes on the treatment of animals — especially the horse. He only got laughed at, and was left to lecture to empty walls. The Swedes are not more harsh or cruel than other nations; but we have not here, as in other civilized countries, any laws for the prevention of cruelty to animals,[1] nor has attention been publicly directed to their characteristics, their merits, their sufferings — to "the sighs of the animals."

Yet there are in this country many women and men who silently feel these "sighs." Foremost amongst these latter stands Mr. Ekeblad, for he has not only thought and pub-

[1] Such laws do now exist since the year 1857.

licly complained in favor of the animals, but he has also acted vigorously in their interest. Not being able by lecturing to prevent the ill-treatment of horses by their selfish and heartless owners, he began buying up all worn-out and broken-down animals, and slaughtered them in a way which gave them death *without pain.*

Honor be to this Christian horse-friend! He has, under hard struggles and with much self-sacrifice, effected much good.

Having now described my present residence and the prospects which it offers, I shall now go back a little in my narrative, in order to relate what I saw on the 26th of April.

I was that day not exactly out of humor. God forbid that a woman before she has reached fifty should be out of humor; that is impossible! That belongs only to old men and old women, doomed to take snuff and play at "patience." But to say the truth, I was not quite in good temper. I sat down to my piano: it was out of tune, or perhaps I was out of tune myself. Even out of the "Magic Flute" came only disharmony. I had recourse to my easel. On it stood a portrait just finished. It stared at me with a squinting, cross look. I turned away from it with disgust, and tried to console myself by writing a verse, but could not find a rhyme for *am;* dissatisfied, I opened a book, but could not understand what I was reading. I threw my talents overboard and sat down at the window.

The April wind played his capricious pranks in the air. The sun, which had only just been shining out brightly, was now hidden by clouds, which in their turn were again dispersed by the merry winds, forming, in so doing, a fantastic triumphal arch for the King of Light. But they returned thicker and darker, now hanging in heavy draperies upon the earth, anon beating it with icy hail-showers, or powdering it with curling wreaths of snow. Through their gradually thinning veil the bright, blue sky soon again peeped forth; it blew, then it became calm, the sky brightened and darkened, darkened and brightened, exactly as in the daily repeated comedy of "Love's Quarrel," or in life's great wonderful drama. A sudden severe hailstorm coming on, I saw the pedestrians in the street, leading into the square, rushing about in wild dismay seeking a shelter from the pelting hailstones. A young servant-maid, walking rather more upon her dress than upon the stones of the street, came running with a jug full of cream and a basket with bread in her hands, stumbled, spilt the contents of the one and dropped what was contained in the other, all for the benefit of a lean dog, who, poor animal, to judge from his insensibility to the hailstones, must have been accustomed to take his meals under the accompaniment of kicks — the good with the bad. With light boots and a woeful countenance, an elegant gentleman skipped across the street to a house, out of whose window a young lady seemed compassionately to contemplate the sorely beset hero, who, with his eyes fixed upon her, and blind as the little God of Love, rushed into the arms of a stout "Madam," who, in her innocence, surely did not think of enveloping in her cloak any body else than her own fat self and her basket full of gingerbread.

Here a woman, with a child in her arms, was hastening towards her home. She unfastened the handkerchief upon her head, in order to wrap it round the child. Mercilessly the hail was battering against her brown curls, while in front of her two gentlemen were butting at each other with their umbrellas, swearing at each other in their blindness and hurry. An ancient horse was philosophically shaking his shaggy head at the unwonted noise, and being left to manage it according to his own pleasure, for himself and for the old friend to which he was harnessed, — a cart, shaky from old age and long service, — he found himself at last induced to do as other people, to drag his appendix and himself, with bent head and drooping ears, into an open covered gate-way. Three cats and two dogs followed his example, but in opposite directions. The sparrows, those little airy optimists, merrily chirping under the shelter of the eaves of the houses, seemed to rejoice that nothing could upset their good temper.

Soon the street became empty. A mummy-like figure was sitting alone and immovable on the steps of the house from which I made my observations. She was sitting as if she did not notice the hailstones, staring straight before her with a look which seemed to feel no more interest in any thing in this world. The crutch lying beside her, and the rags of her tolerably clean dress, seemed to explain to me her listlessness. Poor woman! I said to myself, she is poor, old, decrepit, abandoned, and alone in the world. She has nothing more to fear, nothing more to hope. Why should she have looked out for a shelter? She may well be indifferent about every thing. She is a zero in the world, and to her the world is a zero. I was deceived. The hailstorm ceased; the clouds broke, and the sun shone bright and warm. The old woman looked up — so happy, so gratefully happy — at life's light and joy. Her face, on which old age, sickness, and misery had left deep and dark traces, still retained the expression which the poet so beautifully paints: —

> "There, through sorrow's bitter tears,
> And the beaming rays of joy,
> Hope, immortal, smiles."

Thus sat the old woman, enjoying what nobody envied, what nobody could take away from her — the light. Somebody approached her; she put out a supplicating hand, and did not draw it back empty.

In a summer garb more than transparent, a little pale boy came wandering along with downcast eyes, past the row of houses, he and his dog looking out for some thrown away, but for them precious, morsel of food.

The old woman beckoned the boy to come to her, and with

some friendly word gave him the alms which she had herself but now received. With his hungry four-footed friend he hastened, with merry bounds, to a neighboring baker's shop, where they shared their luxurious meal with enviable appetite and delight.

Their benefactress looked after them with a pleasant smile. A few minutes afterwards she took a piece of soft bread out of her apron, and ate it with evident enjoyment. Again she looked up to the bright sky, so gratefully, as if she had nothing more to wish for in life.

This sight gave me something to think of, and in harmony with the change in the weather, my thoughts were now the very reverse of those which I had entertained a short time before.

This old woman, whom we pity, ought we not rather to deem her enviable? She may have what we all of us want, what we all long for — an interest in every day. The beginning of each day offers to her an eventful future. What she receives at the hands of the charitable, is to her a favor of fortune, or rather a mercy from Heaven, who does not abandon her any more than the sparrow, which, merrily chirping, picks up the grain that has fallen for him to the ground. If occasionally her prayer is refused, why she is used to it; it neither spoils nor embitters her temper, and wanting but little, she still always gets that little. What she gives out of her poverty to others, has, like the widow's mite, a great value in the eyes of the Great Judge who examines the heart and the will. She has no cares for the morrow, and no day goes past which does not bring her some good, which yesterday she did not expect to get. Hardened from long habit against the changes of the weather, she suffers little from its roughness, whereas she enjoys undisturbed and free its more genial moments.

I believe that they who live and move about much in the open air, they who frequently have no other roof over their heads than heaven's vault, feel themselves more vividly and more trustfully to be under the protection of the higher

Being, who, their heart tells them, is up above. Just as in the new-built temple of Solomon, the Lord manifested His presence in a cloud, so in Nature's glorious temple He manifests Himself to us, even to this day, in the atmosphere of the high and the holy which everywhere surrounds us; and although a cloudy darkness still hides the revelation to our eye, yet we feel it in the light, in the invisible, mighty wind, in all the life which surrounds us, and the hidden source of which we are called upon to feel, to pay homage to, and to worship. The ever-varying changes of the seasons; the rigor and often splendor of winter; spring's creative glory; summer's thunder and lightning, and its charms; autumn's ripening life, fogs, and farewell festival; day, night, morning, evening — every thing speaks to the child of Nature, and spreads before its view a picture in the harmonious variety of which it learns to trace a heavenly Master's hand.

And it was surely not in the bosom of full life-giving Nature, where they were created, these systems of materialism, of eternal death, this nothing doctrine of nothingness. Spring's balmy winds did not fan the forehead within which this gloomy phantom was born. It was within the dark walls of his narrow cell, while breathing close and unwholesome air; it was by the dim glimmer of his midnight lamp, that the fallen son of light and truth did exert the whole power of his ingenuity to disclaim his soul, and with it life's every flower. It was there he could deprive suffering and longing man of the angel of hope, and in exchange, give him a skeleton.

Happy, immeasurably happy, art thou, although poor and despised, if Heaven's light, which shines before thy mortal eye, shines also in thy soul. How rich thou art! how little dost thou miss! What is it thou hast less than the mighty and the rich? Want. What more than they? Content.

The golden grains of happiness are sown more evenly than we generally believe; perhaps with a more liberal hand on that side where earthly gold is not found.

I do not know whether Alexander the Great, or whether the still greater Napoleon, ever knew real happiness. I do not know whether the possession of the whole world could have given them contentment; and yet this, the highest for which they struggled, which they needed, was given to a poor beggar woman in a ray of sunlight, and a morsel of dry bread.

And I, who in the silent shadow of an unnoticed life ought sooner to find the hidden violet of happiness, but who find so little enjoyment in many gifts of fortune, I feel that I possess less than thou, poor and yet wealthy woman. I have envied thee thy smile and thy glance so free from care.

By way of penitence I will at once make a pilgrimage across the street to thee, saint of rags, and humbly offering my little gift at thy shrine, earn from thee a " God bless you! " " Amen! " I shall say silently, and pray that He, as His best gift, may give me thy patient contentment. I gave her my mite and returned home.

In the window opposite, the young gentleman and the young lady stood side by side. They smiled. The old beggar-woman smiled with silent satisfaction, and the sun was smiling over us all. My bad temper had vanished, and I smiled likewise.

THE SISTERS.

NOVEL writers have planted the world's fields full of a flower called love; and every one, who, like me at the age of ten years, has collected an herbarium of knowledge of mankind only in their gardens, expects at his first peep into the real world to see the beauteous, wonderful flower blooming in the verdant summer groves; on the frozen snow-hill; in the park; on the heath; in the valley and on the mountain-tops; at sea and on shore; in every cottage; in every palace, and especially in the road-side inns — but, like me, he will be grievously deceived.

This glorious, eternal flower, fed by heaven's purest dew, is in reality very rare. I have seen it growing in the silent sanctuary of the breast of a few noble people, there ennobling and glorifying every thing. I have seen it in a few earthly homes create a paradise. Yes, it *is* found on earth, this flower; I know it and I feel it.

But what we do not unfrequently see, is a kind of love in idleness, blooming for one short summer and then withering away; some passion-flowers with four and twenty hours of life; and a number of love-anemones, which the spring sun calls into life, which come in May and depart in May, and about all of which trifles the world makes a great fuss; but what we see much more frequently is the grassy or ploughed pasture-land within or without doors, without any love-anemones at all.

And then also the novel writers have woven round the world a net of golden threads, on which man dances merrily along. These life-threads meet, resist, follow, or cross each other incessantly; one finds everywhere complications and *dénouement*, and consequently interest; nothing disjointed; nothing fragmentary; nothing of the knots of the life-thread; nothing of this melancholy "we sit where we sit," which so often occurs in reality: on the contrary, one sees always progression, in prosperity as well as in adversity; always a contact of man with his fellow-men, full of interest; and I will wager with you, young maiden with rosy cheeks, with you, young man with downy chin, that you believe you cannot take a single step in this world of ours, without encountering people who care for you; yes, they do, as the spider cares for the fly or the butterfly for the rose. You may, it is true, probably now and then create some interest in this way; perchance frequently meet with people who ask what value you have — in money; but what you will meet with much more frequently is a number of people who each of them look after their own selves, and their bag and baggage, but who do not care for each other, or for you, more than for the man in the moon, and sometimes still less.

It is in the miniature copies of the world's large posting-house, where the truth of this sad sketch is forced upon your experience with glaring colors; and in order to illustrate this, I will here tell, especially for the benefit of those who have never been at an hotel or a road-side inn, how, one fine day, towards the close of September, two handsome carriages, containing a mother with her three daughters, son, and a nephew with moustaches, stopped at the door of the hotel at the Falls of Trollhättan; how these travellers, after having ordered supper and lodgings for the night, proceeded, as it becomes civilized people eager for enlightenment, to see the locks, while they philosophized over man's genius to create water where formerly stood mountains; and how they, thereupon, during all kinds of pleasant chat, went to view the roaring waterfalls, in order to fall, as becomes thinking people, into deep meditations at the wonders of Nature; and how at the the Gullö cataract, in one of the daughters, who, besides very round cheeks had also been gifted with a poetical vein, all kinds of thoughts arose, bedewed with the misty spray of the waterfall, but from which thoughts she hoped that one day the mist might roll away, so as to discover some outlines of certain "Sketches."

It is further worth remarking, how the cousin with the moustaches not only fell into a deep reverie on the Tappö cataract, but was on the point of falling into it himself, and how thereupon the whole company walked back to the hotel, installed themselves in apartments No. 6 and 7 and 8 and 9 and 10, drank tea and ate sandwiches, amidst the sound of merry laughter and pleasant chat.

From another quarter two Englishmen, returning from a shooting excursion, thoroughly soaked and bespattered all over, but in "high spirits," let off their fowling-pieces at the hotel door, and took possession, with a vast deal of noise and bustle, of room No 11, where, on the untuned strings of a harp, they struck distracting discords, at which one of the daughters in the adjacent room, who had a wonderfully acute musical ear, grumbled a good deal, which did not prevent the friend of disharmony from jingling and twanging until midnight.

In No. 1 a dear papa gave his two daughters a spiritual gymnastic exercise: "Have you brought up the portfolio?" — "Yes, dear papa." — "I hope you have not forgotten the travelling-map in the carriage?" — "No, dear papa." — "Where is my pipe?" — "Here, dear papa." — "Do not stand there, Wendla, and look foolish; sew fast my star to my coat; do you hear?" — "Yes, dear papa." — "Fanny, have you ordered tea?" — "Yes, dear papa." — "And coffee for Wendla, and ale-posset for me?" — "Yes, dear papa." "And bread and butter and beef? you think of nothing; I must manage every thing. See now that you sleep soundly and well to-night, so that we may be ready for travelling a little early to-morrow morning."

In No. 3 a young gentleman was writing his "travelling impressions," beginning with these words: "I am now writing" . . . (for posterity he thought, — so I suppose).

In No. 5 two young fellows were playing at cards, and drinking punch; they found it good, and they thought with Kaja in "Noah's Ark," — [1]

"I think our world is the best of worlds,
For far far worse in Hamburg it is."

In No. 15 a married couple sat conversing in the beautiful moonlight. Of the subject of their conversation we can judge best by the words which were most frequently heard in the course thereof: "Expenses, income, living, hard times, electoral sheep, pigs, corn-brandy, barm, steward, eggs, butter, milk, pork, cow-houses, and barns." My young readers, I could go on until to-morrow, reciting all the

[1] A satirical poem by Bishop Fahlcrantz.

various subjects of conversation, and still not find place for the word love.

In No. 18 somebody was continually yawning and ringing the bell, seeming desirous of coming in contact with the other inmates of the hotel, but these (as it often happens in similar cases) did not seem inclined to come in contact with him. Still he made the landlady's seven chambermaids chase each other up and down the stairs.

In No. 20, a small and dismal room, a mother was sitting beside her child's sick-bed. The landlady entered to speak with her about her new arrivals, and to give the pale, poorly dressed stranger a hint to continue her journey with as little delay as possible.

Her eye lighted upon the child, whose sleep was disturbed by frequently returning cramp-attacks, and she exclaimed: "Lor! what is the matter with the brat? It won't live till to-morrow, I can tell you!" The poor mother bent over her child with kisses and tears. The landlady went on: "If you were to put a blister upon its head; or gave it some 'Hoffman's Drops;' or put it in a bath, — or if we could make it swallow some camomile-tea — but what at all events is certain, is, that it won't live over the night; but, if you could afford it, you might buy a bottle of French wine." . . . .

The stranger interrupted her, by asking how far it was to Werna, where the Ladies L—— were living, and whether a messenger could be found at once, to send on to them?

"About thirteen miles," was the answer, "and a messenger you can certainly get; but my dear little lady, if you believe that you can get any assistance from the "Ladies at Werna," you are mightily mistaken. They are proud and hard-hearted people."

"That is not true," interrupted the stranger with vehemence.

"Not true!" rejoined the landlady, much offended. "Whether it is true or not, I ought to know best, who have myself asked a favor of them and have been refused, getting well moralized by Lady Helena into the bargain. Not true! I ought to know it best, who have had a step-daughter in their service. Not true! very well, go to them, go to them, and you will see yourself whether I tell any stories.[1] You will be shown the door, as well as others. Go! go!"

"Had not"—the stranger asked in a tone of deep dejection—"had not the Ladies L—— a sister?"

"Yes, certainly; but she has been absent many years, and I would not advise her to return to her sisters, unless she were very wealthy or married to some Prince, for otherwise they won't acknowledge her. They are very proud women; they associate only with grand folks, and live in style. They have a ball to-night."

"To-night!" said the stranger.

"Yes, and they have one every Sunday night; I say nothing, I; but still I think that on the Lord's day one ought"—

The stranger here interrupted her, peremptorily desiring to be furnished with writing materials and a candle, and to get a messenger, who would for payment undertake to go at once to Werna.

"Oh, certainly!" replied the landlady, with a taunting sneer, "I won't be in the way of your fortune."

A quarter of an hour afterwards, the stranger sat beside a wretched candle, writing in feverish haste. The faint light fell upon her pale and sunken cheeks. She was the very image of suffering.

The messenger, Mother Bengta, was now ready to go to Werna, to which place she also had an errand on her own account, and the last bank-note was transferred from the

[1] Excuse me, my good woman, you *do* tell a story, and a friend of truth must here bear witness, that you look upon the sisters at Werna in such a dark light only because they refused your request to become security for one of your sons, who wished to set up in business as a tradesman, but who was well known to be a good-for-nothing fellow.

stranger's pocket-book to Mother Bengta, in payment for her trouble with the letter, which with real agony she enjoined her to take good care of and to deliver without loss of time.

She then turned again to the child, which had just awakened.

"How the waterfall roars," said the little one; "I feel so uneasy, mamma! take me upon your knee; I shall rest better there."

"How are you, my child?"—"Better, mamma; I have had such a beautiful dream; I saw an angel and a bright light—mamma, you're weeping; kiss me. How the waterfall roars! sing to me the song about the North, mamma, so that I may not hear that roar; when you sing to me, time flies quicker."

The mother sang, and when she came to the last lines, she sang so slowly and with deep emotion:—

> O thou glorious North
> That a cradle me gave,
> In thy well-beloved earth
> Let me sleep in my grave;
> With my little one dreaming
> Where the snow-drifts are gleaming.

And thus she sat all night, rocking her child upon her lap, slowly singing.

Meanwhile, Mother Bengta was trudging goose-fashion along the road to Werna. Have you, dear reader, ever known persons who were wonderfully clever at the trick of losing every thing? It is a curious spectacle! They begin, for instance, with dropping their pocket-handkerchief; and when they stoop down to pick it up, they drop a key, a glove, or a letter, or a memorandum-book, or the pocket-handkerchief a second time; and if they do not drop their nose, it is merely because they do not have it in their hands. Mother Bengta was one of those persons, gifted with a similar talent, and after having (on her way to Werna, beginning with her garter) gone through the aforesaid dropping process, she arrived there at last, minus the letter so anxiously recommended to her care. She looked for it everywhere, but it could not be found.

The early morning-sun shone upon scenes of various kinds at the Trollhätta Hotel.

" Dear papa " in No. 1, loaded his daughters with packages and books to be deposited in the carriage. " Can you carry any thing more ? " he asked one of his daughters, whose head was just visible above the pyramid of packages which she was carrying in her arms. " Yes, with my nose," she replied with that good-natured and merry laugh, such as buoys up body and soul, and two books were accordingly confided to the care of the little nose.

The two Englishmen went out shooting, singing at the top of their voices, without looking even with half an eye at " Gullön," standing there in the golden sunshine so glorious with its yellow autumn birches and evergreen firs, while the cataract, roaring and foaming, rained showers of sparkling diamonds upon its mossy banks.

The youngster in No. 3 tried to rub the sleep out of his eyes; he began slowly dressing, and while looking at himself in the looking-glass, he muttered: " My dear Figge! thou art certainly not so very handsome, but thou art not so very ugly either."

The refined and interesting family's travelling-carriages drove up to the door. My lady-mother and her two daughters, each with her reticule, took their seats, rejoicing at the beautiful morning, while the third daughter went with her brother, who was to pay the heavy bill, in order to assist him in trying to beat down the exorbitant charge, which object — so his future wife will no doubt one day say — was quite contrary to the young gentleman's nature.

The landlord and landlady were not visible, but their seven servant-girls stood all in a heap to defend the bill.

" Nothing could be abated; that was utterly impossible!" His sister, the sage Hulda, moralized and demonstrated; the brother looked black and fierce ; all in vain — the bill did not grow less, and from the ranks of the seven servant-girls was heard a low growling about "a shabby company, that wants to bargain." Then stalked in through the open door the cousin with the moustaches, looking awful and threatening; but he ended by strutting with large strides through the kitchen, thundering between his teeth: "This is scandalous!"

Then the brother made a tack or two round the seven servant-girls, who, in some alarm, had gathered in a knot in the middle of the kitchen floor, while he repeated with the calmness of despair: "This is a confounded shame!" whereupon all three sailed out of the kitchen to the carriages, in which the fresh morning soon made them forget their night's lodgings, the exorbitant charge, and the league of the servant-girls.

When the bright beams of the morning sun looked in through the window of No. 20, an angel bore away a little child's spirit, and carried it to the throne of the Almighty.

With her child's lifeless body in her arms, the mother sat, closing with kisses the eyelids of the beautiful, now lustreless, eyes, and as she had sat all night with her child in her arms, so she sat all day, rocking it silently.

Towards evening she asked whether any messenger had arrived for her with a letter, — but none had arrived. On the second day old Mother Bengta returned, stoutly asserting that she had delivered the letter, but that she had received no answer.

One, two, three, four — five days passed, and the stranger wandered about, pale as a ghost, without either eating, drinking, or sleeping; only asking, ever and anon: "Is there no letter for me?" On the sixth day she laid her little child, with the aid of the clergyman of the parish, in its silent grave, and when it was buried, a light covering of snow spread itself over the tiny hillock, and it comforted the heart of the poor mother. Long she sat beside the grave, and suffered the snow-flakes to fall upon her bare head. Then, with faltering steps, she dragged herself back to the hotel, asking again : " Is there no message, no letter for me ? " But there was none. Then sickness laid its hand upon her heart and head, and whispered to her agonized soul, Enough! enough!

Sickness, bodily pain! Thou hast been called an evil upon earth, but thou art often a good and salutary balm, under whose influence the soul finds rest after its hard battle, and the raging tempests are stilled. More than once hast thou prevented suicide, or saved from madness. The fearful, the bitter words which disappointed expectation and deluded hope have written upon our heart, are gradually defaced in the dark and feverish dreams of sickness. The terrors which lately were so near, fly far away from us, — we forget, thank God! We *forget*, and when at last weak and tottering, we arise from a bed of sickness, our soul often awakens as from a long night to a new morning.

While we are waiting for this new morning to dawn upon our poor sufferer, let us spend

AN EVENING WITH THE SISTERS AT WERNA.

The customary little Sunday night's dance was over, and the young boarders, after lovingly kissing and embracing their kind governesses, had retired to their respective dormitories.

The candles were put out; the cold November wind whirled the snow-flakes round in mad gambols, but the autumn night's cosy fire was burning with a bright flame, throwing its cheering light round the room, in which the sisters, Helena and Amelia, were sitting in their easy chairs on each side of the stove, from which the light fell upon their kindly thoughtful faces.

Once, contemplating an elderly lady's sad countenance, which seemed to bear the stamp of a joyless life, I thought, Oh! how much that is beautiful remains undeveloped in the face of the woman, who has never experienced the blessing of life's joy, of a pure, happy love; it resembles the soil upon which no ray of the sun has fallen, and which, therefore, brings forth only sickly colorless flowers. But in contemplating these two sisters, I said to myself, Oh, how beautiful are not the features of those, who have preserved their soul's peace by patience.

Earthly love, enjoyment, and happiness cannot thus make the human face a bright mirror of heaven. This alone — Oh! do not turn away thy glance, young woman, whose eye is still beaming with youth and hope — this alone can the cross of self-denial, humbly and patiently borne, do; this alone be reflected by a firm mind, sanctified by a whole life, when it says: "Thy will be done, O Father!" And the sisters had said this, and they had borne the cross. When one day they become glorified angels, they will perhaps appear with more beautiful features; but this look, so bright, so serene, this smile, so gentle, so kind — can heaven's children have one more beautiful? I do not believe it; for the angel was already there in the sisters' souls, and smiled and looked out of them, blessing earth. There were lines on their foreheads; their eyes were sunken; there were traces of suffering on their cheeks; but the spirit of humble submission had passed over all and had chased away all gloom. But not only the soul's beauty and peace lay spread over the faces of the sisters; for especially when they spoke, there sparkled a ray of lively humor, of that quiet, good-natured temper, which I believe we begin to feel when the stormy season of passion is past, and we submit to let alone what cannot be altered; when we take man as he *is*, and put the best face upon things, and, above all, when we do not allow the minor business of life to irritate us, or become annoyed at petty vexations. We have much to combat with before we arrive at this delightful peace of mind, but the sisters have communicated to me the prescription, which they have themselves made use of, and this was to consider the Disposer of their fate as more clear-sighted than they themselves, and mankind often troubled with a cataract; and therefore, in misfortunes and troubles, which they had to suffer in consequence of other people's hostility and errors, they merely remarked: "If they saw clearer, they would act differently!"

In the sky it is so arranged, that when all darkening clouds are swept away, the sun will shine out, or the stars will twinkle; and in the same manner, when clouds of doubt or bitterness no longer hide the soul's heaven, the mild bright light of cheerfulness will shine forth, and in its rays are kindled these lively fancies, this innocent mirth, these merry jests, of which the airy and animating fire-works of every-day life are composed.

At a little distance from the sisters, opposite the fire-place, a young girl was seated on a low stool, her head leaning upon her small hand. She was watching, with a pensive mien, the dancing flames, which, to judge from the expression of her face, spoke to her more of life's play than of life's earnestness. She was pretty, eighteen years old, and her name — Emma.

To her Helena turned round, after a short pause in the conversation, opened her lips, and began as follows: —

"I have got a Bible for you, my dear Emma. You shall take it with you when you part from us. I think you can find a place for it in your portmanteau."

"And I have got a large cookery-book for you," said Amelia, with an arch smile; "you must not forget to take that with you, also. It must not be said that you come from the sisters L——'s house, soon to enter your own, without being well provided with that which can teach you how to become a clever housewife and mistress in your own home."

"As to your housekeeping," chimed in Helena, "it is necessary that you should always attend carefully and have an eye to the garret, the cellars, and the kitchen, and keep a sharp lookout after the cook. But be careful, my dear child, not to make all the fuss and bustle that so many mistresses are in the habit of indulging in from morning till night. One would think that no fire could be lit and would burn, and no fish could be fried, without their poking their nose into every thing. Believe me, the cook pestered by her mistress, while she herself is bustling about amongst her pots and pans, will do her work much worse than if she were left to manage for herself. Let every body in a household rule and govern in his own province, while the head thereof, that is to say, the housewife, superintends and rules the whole. But to do this properly, she must be herself a pattern of order and regularity."

" Above all," observed Amelia, " it is necessary to be strict and even-tempered in your treatment of the servants. They ought each of them to have their certain and distinct duties, and be kept to them strictly, but with kindness."

" So that not," interrupted Helena, " as I have seen it somewhere, when any thing is to be done, the man-servant tells the lady's maid to do it; the lady's maid tells the house-maid; the house-maid tells the cook; and the cook tells the scullery-maid; and that at last the mistress has to light the fire herself."

" Besides," said Amelia, " there is a certain quiet, regular clock-work in household affairs, which is much to be recommended. And, moreover, that part of the house which is occupied by the family, ought, if possible, in so far to resemble a fairy palace, that every thing in it is kept in the greatest order; free from every particle of dust; perfectly clean and ready, without any body, except the fairy herself, knowing how and when all has been managed."

" Yes," said Helena, " by all means manage so that your husband may never have reason to complain, like Captain Knock—, Knack—, I forget his name, who never observed when his room was scoured, except when he stumbled over the water-pail."

"To praise in proper time and to blame in proper time," remarked Amelia, "is an effective means by which a housewife can use her influence. I have heard many complaints made in this world about servants, but I have almost always noticed that the principal fault which caused all the complaint, was owing to the master and mistress themselves. Wherever those who are to command are morally and intellectually superior, which, in consequence of their higher position in the world, they ought to be, the inferiors will, if they are treated with justice, common sense, and kindness, in general be not only obedient, but also willing, respectful, and often become sincerely attached; in most instances the faults of the master or mistress are the cause of the faults and errors in their servants."

"You have, my dear child," said Helena, "a little fault, against which I must warn you, especially on account of the annoyance which it may cause your husband. You think you are always right, even in the greatest trifles, and you become therefore frequently irritable. In such little altercations a straw often becomes a large forest and a pin's head a cannon-ball."

"Which often," remarked Amelia, "make a breach in the wall of domestic peace."

"Alas!" continued Helena, "here in this life, where so many real cares and misfortunes can befall us, the greatest wisdom consists in letting, especially in less important matters, five be an even number, in order to preserve domestic peace."

"You have also," said Amelia, "another little fault, which, at your age, it is important to overcome. This is a carelessness in dress. How often have we not been obliged to say to you: 'Emma, your shawl is all awry.'"

"Or," observed Helena, "your shoe-string is broken."

"Or," said Amelia, "your collar has been put on with

the wrong side out, or, your dress looks more gray than white! My dear child! you cannot imagine what a discomfort a woman brings with her who is disorderly in her dress; and on the other hand, what a comfort it is to one's self, or to those who are around us, to be strictly attentive to the neatness of one's personal appearance. This attention to neatness can supply the want of beauty, and no beauty can have any charms without it, in the long run. Remember the words of a great author: 'God alone sees the heart; manage thou so, that also others may see something tolerable.'"

"You have," said Helena, "a quality for which you cannot enough thank kind Nature, and which you ought to try to preserve through all the changes in life, and that is, a cheerful, happy temper. This, as it were, blows away the dust from the leaves of life's tree, and they will grow all the more fresh and green. I have always sincerely pitied those husbands, whose wives have a face like a gloomy November day."

"Unless," interrupted Amélia, with liveliness, "the husbands themselves are the autumn wind which had caused that gloom."

"Of course," added Helena, "every season must have its own days; but he who is to become our Emma's husband, unites with a noble character a gentle mind; and as far as he is concerned, nothing will prevent her from looking like a bright May-day."

"Create then a spring in your home, my child," said Amelia. "The son of the North has his world in his home, more so than the children of more genial climates. Nature, here in our North, does not, as in the South, give to man a home in her bosom, and a treasure in the sun and in the air, full of joy and love of life. Severe and cold, she here compels him to seek a shelter against her inclemency; and he looks for it in his home at his hearth. If he does not find comfort, delight, and love of life there, then life in this our North is to him nothing else than a long, bleak, autumn day. My dear child, create a spring in your home."

"And do not forget the flowers, my little Flora," said Helena, — "your singing, your music, your painting; in a word, your talents are the flowers which you must carefully tend, to decorate with them the altar of your home."

"And then," said Amelia, "I can predict that a little god, who thrives well amongst flowers and spring, will come and build his nest in your home: guess what he is called?

Emma did not by any means look stupid.

"Above all, my dear girl," Helena went on to admonish with gentle but deep earnestness, "lay one thing on your heart, the only one necessary. Think, think often, of *Him* who gave thee here on earth a mission to fulfill and talents to improve. Life is changing in all its stages; greatness and lowliness, enjoyment and pain, relieve each other in turn; if in these changes we have nothing to lean upon, we shall be tossed about like a reed in the wind, and this support we have only in an enlightened and sincere fear of God. Pray every day to Him, in whom alone is light, this prayer so full of wisdom: 'Enlighten our understanding in Thy knowledge, and teach our hearts to make Thee an offering of true obedience!'"

"Then," said Amelia, "you shall in your walk through life, in all your actions, be able to maintain that order, that loving spirit, full of truth and peace, without which a woman never can properly fulfill her beautiful mission on earth. Your husband will then lean upon you with full confidence, in joy as well as in affliction, and all those who surround you will, through you, reverence and love true Christian virtue. In success you will not then become proud and overbearing."

"And in adversity," continued Helena, "you will not allow yourself to be crushed, but have hope, and forget yourself in order to comfort others."

"Around all life's joy," said Amelia, "you will spread the all-beautifying radiance of innocence."

"And in the depth of your sorrows," continued Helena, "you will not feel bitterness, but be able to say with the suffering 'Vitalis'" (here Helena unconsciously clasped her hands, and in her serene face one could read the pain and the beauty of self-denial mingled, while she recited with deep feeling):—

> "'Let my will-offering in thy sight find favor,
> O Thou! who dost my inmost spirit read;
> With love I take the cup, nor will I waver
> Whene'er it doth from thine own love proceed.'"

"And then," said Amelia, much moved, "may the love of your fellow-men and the peace of God's angels follow you through life!"

Emma wept and embraced her kind governesses.

"I will," she exclaimed, "become good, make you happy, and try to merit God's approbation and my Edward's love. Oh! that my power to do so could equal my desire! I often feel anxiety, when I think of the duties which await me; and I fear that in the active life upon which I am about to enter, while still so young, I shall not always be able to distinguish the right from the wrong."

"There is," said Amelia, "one way of acting, one maxim, which, if we follow it, will enable us easily and surely to accommodate ourselves to all circumstances in life, according to the will of the eternal Goodness."

"And that is?"

"*Between two different ways of acting, if you would know to which you ought to give the preference, weigh the consequence for the better or the worse, and choose the one which promises to insure the greatest amount of real happiness.* In order to arrive at clearness and certainty in your choice, you require above all, an enlightened understanding; but of this and how to gain this understanding we have already spoken."

"And now," said Helena, "go to bed; it is growing late, and you have heard a longer homily than you may perhaps be able to remember. Never mind your portmanteau to-night; I shall to-morrow morning put into it your Bible and your cookery-book, and some trifles which we have made for you. Good night, my own dear girl."

Emma kissed, wept, and thanked, and in the fullness of her young heart did so again and again. There is a period in life, when we think we can never show enough of gratitude and love. Emma went away at last, followed by the sisters' blessing.

The two sisters were now left alone. The fire was burning with expiring flames, and around them it grew more and more dark. The gale began blowing in louder and louder gusts round their dwelling, intermingled with strange sounds, like human sighs. Gradually their hearts were seized with deep melancholy. It is so with us in this life when once we have experienced a deep sorrow, that even the smallest additional pain suffices to make the old wounds bleed afresh, even if time has succeeded to throw over them its healing balm. Love and sorrow in our soul resemble the fire in some deep mines; it may for a long time be apparently smothered, we fancy that it is entirely extinguished, but — some sudden draught, some ashes dropped, and the flames, wild and consuming, will break forth with redoubled fury.

The two sisters had, during four years, directed Emma's education; she had become dear to them, and they felt painfully the impending parting. But she would be happy, and then, as Helena used to say in similar cases, "all was well." But the new impression of sadness which they had just experienced, awakened within them another feeling of pain, often conquered, but as often returning with the same intensity, and which now, when their hearts were stirred, forced itself upon them more vividly than ever. An empty chair was standing between the two sisters, and on it their eyes were fixed. Now they were but *two*, —

formerly they were *three.* Cecilia should have sat there, sat between them, if she had not, blinded by love, contrary to their advice, united herself to a man who was not worthy of her, and allowed him to tear her from their side; and now rose again before their fancy the sister's image in all its melancholy beauty. Cecilia whom they had so sincerely loved — Cecilia with her loving, warm soul, her rich natural gifts, had died in a foreign country, poor, lonely, and deserted. Surely, she must have longed for her home, have tried in vain to come back to it. Alas! she had suffered alone, so long, so deeply; no loving look had comforted her in the hour of death, no friend's hand had closed her eyes, and she had till the last struggled — struggled with stern necessity. Perchance she had doubted her sisters' tenderness; perhaps she had called them and they had not been able to answer her. Oh! bitter, bitter memories. The sisters' eyes met; they were full of tears. Helena rose, and, to conceal her agitation, she seized the fire-shovel to rake together the dying embers; but while she did so, anguish was depicted on her features; tear followed tear, and fell upon the cold stone. Amelia saw it; she rose, embraced her sister, leant her forehead upon her shoulder and whispered: " Cecilia!"

They were here interrupted by a servant-girl who came to inform them that a poor woman was standing in the kitchen, wishing to speak to them.

Helena desired the servant-maid to show the woman into the room, declining at the same time her sister's proposal to have the candles lit, " because," said she, " her eyes smarted so much, that she did not think she could bear the light."

After a short while the stranger entered. In the dying light from the fire-place her features could not be distinguished. She stopped short at the door, and stood there in the dusk like a shadow, silent and immovable.

A kind of awe came over the two sisters, and with uneasiness, which betrayed itself in the tone of her voice, Helena asked her what she wanted.

The shadow remained silent; but a faint sound, proceeding from the handle of the door, showed that her hand, which held it, was trembling.

Helena repeated her question in a more serious tone, receiving an answer, but so indistinct that it was impossible to find out any coherence in the broken words and half sentences. So much she could, however, understand, that the stranger wanted some assistance, and that she asked to be taken into the service of the two sisters.

With some surprise and with some severity in her voice, Helena said, that "the proper time for changing servants was already past; that they did not want any more servants than those which they had at present, and that, besides, they did not know her."

The shadow was silent, and the sound proceeding from the door-handle became more distinct.

"Have you got," asked Amelia, "any certificate to show us?"

"Yes," answered the shadow.

"From whom?" Amelia again inquired.

"From Misfortune," was the reply.

"Who are you?" asked Helena.

"A shadow of what I was formerly."

"Where do you come from?"

"From the grave," sounded the answer.

Not without some impatience Helena said: "I do not know what your meaning may be with these mysterious words. Say at once what you want and who you are, if you wish that we should help you, which, however, I doubt that we shall be able to do."

"If *you* cannot," the shadow said slowly, "nobody can;" and in a lower tone she added, "Do they then not know me by my voice?"

"God can help," said Helena, "where mortals do not

see their way; if we only confide in *Him*, and pray to Him with a humble mind."

"God helps by man or by death," answered the shadow. "If the former casts me off, I must seek my refuge in the latter."

"Those are very sinful words," said Helena, gravely. "God allows no one to despair, who trusts in Him. By doubt and impatience we frustrate our own fate."

The shadow here interrupted her in a bitter tone of voice: "This is beautifully said; 't is only a pity that such reference to God's mercy generally flows from a want of mercy in ourselves."

With some indignation Amelia exclaimed: "We have not deserved this. If you have come hither to insult us, you only injure yourself. We cannot talk to you any longer to-night; but the night is dark and tempestuous; we will give you a bed here and food." She rang the bell, and added in a milder tone, "To-morrow at daylight, we may perhaps understand one another better. Go now!"

"Go!" reëchoed the shadow in a low voice; "go! but whither, whither?" and suddenly letting go the handle of the door, she dropped on her knees, ejaculating in a heart-rending voice: "Sisters! sisters!"

Oh! God. Then it was she, the lost, the beloved, the long wept-for sister; it was Cecilia!

Trembling with joy and fear, the two sisters would have asked in that moment whether there were really spectres; whether the inhabitants of the grave can revisit the earth. The sisters did, however, not ask these questions; the first agitating impression which they experienced was: It is her spirit; but then they thought: To her, to her, even if she came out of the grave; and under an irresistible impulse they hastened with open arms to the kneeling form, with feelings in which heavenly joy and terror were mingled. Unable to speak, the three sisters embraced each other.

O Death! if thou then hadst taken them in thy arms,

thy bitterness, thy pangs would not have been felt, and no look of regret would they have turned back to the friendly, earthly home. Regret? yes, for who can deny that it is good and beautiful to live here in this world, when we have there built a bright and peaceful home; when every day that passes leaves behind a kindly memory; when every day that dawns upon us is greeted with silent hope. When life, notwithstanding all its shadows, still has a bright side, then death, at least for a while, appears to us a dark angel. But it was not now death which reunited the sisters; it was life, it was joy.

And when they arrived at the full consciousness thereof, when they found themselves locked in each other's arms, meeting again in a life full of love, then they felt what I feel in my heart for them.

I remember having seen a beautiful engraving of a painting, in the Vienna gallery of paintings, representing the return of the "prodigal son" to the parental home. The father bends his head in joy, in love, and in sorrow over the son, who, kneeling before him and contrite, hides his face upon his father's knees. Only a small part of the profile is visible—a large tear rolls slowly down the furrowed cheek. I will follow the painter's example, and leave it to the feeling and loving heart to imagine what pen or pencil would vainly try to tell.

THE MORNING.

Oh! that I were like the ray of that bright autumnal sun, which, on the morning after the events which I have now related, peeped through the snow-white curtains into "*Cecilia's room,*" and that I could shed the same cheerful light and life over my narrative, as that which this ray shed over the little world in that room! Then would my reader exclaim: "It is the home of comfort and of bliss!" Comfort! Let me see if with the help of the pen of the blessed "Beata Commonplace," which she has bequeathed to me, I can make your lips pronounce this word, dear reader.

But first, a general observation. There is in our language a pleasant little word with a corresponding pleasant idea attached to it, and this is " rum-trefnad,"—"room-cosiness." This word expresses a thing which constitutes a part — a quality of the room itself, and which makes, that in it a feeling of delight and quiet enjoyment steals over our senses; a something which has a soothing influence upon our soul. This lies in a certain comfort displayed in every thing, yet without any thing affected or any thing prim or stiff; a certain *juste-milieu*, bright, cheerful, genial, which we feel instinctively, but cannot describe, and which, I believe, strikes us in its refreshing delight, especially where a gentle, order-loving woman has set the impress of her own inward being upon the outer world in which she moves.

In the room now arranged and decorated *con amore* by the two sisters, and which had been hitherto left empty in order one day to be occupied by Cecilia, this kind of comfort was found. Genial warmth, pure air, pervaded by a slight fragrance of flowers; furniture of a graceful, simple, and commodious form; a proper arrangement in every thing, so that one found a chair in the very place where one wished to sit down, where nothing stood in one's way when one moved about the floor. Not the slightest particle of dust on the green carpet; on the bright polished tables, not the smallest speck. Harmony in all the colors, every thing was pleasant, and the large looking-glass did not, as they sometimes do, reflect a parody of one's face, but showed a true and exact copy of it. Against the bright window-panes monthly roses and mignonette displayed their fresh verdant leaves and their flowers.

It happens sometimes that Nature smiles upon man's joys as if she wished to share and heighten them, like a mother sharing in the sports of her children. Now she was smiling kindly upon the sisters' home; the air was bright and mild; beautiful clouds sailed in stately array over the clear azure of the northern sky. A dazzling carpet of snow lay spread over the landscape, and seemed to be studded with millions of glittering diamonds. A little bird sat in the leafless tree beside one of the windows, singing and chirping so merrily and sweetly that one could almost be tempted to believe him to be one of Nature's messengers, sent to congratulate the reunited sisters. The sun, which I shall now try to resemble in clearness and slow progression, was shining on the breakfast-table, making the dazzlingly white damask table-cloth more dazzling still.

The breakfast cups were standing upon the table, and one with a broad, gold edge stood between the other two; in the crystal cream-jug, in the shape of a nautilus, the rich cream, not whipped, was frothing from its own inherent richness. Snow-white pieces of sugar, not resembling the atoms shaped in primitive chaos, pointed, triangular, and octangular, such as we often see them in the sugar-basins of even fashionable people, but square and even; rusks, which in their light brown color did honor to the flour, the yeast, the oven, and above all to the baker; and then the mysterious coffee-urn, which, by its curling, aromatic steam, gave notice of the comfortable beverage contained within it. Oh! my dear female reader! is not all this enough for " comfort?"

And for happiness? Look at the three reunited sisters, the long lost one now returned, between the two others, at home, in her own home (for her is the cup with the gilt edge intended). Remark in the two elder ones, the moist and happy glance of the eye, the low voice, the tender, broken words, the lip quivering with joy and delight, the warmth and indescribable expression of features which cannot find words and yet so distinctly says: "All that we possess is thine, thou our joy and darling! Thou hast again been given to us — we shall now be able to tend, to love, and to make thee happy!"

And in the third returned one, mark the repose, the hope, the consciousness of home, of peace, of sisterly love, this love so tender, so pure, so rich, so powerful to create happiness. She wants words, but the tear that glides from her eye is one of joy, and speaks volumes. There is a rosy hue on her cheek; there is happiness in her heart; she presses her sisters' hands and feels that she can be happy yet.

And why should she not again be happy? The home which shall again hold her, the port in which she has cast anchor, is that of kindness and peace. Kindness led by wisdom has a great, a wondrous power, and few are the pains which it cannot assuage, few the afflictions the memory of which it cannot gradually efface.

The effect of its power seems natural when one sees and marks how this power is wielded. Life is an aggregate of moments (any body less clever than I am, may make this wise observation); kindness seeks to seize these moments in order to lay down in each of them a seed of comfort for the sufferer.

Now it is called rest, anon cheerfulness, sensation of comfort for body and soul — aye, even flattery; kindness can flatter, but only the unhappy one. It acts like the sun in spring; melts slowly away winter's snow and ice, and sheds warmth everywhere; and then earth begins to get green, and then come the flowers — the wish to live.

In this world, so full of suffering and of enjoyment, of splendor and misery, of greatness and littleness, of strength and weakness, of life and death, above all others, happy is he in whose soul lies active kindness, holiness, and peace. He alone stands in this restless world as if it were a paradise, whose sanctuary no tempests can reach. He alone goes on his way in joy and affliction, in wealth and in poverty, in life and in death, calmly and unwaveringly; suffers and enjoys alike silently, loves, forgives, does good, and feels peace. In order to work on uninterruptedly, in order not to weary in his work for the weal of fellow-men, he does not want the "desire of a name which shall survive him;" not glory's beautiful *vision*, which a great Roman calls "the only passion of the wise," and without which to many a one "the past were nothing, the present a narrow and sterile sphere of action, and the future vanished." No, no laurel-wreath shall be laid upon his forgotten grave; no line in a funeral-oration shall be dedicated to him; no patriotic bard shall sing what he did for his native country. He will be forgotten, he knows it, and yet he labors night and day, and his lamp is not extinguished until with his life's last spark. Here a fellow-creature has been comforted, there another has been given work to do, and with it hope; here a seed has been sown of a future noble laurel, which will confer honor upon his native country and upon mankind; there again a spark has been kindled, a flame kept burning, and here happiness secured — the good has been done; that is enough.

"Doth pure religion gather here below
A harvest of unfruitful treasures? No,
Unpaid, unthanked, she with unceasing toil
Sows seeds of blessedness in sorrow's soil."

Fall freely, O days of our life! — silently, like yellow leaves from life's tree; cover its stem and branches, ye wintry snows; oblivion! take his memory. What to him is all this? The good has been done — that is enough.

Yes, it is enough for *him*, but not for *me*. Like a bee I would wish to fly over the world's fields, to gather honey out of these beautiful, but hidden and modest flowers, and store it in the hives of memory, in order that men might see and taste how sweet it is, and rejoice at it.

I pause. Friendly reader! when I invited thee to enter into my balloon, I promised to carry thee to "the home of comfort and happiness." I have fulfilled my promise, and I will not now, like a honey-bee, persuade thee to a fresh excursion, but I may perhaps during my journey visit thee (unknown to thee and unexpected) to imbibe out of thy life's flower a drop of honey, clear and sweet as that which I got from the sisters.

THE LIGHT-HOUSE.

"Look, Axel, look how the bridal-lights are gleaming upon yonder height! And look how the bridal guests are dancing down below it! And now, behold how the lights themselves are dancing about! Look how they waltz and swing round! How droll! But now, now they become paler — now they die away — now they are gone! Why are the bridal-lights extinguished, Axel? Why has the chandelier up there gone out? Ah, see, now they return! There the bridal-lights are again, so bright, so joyous, and they shine upon the waves far, far out at sea, and upon you too, and make you look so handsome! But, Axel, why are they gone sometimes, and why do they then come back?"

And the young wife, who, herself radiant as a happy bride, thus asked, stood fondly leaning upon her husband, while she pointed to a group of lights which were lit, as it were, high up in the air, shining against the dark evening sky, and slowly swinging round the same point, now hiding their lustre, and anon shining forth in full splendor, throwing a bright gleam over the rolling billows of the sea, and into the silent sombre room in which this new married couple stood at the window of their new home.

"It is a light-house with a revolving light, little one," said her husband, amused at his young wife's ignorance. "It revolves in this way in order to tell the sea-farer, in the night, where he is; and the shadowy forms which you see moving about below the flames, are the men who kindle the beacon. Do you understand?"

"Oh, no; they are bonfires, they are bridal-lights," said Ellina, smiling. "Oh, how I love them, the beautiful friendly lights. How pleasant it will be to see them every evening and every night. They remind me of our wedding-night, Axel. Oh, those lights! I cannot forget how they dazzled my eyes when I entered the room to be married. For some time I could not see any thing. But soon I fancied that every thing, that the whole world shone. There were so many, many lights!"

"But you yourself shone brighter than all the bridal-lights. I saw not them, I saw only you;" said the fond husband, pressing his young wife to his bosom.

But she could at this moment see and speak only of the bridal-lights on the height, and however Axel tried to explain the phenomena of the revolving light, its fires and reflectors, still Ellina would inwardly make an explanation of it of her own. And at night, on her pillow, sleep she could not, but was constantly looking at the light as it revolved, now illuminating her room, and anon leaving it in utter darkness; she would listen to the wind as with deep-drawn breath it was sighing round their dwelling; listen to the monotonous rushing of the sea as the waves unceasingly broke upon the rocks. For it was now autumn, and the weather was tempestuous. And this ceaseless again and again, this endless heaving without rest, without aim, awoke in the soul of the young wife thoughts and presentiments almost sad. It was the first night in her new home.

In a peaceful home in one of the most beautiful valleys of the south of Sweden, surrounded by loving parents, sisters, and youthful companions, she had dreamt a quiet dream of childhood. There was in the neighborhood a large town with a university, and from it came voices and visions of fountains of wisdom, of the fine arts, and of intellectual ornaments of life. Much that was beautiful Ellina beheld around her in Nature and in her home; but she knew that beyond this her quiet world, there existed one still more beautiful and splendid, which she would see when she had grown to be a woman. And thus the child grew up in joyous presentiment of life, thinking constantly,

"When I am older, then I shall see, then I shall learn much more; then will come something still better, something more beautiful still." But what this was to be, she did not clearly understand. And what young girl has a name for her beautiful visions? But it was to be something in feeling, something in thought, which made her life seem to stand forth in radiant glory; which let her step forth out of darkness into the light of life and joy; which answered all her young soul's silent but earnest questions and aspirations; something of that kind it would be, something of that kind would come. Thus thought Ellina, and thus almost all happy young girls think. And then came a young man and offered the lovely young girl his hand. Her parents said "Yes," for Axel Ern was an excellent young man; Ellina did not say him "Nay;" for bridegroom, bridal-wreath, wedding, it was that which was to come first, which was to be the commencement of the brilliant vision. Her parents would be so happy; Axel would be so happy, and how then would not she also be happy! To be sure, she was still rather young, and was reluctant to leave her parents and brothers and sisters, but they all said that it was to be, that she would make them all happy, and she said "Yes;" became affianced, courted, teased, and adorned. And then came the wedding; and that evening when Ellina saw "so many, many lights," when she thought that a life of light was to begin for her. And so she accompanied her husband to the place where he had built his nest.

It was situated amongst rocks, surrounded by the sea, in the neighborhood of one of the fortresses on the western coast of Sweden. I shall not say whether it was the fortress of Elfsborg, or Carlstén, or Bohus. But the place was far distant from Ellina's childhood's home, and very different from its beautiful valleys. *There* were leafy forests and nightingales; *here*, only islands, and barren, gray rocks, and round them the surging, dangerous Cattegat. Such is in general the rocky coast of Bohuslän. Many find

Nature there ugly, terrible. repulsive. I love her. To me she has in her something more attractive, more pleasing, than landscapes of soft verdure, cultivation, and fertility, which one can, as it were, look quite through. Reader, canst thou love a nature without mystery? I cannot do it, and I feel sure that thou canst not either do it, in case it were question of a human nature, of a human soul. But beware of saying (I am now speaking to myself), this nature has no mystery! Is there, I ask, generally speaking, any human soul devoid of an unknown depth? Say then: This soul has not yet had its Whitsun festival; no tongue of fire has breathed upon it with reviving breath, and one knows not what is in it.

But to return to the islands on the rock-bound coast of Bohuslän, and their mystery. They possess such a mystery: they resemble those human natures, whose surface is hard and harsh, but hide within fertile and beautiful valleys. Approach nearer to these granite islands, these naked rocks, and you will not find one amongst them which has not grassy spots and beautiful flowery paths. These gray rocks drink in the sun's rays, and long retain their fire in their granite bosom. They communicate it to the soil round their foot, and in their bosom and out of it blooms forth life in its fullness. Out of every crevice honeysuckle and blackberry bushes spring forth in wild profusion, encircling with their flowery arms the mossy boulders, and transforming them into beautiful monuments upon the graves of the ancient Vikings. Bouquets of golden "Iris" and of wild roses are blooming amongst the granite rocks, and high up on their rugged tops, where only the goat and the sea-mew can find a footing, tiny white and yellow flowers are nodding in the breeze, whilst the wild breakers of the Cattegat are foaming round their base. Even upon the smallest of these rocky islets the sheep find nourishment and fatten, and upon the larger islands one finds hidden from the eyes of the world a small blooming paradise, full of roses, lilies, and fruit, where some son of Adam is living with his Eve, peacefully and — happy. We would gladly believe the latter if there were not some peculiar circumstances attached to these secluded paradises. Things did not turn out quite well in the first one — we know that — and they do not turn out much better in the later ones, provided man remains there long. Life in solitary islands is rarely beneficial. The sameness in the surrounding objects, the want of diversion, of amusement, of something new, of intercourse with the great, changing world, cramps the soul, and feelings and thoughts become one-sided on certain points and there stick fast, as it were. We see this in Iceland; we see how in Corsica, under the ceaseless and repeated pressure of many years, and the beating of the same bitter billows upon the heart, secret animosity grew into hatred, hatred into revenge and sanguinary retribution. We see it even to this day in the Farroe Islands, in the silent, half-witted forms wandering about amongst the mist-enveloped hills, and who have become such, because when misfortunes and adversity came, they had no place to go to, nowhere to seek a refuge from these gloomy impressions, these frowning rocks, and heavy, misty atmosphere. The mails from the outer world are sometimes from seven to eight months in reaching them.

But loving solitude, as I do, and the undisturbed communion of the soul with itself, I cannot pursue the argument, to which these examples lead, any further than by saying, that it is not good for man to be alone for any length of time.

And so let us return to one young couple — Axel and Ellina. It was as if an eagle had carried a pigeon to his eyrie. The strange and solemn surrounding scenery, the solitude, the roar and turmoil of the breakers, the autumn gales — all this filled Ellina's bosom with fear and nameless anxiety. But she had her own home — and there is no woman who does not feel this as a blessing — she had her household duties to attend to in this home. And then there was the light-house, the revolving bridal-lights on high, which reminded her every dark night of the most beautiful evening in her life, her wedding, when she saw " so many lights, oh, so many lights." And there was first and last, and above all, her husband, and this husband was a noble-hearted man, and still more he was an excellent husband.

It is perhaps as well that I avail myself of this opportunity to make a confession, which has frequently hovered over my lips, but which I have hitherto hesitated to give to the world, out of fear that I thereby should incur the hatred of all married ladies. I dread this even now, but — never mind, I must unburden my heart. I confess, therefore, that I have never found, that I never find a man more amiable than when he is — a married man, that is to say, a *good* married man. In my eyes a man is never more noble, more perfect, than when he is a married man, a tender husband, a father of a family, supporting with vigor and with manly kindness his wife and the domestic circle, which, by his entering into the wedded state, has closed round him as a part of his home, of his world. He becomes thereby not only more worthy of love, but in reality also more dignified. Therefore the excellence of a man consists in his being a good married man, and only with such a one am I tempted to fall in love. But this being strictly forbidden, and Moses, as well as all other legislators, having pronounced it to be a sin, all married ladies will consider it a sacred duty to stone me.

Nevertheless, I cannot help this. My only hope of reconciling the offended parties lies in proceeding in my confession: that no happiness makes me more happy to behold, no love touches me more deeply, than the mutual love of husband and wife. I am myself astonished at this; for it seems to me that being myself not married, I have very little to do with that happiness. However, so it is, and so it has always been. I was yet a child, when one day I saw my father enter my mother's room, laying down before her a present, which gave her great pleasure. She took hold of his hand, and kissed it, and words and looks of love passed between them. Never shall I forget the sensation of happiness which filled my soul, where I stood alone in a corner of the room, playing with my doll. It was as if heaven had lighted upon my heart. I stood silent, overwhelmed with the power of this sensation, when the eyes of my parents discovered me. "You blush so prettily, little one!" said my mother, tenderly, and my father came and laid his hand gently upon my head. Never shall I forget this.

Something of this first sensation I experience still, when I witness the happiness of husband and wife some distance beyond the honey-moon.

. . . .

Ellina was very young when, for the first time in her new home, she beheld the "bridal-lights on the height." Many years had rolled past since, and Ellina was now no longer young. She was now the mother of seven boys. Serious illness, many cares, much work of all kinds, and narrow circumstances, had wrought a great change in her — inwardly as well as outwardly. But she was still a pleasing woman, though the bloom of her youth was gone; and her soul — that soul which had foreboded so much that is great and beautiful in life, which believed that it would progress from one light to another, until the whole world and her own heart, her own life, should stand glorified in radiant light — had said farewell to all its hopes, one by one, had said farewell to all its dawning thoughts, until it had spun itself round by innumerable threads into the web of her domestic duties and cares, which were renewed every day, like the beating of the waves upon the rocks, like the revolving shadows of the light-house, like the deep-drawn sighs of the autumn wind. And Ellina faithfully spun her thread, faithfully fulfilled her duties. But happy she was not, for the road of duty, although it certainly leads to happiness, as the working-days of the week lead to the Sabbath, is yet not happiness itself. Ellina was no longer merry, as formerly; she felt that something living and beautiful, which in days gone past was within her, was gradually becoming buried under the weight of years and petty cares. She found herself changing sadly. She had imagined life in general, and her own life in particular, as something quite different. Sometimes she felt an indescribable longing to weep over herself.

It is thus with a great many women. They feel themselves born to conceive life and things in beautiful harmony. They believe themselves progressing in knowledge, in love, in enjoyment of all that is good and beautiful, as in an elevating metamorphosis. But life's current comes and bears them away to barren and desolate regions. They are spun round by earthly anxieties; are surrounded by the trammels of petty cares, of trifles, of mean interests, and upon these at last they themselves spin. Then life loses by degrees its beauty, the mind its rosy tint, the soul becomes oppressed, their temper soured, and their horizon becomes narrower and more dim. In some silent hour perchance they look round now and then; look into their own soul with melancholy surprise, and exclaim: "Was *this* to be the end of it? Is life nothing else? Was it for nothing else that I was born?" And they recall the illusions, the hopes of their youth. "Dreams!" they say, and they suppress a sigh, wipe away a tear, and weave again the daily web, until they have woven their shroud, and their earthly days are closed.

But such is the fate not only of many women, no, it is the fate also of a great many men, with warm, rich souls. At the yard-measure, at the needle, at the weighing-scales, at the writing desk, under the withering influence of dead figures from morning to night, they feel themselves gradually becoming blunted and like a stock; they feel the poesy, the sensitive, loving, creative spirit within them, buried even before it has had time to live. Also they sometimes look up sadly, asking: "Why do I live? Is life nothing else?"

These all are souls awaiting their Whitsuntide. Expectant souls! could I but let you feel and believe, as firmly as I do it myself, that it is coming, and the glory of its reality shall exceed your most beautiful dreams.

Some of my fair readers have probably already guessed, from the change which I have mentioned as having taken place in Ellina, that her husband and the first conjugal happiness also had changed. It was so. What husband and what marriage remains the same during a period of nineteen or twenty years? Ellina's husband was a noble and good man, as I have said, and I repeat it. But still he was too one-sided manly, as Ellina was too one-sided womanly. His was a nature energetic, practical, looking at the outer world; hers poetical, sensitive, living in the world within her. In several points husband and wife never harmonized. They harmonized less and less, when, during succeeding years and with an increasing family, the support of the same necessarily claimed a greater exertion of his industry, and when his time and his mind became more and more taken up by outward, practical life. She felt herself more and more lonely, and too proud and too wise to complain of the unsatisfied wants of her soul and heart, she shut herself up more within herself. She became still more like the steep, rugged rock; she resembled the solitary lily near it. Besides, there was between them another subject of dispute and discontent, which, though frequently dropped, was still as often renewed. And thus they became gradually estranged without clearly knowing how; between them rose a something, a darkening cloud, an invisible wall, — something nameless, they knew not what, which made them more and more strangers to each other.

Husbands and wives! ye who have wandered together through life some distance beyond the "halcyon-days," tell me, is it not an every-day story, this one which I have sketched here; is it not the history of nine married couples out of ten? Where the mutual relation proceeds in this downward direction, married life is transformed into that *Dead Sea* on whose shore no flower is thriving, no bird is singing; over whose surface pestilential vapors are hanging, and in whose depths one can occasionally descry the ruins of a once beautiful, but accursed city. Married life is as little stationary on earth as any other life. Within it a slow but continual change upwards or downwards takes place, according to the will or the fault of the husband or the wife. The causes may be different in all marriages, but in all there are moments, crises, from which we can guess how time advances, what " the clock strikes." And in them all arises a temptation, when the first flame has burnt down, to let the deeper union dissolve, let the spirit fly. And it will do so.

> " Should not the heavenly Amor then
> Hold fast his Psyche with new bridal kiss,"

and consecrate her to a higher, truer union?

There will not be wanting Nicodemus'-heads in the world, who will ask doubtingly, " How can these things be?"

We have little else to reply hereto than this: That we know that they are; but we know no other fundamental cause for it than the one upon which every good result depends, the driving-wheel in life's steam-engine, the axis of life's revolving-light, the earnest, hearty *will* of the parties concerned. But to continue my story. I wish (I whisper this to myself) that I could avoid lengthening it by reflections, which the reader can make himself without my assistance.

The first subject of discord which arose between Axel and Ellina, and which we have alluded to, was the education of the boys. The father averred that the mother petted, indulged, in a word, spoilt them. Very possibly he was right. However, I believe that she did it in the right way. The boys were obedient and adored their mother. No *really* spoilt children do this. But the father was too severe, where he found the mother too weak. He was very anxious to send the boys out of the house into a good school, that they might " learn something," and that they might " be made men of." Six eaglets had already left the eyrie and winged their flight to distant parts. The mother's heart had said " Nay " to each flight, but her reason had said " Aye," and so it was done as the father wished it. The youngest boy alone remained now. "He also," said the father, " must go away, must out in the world." But now the mother said " No, he was still too young, too tender, too weak." — "Just therefore," the father argued, "he must go away from home, out amongst other boys, to lead a more vigorous, a fresher life; the boy was already nearly ten years old." The father's will triumphed over the mother's; but when he tore her youngest one out of her arms, he broke the thread which tied her heart to her husband. So Ellina felt, for she fancied that he had used her harshly. When she thus found herself alone, she found herself doubly alone. She had not any longer a little curly head to fondle when she went to bed at night; no warm, tiny breath near her pillow rocked her heart to rest and sleep; no little arms full of trust encircled her neck night and morning; no childish prattle in the day made her forget what her soul had lost. Gone was every thing, and the worst of it was, that also Axel was away, not only from home, but also — from her heart. She felt it so empty that it almost frightened her. Yes, it is probable that she would have borne the absence of her boys and her loneliness very differently, if she only could have held fast in her heart her husband's image, as bright as it was in days gone by.

Again it was autumn, and all the domestic duties for the autumn had to be attended to, all those duties which Ellina had never loved, and which now appeared to her more irksome than ever. Bullocks and sheep were to be killed for the winter, meat to be salted down, bread to be baked, sausages and black-puddings to be made, candles to be moulded, etc., etc. The autumnal gales came on, the billows roared and thundered against the rocks, the wind howled round their dwelling, and the lights in the lighthouse revolved with the same lights and the same shadows. This eternal sameness had an almost suffocating effect upon Ellina's desponding mind.

Axel stayed away a long time, — much longer than was required for placing the little boy. When he returned, he brought with him three strange gentlemen as guests. Ellina did not belong to the impossible women (read: *impossible women*) who make impossibilities and grim faces, when occasionally their husbands come home to dinner or supper, bringing with them an unexpected guest. But three at once, and at this moment too, when her heart was sore and heavy and the larder empty — that was too much! When Axel folded her warmly and affectionately in his arms, she stood in this embrace cold and pale as the lily in the mountain-cleft, and gave him no pressure of the hand, no kiss in return. He turned therefore to his merry guests, occupying himself with them. Ellina went out to arrange about the supper and to prepare what else the new-comers might require. Perchance husband and wife felt dimly that it would not be good for them to be now left alone together.

When the goblet is full, it wants only one drop more to make it overflow. This drop came now to Ellina in the shape of her help in house and kitchen, — Miss Unready, the gentlest, most faithful, and also one of the most efficient persons in the world, but who had a great inclination to look at every thing from a tragic point of view, and who in all emergencies always began by saying that "she knew of no living means," on account of which Ellina used to call her in earnest and in jest, "my Miss Unready." But as Ellina herself always found out some ways and means, and

Miss Unready really excelled in doing all that her mistress desired her to do, they managed beautifully together; although Ellina's patience was put to the proof now and then, when she spoke about the dinner, and "Miss Unready" stood before her, straight as a post, rubbing her long thin arms, " knowing of no living means," and having nothing to suggest except — spinach. If the moon and all her supposed unknown inhabitants had tumbled down upon earth and into Miss Unready's kitchen, she would have looked scarcely more irresolute, terrified, and bewildered than now, when the master of the house came home unexpectedly with three guests; and of all evenings in the world just on that evening, when preparations were to be made for baking bread for the winter, and when the larder had not yet been stocked with its winter provisions.

At the sight of her Ellina could scarcely suppress her vexation, and she said to her in a half angry tone: "It is no use, Unready, looking like misery itself, but advise me now what you think we can have for supper."

Miss Unready rubbed her right arm, that hung straight down, with her left hand up and down, and down and up, but " knew of no living means."

Ellina: " Have we got nothing in the larder; cannot you invent something, which can be ready in a short time?"

Unready rubbed her left arm with her right hand up and down, and stammered: " Yes, spinach!"

Ellina, impatiently: " Spinach! — but how can you, Unready, think that four gentlemen can be satisfied with spinach?"

And it ended as usual: Ellina herself had to find ways and means, and to be this night both head and hand in the kitchen, because Miss Unready had completely lost her head, and, besides, every cranny, bin, and shelf in the larder was unusually empty.

Ellina succeeded only with great difficulty in providing what was necessary for the moment; but when supper was finished, and she saw the four gentlemen seated at the whist-table with their cigars and punch, she drew a long breath, bade the whist-players and smokers a good night, and retired to her room. She felt weary both in body and soul.

Her soul was wearied, yes, but yet like an agitated sea. Within it moved a something which Ellina had never before experienced. It was something like discontent and bitterness against her husband — voices rose out of these agitated waves, whispering: "Has it come to this? Am I to him nothing but a housekeeper, a servant, destined to attend to his whims, his pleasures, his comforts? My feelings, my pain, my heart's life — do not they deserve some consideration, some forbearance? Am I really so fallen? And he — he who " —

"Be silent!" Ellina interrupted resolutely the resentful voices, pressing her hands hard upon her beating heart, as if she would have stifled its throbs; "be silent! not a word against him; whatever he may be, whatever I may become to him, I shall always know how to fulfill my duties faithfully. He shall not see the agony of my soul, the cloud in my heart. He shall miss nothing; he shall never find cause of complaint!"

With this determination Ellina tried to calm her feelings. She covered up the windows closely, so that "the bridal-lights on the height" might not shine into her room. She would not see them now. Chilled, indifferent, and sad in her mind, she laid herself down upon her sofa, shut her eyes, trying to feel nothing, think nothing — to sleep. In vain. The misery in the depths of her heart was too great. Again and again returned the galling wave; again and again was heard the complaining, resentful voice, and heavy tears gathered under her burning eyelids. Every moment she felt more uneasy, more unhappy — she could not rest, she could not even pray.

When she again opened her sleepless eyes, she found her room light, — not from daylight, because it was now near midnight; not from the unsteady gleam of the revolving light, but from a mild, steady, though faint glimmer. Ellina rose, went to the window, and drew up the blind. She saw then that the clouds, which for many days had hung like a heavy canopy over the sky, had been dispersed, and had given way to the moon, which now in her first quarter, stood with her pointed horns turned upwards, bright and beautiful over the distant hill-tops. The gale had subsided. Ellina opened the window. Warm, and refreshing at the same time, the wind fanned her burning temples. The moon's rays fell so peacefully upon rocks and waves, on the greensward along the shore, and on the dew-drops hanging on the leaves of the trees. It was as if they had whispered to her: "Come out! come out!"

Ellina threw round her a large shawl, tied a veil over her head and stepped out. As she passed her husband's door she stopped involuntarily. She heard that he was still up, and she thought: "If I were to go in and lean my head upon his shoulder, and — I did not receive him in a loving manner to-day. Perhaps this has given him pain. If I were" — "No," said another voice within her; "he cares little for me and he does not deserve it." And she passed on silently and quickly. How many good feelings, how many a moment of reconciliation does not thus pass by disregarded, and time passes also, and then it is too late.

Ellina stood upon the terrace near the shore, outside their house. It was a beautiful September night, such as we see so frequently on the west coast of Sweden. A repose had come over Nature after the last days of stormy weather. The leaves dropped down yellow from the trees, and the flowers upon their stalks drooped their withered heads; but in the glittering drops which trembled in them, glimmered the moon's silvery beams, and they stirred gently under the caresses of the balmy breeze. It was as if some power of love was here busy to reconcile, to beautify. Even the billows of the Cattegat seemed charmed;

they rose and fell slowly, as if lovingly murmuring, and laid themselves to rest upon the granite bosom, which so often had chafed and broken their surge.

Ellina contemplated the fallen leaves, the withered flowers, the soft moonbeams, the charmed billows, and a feeling of indescribable pain, at this moment nearly approaching to despair, overpowered her. She, who was ordinarily so calm, now wrung her hands, raised them on high, and exclaimed, while long suppressed, bitter tears, chased each other down her cheeks: —

"Oh, that I were a seared leaf, a withered flower! Oh, that I might fall like them! that I might die before my heart dies, before I become wretched and embittered! Father in heaven! take me to your mansions, for I have done with earth. Gone away are my children, and my husband loves me no longer. Youth, health, joy, love of life, love, and faith — all are gone, gone forever!"

But before her outstretched arms had again sunk down, other arms seized her, and a voice whispered in her ear: " What is gone, gone forever?"

It was Axel's voice, but Ellina was too agitated to be able to make any answer. She turned her face away from him and wept, only wept, while he still was holding her in his arms. When she seemed to be a little more composed, he said : " Come, go with me to our resting-place on 'chat-island.' The night is fine, and I have something to say to you."

Ellina followed him down some steps into the little green-painted gondola, the boys' boat, the " North Star," which now, impelled by Axel's powerful stroke of the oars, flew swiftly across the calm waters.

They sat both silent — Ellina with downcast, tearful eyes; she felt that Axel's glance was resting upon her, and her heart beat in uneasy expectation. It was not long before they arrived at a small rocky islet, higher than the others with which the coast was dotted. A high granite wall constituted its protection against the north and east, gathering on the south the rays of the sun as in a focus. Nature herself had cut out a "*causeuse*" in the rock, a small seat for two persons, which Axel had made more comfortable, and round which he had trailed the luxuriant ivy and honeysuckle. This he had done during the earlier period of his love, and he had frequently brought his young wife thither. Many a dark evening, when the sea was glittering with phosphoric light, and the wind was softly whispering, had they sat there exchanging words of love and looking with hopeful, bright eyes at future, coming days, while the light-house on the fortress threw its dazzling light upon the rising and falling billows.

A very long time had elapsed since they last had been there — many years.

The honeysuckle and ivy tendrils grew as luxuriantly as ever, but they were hanging round in wild confusion for want of a tending hand.

Husband and wife sat again side by side, with the wide sea around them, over which a gentle breeze came sweeping to them which seemed to whisper: Speak! speak!

And Axel spoke, saying, while he drew Ellina closer to him: " Ellina, what is it that is gone, gone forever?"

Oh, that voice! It sounded as in former happy days. Twenty years gone by, rolled in a moment past Ellina's soul. She leant her forehead upon Axel's shoulder, saying only, " Axel, do not ask me!" but she felt conscious that he had read her heart, and she therefore added, in a scarcely audible voice, " you know it."

Again they were silent, but the friendly breeze whispered: Speak! speak!

" Yes, I know it," he said slowly — " yes, I know how it is. I have seen it for some time. Ellina, you cannot any longer live here. You must be nearer your children, nearer objects and persons who can give you what your heart, what your soul, longs for, and what I cannot give."

His voice trembled. Axel's nature was like unto the scenery of his birthplace. A granite nature was his, but when it revealed itself, life was blooming forth luxuriantly; paradise opened itself. Generally taciturn, he then became eloquent.

"Do not believe," he said with a violent exertion, which caused his cheeks to become pale, and forced the tears into his piercing eagle eyes, "do not believe, Ellina, that I am blind to the dissimilarity between us, and that I do not see that in much I am not sufficient for you. You stand above me in many things; you have more exalted and noble aspirations, which it is beyond my power to satisfy. I have sometimes endeavored to conceal this from myself, because it has pained me. I have tried to harden myself against this feeling and against you; I have walked as if in a fog, and placed a rock upon my bosom to appear strong and manly. Your gentleness and your tears have blasted the rock. O Ellina! I see by your pale face that you are unhappy, and that it is I, who — but no! I will not make you unhappy, I, who have sworn to live for your happiness. Already, when last time I had to go away from you, my resolution was formed, and I will now tell you what it is. I have applied for some other employment and to be removed from here. If my application should be granted, which I hope it will be, you will then be near your childhood's home, near the town in which our boys are, and where you will be able to find that circle of friends and those pleasures which you long for. You will then be able to see our sons once a week, if you wish it; they shall often come to see us. Believe me! I will not remove them from your influence; I only wanted to remove them from too effeminate an education at home. I know that there is in life but one true high-school, — that in which the heart is educated, and to do this a mother's heart is required. I have long been desirous of removing from here, although it cannot perhaps be done without some serious pecuniary sacrifices. It is possible that I may have hitherto overestimated them. And now, if my plans should not after all be realized, if the hopes which I have raised should after all be disappointed, or be so, at any rate for some time, will you submit to this patiently, Ellina; will you still try to be happy, to love me — as formerly?"

"No, not as formerly, no, but a thousand times more!" ejaculated Ellina with overflowing heart. "Oh! why speak of missing, of waiting, of disappointed hopes now, when I see how you think of me, when I see that you love me!"

"But how — how could you have doubted?"

"Alas, Axel! you have been so very much changed; therefore every thing round me has become changed."

"And you, Ellina, have you always been the same as formerly? Have you not often been cold, when I approached you with warm feelings? Have you not in later years often stood aloof from me, when — and this very evening — yes, *I* might have reason to doubt that you still love me."

Ellina was silent and looked down. She felt conscious that it was as Axel had said.

He went on: "I am too proud, Ellina, and perhaps too sensitive also, to enforce a love which is not voluntarily yielded to me. I have stood aloof, because — you stood aloof. But perchance, I have been more proud than I ought to have been, more distant than I wanted to be. It is difficult, Ellina, to see how far we err. But one thing is certain. I cannot, I will not go on as we have done now for some time. Give me your hand, and — if you can do it — give me back your heart; read mine and you will see what I mean, and — pardon me."

"Oh, hush!" said Ellina, kissing away the words from his lips. "Oh, say nothing more! Oh! that I had rightly understood you, you would not then have had any reason to complain. But now — God bless you for having said what you have said! Be it with our removal from hence as it may, good will come of it, I feel; for you have again taken up your abode in my heart, and I feel again at home there. And now — look! I am yours, your wife, your servant, every thing you wish, Axel! I feel that you again are mine. Come death, come life, cares, sorrows, still I shall be happy in you, in your kindness, in your love, with the certainty that you are mine and that I am yours."

When such words have been uttered between husband and wife, there is not much more to say. There is then only one language, silent yet eloquent, one which can express the fullness of the feelings. Ellina felt the glowing words fall like a dew upon her throbbing forehead, upon her cheeks, upon her eyelids. Every wrinkle of time, and sorrow seemed to be effaced by these words. It was as if she had become young again. Paradise was again blooming within and round the two.

When Axel rowed Ellina back to their house, the moon had gone down behind the hills and the night had become quite dark. But the sea shone and sparkled at every stroke, and fiery pearls dropped from the oars. Over the heads of husband and wife the stars peeped forth out of the fleecy clouds, and "the bridal-lights on the height" shone and danced brighter than usual against the dark sky. "The bridal lights" shone again in Ellina's heart, and everywhere, in the sky and on the earth, she beheld again as on her own bridal-night, "so many, oh, so many lights."

And it was never more to be extinguished, the steady beam which fell into her heart; its waves might rise or fall, but light would always be there. The consciousness of this filled Ellina with celestial, child-like joy. Yes, she was so happy, so confident, that she became almost like a child. She toyed with the glittering ripples — they also were full of love's life — she splashed her hands in them, and made them glisten and glitter, and in wanton delight she sprinkled Axel's hands and face with water, while he was paying her back the showers of fire and water which she gave him. Their eyes sparkled in the dark, starry night — their soul's wedding-night.

But when Ellina on the following morning entered her kitchen, she looked like the rosy tint of the young day, illuminating "Miss Unready's" soul and mind so that they threw a reflected light into the darkest corners of the cellars and pantry. Ways and means for every thing were found at once. "Spinach!" No question about spinach any longer; no thought of poor spinach, mean, miserable food! Sausages, roast joints, the fish of the sea, the birds of the air, came as if by enchantment. Kitchen and table became full. Nothing was wanting, or if any thing was wanting it was not noticed, which is better still.

And they who know what a mighty wizard a joyful stout heart is, and how it knows the primordial word which is the key to and can command every thing, will not be astonished at this.

I will not tell you any thing about the projected removal, whether it took place or not, because I do not know any thing about it. But I must tell you that within a year a girl was born, who was christened after father and mother, Axellina. And if you should want to know how the sun's light and joy can become, as it were, embodied in a human face, I would then show you the face of this child, show you its bright curls and laughing eyes. No language is more incomprehensible and more charming than the words which flow from its little mouth, chirping bird eloquence. The honeysuckle tendrils cannot be more wild and lissom in their growth than this little girl. You should see her in thousand graceful, ever varying attitudes, twining her arms around her father, or playing at his feet. And if ever a strong, firm man can be conquered and ensnared by the witcheries of a little child, it is Axel Ern, when he holds in his arms the wild, supple, laughing, charming little girl, pressing her in silent eloquence to his heart, or sitting at night beside her little crib, hearing her saying her prayers, while from her — *he* again learns to pray. Yes, he is not a whit better than Hercules spinning at the feet of the young Omphale. I think that he is even a little worse and more weak, being fettered by a yet weaker and more childish being.

Ellina threatens sometimes — and you may guess how seriously — to send the little girl out of the house to a boarding-school, as otherwise, " she will be perfectly spoilt " by her father, and she ought in time to learn to become " a sensible woman." The father says nothing to these threats, but he lays the child in the mother's arms and then embraces them both. He is meanwhile very anxious for all the boys to come home during the holidays.

Ellina is no longer pale and suffering. She is a blooming middle-aged matron, with the calmness of happiness in her whole being, and she likes to say to young married women: " When the time of first love is passed, then comes something better still, something more beautiful; then comes the *second love*, the faithful friendship, which never changes, which makes every thing bright and peaceful. But we ought to manage so that it *does* come. Then every thing changes, every thing turns to the best."

Miss Unready was also changed, metamorphosed into Mrs. Sheriff Ready. But whether her spinachomania has also changed, I am not aware.

The eaglets have grown up to be young eagles. When from their flight over earth's or thought's sea they revisit their eyrie with tales from foreign lands, and with new discoveries in science and art, then much is added to the wealth within it.

> But Bohuslän's rocks, they stand now as before;
> The waves of the Cattegat flow as of yore ;
> To-day they roll on
> As in centuries gone.

The flames of the light-house — kind reader, pray
Think of the nuptial torches so gay,
They 're turning and turning and turning to-day.

THE EAGLESS.

IT was morning, and the sun was shining brightly. The Eagle's sister sat in her eyrie upon the cliff, looking with longing eyes into bright space, involuntarily raising her wings, untried as yet. Proudly heaved her breast.

"Towards the sun! Up, towards the sun!" thus a voice seemed to say within her. "Why should not I also see the glorious one nearer, bathe my eye in his light, and drink strength from his rays? Why should not the pilgrimage of the Eagless to the sun be praised in song, as well as that of the Eagle? My sight is strong, my wings young, my will powerful; up, up, towards the sun, towards the sun!"

She flew. The morning, the sunlight, and the freshness of endless space, the feeling of youthful vigor and energy filled her breast with delight.

In order to rest herself awhile, to look round and enjoy the new, beautiful life, she perched upon the top of an oak.

In the woods below all kinds of birds had flocked together. They had witnessed her bold flight.

"Trillili, well, well, trillili!" sang the larks, exultingly; "fly on, Eagless, thou wilt be the glory of thy sex!"

"Courage!" cried a noble heron, "courage, my little friend!"

"Hail, sister, hail!" sang the white swans, sailing among verdant islets.

"Croak, croak!" croaked the crow, "that flight is dangerous; take care of yourself, my dear young lady."

"Coo-coo-coo!" cooed the dove; "why dost thou seek happiness so far away? Stay at home in your nest; warm yourself beside your mate; hatch your eggs and feed your young ones, and you may live many, many years! Coo-coo-coo!"

"Kle-vit, kle-vit!" screeched an owl. "Some mischief will be done here."

"Some mischief will be done here," repeated starlings and parrots.

"All goes well, all goes well!" cried a flock of merry wild geese; "very well!"

But a young and noble Eagle came and perched beside the Eagless, saying gently and tenderly: "Thy flight is beautiful, but the road is long and thy strength is not yet sufficient.[1] Let me accompany thee; when thou beginnest to break down, my wing shall support thee; it shall shade thy eyes when the sun begins to dazzle them; and when danger approaches, or when thou tirest in thy flight, I will lead thee to my safe nest, yonder, upon that far off cliff, and stay beside thee!"

Gratefully declining his offer, the Eagless bent her head to the noble bird: "I will be alone," she answered; "alone will I work out my destiny!" The cries of the other birds she took no notice of. She hastened only to the voice in her own breast: "Up towards the sun, towards the sun!"

And again she raised her wings. Enraptured by the sun, by the freshness and joy, she rose higher and higher, far away from all the others.

Sadly and gloomily the young Eagle shook his wings, turned his eye away from the daring one, chose another mate, and conducted her to his eyrie on the distant cliff.

Meanwhile, the Eagless pursued her flight alone, and approached nearer the sun. But alas! her eyes were suddenly dazzled, her head became dizzy, and she could not any longer clearly see her road. Still she flew on, but unconsciously she had lowered her flight towards earth. A sportsman saw her; he aimed at her with his murderous weapon; he fired, and — the lead was buried near the Eagless' heart.

[1] Ornithologists must excuse the authoress for having in her poetical allegory depreciated the physical strength of the Eagless.

On she flew still, but not upwards; she flew towards the deep, deep forest. She felt herself struck by death.

Far into the dark forest she flew, and the dark forest closed rustling around her, concealing her from all eyes.

With bleeding bosom and a tear in her dimmed eye, the Eagless perched upon a fir-tree's branch. "Happy for me," she sighed, "that I die unlamented and alone!"

Then she heard the dove coo to her young ones: "Daughters of mine! Do not do as the Eagless! The proud silly one will surely come to grief in her flight. Stay at home in your valley, in your peaceful nests, and you will live many, many years."

"I have erred!" said the Eagless, but proudly her heart swelled under the deadly wound; "from youthful presumption have I erred and am punished. But silently I submit to my fate; may others be more happy! I do not complain, for I have beheld the sun nearer!"

"Kle-vit, kle-vit!" screeched the owls.

"Kle-vit, kle-vit!" repeated the starlings and parrots.

"All goes well, all goes well!" tauntingly sang the wild geese, while they sailed away over the forest.

"I die," said the Eagless, with expiring strength; "I die, but — the sun! I have beheld the sun nearer! Happy for me!"

And from the branch on which she had perched, she fell down with expanded wings, and was no more.

THE NOVEL AND THE NOVELS.

"This is the time for Novels; but what is to come after the Novels?" a literary man said to me one day, half in jest. I do not now exactly remember what I answered — something thoughtless, I believe; but I began afterwards to ponder on this subject — the Novels.

I had read, nay devoured, in the course of my life — I cannot tell how many dozen novels, and I had wept and laughed over them, loved, reveled, lived, and almost died in them; my soul has transmigrated through their Sophias, Julias, Rosas, Amandas, Alices, Elizas, until I was on the point of losing myself, when, in a fright, I vowed a deadly hatred of all novels; wished their eternal thema, *Love*, at Jericho, and determined to live for reality, and to cultivate friendship and potatoes.

About this time I began myself to write; not novels, oh dear, no; but lo! before I knew a word about it, it turned out to be a novel after all, or something very like it. Gracious Heaven! had I not then suffered enough from the poisonous stuff? And was I now going to poison others with it? And yet I wished to do something quite different. Have I not known young ladies, who, through romantic whims, had mistaken the aim of their life, failed to become real human beings, because they had failed to become happy heroines of romance; who for the love and moonlight of the novel had forgotten life's real light; sighing for grand dramatic effects, until they had forgotten the significance of their own part in the great drama of life? Have I not known young men, who, enamored and dazzled by romantic scenes, had forgotten to be honest men, and who, when they came out of the world of illusions into the world of reality, saw therein nothing but prose, and want, and "reality's barren rocks," on which no beauty and no happiness could grow. Have I not at one time been so "novel possessed," that every time I went to church I expected to be carried off on the road? No, no; by no means — no more novels; away with them all!

So I exclaimed, but at that moment I saw marching up before me silently the whole host of novels in formidable array. From England they came, from France, from Denmark, from North America, aye, also from China (whose long novel, "The Two Brides, Miss *Li* and Miss *Lo*," one cannot praise without being one's self a Chinese, or Mr. Abel Rémusat [1]). And I saw this host rising out of the

[1] The name of the translator.

bosom of even my own native country, all forming an army of millions, billions, trillions of volumes. They marched towards me, and I heard them say in a voice like thunder: —

"Behold in us a power upon earth: we are mighty under the sun; citizens in all enlightened countries; beloved by all enlightened nations; at home in the enlightened home of all enlightened nations; enjoying the friendship of old and of young, of professors and of students, of octogenarian matrons, and of maidens still in their teens. He who would combat us, must first be prepared to conquer all these."

What a terrible prospect; enough to make even a Napoleon beat a retreat! What, then, could such a dwarf as I am, do? Must I not lay down arms, rescue or no rescue, and own myself vanquished? Or shall I, like another Charles XII, fight against the Turks (the novels must, in that case, represent the Turks, although they, as I believe, are not guilty of writing novels), and gain immortal glory even by my own overthrow? This would be a prospect which might inspire me with courage. I might try it, but the worst of it is, that — yes, I feel it — I would then have to fight against myself also.

I hold the firm belief, namely, that what has occupied mankind for a long period, must have some reason in it, some common sense, something connected with what is eternally true and rational. And as now mankind, since more than a century, writes and reads novels, and as this taste for them, instead of decreasing, is increasing more and more, and is spreading further and further, therefore, my friend! I hope that you will see the conclusive argument yourself.

And then, after carefully sounding my own soul, was there nothing in it, which spoke in favor of the worth of the novel; of the many delightful moments, the warm feelings, the beautiful pictures, which it has given me to enjoy? And did I not, amongst the many weeds which the novels have sown, note also the seeds of noble plants, of shading trees, which have since grown and become developed? And now, when the soul has grown older and calmer, has it not often been awaked by the novel to warm sympathy with man's joys and sufferings, and did not the novel call forth kindly and generous feelings? Yes, yes, it is so, and the result of it all is that —

Novels certainly must have a sensible, good aim; must have the right of citizenship in the world.

But, what is it they really aim at? Do they want merely to amuse, to awaken sympathy, to excite the imagination, to light up playfully the depth of the human soul, and the innumerable winding passages and mazes in life's labyrinth? Are they to be looked upon as resembling those millions of butterflies which, coaxed out of the chrysalides by the warm sun-rays, flutter about, delighting us a short time with their splendor and with the brilliancy of their colors, and then die? Nothing more? Impossible. There must be something more in it. But what?

Think only, if those legions from all nations and countries should have an invisible leader, a commander-in-chief round whose standard they gather, for whose plans they fight, consciously or unconsciously, bravely or timidly, according to circumstances. But if this is so, I must look to this leader, the Napoleon of the novel army, to discover the movements of the grand army and its object.

A bright idea!

Goethe searched for the primeval plant; the philologist is seeking for the primeval language; the Finnish exorcists searched for the primeval word of things, and I went in search of the primeval novel.

I called up the spirits which have made the greatest impression upon me, from Grandison, Joseph Andrews, Corinna, and Rousseau's beautiful Héloise, up to the variety of works of our own days, and I adjured the Spirit of these spirits to reveal to me his nature and his aim.

And I heard him answer: —

"In me thou seest a picture of man's inner development. I represent the metamorphoses of human life, ascending and descending in accordance with eternally ruling laws. What thou seest in me is thy own past, or present, or future history. Therefore thou learnest of me, whilst thou lookest into my mirror, or beholdest how this world goes on. And out of my lesson I create for thee a pleasure. For I take the flowers of the day, and the stars of the night, and I dye my robes in Aurora's roses, in order, beloved one! to come to thee and make thee happy with my beauty, by showing thee life's dark mysteries, making them light to thee, through my earnestness. On my arms I raise thee above the earth, and let thee behold the struggle which agitates man's bosom. Wherever thou seest powers wrestling with each other, developing themselves under liberty's banner, either for good or for evil; wherever thou seest life's most secret history, lighted by the torch of heavenly love, there also thou seest me — the novel."

"Yes, the genuine one," I exclaimed involuntarily. "Beautiful Genius! I understand thee, but" .... I understand also clearly why the world loves the novel so much, but I learnt to distinguish more keenly between the genuine and the false; between the enlightened and the blind imitators of the genius whose words I have just quoted. I beheld a countless number of novels, so widely differing from him, that in order to find again the primeval novel it would be necessary to refer man from his books to his own life. For even in the most commonplace human life we discover the metamorphoses which constitute the nature of the novel — life's changes, its transitions. In whose life are there not struggles, if ever so silent, defeats, and victories? Where do we not see obligations between people, be they lovers, or brothers and sisters, married couples, parents or children? where do we not see the deepest of all relations, the tenderest, the mightiest, the most romantic — the relation between man and his highest, his best, his first and his last friend? I also have a little objection to novels in general, when I compare them to the novel of novels — real, living life.

It is because they occupy themselves too much with conjugating, in a certain exclusive sense, the eternal verb, I love, thou lovest, we love, etc., etc. Yes, I object a little to this, for I find that it is not so on earth. I am of the opinion of England's great Dr. Johnson, when he says in his preface to Shakespeare's works: "Love is only one of many passions, and as it has no great influence upon the sum of life, it has little operation in the dramas of a poet who caught his ideas from the living world, and exhibited only what he saw before him. He knew that any other passion, according as it be regular or exorbitant, is a cause of happiness or calamity."

There are novels which are free from the one-sidedness of which I have complained, and which contain much of the best which characterizes the genuine novel. Their worth lies above all in the moral tone which breathes through them like a healthy, invigorating breeze, and which holds up to view the influence of good over circumstances, and also man's power to help himself. We see in them the good intent, the pure purpose, perseverance, industry, patience struggling with all kinds of difficulties, conquering at last, and man becoming the creator of his own happiness. These novels can have a beneficial influence upon youthful minds on the point of making the acquaintance of life and the world.

All novels which approach the primeval novel, I wish every success and an inconceivable number of readers. These readers I wish mind and sense rightly to understand them; for true is the saying of Lichtenberg: "If, when a book and a head happen to knock against each other, it should sound hollow or discordant, it is not always the fault of the book."

And if any body hereafter should ask me, "What is to come after the novel?" I intend answering: "The day of judgment."

But who can answer for, that after the day of judgment a new evolution of an entirely new romantic literature and new novels shall not take its beginning? This seems very probable.

THE ROMANCE, THE EPOS OF OUR DAY.

ADAM OEHLENSCHLÄGER has said truly and to the point, "The romance is the Epos of our day," and although learned men have proved that the ancient Greek Epos is not strictly an heroic poem, not the same as the epopee, still they grant that the "Epos" is a narrative of actions or occurrences in which *one* person is the principal figure, who therefore becomes the hero or heroine of such a narrative.

A German scholar says that the distinguishing characteristic of the heroic poem is, "that it contains what interests all mankind." But so does every narrative which tends to the honor of humanity. The ancient "Epos," and its younger brother the romance, appear thus both to come so near the heroic poem, that they may lay claim to its title, honor, and dignities. The hero of the modern epic poem is quite different from that of the ancients, and his life and achievements are measured by a different standard. The hero of the ancient "Epos" is, generally, a gladiator, who conquers by means of assassinations and cunning, and who slays a great number of people. He is handsome, brave, fortunate, and his grand achievements consist in battles. But the hero of romance is, above all men, the feeling, thinking, moral man, in his struggle with the world on his road to the goal which his genius points out to him. The ancient "Epos" knows only a few human beings, and they are the favorites of the gods; they are the great and gifted ones upon earth. All the rest of mankind is merely rabble, good enough to serve as stepping-stones to the advancement and rise of the hero. In the Epos of modern times every man can be the hero, every woman the heroine; for *man* is the chosen favorite, loved by God, called to great destinies, to the possession of a measureless realm.

This is owing to the ancient Epos being a Pagan, whereas the romance is baptized in the life of Christianity. Christianity attributes to every human soul an infinite worth before God, and an infinite possibility of perfection. It makes man the inmost essence of creation.

The romance, the novel, understood this doctrine, and grouped round its hero, round the loving, searching, struggling man, as his world, nature, science, arts, society. To the romance, *man* is the centre of life, and it is his task to explain life. In the romance man is still a conqueror, but to bless; and his first and greatest victories are won upon an inward battle-field — within his own breast. If victorious there, he conquers the world.

The romance became thus essentially a biography. In the delineation of the individual man, it purposes to show the *human* in every sphere of the existence. The hero, or the heroine, is the representative of the higher, the spiritual humanity, who through it vanquishes devils and goblins, and is declared, though often not before death, the victor. The romance preaches to every body this counsel, "Learn to conquer!" It is a multifarious paraphrase of the words "Behold the man."

The romance says further to man, "Behold thy world, in all its beauty, its deformity, its greatness, its littleness, its pleasantness, its bitterness, in a word, in all its reality."

To a clear-sighted criticism no doubts can therefore arise of the great importance and value of the romance in literature as a means of higher cultivation. To a clear-sighted criticism therefore the romance ought to present itself as one of the most deeply influencing art-productions which civilization has produced.

The great development which romance literature has attained during this century, is a proof according to my opinion of the great humanizing development of the age; and the fact that romance or novel-reading has become a favorite study throughout all classes of society, shows their sound taste and clear eye. We are here ready to say with Madame de Sévigné, "*Mon ami, le public a bon nez et ne se méprend guère.*"

The question of the value of the romance in general ought to be restricted to a question of the value of such or such a romance in relation to its purport *as* a romance, *as* the epic poem of mankind.[1]

We do not deny that the romance has frequently mistaken its aim; that it has often carried darkness and poison in its leaves instead of light and healing life.

This constitutes its sin. But this sin ought to be as little ascribed to the whole race of romances, as Nero's abominations ought to be laid at the door of mankind.

Far more frequently the romance has carried pleasure, comfort, hope, strength, healing life to man's heart. It will do so in a far greater measure when it has learnt better to understand *itself* and its mission.

Rousseau's "Héloise," Richardson's "Pamela," St. Pierre's "Chaumière Indienne," and in later times "Consuelo," by Madame Du Devant, are beautiful human epic poems, justly admired by all nations and models of the Epos of our time. Higher still than they stands "Uncle Tom's Cabin," the book of our own days, which is being read most and is most liked; for not only does nature, family life, and life's moral questions group themselves round the man who is the centre of the narrative, but the

[1] We can discover in romance literature two leading tendencies, like those which in painting are called the Italian and the Flemish school. The former tries to represent the ideal, the latter strives more to show a vigorous and pithy reality. Our Swedish literature has to thank Mrs. Emilie Carlén for exquisite pictures of this latter kind; pictures which have scarcely been equaled.

profoundest and most weighty questions of life, of the state, and of society, throng along this lonely, loving, bleeding human heart to receive light and judgment.[1]

And what is the man who is here the hero; who makes our hearts beat, our eyes shed tears; who lets the people of two worlds feel the same interest, the same sorrow, make the same reflections, and converse on the same common subject; a subject which belongs to — humanity at large? He is the humblest, the most defenseless, the most despised of men; a man who can scarcely read, who cannot write at all — a poor negro-slave. But he is a *man* in the highest acceptation of the word, for he is a Christian. And humanity rejoices in him over its highest life.

Thus far the divine hero has advanced, and thus far the romance has followed his footsteps in raising man.

The romance, and its sisters the novels and sketches, have likewise this merit, that they make us acquainted with far distant lands and nations, in a more hearty and living manner than other books are capable of doing it. Travels give us a description of outward things and situations. Scientific works can inform us of a country's geography and geology, of its Flora and Fauna, etc., etc., — and of the character of its people. The romance, on the other hand, lets us see the heart of the people and its inward life. It opens to us the home; shows us the father, the youth, the maiden, the child, the servant; shows us what constitutes the aim of their life, their joys and sorrows, their work and pastime; shows us the trees which afford them shade, and the flowers which delight them; lets us, in a word, see man in his human world, and lets us see that world in its peculiar form in such a land and amongst such a people.

And we know scarcely a greater, and at the same time a

[1] The English novels "Mary Barton" and "Alton Locke" discuss likewise the great social questions of the day (in England) in their relation to man, who in them appears in his highest signification as a member of society. The political or social novel thus appears upon the stage.

more useful enjoyment, than to be transported from our quiet home, as if by a magician's wand, to foreign countries, and to make the acquaintance of new characters, and a new state of things, and to learn from them, at any rate, what is going on in the world.

For although Sweden's noble and amiable poet, Franzén, did characterize the romance as "an occurrence which has never occurred," still we venture to assert that every thing which the *true* romance describes, has really happened and happens every day, if not *exactly* in the same way as told in the romance, yet in an analogous manner, and that no romance is so romantic as is frequently actual life.

We would wish that every young man and every young girl would understand their life in its truly romantic signification, and that they would at an early age think of writing their autobiography. The romance in it would be more than a little love-story.

But if it is a love-story on a grand scale, so much the better.

The genuine romance is such a biography.

But let us return to the mission of the romance — to bring near each other far distant people and countries by a delineation of their inner life.

The American people have been glad to become acquainted with Sweden and its home-life through Swedish novels. Swedish readers who, through "Uncle Tom," have been introduced to North American houses, natural scenery, and social conditions, will no doubt with increasing interest renew the acquaintance with America through American novels and sketches. They who, with a beating heart, have followed "Uncle Tom" through his checkered life, will willingly follow her who has described the same in her sketches of characters and scenes amongst the descendants of the Pilgrims, given in the "Mayflower," the first full-blown flower of her talent as an authoress. She was, while writing that work, a young mother, taken up by domestic cares, of which the little sketch, "A Mother's Trials," is a humorous picture.

She wrote these sketches in her leisure hours, for a small circle of friends, without at that time thinking of publishing the same.

They are the firstlings of a youthful, richly endowed soul, and although they carry the impress of firstlings, and lack artistic finish, yet we find in them the same qualities which are so essentially characteristic of "Uncle Tom;" an acute perception of the peculiar and national, an overflowing vein of humor, and a deeply religious mind.

Washington Irving, Caroline Kirkland, Catharine Sedgwick, Fenimore Cooper, and Nathaniel Hawthorne have given us masterly sketches of America and of her people, but none more striking sketches of character, none more *American*, than those of the authoress of the "Mayflower" and of "Uncle Tom's Cabin."

THE CHILD'S PRAYER.

"In my childhood," relates the great and brave Captain G——, "I was exceedingly strictly educated. Every fault even the most trifling, was most severely punished by my mother, — a woman strong both in body and mind. This severity filled me with great dread and terror, which easily might have led me to falsehood and hypocrisy, if these sins had not been even more severely punished than all others. Meantime I was often very unhappy. In my extremity I had recourse to prayer, prayer to the invisible Father, whom I knew to be watching over me and over all. A flat stone behind one of the hedges in our garden was my oratory. Often have I been lying there on my knees — praying and weeping.

"One day I had undertaken the praiseworthy labor of weeding the hot-beds in our garden. In doing this, I worked especially very hard at a large plant with such deep and strong roots, that, notwithstanding all my endeavors, I could not tear up the root entirely. One piece of it, deeply imbedded in the earth, I was obliged to leave behind. Delighted with my work, I went to the gardener, saying to him, 'Well, now I think I have very nearly pulled up all the weeds from the hot-beds. There was only one large plant, which I could not quite tear up, but'—

"'What in the name of goodness have you been doing?' exclaimed the gardener in evident consternation; 'I hope you have not torn up Mistress's chervil?'

"He ran to the garden-seat; I followed him, trembling. Alas! it was indeed so; the only chervil-plant in the garden, my mother's favorite herb for cabbage-soup, I had in the sweat of my brow labored to exterminate. Oh, how I prayed and entreated the gardener not to mention my misdeed. He promised not to do so, but only conditionally. As long as nobody asked him, he would be silent; but if his mistress discovered the mischief and wanted to know the cause of it, he considered it his duty to tell her.

"From this moment I listened every day with indescribable anxiety, and especially every Sunday, to the orders which were issued to the cook about dinner, trembling from fear that I should hear the dreadful word, 'cabbage-soup.' For three weeks it was never once mentioned, and my anxiety had gradually become less intense, when one Sunday morning I heard my mother saying to the cook: 'I suppose we must soon have cabbage-soup again; I was thinking of having it to-day. The chervil ought by this time to be large enough.'

"More I could not hear. Half frantic with terror, I ran down into the garden; I was almost in despair. Again I had recourse to my oratory, and there I sent up as fervent prayers for delivery out of my misery, as ever passed child's lips. Having prayed long, I rose, saying in a gloomy frame of mind: 'I shall now see whether there is any efficacy in prayer, and whether it can do any thing to help us.' And with quick steps I hastened to the fatal hot-bed, which during all the time I had never thought of visiting. I approached it; with a heart beating almost to bursting, I threw at it a terrified, searching glance, and behold! a luxuriant chervil-plant stood there verdant, a foot high, on the same spot where the former one had stood. My surprise and my joy cannot be described. It was the root which had been left behind, which had shot up. The matter could easily be accounted for, but upon me it made an impression never to be effaced. And it was not difficult for me afterwards to follow the advice which my father gave me many years later, when I left my parental home to enter the great world as a military officer. 'Above all,' said he, 'do not forget prayer; let it be the beginning and the close of your day; for however our fate may vary, to *that* we always return!'"

MAY THOUGHTS.

GENTLE breezes, pearly dew-drops, warm sun-rays, *spring*, spring life, blessed, blessing all, welcome to all! How the earth quickens; how it stirs in the seed, in the bud; how it sings in the air, in the waters! Glorious life, giver of joy and of beauty, receive our thanks for having returned; for again awakening earth with kisses and warmth; for again awakening hopeful feelings and thoughts in the souls of men! Over *them* also snow was lying — winter's sleep and heaviness; but they feel thy spirit, and they breathe again, and send forth into life an "Ah!" of longing and of hope.

Spring, which so often I have seen come and depart, bloom into beauty and — die away on a bed of withered leaves; enchanting, but ephemeral season, why do I now greet thee with so much joy? Is it for the sake of thy verdant fields, thy tender foliage, thy flowers, thy butterflies? They must all soon perish. Is it for the general joy which thou callest forth amongst all people, my brothers and sisters? Oh, yes! But with thee this joy must also die away.

Delicious spring-time! no, it is not at thee that I rejoice so much, but at the life of which thou art the symbol, whose spirit thou bearest; at a spring which I feel is approaching; a spring which does not wane; a life which does not die, and which, like thine, imparts its all to all.

It is the spring of community, of universality; it is all mankind's participation in the communion of God's good gifts.

That spring is spiritual life; that life is eternal.

It descended from heaven to exalt and to bless earth. During eighteen centuries it has breathed upon generations, melted icebergs, burst fetters, cleansed, purified the air, and penetrated in innumerable individual hearts. Now it penetrates public life, *Society*, and also its movement has become a downward one, in order to elevate.

Associations are formed for the propagation of God's kingdom upon earth in goodness, in wisdom, in beauty. Weak men join their hands in long chains, which gives them power; and the electric current of God's love runs more rapidly along them all.

And the neglected children are adopted, educated; the ignorant are taught; the erring improved, and the condition of the poor is raised nearer to that of the rich.

Science steps forth from its study, and in bright beams gives to the people the light which it has discovered — the truth which it has gained during solitary labor and watching. And man learns better to conceive the God in whom he has believed; learns better to understand himself, to know the world in which he lives, the stars which shine above his head, the flowers which grow at his feet. Thus he wanders more securely and more happy upon earth. More securely, but also more humbly, more peacefully, and — " Blessed are the peaceful!"

The social system becomes a general and sacred system,

and social life expands to receive more and more citizens, participators of the same noble duties and rights.

Art descends from sun-lit heights to throw — like the sun itself — its light into obscure, hidden valleys; into the cottages of the poor — life-giving, cheering. Beautiful pictures adorn the lowly cot. Poetry and song fall like fertilizing dew out of warm spring clouds upon the soil of the mind, quickening the noble, slumbering seed.

And upon earth breathes — although in various tints and degrees — one heart, one reason, one sense of beauty; and from earth one common, bright, radiant eye is raised towards heaven.

Spring of the human race! Day of participation for all! Alas! it is yet only approaching. It is obscured by the dark shadows, the heavy crust of ice which still rests upon earth. But the tints of its dawn are visible in the sky; its spirit breathes through space. It is coming, it is coming, God's "Let there be light!" His first commandment to the world has been given to us to repeat, to realize until the last day of time. May herein every one of us be a spark, a ray!

Go then, when thy time is up, beautiful, earthly spring! Thy farewell, thy withered flowers, thy death, shall not discourage us. The spring life which knows of no death, the bloom which does not decay, is approaching. In it we shall unite; in it we shall labor as thou laborest for all, every one according to his individual powers and in his place, if even only as a breath of air, as a drop of rain, aye, even if only, as now here, by — a drop of ink!

THE GRATEFUL LITTLE FLOWER.

THE closed bud of a tiny flower was shooting forth unnoticed amongst the grass, while the vapors of a May morning were sweeping, like dreams before the soul of a slumberer, over earth, yet sunk in sleep. Still every thing was dusky, but in the bosom of the tiny flower a dim dream was stirring, a presentiment of light, of joy, of something that was to develop and beautify its little life. Thus dreams the child of the sun which shall rise over its noonday. Thus man divines, through life's long dawn, the new light, which, at the command of a new " Let there be light," shall beam forth and annihilate every particle of the dust of ancient chaos. Dreams sometimes become truth. How beautiful to awake from a pleasant dream to the joys of which it has whispered to us. Such was the fate of the tiny flower.

The sun threw a ray upon the lonely one. Delighted, it felt light and warmth develop and beautify its life. The wandering wayfarer cast his eye upon it, saying, " See how beautifully the sun lights up the little flower!" Deeply the flower felt the beneficence of the king of the firmament. It could acknowledge it only by trying to preserve unspotted its inner part, which light had deigned to look upon, and it followed, with an eye never turned away and with joyous and humble adoration, the course of the glorious one as he moved along his path in the heavens. Occasionally it whispers to a passing breath of air, hoping that it will carry with it and carry to him its sigh: " Oh, if the sun could but know how grateful the little flower feels!"

THE UGLY HAND AND THE BEAUTIFUL HAND.
A TRUE STORY.

"Now you shall hear," said Grandmother one day to Peter and Lotta, who were seated on the floor before the stove, in the light of the fire, looking with curious eyes at the old woman, who sat herself down opposite to them in the shade. Mother was baking the pease-flour pancake in the hearth fire; father was sitting at his joiner's bench, but they all listened attentively to Granny when she began.

"Now you shall hear: listen attentively! There was, once upon a time, a young peasant lad, who married a young peasant lass; and her name was Gertrud and his

name was Sven. Oh, what a grand wedding that was! She
was dressed at the parsonage, and she looked so splendid,
oh, so splendid, that all the people crowded round to get a
look at her. And she was so fine and so grand, where she
was riding on horseback, with a large nosegay stuck in her
stomacher, and with fiddlers riding before her. And so
they went to church, and were married. And the church
was cram full of people to look at her. And so they went
home and had a grand feast. And while all the dishes
were brought in, the fiddlers scraped away, and then they
ate and they drank, and they danced nearly all night.
That was the wedding. Then the newly married couple
went to their own cottage; for they had their own cottage
with two rooms in it, and before it stood a mountain-ash,
in which the birds sang; and a farm-yard they had, too,
with a cow, and sheep, and pigs; and furniture they had,
and meat and drink as much as they wanted. All this
they had got from their parents. And they were very
happy, and said: 'Now we shall be merry and enjoy our
life thoroughly.' And so they began eating and drinking
and sleeping, and they rose late in the day, and slept also
during day-time. But for all that they were not happier,
but only more sleepy, and yawned all day long. One evening, just as they were going to have their supper, they saw
coming into the cottage — but whether it was through the
door or through the window, they could not tell — a large,
ugly, black hand with long fingers: look you, children, in
this way it came, so slowly, stretching towards the table,
seized the basin with the porridge, and carried it away right
before their noses, which grew so long — so long, that they
would have knocked against each other, if both Sven and
Gertrud had not tumbled backward from sheer fright, when
the large ugly hand came and took away their supper and
disappeared with it, they could not guess how. 'But,' said
they, 'we won't mind it, but we shall go to bed, and it will
be all right to-morrow;' and they went to bed, but they

did not sleep, because the horn-owl sat in the mountain-ash, crying all night, 'Uh, hu, hu!' and they fancied that the ugly hand was moving about in the kitchen, but it was so dark they could not see. At last they fell asleep, and when they awoke it was broad daylight, and then the gudeman said: 'Get up now, gudewife, and light the fire and make some coffee.' And she went and lit the fire, but just as she was going to take hold of the coffee-pot, what do you think she saw? Why, the large, ugly hand; it caught hold of the handle of the coffee-pot and was off with it in a trice, as if it had flown through the wall. Then the gudeman flew in a rage, clenched his fist, and said: 'Well, come once more if you dare, you great ugly brute, and I'll squeeze you so that you shan't forget it in a hurry: and now I'll go to the bailiff.' And he got out of bed and dressed, and wanted to put on his holiday coat; but just as he was going to take it down from the peg, he felt something pulling at it that was stronger than he was himself, and when he turned round, lo! there was the large ugly hand, grasping his coat and flying off with it before he had time to understand how it was done. And thus it went on every day. Every day came the ugly hand into his cottage, and took away something or other, either victuals, or clothes, or household furniture. And then husband and wife got very frightened, and they asked each other: 'How will this end?' One day they heard the cow lowing, and they saw the ugly hand dragging her along by the horns into the forest. And the poor cow was so lean, and looked back imploringly to the young wife, and then disappeared in the forest. Then the wife began to weep so bitterly; but the husband said he did not like to see all this misery, and so he emptied the brandy bottle and fell asleep, and slept as heavily as if he was dead; and the wife did nothing but cry, and did not know what to do. 'Now I have not got a single drop of milk to give to my husband; what *shall* I give him to eat?' And she thought more of her

husband than of herself, for she was, after all, a good soul
While she was crying and staring up at the sky and praying to God for help, she thought she heard a bird in the tree sing : —

> "'Industry wins bread,
> Stands us in good stead;
> If the handsome hand is busy,
> Sure the ugly one's away.'

"And when she heard this, the scales fell from her eyes and her heart became light. She dried her tears, took her spinning-wheel out of the corner, where it had stood forgotten with the flax upon it for many weeks, and she began spinning: whirr, whirr, whirr-irr-rr. She thought it sounded so nice — she had almost forgotten the sound. 'What is that strange music?' asked her husband, when he awoke. And the wife told him how she had felt, and what the bird had been singing in the tree, and how she had thought that if they were to begin to work, things might perhaps turn out better for them. And he scratched his ear and said that 'There might be something in that.' And then they kissed each other, and promised one another to begin living in a different way. And all day long they worked away, and that day the ugly hand was not seen to take any thing away from them. But it is true there was not much to take now, for the ugly hand had already carried off so much. They had only one kettle left, and a few potatoes in a basket, but no bread. When therefore the young wife was boiling the potatoes in the kettle at night, she said: 'Think if the ugly hand should come now and take away the kettle also!' And she was in a great fright. But no, no ugly hand did she see; and when the potatoes were ready and she was going to put them on the table, she saw a pretty little white hand, placing a loaf of bread upon her plate and one upon Sven's plate. And the bird in the tree sang :—

> "'Industry wins bread,
> Stands us in good stead;

> If the handsome hand is busy,
> Sure the ugly one 's away.'

"She was so glad, oh, so glad, that she had almost let the potatoes drop on the floor, for she was so anxious to run and kiss the blessed little white hand; but it was gone, and at that instant her husband came home from his work, carrying a large bundle of wood, and the wife told him with joyful tears what she had seen. And he was also heartily glad, and they sat down to eat. And for many, many a day, their meal had not tasted so well. They were happier than they had been for a long time, and they thanked God. And now they began another life. Every morning they got up at daybreak and worked all day long, that often, when night came, they were so tired, oh, so tired; but then they had encouragement, for every day they saw the white hand come in, bringing back some of the things which the ugly hand had dragged away; yes, and one day it came and put the coffee-kettle on the fire, and hung up Sven's holiday coat on the peg; but the funniest thing was when they heard one evening a lowing outside the window. 'My cow, my cow, my blessed "May-rose!"' cried Gertrud, and ran out, and behold, it was 'May-rose' that had come back, led by the horns by the white hand, and she looked at Gertrud with her large, friendly eyes, and lowed so merrily. Gertrud could not sleep that night, for she longed so to get up in the morning to give her dear 'May-rose' her fodder, and caress and milk her.

"And now Gertrud was much more industrious than any wife in the whole neighborhood, and she had woven such beautiful stuffs out of her yarn, and she sold them to the people all round. And the husband wrought weaving-looms during the winter for those who wanted to weave, and Gertrud taught them how to do it. When now Sven and Gertrud had become rich, they took his old mother into their house, and made her old age happy, for which God blessed them. And He did so indeed, for He gave them two nice little children. a boy and a girl, and they liked much to hear stories told to them, just as you do, children.

"And then there was a great fuss and a loud cry all round the neighborhood: 'The King is coming! the King is coming!' And, sure enough, it *was* the King himself, who sat in a large, large carriage beside his Queen. And every body ran to see the King and the Queen, for he was a very good King and she was a very good Queen, and they thought only of how they could do justice to all, and make the people happy. And when the large carriage stopped at the inn, there were so many people that it looked like an ant-hill. And the King and the Queen went about amongst the people, and spoke in such a friendly way with them all. And the King was such a fine gentleman, with dark hair and brown eyes, which shone like the sun; and the Queen was a tall, beautiful lady, and looked as good as an angel in heaven. And they saw that all the women and girls had such nice clothes of homespun stuff, and they asked, 'Who is it that weaves such stuff here in the neighborhood?' And the people answered that 'Gertrud does, Sven's wife.' Then Gertrud was told to come before the King and Queen with her husband, and they praised them, and said that they would buy some of their stuffs. And so they ordered fifty ells of cloth, and six dozen handkerchiefs with red and blue checks for the little princess. And the King made Gertrud and her husband a present of a silver medal with his portrait on it, as a remembrance of him, and he said, 'I wish you every happiness, my children.'

"And it became known through all the neighborhood how that the King had spoken with Sven and Gertrud, and every Sunday they had to take out the silver medal, for all wanted to see the King's portrait.

"This was a great delight to Sven and Gertrud, as you may believe, and they became still more industrious, and more and more rich; and they joyfully helped poor people out of what they had earned, and told them their own story, and all about the naughty hand and the kind hand. But never again did they see the naughty hand in their cottage.

"For look you, dear children, the naughty, ugly hand, that was *Want*, which drags every thing out of the house, when laziness, and extravagance, and carelessness enter into it; and the kind, beautiful hand — do you know who that was? Well, that was *Industry*, which brings every thing into the house, and makes comfort and independence dwell therein. And the King, that was our own King Oscar, God bless him! And the Queen was our Queen Josephine, and they like to see their people happy and industrious, and to reward them that are honest. So you see that this whole story is nothing but the real truth. And now my tale is finished, and just in good time, for now mother has just baked the last pancake and we are going to have our supper."

Peter and Lotta jumped up from the floor; Granny also got up from her chair, and all sat down round the table where the pancakes were smoking. And the husband and the wife winked at each other and smiled, as if they meant to say: "*We* know that story, *we* do!"

And when they had sat down to the table and were all so pleased, they heard the swallows outside the window chirping to their young ones: "Be busy, be busy, be busy!"

"Hark!" said Lotta, "what the swallows are teaching their young ones. That they have taught themselves."

"Lotta is stupid," Peter said; "God has taught it them."

CHRISTMAS EVE AND CHRISTMAS MATINS.

I SHALL now relate to you, my dear little children in Stockholm, how Christmas is celebrated in the country, for you probably do not know this; but I know it, for I have often taken part in it myself, and seen it with my own eyes, and have enjoyed it vastly; and I know that it will interest you to hear all about it.

But the mother and children of whom I am about to tell you, I have not known myself; a good friend of mine has told me all that I am now going to relate to you.

Well, you see, children, there was a cottage lying on the margin of a dark-green pine forest, and upon it and round about it the snow fell in large flakes, one dark winter's night. But the interior of the cottage was light, for the fire was blazing merrily upon the hearth, and threw its friendly glare upon the pine-tree which stretched its heavy snow-laden branches against the outer wall of the cottage, and the fire also threw its light into the forest where the large owl sat screeching, "Uh, hu, hu, hu!" Merrily the smoke was curling up through the chimney, and the sparks danced about amongst the snow-flakes so that these became quite giddy, and tumbled down through the chimney into the porridge-pan, that is to say, they would have tumbled into it, if they had not melted on their way through the smoke.

It was the Christmas porridge which sputtered and bubbled on the hearth, besides other Yule fare; for it was now Christmas Eve, and according to the custom in the rural districts in Sweden, the food for the whole Christmas holidays was to be prepared, so that it only required to be warmed up for the meals during those days.

It was not, you may believe, rich man's fare which was being cooked in the cottage. For in it there lived only a cottar's wife — and she was a widow with three children. But she was an industrious and thoughtful woman, and a good mother, and had now, in honor of Yule time, prepared the very best; and that was not to be despised. Three pounds of meat she had bought, and it was now boiling together with parsly-roots and celery, and promised to make a savory soup, with cabbage, on Christmas Day. For in the country people must have cabbage-soup on that day.

There was also "lutfisk," quite white and soft in a pan, and potatoes, as a matter of course.

The Christmas cake was already placed upon the table, and there also stood the "*Yule-Kuse*," with long horns. And there he was to stand during all the holidays, in the midst of all the Christmas fare. Have you heard, children, what a "Yule-Kuse" is, and why he stands upon the Christmas tables in the country? I will tell you.

The "Yule-Kuse" is a large lump of dough, which is kneaded and made into the shape of a large goat, with long horns. When he has stood upon the Christmas table all the holidays, he is put into a wooden chest, where he rests in peace until spring comes, and the fields are to be ploughed. Then the "Yule-Kuse" comes forth again out of the chest, is chopped in pieces, and given to the horses and oxen that have to labor in the fields, and which through the "Yule-Kuse" become doubly as strong as before.

And if the fields are well ploughed, the grain will grow beautifully, and a vast number of sheaves will be brought into the barns, and a great deal of grist to the mills, and much bread into the house, and all this the "Yule-Kuse" does, that wonderful animal.

Two little children, Pehr and Maja, were running round the Christmas table, and could scarcely conceal their delight at the "Yule-Kuse," and the cakes, and at the Yule fare boiling on the hearth, smelling so nice in the cottage, and at the Christmas Day matins, which they were going to attend the following morning with their mother. Brother Anders was going to take them all in the sledge drawn by old Polle. And the children had never yet been to the Christmas matins, and did not quite know what it meant; but something grand and beautiful it was to be, and that they had heard and could well believe.

Brother Anders was still standing upon the hillock behind the cottage, cutting wood, that there might be plenty of fuel for the whole week, from Christmas Eve until

New Year's Day; but if any body had seen him where he stood, with gloomy looks and his hair hanging down over his forehead, he would have seen that Anders did not think that Christmas was a merry time, and that he was not much satisfied with the world.

The mother was busy at the hearth. But why does she always stand thus turned towards the fire, as if anxious to keep her face away from the merry children? The flames might tell us, if they could speak, for they see that her face is sorrowful, and that now and then tears roll down her cheeks. And she does not wish the children to see this; she will not spoil their pleasure. But she cannot help it; she must this evening again and again think of her husband, who died only three months ago, and how happy she was with him last Christmas; how good he was, how honest, how industrious, how kind and loving to her and the children; how they two together had labored to overcome many cares, and how their circumstances had improved year after year, so that they began to look forward to the future with pleasure. She thought of how faithfully he had assisted her in every thing, and how he sometimes said: "We must work hard for some time yet, my little Margret, but then you will see that all will be well for us and the children!" And she remembered how, when he felt that he was dying, he had comforted her, and had told her that "it was to be so: that if one of them was to be taken away, it was better that this lot fell upon the husband than upon the wife, because she was able to take better care of the children than he could!" But the wife thought this a heavy burden to bear, and she had much anxiety for the future. For she felt now so lonely both in her heart and in her cottage; and the eldest son, her stepson Anders, who had hitherto been out at service in another parish, but had now come home to assist his mother in her little farm after the father's death, was of a sullen temper, and was evidently unfriendly and bitterly disposed towards his step-mother, which she had hitherto in vain tried to overcome by kindness.

Anders was in the house like a dark cloud; he was always dissatisfied, and rude in his language. This was a great trouble to the mother. And especially this evening, when she had determined, for the sake of the festival and the children, to get rid of all anxious thoughts, just this evening they crowded round her thickly, thickly as the snow-flakes upon the pine-tree, and whenever she tried to shake them off, look — they were there again, worse than before, and seemed almost to crush her down.

But the children, little Pehr and Maja, they could not think of any thing unpleasant, not they.

"Oh, but look at the Kuse, Maja! see how he stares at you with his large black eyes! take care, he will butt at you if you touch him. He says: If you come near me, I will butt you with my long, long horns!"

"Oh, do you think that he will butt? Do you think that he really lives? Oh, how nice the soup smells! Is it not soon ready, mother? And may we not soon go to May-rose and Doll and let them look at the star and taste of Christmas?"

Yes, all right; the soup was ready and lifted from the fire. And the mother lit the candle in the lantern, and round the candle was put a beautiful star made of yellow paper, which was illuminated by the candle, and which again illuminated the candle. And the children got each a small loaf of bread, and the mother filled a large stone-jar with new Christmas ale, and so they went off to the cow-house to let the cattle know that it was Yule.

For it is the custom everywhere in the country, in Sweden, to let the cattle also have the benefit of Christmas, which is both right and good. For every creature upon earth ought to rejoice at the birth of Him who gives new life to the world, and who sent out His Apostles, saying to them: " Preach the gospel to all creatures."

It is chiefly the domestic animals to which, according to old Swedish custom, they give a treat at Christmas. But in some parts of Sweden, and in the country throughout the whole of Norway, it is usual to place outside the house and barn doors, oat and barley sheaves on the top of high poles, or pine-tree saplings, so that the little birds may eat their fill. And when I was one year in Norway, I had two such poles before my window, with large barley sheaves on the top of them, and swarms of little sparrows, and green finches and bull-finches had their Yule feast in them, and seemed incessantly to be twittering " It's Christmas! it's Christmas!"

There was so much rejoicing, and they made such a noise, that you could scarcely hear any thing else. But to return to our cottage in Sweden.

May-rose and Doll did certainly not think of any thing where they stood in their cribs, chewing their straw, when the door of the cow-house was opened and a light shone into their eyes. They turned their heads towards that side, looked a little astonished, lowed and snorted a little to signify that they knew those who entered, and that they were welcome. But when the children in their zeal ran forward, each holding out their cake, screaming in May-rose's and Doll's ears: " It's Christmas now!" they stepped back a pace or two, shook their heads violently, and stared at them with their large eyes as if they would have said: "Ah, what sort of a thing is that?"

But being both very sensible and good creatures — of brown color, with white spots — they soon recovered from their surprise, put out their tongues for the bread, smelt at the Christmas ale, had both a good drink of it, and seemed to be vastly pleased. And when mother had strewn fresh straw under them, and filled their manger with the best sweet hay, and had said to them, as she went away: " God bless you now, dearies; now you have got your Yule fare!" then they seemed to understand the matter, stared at the candle and star, which the children tried to make shine right into their eyes, and with a large tuft of hay in their mouths they laid themselves comfortably down to think the matter over. However, they said nothing but boo-o!

Then they were off to old Polle, to let him also have a taste of Christmas cake and Yule ale, and let him also know that it was Christmas. And Polle pricked up his ears, lifted up his head, and looked as if he would have said that he expected these news, and that he also bade them welcome. Polle was an old stager, and had during many years tasted Christmas. And horses have a wonderful good memory.

The sheep were bleating with delight, and licked the hands which gave them their Christmas treat. And the little pigs jumped and ran about as if they had been crazy.

And if you could but know, my dear children, how much pleasure we can have from the domestic animals in the country, how happy one can live in the cottage and in the farm where one is daily surrounded by, and is, as it were, on friendly terms with the gentle, tame animals, so useful to us, I believe you would then all wish to live in the country.

Puss on the hearth was just beginning to find that time was getting a little too long, and that it was rather dry work to lick her paws, when the mother entered the cottage with the children. Puss now got a whole saucer full of thick creamy milk.

The chickens were very unruly this evening, and would not go to roost upon their perches in the hen-coop; they flew up and down, clacking all the while, and had a great deal to say which nobody could understand. But now when handfuls of golden grain rained over them, and the children shouted to them, "Now it's Yule!" they began clacking and flying about worse than ever, making a dreadful noise; the cock crowed as if it had been morning, and his wife, the white hen, laid an egg.

Anders was also in the cottage when the mother came in with her children. He was a tall lad of about seventeen, and had a sullen and gloomy appearance. The mother gave him an anxious look. Ever since his father had married a second time he had borne his step-mother a grudge, and would not remain in the house after she came into it. He had, therefore, gone into the service of a peasant in a neighboring parish, who certainly was a well-to-do, but not a good man.

Anders now sat with his elbow resting upon the table; he was gazing silently at the fire, and seemed neither to notice that the housewife put the eatables on the table and made every thing so comfortable, nor little Maja's prattle, who wanted to tell him about all the animals, and how they had got their Christmas supper.

For Maja was a nice, friendly little girl who loved every body, and seemed particularly to like brother Anders, although he rarely was friendly to her.

When they now were all seated round the table, and the mother had poured out the Yule ale, the little ones peered at each other, at their mother, and at Anders, winking at one another, and looking so sly, as if they would have said: "Now it comes!"

And now the mother raised her glass, and the children took up their little pewter mugs, and all three said, "Here is to you, Anders!"

Anders looked up, as much astonished almost as Mayrose, when they shouted to her that it was Christmas. But when the mother added, "And much happiness to you, my son, for on this night you were born," Anders said in a sulky tone, "Well, what is that to drink to, and what sort of happiness is that? It would be much better not to have been born."

The mother answered gravely: "Those are sinful words,

my son. When God has given us health and strength to strive and work"—

"Yes, but why must one strive and work?" interrupted Anders in a sullen tone.

"My dear boy, how can you ask so?" she said; "one must live, I should think."

"And why should one live?" retorted Anders.

The mother was silent, for she could not immediately find an answer to that question, and it pained her that the lad so often used such dissatisfied and bitter words. Anders went on:—

"When one has neither father nor mother, nor money, nor any thing in the world to live for, it would be just as well to be dead. One would be out of all bother then."

"Am I not your mother?" said the widow, while the tears rose to her eyes.

"You are only my *step*-mother!" retorted Anders harshly. "Had you been my *mother*, you would have thought more of me than you have done, and I should not then have had to go in this old coat of my father's, but you would have got me a new one."

"That I would have done, if I could have afforded it," answered the widow, blushing from indignation at the unjust accusation. "But you know that I was obliged to sell your father's best coat, to be able to get him decently buried. And you know also that I am busy spinning wool for a new coat for you."

"Aye, but when will it be ready?" said Anders. "You might have sold the old brute of a horse, Polle, and have got money for him, instead of selling father's best coat. But you are proud, and want to keep Polle only to drive to church with him, although he is of no use, but eats up the fodder for the cows. The wisest and best thing would be to sell him."

"My son," said the mother, "Polle is old and has served us many years, and therefore I am unwilling to sell him, but not from pride. And I know also that Polle brings us in many a rix dollar, when our neighbors hire him for their journeys; but if it is so, that it is best to sell him, I shall have no objection to it, if I can only find him a kind master. But it will be painful to part with the faithful animal, and then I shall never again be able to go to church, as I cannot any longer walk there, ever since I have got the pain in my side! But — it cannot be helped!"

"A gentle word turneth away wrath," says the Scripture, and the mother's words were uttered so gently and with so much dignity, that Anders could not say any thing in reply; but he felt a sting of conscience, and he rose hastily, pushed aside little Maja so roughly as nearly to upset her, and went out, violently banging the door after him.

All this hurt the mother very deeply. And if you knew, my dear children, what pain parents suffer when a child is naughty or ungrateful, and what a bitter root grows up from malicious and hard words, you would then certainly always be on your guard, even for your own sake. For, believe me, you will one day surely have it back again. And the child who causes his father or mother a sorrow, will one day have to bear sorrow from his own children, and must then feel how it tastes.

Now, the mother felt within her that she had a motherly love for her step-son, and that she did not deserve his harshness.

But she felt also, that he might be right with regard to old Polle, and that it would be most prudent to get rid of him. And the thought that she could not any longer go to church — a distance of a couple of miles from the cottage — was very painful to her.

The children could not make out what was the matter with their brother. They ate, however, and drank to their heart's content, and thought that nobody could be better off than they were, and that it was very pleasant to live.

When the mother saw that they had eaten enough, she proposed that they should put aside a part of the supper for the "flower-woman" in the parish poor-house. The children were heartily willing to do this. Bread and meat were accordingly tied up in a blue-checked handkerchief, and the bundle was put away on the shelf until the following morning. They would take it with them when they went to church to attend the matins, and they got permission to go themselves to the poor-house and give it to the "flower-woman."

Then the children went to lie down on a large sheaf of yellow straw, which they had dragged into the cottage for Christmas: because in the country people must dance and sleep upon straw at Christmas, if every thing is to be done properly. The children did not undress, that they might the sooner be ready in the morning. And they got from their mother each a white pocket handkerchief to put upon the straw under their head, and then they lay down and were soon fast asleep, side by side, while the light from the fire-place was dancing over them and seemed to kiss their cheeks.

Anders came in silent and sullen, and went to bed without saying good-night.

Last of them all the mother went to bed, after having put all things to rights in the cottage, washed plates and dishes, and put every thing in its proper place, and after having thrown more wood upon the fire, for it is the custom in the country that the fire shall burn during the whole of Christmas night.

As she was now lying on her bed, she could not sleep, for she had anxious thoughts, and she heard that Anders was turning and tossing about in his bed, as if uneasy thoughts had been tormenting him also. And she said to herself: "I wonder whether I ought to speak to him; whether I ought to tell him that he has grieved me and done me wrong; that I bear a motherly heart to him, although I am not his *real* mother; that I would love him if he only would let me; but — I have told him this already more than once. What shall I do? It is Christmas Eve, and then one ought not to part in unkindness!"

In a low voice she called out: " Anders, are you awake?" But Anders did not answer; he was perfectly still and silent. And so she thought: " He has fallen asleep."

And she remained, therefore, silent, but turned her thoughts to God, praying that he might change the boy's dissatisfied and bitter mind. And so, without knowing it, she followed the advice of the pious Thomas à Kempis, when he says: —

" When you have reproached any body for a fault once or twice, and if he then does not mend, then say nothing more, but leave it in God's hands."

And this is a wise and a pious advice. For you do not make any one better by continually scolding and railing. But when nothing else avails, prayer will do it.

Believe me, children, prayer *will help* in one way or other, and although it sometimes feels and seems to him who prays as if God did not hear his prayers, yet he will, in good time, find that the Lord is faithful, and that " He who prays will be answered, and he who seeks will find." For it is with our prayers as with the vapors which rise out of the earth; they return to it again as fertilizing rain. And if the hearing of our prayers sometimes does not manifest itself in the way you expect, you will still find, sooner or later, that it does come; that the load which you have prayed might be taken away from you, has been removed; that the blessing which you have prayed for has been given to you, and that you have got much more (although, perhaps, in another way) than you have prayed for or even dared to think of. Yes, children, hold fast to prayer; it is, when all comes round, the only thing that is sufficient on this earth; it is the most wonderful and also the most effective and powerful in man's life. For it is like a thread which unites us to heaven, by which God's life and power comes to us. The Lord himself has given this thread into our hands and bade us use it rightly, that we through it may get all the good which we stand in need of. But good is nothing, after all, without God's life and light in our hearts.

And the mother prayed for this and for her children, and for a blessing upon them all. And while she thus prayed, she became more calm inwardly. She then turned round to look at her little ones, on whose rosy faces the light from the fire was dancing, and while she thus lay looking at them she fell asleep.

When she awoke it was totally dark in the room, and she felt fear and anxiety come upon her, and a heavy weight in her heart and head. It was as if a large, heavy tear had gathered there and would not drop down, but was lying heavy as lead. The death of her husband, the gloomy mind and bitter reproaches of her son Anders, her loneliness, and the dark future which was before her, all came now upon her like a snow avalanche, and seemed almost to overwhelm her. She heard in her soul Anders' bitter words: —

" Why should one live? " and she thought she would like never to rise, but lie still forever.

But yet she got up and dressed, and lit the fire as usual, and put on the coffee-pot. For although she was not one of the wasteful housewives who drink coffee every day, still the whole household should now be treated to coffee in honor of Christmas.

And then she lit the candles in the Yule tree at the window, which had been prepared the previous evening, and then she awoke the children.

" Christmas matins, children ! Christmas matins ! "

The little ones started up bewildered, rubbing their eyes, opened them wide, and saw the candles burning in the Yule tree. Then they remembered that it was Christmas, and that they were to go to matins. Then they jumped up and were soon wide awake.

The mother prepared the breakfast for them and for Anders, and then went out to milk the cows and look to the other animals; when she came back she dressed herself and the children for breakfast, while Anders, always sulky and taciturn, went to harness Polle to the sledge.

When the sledge stood at the door, and the mother stepped out of the cottage in her holiday dress, with her Psalm-book and white pocket handkerchief in her hand, and with her two children, one on each side of her, she looked so pious and pretty; and Anders, who looked at her stealthily, perhaps thought so too.

The morning-star and the moon shone so bright on the firmament over the dark pine-forest, and shone so friendly in the bright, frosty morning upon the new-fallen snow. The widow thought: "How much that is beautiful has not God done for us!"

And she inhaled the fresh wintry air (not very cold this morning), and she felt her heart becoming lighter.

Polle, poor old Polle, had no idea that they contemplated selling him; he was in high spirits, neighed, pricked up his ears, turning his pretty head now to one side and now to the other, pawing the snow with his fore feet, and was as merry as a foal.

The widow and the two children were soon seated in the sledge. Anders stood behind driving, and Polle's bell was tinkling right merrily, while they were driving along the village road through forest and field, and the morning-star shone upon the white snow fields, and upon the pine-trees heavily laden with snow, and here and there a light was seen twinkling in the forest. The little ones were very talkative.

"Oh, look," they cried, "look how the candles are shining in the Manor-house; candles in every window! Is there not to be a grand ball the day after to-morrow, mother? And look! there is also a light at old Mother Brita's on the hill. And look there! far, far in the forest is also a light! And look there! well, it is wonderful, three lights in the window at the turnpike's, three candles in their Yule tree in the window; see how they shine all along the road! How beautiful! Is it more beautiful in the matins, mother?"

"You little gooseys," said the mother, "the matins are beautiful in another way!"

And now they came out upon the high road, and a great many people came driving, all going to church; there was a long line of sledges, and such a tinkling of bells that the children became almost giddy in the head. When they came out of the forest upon a height, there was lying before them an open valley, and yonder, with the dark forest as a background, lay the white church with its spire pointing high up towards heaven, and with lights shining through the windows as if there was an ocean of light within. Just then the bells began ringing to summon the people to church.

The children became quite silent; a solemn and strange feeling came over them.

They were soon at the church. The bells were pealing and light was streaming out of the church, and the song and the organ burst forth. All around was dark; the moon had gone down.

All round the church small sledges and horses stood closely packed, the horses munching their hay. And amongst these Polle got a place and a large bundle of the best fodder for Christmas breakfast, and a horse-cloth over him, so that he should not feel the cold while waiting. And the widow patted his neck so kindly, thinking, "Thanks, old friend; perhaps this is the last time you take me to church!" And she could not help sighing deeply.

The widow with her children walked across the church-yard between the silent graves, which during the night had been covered with a thick mantle of snow.

"Do you remember, children," she said, while slowly walking forward, "what I have told you about the Christmas matins, and why we have Christmas matins?"

"Yes," said little Pehr; "it is, it is — because " —

"Because our Lord and Redeemer was born on the Christmas night," said little Maja.

"And do you remember," continued the mother, "what I have told you about Him, and of the good which He has done to us and to all mankind?"

"He has taught us" — stammered the children, uncertain what words they should use.

"Yes, dearest children," said the mother, "I cannot tell you all that He has done for us, for it is more than either you or I can understand. Recollect only, that He has lived and died for us; that He has revealed to us God's heart and God's will with us; and that without Him we should not know God as He is, nor have any certain hope of an hereafter. He came to this earth to make us understand God's love and to teach us to love God."

"And is it His birth which we celebrate in the Christmas matins?" asked little Maja.

"Yes," said the mother. "He is the light of the world; and He has made life light for us, and therefore we light candles on His birthday."

And just then they entered the church, and the whole congregation sang, —"All hail! ye radiant morning hours!"

But the children did not think of the singing.

They could only stare and be astonished. There was so much light, so much light! They could scarcely see any thing for all the light. The four large chandeliers which were hanging over the middle aisle were quite full of candles, and on the altar candles were burning in large candelabra. There was a long row of candles along the gallery, and on the walls were gilt sconces carrying whole bunches of candles, and at every seat a candle was burning, so that the aisle looked like an avenue of flames. Wherever one looked there was nothing but candles.

The seats were crowded with people who sat close together. The children had never seen so many people. And they thought that they would never get a seat. But they got a seat in a pew where the people made a little room for them. An honest peasant woman took little Maja upon her knee, and the widow took Pehr upon hers, and so they could all sit comfortably.

The children kept gazing about, and had eyes only for the splendor around them. But the mother soon forgot this and every thing else about her; for just as she was going to open her Psalm-book to join in the singing, the congregation struck up the verse:—

> "Yea, even as we our Lord shall weep,
> Shall know our wants, watch o'er us keep,
> With holy strength us fill;
> To us His Father's law repeat,
> And everlasting mercy sweet
> In sorrow's cup distill."

Then the leaden weight which had been lying upon the widow's heart melted away and was dissolved in tears, which, though painful at first, became more and more sweet. They were like a balm to her.

Now the clergyman came into the pulpit. He was a young man with a good face, expressive of much earnestness and hearty kindness. He was a son of the old incumbent of the congregation, and it was known that he was a pure-minded young man, who, although poor himself, had yet done a great deal of good; was always cheerful while visiting the cottages, consoling the sick, and teaching and conversing with the children. And it is a great thing when the clergyman who is to teach others lives according to what he preaches, and when one knows that he is a good Christian. For then the people believe in his word, and in the power which works through him.

It was a strange feeling for the widow (and for another person, too, in the church), when they heard the young clergyman's first words : —

"Why are we to live?"

She could not help stealing a hasty glance at Anders, and she saw that he looked up at the clergyman in astonishment, as if he had said this to him personally.

And he did so, for he spoke to *all* as well as to *himself.* And especially he spoke to all the poor, all whom in the world are called lowly and simple. He showed how the Saviour had let Himself be born like one of them, in order to wander amongst them, to show them what they should live for, and how beautiful life is here and still more hereafter, in eternity, if we follow Him and become one with Him, and through Him with God. When he then spoke of this life, how great it could be, even in the lowliest cottage; how every, even apparently insignificant, human being could through his life labor for God's kingdom, and for the advent of that glory for which we all long, and how every one could in this labor follow the heavenly Redeemer, "as mother, sister, or brother," and afterwards be received in the heavenly mansions, where they shall see His glory, — then this little life appeared so great, so rich, so wonderful, and so full of the future and of happiness, that the widow when she heard it (and she thought that she had never before understood it so) thanked God for having been born, and for being allowed to live for so beautiful and great an aim. She felt at this moment as if nothing could be too difficult for her any more. That every trouble has a change; that is certain. God's goodness and glory lasted eternally; that was likewise certain. And the young clergyman spoke of this with a joy which lit up his whole face, so that it appeared to the widow like an angel's.

When the sermon was finished, she felt an impulse to turn her head towards Anders, and then she saw also his eyes bright, as she had never seen them before. It was as if a light had been lit within him.

The congregation sang another psalm, after which some of them left the church. But some remained, because in half an hour the usual morning service was to commence, and the people do not all go home between the two services in the country, where they often live at a great distance from the church. It was now daylight and all the candles were put out.

The widow left the church with her two little children, because they were to go to the poor-house and take the " flower-woman " her Christmas treat.

The "flower-woman" was a handsome, pale, aged woman, blind of both eyes, so that the black spot in the pupil of the eye was completely gone. They had become so, she said, when she had her eye-teeth taken out, from which she had suffered severe pain. This was now ten years ago. Formerly she used to wander about the country, teaching little children to read, and making beautiful bouquets of flowers of colored paper, which she put into platted paper flower-pots, and gave away in those houses where people had given her shelter and been kind to her. Thus she had wandered about and lived in the district for fifteen years, and nobody knew her name, nor whence she came; they only knew that she came from a distant part of the country, and never would speak of herself or of her family, nor give any account of herself; there was, however, something in her manners and in her speech which made people say that there was something "strange" about her, but that one could easily see that she belonged to the better class; and being very gentle and pious, and besides, neat and well-mannered in her person, teaching the children so well and making such beautiful bouquets of flowers, she was liked everywhere, and was called the "flower-woman" by every one; and peasants and farmers all liked to have the "flower-woman" in their house for a few weeks at a time. After she became blind, and was not able either to make any more bouquets, or to teach the children to read, or to provide for herself, she had been admitted into the parish poor-house. And people who still had some of her bouquets, used on Sundays to come and give her a little "grub," as they called it in the country — a few eggs, some butter, or some such things, which a poor old body might relish.

When our widow from the cottage in the forest entered the poor-house, she found the "flower-woman" sitting on her bed, and four other old women sat there also on their beds, all in their holiday dress, and the floor was strewn with juniper, and it smelt as sweet as in the forest. The "flower-woman" was paler than usual, but the gentle intelligent face looked more happy than it did usually since she became blind. And when the widow had chatted with her a little while, and asked how she felt at present, she answered: —

"God be praised! for since some time I have had much comfort, for I have lately occasionally seen a *light*. It is not sunlight, nor is it *light from the flowers;* but I believe it is a light warning me that I am approaching that country where the eyes of the blind shall be opened, and shall behold the glory of God!"

The widow kept these words, and the light from the face of the old blind woman when she uttered them, in her heart, amongst the bright impressions which she had received this morning.

Then, before the morning service began, she was seen standing beside Polle with the farmer from "the Manor-house," and both were patting and stroking Polle. And the "Manor-house" farmer, some said, looked afterwards as if he was richer by a horse.

The sun stood high in the heavens when the service was over and the bells were ringing the people out of church.

In a few minutes it was entirely empty, and now the church people were seen running and driving away in all directions along the roads and foot-paths, over snow-clad hills and dales, trying who should get home first. For it is a saying in the country, that he who reaches home first on Christmas Day will be the first to get in his harvest in the autumn.

But this is more a saying than a truth, and certain it is that the people, while driving and running away over hill and dale, looked so merry, that it was easy to see that there was more fun than earnest in it.

The widow was not in any hurry, but was the last to leave the church with her children. The sun shone brightly over the earth, which was now sleeping its winter-sleep under a shining white coverlet, and the dark pine-forest looked sleepy also, as it stood there with a white night-cap upon its rugged head.

In silence the widow drove home with her children through the forest.

Serious, although not gloomy thoughts made her silent. The little ones were hungry and cold, and what Anders thought, they did not know. But Polle was thinking of his dinner, that was clear, for he trotted home as fast as ever he could, and his bells were tinkling merrily through the forest.

And soon after Polle was standing in his stable, and gave himself a treat of Christmas fodder, so that you could almost hear how he enjoyed it. And the widow with her children was also soon seated at the dinner-table, eating a delicious dish of cabbage-soup and beef. And I cannot describe to you how well it tasted. Certain it is that the king's cabbage-soup could not taste better. After dinner they had a cup of coffee in honor of Christmas Day.

Now, when it was dusk and they were all sitting in the cottage, where the Christmas log was flaming and crackling on the hearth, the widow said to the children: —

" Well, I wonder whether my little ones remember anything of the sermon at the matins, and what the young clergyman told us about Christ, and what He has taught us, and what we ought to live for."

But alas! the poor little things did not remember a single word; no, they had not heard even *one:* "There was so much light," said they; "they could not listen for all the light!"

Then the mother told them what the clergyman had said, not so well and in such beautiful words, yet clearly and beautifully after her own fashion, so that the children understood it much better than if the clergyman himself had told it them. For a good mother is always the best teacher of her children, and can put her words so that they go direct to the heart and remain there. Therefore, also, one of Sweden's greatest kings[1] made it a necessary point, that before a woman was allowed to marry, she should be able to prove herself well instructed in the Christian religion, "for," said he, "it is the mother who is to teach the children."

Pehr and Maja were good and intelligent children, and understood what the mother told them, and remembered it in their hearts. Then they were allowed to go and play with their paper flowers, and some toys which the "flower-woman" had given them, and which she had kept since the time when she still could see.

The mother and the son Anders remained sitting alone at the hearth. Anders was sitting with folded arms and bent head, while he was intently gazing at the fire. The mother looked at him. Hitherto he had not said a single friendly word to her since the previous evening; but yet it appeared to her as if something had softened within him.

After a while she said, suppressing a rising sigh, which almost choked her voice: —

"Anders, I have been thinking what you said last night about Polle, that we ought to sell him, and I have spoken to the farmer from the 'Manor-house,' and he told me that he would take him for one hundred rix dollars. He will come to fetch him away to-morrow, and pay half the

---

[1] Charles XI.

money at once. This shall be yours, Anders, and you may do with it what you like; you are sensible enough to manage your own affairs now; only — my son — don't again say that I am only your *step-mother;* for your father was very dear to me!" The widow could not keep back her tears.

Anders rose from his seat. It was as if the ice about his heart had at once broken up and the snow over it had melted away. His lips trembled, and his whole frame shook with emotion, while he said: —

"No, mother, you shall not sell Polle; the farmer from the 'Manor-house' shall not have him; you shall keep him, and every Sunday, if it pleases God, I will drive you to church with him. . . . . I have done you wrong, mother; . . . . I know now that you love me, and I know now for what I shall live! I have not known it before; but now, henceforth it shall be otherwise. . . . You shall see it, mother! This farm I shall manage so that we have credit of it, and fodder enough shall Polle have until his dying day; . . . that shall be my business. Everything shall henceforth be different; . . . I do not know how it is; but I feel so strange within me since this morning. Do not be sorry any longer, mother! God has "— He became silent and could not continue; and as now little Maja came to him with her flower-pot, asking him to smell it, he took her and the flower-pot in his arms, and kissed her again and again, and cried over her and over the paper flowers so bitterly, that little Maja, quite alarmed, began also to cry with all her might.

"The peace of God be with you!" said a happy and friendly voice at the door, which slowly opened, and in stepped the young clergyman who had preached in the matins, and who looked as if he had brought all the light from it along with him. He had heard the sorrowing widow in the forest cottage spoken of, and came to speak words of comfort to her, and if possible to bring happiness into the house of mourning.

But he found it already there, for before him had been *He* of whom he had preached in the morning, and whose message he wanted to bring to them.

But yet he remained a long while in the cottage, conversing with the widow and Anders, whose heart now seemed to be, as it were, new-born. The young clergyman promised to lend him books, and invited him to come and see him.

He wished to instruct and make some young men amongst the country people practice singing quartettes, and he wished Anders to join them, for he had heard that Anders had a good voice. And so he had.

When the friendly young clergyman took leave, and shook Anders' hand, then Anders' eyes sparkled more happily than they had ever done before. He felt as if he had that day got father, mother, brother, and the whole world.

He wondered inwardly how every thing could have changed so much in such a short time.

And from this moment Anders became quite a different being to what he had been formerly. Not exactly that he became more talkative or more lively, for every body has in this respect his own humor, but he became very industrious, and friendly to all. Every body liked him and one could see that he now liked to live. In the church he sang so that it was a pleasure to hear him. At home the widow forgot that he was not her real son; for a real son could not have been more loving to his mother. And although he was taciturn, yet he was never sulky; nay, his very outward appearance became changed. It seemed at times as if something was shining within him, so brightly shone his eyes. And the little brother and sister, who noticed it, used then to say to each other and to their mother, —

"Now there's Christmas matins in Anders!"

POEMS.

*HYMN.

Lord God, we worship Thee!
Heavenly Father, we give thanks to Thee,
    For Thy word,
For Thy love made manifest on earth, O Lord.
  Thou who hast saved us,
  From death's bonds delivered us,
  Called us to life eternal,
    Glory be to Thee!

  Father, O bless us,
  Cause Thy face to shine on us!
    Let Thy light
Guide our steps to Thy mansions bright!
  O let Thy Spirit
  Thy fallen image glorify,
  That in Thine image, O Father,
  Thou may'st be glorified!

*GOSPEL TIDINGS.

O God, we never knew Thee,
We walked in darkest night,
Till thou didst send the Saviour
Clothed in Thy power and light;
To Thee be praise and honor,
In heaven and earth, O Lord,

For the blessings of our Christian faith,
And for Thy gospel's word.

Oh blest are those who treasure
The word of life and love,
Who tread the paths that lead them
To God's own heaven above.
And they shall learn forever
How precious is the Lord,
How those who love His holy name
Shall reap a rich reward.

*THE LORD'S SUPPER.

Oh, miracle of grace!
  On thee our thoughts shall dwell,
In hours of lonely peace,
  With love unspeakable.
God gives Himself for me,
  Hid in this wine and bread,
That I in life and death may be
  One with our living Head.

He is our meat indeed,
  Our drink, life of our life;
Thus sanctified He'll lead
  Us to eternal life.
Fain would He see our hearts
  Holy and pure as His,
As strong 'gainst sin and sorrow's darts,
  As full of tenderness.

So God this earth did seek,
  Of human form possessed,
Salvation's word to speak,
  And clasp us to His breast.

Then hopes of life immortal
  Rose in this vale of death,
Those hopes that ope heaven's glorious portal,
  To all on earth beneath.

He still draws nigh this day
  To us, that Saviour good,
And would our thirst allay
  With His most precious blood;
Would make our hearts more pure,
  More chastened and upright,
And grant our union firm and sure
  With God in endless light.

O Thou! once pierced for us,
  Who didst our souls deliver,
Thou who hast died for us,
  Of life and light the giver!
Accept us, Christ, we pray,
  While we, in holy peace,
Renew with grateful hearts this day
  Thy covenant of grace.

Be Thou our hope most sure,
  Our strength, life's precious bread!
Within Thy church secure
  E'en death we need not dread.
Our life, our resurrection,
  Thou evermore shalt be:
To Thee all worlds are in subjection:
  Glory, O Lord, to Thee!

*TO MY SISTERS.

How blest is he that, like Tobias, goes
    Upon his way by some good angel led
Who gives him light when midnight shadows close,
    Who gives him strength when sinks his weary head.

Thus once my way was dark; oh, fain would I
    That none might tread a path so full of gloom;
I knew not whither from deep woe to fly,
    From anguish that my life-blood would consume!

My cheek was pale, my eyes were running o'er
    With bitter tears. My heart in desolation
Saw suffering, like a vast and rankling sore,
    Prey on the vitals of God's fair creation.

I looked for dawn, I found but nightly gloom, —
    No hope of happier days, no blessed faith;
Life burned, like some wild meteor in a tomb,
    In my sad heart: I only prayed for death.

Then spake a voice, like angel-whispers blest,
    And at those tones of love, so soft and clear
Stilled was the tumult wild, peace filled my breast,
    And lo! those angels were my sisters dear.

The skies grew bright; my tear-dimmed eyes once more
    With hopeful gaze I raised to heaven above;
I looked around; earth smiled from shore to shore,
    For joy had wooed me in my sisters' love.

O God, 't is sweet such solace to receive,
    With nobler aims to see new springs draw nigh!
My sisters, lo! wild storms no longer heave,
    My soul is calm, my tears are tears of joy.

Pure, gentle ones, I turn with fond emotion
  To you, and would to all the world express,
That all I have I owe to your devotion, —
  My mite of strength, my hope, my earthly bliss.

Oh, it is hard to feel such loving debt,
  Which by our deeds can ne'er be canceled quite;
To throw it off I wrote a book, — and yet
  That pleasant burden never grew more light.

Sisters, if in these pages, now to you
  Inscribed, you find some balm for tears that fall
From sorrow's eye, some thoughts both pure and true,
  From my good angels' hearts I've called them all.

*THE CRADLE OF LOVE.

Rock, rock, cradle of Love!
Flow, O Song, with thy silvery strain;
Throbbing hearts shall its sweetness prove,
  Soothe this earth in her tumult and pain:
    Rock, rock, cradle of Love!

Lull the memories of bitter wrong;
Bid each tender and holy dream —
Herald of truth — round the slumberer throng;
Launch the keel, but on Love's broad stream,
  Guided by Hope, the immortal, the strong.

Thoughts soar upward to realms above;
Fight, strong arm, in our stalwart North;
Champion of truth and of right thou shalt prove;
Over all this tumultuous earth
Flow, O Song, let thy strains go forth:
  Rock, rock, cradle of Love!

*THE STAR.

GLITTERING in the skies I burn,
    Brilliant as when erst,
Singing on my natal morn,
    I from chaos burst.
Far in azure space, where I
    Dwelt since thousand years,
I have seen the storms sweep by
    Round yon lower spheres.

Mortals! gazing silently
    With unchanging ray,
Every lurking snare I see
    On your mazy way;
See how passions wild enthrall
    All the race of man;
How his empires rise and fall
    Silently I scan;

See men lavish wealth and state,
    See them idly fret;
How eternal love and hate,
    Yet full soon forget.
I have seen how pleasures showe
    Then as swiftly fly,
Beauty fading like a flower,
    But unchanged was I.

He whose sceptre ruled the world
    I have seen forlorn,
From his throne imperial hurled,
    Pointed at with scorn.
Heroes, sovereigns, and slaves,
    All to dust must turn:

Silent o'er forgotten graves,
  Still my lamp doth burn.

Oft when in the dead of night
  Some sad eye was raised,
Tearful, to my placid light,
  All undimmed I gazed.
On the mourner still I'd shine,
  By her prayers unmoved,
For I knew she soon would join
  Him she fondly loved.

Oft when innocence opprest
  Bows her troubled head,
And with anguish-stricken breast
  Cries to Heaven for aid,
Then I beam more golden bright,
  Knowing she will shine
Once 'mid angels with a light
  Clear and white as mine.

Mortals! 't is decreed by Heaven
  Ye like flowers should die,
Yet accept the promise given
  Ere your hour draws nigh;
Know God's faithful ones shall be
  Stars of heaven bright,
When I and all these orbs with m
  Long have lost our light.

*THE POETRY OF SPRING.

Now the trees their snow-capes doff,
  While the swallows, light of wing,
On their airy trips set off,
  Merry harbingers of spring.

Zephyr with his team is dashing
    Swiftly over land and sea,
Where he sweeps — the waves are flashing,
    Banks are green, and streamlets free.

'Neath the azure skies of spring,
    All the budding groves among,
Little birds in joyous ring,
    Gather for their feast of song.

Charmèd by their strains, each bud
    Opes its eye in field and brake;
While, applauding in the wood,
    Tender leaflets thrill and shake.

Merry midges loudly cheer,
    Dancing in their chambers bright;
Round the honeyed blossom near
    Bees are murmuring with delight.

In the golden sunbeams flash
    Purple-wingèd butterflies;
O'er the flow'ry meads they dash,
    Full of fluttering hopes and joys.

Spring all living creatures hail;
    Whilst man claims, with yearnings high,
Promises that ne'er shall fail,
    As he gazes towards the sky.

For this short-lived spring, this clear
    Crescent moon of life, was given
As a type, foreshadowing here
    That eternal spring of heaven.

When life's wintry days have fled,
  To that spring of endless joys,
By a law eternal led,
  The heaven-born bird of passage flies.

*AUTUMN SIGHS.

COME, Nature's sleep, come, silvery snow,
  Life's solace in the North,
And a shower of downy blossoms throw
  O'er the poor, hard-frozen earth.

O'er all the fallen, frost-nipped leaves,
  And the withered flow'rets small,
O'er the herbs of the field thy finger weaves
  A cold and solemn pall.

It seemeth sad, that snow-white pall,
  Yet peace beneath it dwells,
And 't is ever in peace God worketh all
  His wondrous miracles.

The snow shall melt at the breath of spring,
  And moisten the lap of earth,
And the germs in her bosom slumbering
  Shall wake to sunshine and mirth.

In tears the snow-drift melts away,
  The brook makes a tender moan,
And earth grows green as the soft winds play,
  Nor thinks of the days that are gone.

The tree that braved the wintry storm,
  With branches bare and brown,
As the brooklets sing in the sunbeam warm,
  Puts on its leafy crown.

And we who have buried hopes and joys
  On dark Oblivion's shore,
Oh may not we, e'en we, arise
  To live and praise once more?

Then fall, O snow, tired Nature's sleep,
  We 'll rest and forget while 't is night;
But in winter's slumber, calm and deep,
  We 'll dream of the spring-tide bright.

December, 1847.

*THE CRIPPLE'S MISSION.

On bed of straw, all racked with pain,
  A wretched woman lay;
For twenty years she thus had lain,
  And suffered night and day:
With crippled limbs, with joints awry,
She writhed in bitter agony.

No friend or kin with watchful care
  Her bed of pain did tend,
But she was wont in silence there
  Her lonely hours to spend:
'T was but the hand of charity
At times would food or aid supply.

A worthy pastor heard one day
  This tale of hopeless woe,
He took his staff and went his way
  Some comfort to bestow:
And by her bed, in accents meek,
Of peace and love he fain would speak.

And when he saw her thus laid low,
  All comfort he forgot,

He could but falter: "Child of woe,
  Thine is a grievous lot."
And at that fearful sight amazed,
To heaven his tear-dimmed eyes he raised.

Thus the consoler found no word
  To soothe the sufferer there;
Yet not a single plaint he heard, —
  No murmur met his ear:
And — wond'rous sight — with glances mild
She turned to him, and gently smiled.

"Thanks, reverend Sir, for this warm tear!
  Yet, should it please the Lord
Still twenty years to keep me here,
  I'd speak no fretful word."
She said: surprised, once more to try
Her faith, the pastor made reply, —

"What! pray'st thou not that God above
  Would end thy misery soon?"
"I'm thankful, thankful for His love;
  His will alone be done."
"But such fierce pains are hard to bear."
"In bitterest pains my God is near."

"But what if God forgetteth thee?"
    His own he'll ne'er forget."
"He dwells so far from thee and me,
  Where thousand stars are set."
"The sparrows small His eye can see,
Far more He'll watch o'er thee and me."

"O daughter! sure such faith is rare,
  Whence was this grace obtained?"
"In God's own word, with many a prayer,
  This certain trust I gained,

And oft in mine own breast I hear
My Father's voice that whispers cheer.

" He says : ' Yet bear a little while
   Thy cross with patient love,
And thus to men, by thy calm smile,
   My strength in weakness prove ;
Such be thy work, — perform it well,
Then come with Me in bliss to dwell.'

" Oh, blest even now, the captive may
   Bear witness of His love,
Till, freed from bonds, as clear as day
   She sees His face above.
To serve Him there as here, aright,
Is my desire, my sole delight."

Struck dumb, but not, as erst, with dread,
   The worthy pastor stood:
" O gracious God! " he inly said,
   In grateful, melting mood,
" Take health, take all my earthly bliss,
But give me, Lord, a heart like this! "

*THE SONG OF THE WEARY ONE.

Oh that day will come, it will come at last,
   When my weary eyelids close,
When I lay me down to my long, long rest,
   And this aching heart shall repose.

All bitter memories — oh, thought of peace ! —
   Shall fade when my breath is fleeting ;
And the anguish that racks my heart shall cease
   When that heart is no longer beating.

Oh, even to rest and forget were a boon,
   Nought more would I pray for now;
But I know that the Lord in his mercy soon
   A happier fate will bestow.

I know, oh, I know that a morning will break,
   When from death's dark sleep I shall rise,
When the soul, no more toil-worn, wayward, and weak,
   Shall plume its bright wings for the skies.

I know, oh, I know that once more I shall see,
   In glories that tongue cannot tell,
Those eyes that were wont to look fondly on me,
   Those friends that have loved me so well.

I know that the discords that harassed us here
   Shall melt into strains of joy;
For love is the sun of that heavenly sphere,
   And its light is in every eye.

I know that the radiance of heaven shall illume
   Life's pathways on earth, and show
Why the pilgrims who seek their Father's home
   Oft must wander through toil and woe.

I know that beside the pure waters of life
   The weary will find repose;
Will drink new strength, after sorrow and strife,
   From the fountain that ever flows.

Then be of good cheer, and wait, O my soul!
   And take what the Lord shall provide;
All things are done well by His loving control, —
   In His keeping securely abide.

And whilst thou art wandering, oh, list to the song,
   Through earth's wide chambers it rings:
"The day shall be dawning, it cometh erelong,
   When the slumberer awaketh — with wings."

* RESIGNATION.

In the flower, the billow, the beams of the sun,
   O God, we can read of thy might!
It gleams in the gorgeous garlands of June,
'T is traced in the insects' dances at noon,
   In the star-spangled garments of night.

But brightest those heavenly features glow
   In a suffering mortal's breast,
When he calmly tastes of the banquet of woe,
And drains its cup to the dregs below,
   With a saint-like patience blest.

On his lips unmurmuring a smile doth play,
   Whilst of hope and faith they tell;
We see him go on his weary way,
And we laud our God, and humbly pray,
   That in us, too, His spirit may dwell.

* CONSOLATION IN NATURE.

O child of sorrow! Thine eye is dimmed
   By the mists of bitter woe;
O'er all this earth thy glance hath skimmed,
   Yet it could not read nor know
That holy writ, full of solace sweet,
Which springs from the sod beneath thy feet.

Oh, wipe the tear-drop from thine eyes,
   God's writing it must not hide;

See how the beams of morning rise
   From the darksome ocean's tide,
And how the sweet spring breezes play
When the stormy winter has passed away.

And learn that symbol's message blest:
   A brighter dawn shall come;
Soon in thy anguish-stricken breast
   The spring of peace will bloom.
And as yon lowering thunder-cloud
   Is swept from heaven away,
The shades that now thy spirit shroud
   Shall yield to perfect day.

And when thou seest the bud that opes
   To a flower of gorgeous hue,
Know that erelong thy heart's fond hopes
   Shall bloom and blossom too.
But let the seed of the withered flower
   Teach thee, O blossom fair,
That thou must die — in happier hour
   Yet fairer flowers to bear!

CRADLE AND GRAVE.

Earliest, latest,
Sacred to mortals,
Consecrate places
Of slumber and peace!
Tranquil asylums,
Sheltering harbors,
Shrouded in airy
Fugitive shadows,
Where tears of humanity
Have their beginning,
Have too their ending,

Mortals have called you —
Cradle and grave.

By you, twin-brothers,
Mystical cherubs
With torches low-drooping
Stand ever watchful;
Slumber and Death,
Innocent children,
By you stand weaving
Garlands of poppies, —
Garlands of lovely
Blossoms immortal;
Placing them softly
Now on the hoary
Head of the old man,
Now on the young child's
Bright golden curls,
Now on the thoughtful
Strong man's brow.
Whisper: "Sleep sweetly!"
Straightway they slumber,
Moments speed onwards,
Sorrows lie silent,
All is so well.

Ye blessed, ye radiant
Visions of childhood!
Haply the sleeper —
The sleeper low lying —
Once more beholds you!
Haply he findeth
In peaceful seclusion,
Not as delusion,
His cradle's dream.

Rose tints of morning,
Evening clouds golden!
Gleams of eternity
Beckon from both;
Breathe in the flowers
Love scatters over
The bed of the sleeper;
Echo in music
Of lullabies tender,
Which love singeth softly
By cradle and grave:
"During thy sleep
An angel doth keep
Watch over thee;
Waiting the hour
When thou, by the power
Of love's kiss, wakened shalt be."

Cradle of childhood!
Sweetly I slumbered
On thee, thou tiny
Snowy white bed:
Grave ever yearned for!
Laid in thy harder,
Gloomier bosom,
I long to lie sleeping, —
Long to find coolness
For heart-burning fever, —
Long to find rest.

O! might I only
Slumber so calmly
In motherly bosom,
Lying so peaceful
In motherly earth!
Blessed and thankful,

My vision departing,
Then with my final
Sigh would bear witness:
" Fair was my morning,
Sweet is my eve."

M. R. W.

*MY MORNING SONG.

August 24th, 1828.

O THOU, of life the light, the joy,
Thou morning sun, God's glorious eye!
Now do I hail thee, bending lowly,
And bless the love, so pure, so holy,
That lights thy beams o'er earth and sky.

Eternal Lord, how bright, how clear,
How warm, Thy being all divine,
In Nature imaged, meets us here!
Father of light, in light's own shrine
Revealed, we see Thy glory shine.

E'en as the smallest meadow flower,
Thus lowly am I in Thy sight;
Yet on us both Thou deign'st to pour
The fullness of Thy blessed light,
Making our hidden paths look bright.

A grateful heart that lowly one
Doth bring; what else can she bestow?
O Father, look Thy child upon:
'Midst all thy children, high and low,
She humbly brings this offering now.

*PEACE.

October 24th, 1828.

ALL is still; sweet Peace descending,
  Bids my heart no longer languish;
While the hours too swiftly wending
  Wake no restless sigh of anguish.

Beauteous stranger, whence art coming —
  Coming, when my need is sorest?
With thy lilies ever blooming,
  Thou this drooping heart restorest.

Com'st thou like some nightly vision,
  O thou flattering deceiver?
Shall thy fountain's stream Elysian
  From my lips be snatched forever?

Art thou like the north light beaming,
  When my charmèd eye beholds thee?
Like the flame o'er tombstone gleaming,
  Swiftly quenched when darkness folds thee?

Like the west wind softly blowing,
  That of summer's advent speaketh?
Like those tears repentant showing
  When God's voice the sinner waketh?

Com'st thou from bright regions soaring,
  With some blessed salutation?
Then with psalms I'll turn adoring
  To the God of my salvation.

Sure some glimpses thou wilt waken
  Of that home with all its treasures;
Make this heart, with anguish shaken,
  Fit to taste of heavenly pleasures.

Soon, methinks, on loosened pinions,
  Hope reviving in my bosom,
I shall seek those blest dominions,
  Where thy silver lilies blossom.

Where no tear the cheek shall furrow;
  Where no heart with pain shall quiver;
Where the ransomed sons of sorrow
  Rest in arms of peace forever.

* THE VOLCANO.

'Tis done, burnt out is the volcano's fire,
  The lava flood no longer wildly dashes;
Gained is its object: lo, the fierce destroyer
  Grows calm at last, for it is burnt to ashes!

Know'st thou the spot where rose a fiery pillar,
  Fearfully bright, in night's embraces lost?
Seest thou in blaze of noon yon dim cloud-pillar,
  On funeral pyre? 'Tis the dead mountain's ghost.

And know'st thou where the seething lava streams,
  Poured from the giant's heart with terror rife?
Behold yon Eden, fair as childhood's dreams,
  From the "destroyer's" breast it sprang to life.

O'er sunlit uplands golden harvests spread,
  And cities rise with hum of toil and mirth;
The mountain sleeps — even as the mighty dead,
  That from their graves yet wake new life on earth.

CHILLY BLOWS THE WIND.

Come, O Bertha, from the storm!
Come to my embrace,

Come into love's sheltering place;
By my heart thy bosom warm:
   Chilly blows the wind.

To my breast O woman turn!
Wilt thou be my own?
Let the whole world freeze like stone,
Ever I for thee will burn:
   Chilly blows the wind.

Bertha, by love's radiance taken,
Lover's vows believes;
But for distant shores he leaves:
O'er the heart of the forsaken
   Chilly blows the wind.

Bertha prays as time goes slowly:
Lord, be kind to me;
Take my child and me to thee,
Let me in the grave lie lowly:
   Chilly blows the wind.

'Tis the last hour — by the dying,
Weeping kindred stay;
Sorrowful for her they pray,
In the dread death conflict lying
   Chilly blows the wind.

Farewell! Brothers, sisters, hear me!
Pardon me, O Lord!
And to him thy grace afford;
Death approacheth — standeth near me:
   Chilly blows the wind.

In the grave is Bertha sleeping,
Late so young and warm,

Cold her baby on her arm;
O'er her broken heart is sweeping
    Still the chilly wind.

M. R. W.

*HAD I STRONG FAITH.

Had I strong faith, then all unmoved I'd gaze
  On earthly storms, safe in my port of rest,
Unscared by jarring cries, or troublous days;
  For that safe haven is God's loving breast.

Had I strong faith, oh how serenely then
  My heart the tangled knots of life should ope;
Whilst cradled lovingly, both joy and pain
  Would rest in the soft arms of heav'nly hope.

Had I strong faith, no passions wild would sway,
  No evil thoughts have power to torture me,
No galling fetters on my soul should weigh;
  Had I such faith, then were my spirit free.

Had I strong faith, I should indeed be strong,
  Unmoved, unscathed, though evil-doers smite;
Even as the sun o'er clouds, I'd pass along,
  Turning all cold to warmth, darkness to light.

Had I strong faith, Thy holy peace, O God,
  Would ne'er, as ofttimes now, abandon me;
I'd fight my fight on earth with dauntless mood,
  And find eternal peace and bliss in Thee.

November 17th, 1844.

*I TRUST IN THEE.

TO A FRIEND OF MY YOUTH.

WHAT is't to me,
If thou at times dost look askance
And give me a less loving glance?
  I trust in thee!

What is't to me,
Even if I thought thou did'st forget me,
At times, when many cares beset thee?
  I trust in thee!

What is't to me,
If I perchance thy words should find
A little colder and less kind?
  I trust in thee!

I trust in thee:
I know that beyond time's control,
Even in the depths of thy undying soul,
  Thou lovest me.

Thou lovest me!
And though all earthly ties should sever,
My heart's clear torch would burn as bright as ever:
  My peace in thee!

April 15th, 1841.

*THE SAGE AND THE CATARACT.

TO ERIK GUSTAF GEIJER. 1846.

A STRANGER rapt in thought stood by the river,
Where it leapt down into a cataract;

He watched its rushing course, he saw it battle
With toppling crags, with broken forest stems,
Yea, even with its own waves, with its own might;
He saw the foam dashed up to highest heaven,
He heard the thunder in its deep caves growling;
He saw, — and gravely shaking his wise head
With disapproving mien, demanded: " Wherefore,
And to what end, is all this toil and tumult?
What frenzy goads thee on to such fierce warfare,
Such strife for life and death with all around thee?
In this wild vortex thou dost lose thyself,
Thy calm, thy crystal brightness. Better far
In yonder silent, solitary valley,
Where thou didst glide serene 'twixt shelter'd margins,
Reflecting every flower and tree that crowned them,
The craggy peaks, and lustrous vault of heaven!
Then thou wert clear and bright, and blue libellulas,
With emerald flashing wings, shot downward, rocking
On the broad leaves of silver water-lilies,
That, heaving, lay upon the crystal billow,
Calm as an infant in its mother's arms;
Then in thy lap the golden sunbeams showered;
The queen of night with her pale lustre kissed thee;
And blooming village maidens, gayly tripping,
Went down to fill their pitchers at thy waters,
And there the weary laborer quenched his thirst
With thankful spirit. Say, what would'st thou more?
Oh let thy life be spent in peaceful labors;
Sweet is it thus to bless and to be blessed,
And then to sleep on flow'ry meadow's breast!
Say, is not this enough?" Thus asked the sage;
But all regardless of his questions, onward
With headlong speed the cataract rushed impetuous,
Cleaving the rocks that barred its foaming current.
Yet one reply it made; even in that power
Which mighty spirits exercise, constraining

To follow when they lead, to watch their workings,
To mark their onward course, the end that waits them,
And the deep meaning of their life and struggles.

And thus the sage pursued the river's windings,
Saw how at hasty intervals reposing,
Its calm and radiant eye looked up to heaven,
With childlike spirit and with childlike glances
Reflecting back that image on its bosom;
Then wildly rushing on to wage fresh warfare
With open foes or hidden obstacles,
And plunging boldly over heights and depths
With an intense indomitable purpose,
As to some fixed and ever bright'ning goal,
He marked it grow more calm in broadening channel,
Clear to its inmost depths, like some brave spirit,
When the good fight is fought; then free and peaceful,
A glorious river 'mid rich margins flowing,
Calmly it rolled toward the ocean, bearing
Not only its own waves, but on their bosom
A world of human labors, human hopes,
Set free by the same power itself that freed.
He saw the stately ships, the barges slow,
Alike from city and from village borne
Upon the river's arms to world-wide marts
Of commerce, while light winds their sails were swelling,
And joyous songs rung in the evening breezes.
The sage rejoiced; he felt the answer given,
And graven in his heart. The river's answer
Lay in the tenor of its noble life!

April, 1847.

And thus it was one day, on banks of Clara river,
   With thoughts all fixed on thee, fair Wermland's lofty
      son,
   That *one* who loved thee well, whom thou hast called " thy
      friend,"

Did sing this song, borrowed from thine own life, to thee.
A year has passed away, and lo, thy noble spirit
Too soon has burst its narrow bonds, and winged its way,
Freed from the burden of this earth, to cast itself
Into the ocean of God's endless love.

His name confessing, in whose name thou still hast striven,
Before the sons of men,[1] — in thy last prayer on earth,
The battle thou didst quit, at peace with life, at peace
With thine own self, to seek th' Eternal God, who rules
O'er strife and peace, and reap thy labors' rich reward.

Yes, thou art blest, for blest is he who thus hath ended!
Glorified Spirit! Do thou still the path illumine
Of those that loved thee well; oh, shine upon thy people
Whose annals thou did write; thy wife, thy children, friends,
And — even on her, who now looks up to thee through tears.

*ON READING BISHOP ESAIAS TEGNÉR'S POEM, "RESIGNATION."

Hush thee, vain, thoughtless world! Hush, *he* is speaking;
Once more *he* speaks, old Svea's minstrel-king.
He has aroused him from his bed of suffering,
'Mid Œta's flames, the funeral pile of Genius, —
He strikes his harp. Listen ye young and aged,
Hear how the spirit worketh in Esaias,
Hear what the Lord hath to His servant spoken
In the dark midnight hours of pain and anguish.

.   .   .   .   .   .

Well didst thou sing, O bard, of "Resignation,"
Thy "song of songs," life's loftiest it is;

---

[1] See Geijer's confession of faith in his last printed work, *A Word on the Religious Questions of the Day.*

Led by this power to God in adoration,
Te deums we shall sing in realms of bliss.

How noble is thy song! So Phœnix springs,
Fed by a fire divine, from fragrant ashes;
And o'er the desert spreads his shining wings,
On which the dawn of brighter eras flashes.

Our hearts within us burn! Oh speak again, —
Our ears yet more thy glowing words would drink:
Oh speak once more! Teach us in strife and pain
Like thee with noble aims to feel, to think!

Racked by fierce pain, Heracles stormed with ire,
Wild were his shrieks and loud his maledictions;
Thou suff'rest, too, but from thine altar fire
Ring words of gentle peace — and benedictions.

Heracles lives in many a tale of yore,
But thine, Tegnér, a fairer fate shall be;
A life that knows no grave — yet evermore
A life on earth — of immortality.

Where is that home, in which 't is good to be,
Safe from the surge of time on shelter'd shore?
O Svea's bard! *Thy country* answers thee:
Here liv'st thou, and shalt live for evermore.

There is a public, light as ocean's foam;
A people, too, there is, that *ne'er shall die;*
Within its arms was laid thy children's home;
Within its heart shall live thy memory.

*THE SOUND IN TIME OF PEACE.

Hurrah! How briskly the south winds blow,
Crisping the Sound as it sleeps in the sun.
Hurrah! What sails sweep to and fro,
Swelling and scudding and hurrying on ;
Of every nation,
Color and fashion,
Foe or confederate,
From cities small and great,
On the blue waters that dance round each prow,
Glowing in sunlight they come and they go.
And Denmark's green shores, how they gleam through the mist,
With gold waving harvests round " Marienlyst ; "
And " Kronoborg's " castle, that fortress of pride,
Where " Holger the Dane " is still said to reside ;
There rise Odin's heights, there the royal town
With its palaces, churches, and towers looks down
O'er the placid wave. But from Svea's strand
Frowns the dark cliff of Kullen, her pride and her boast ;
A greeting it sends to the opposite coast —
A greeting of peace from the " Jernbärar " land [1]
And Scania's parks, and the island of " Hven,"
Where rose Brahe's tower on the starlit plain ;
Those shores, once ringing with warlike cries,
Now bound by a thousand peaceful ties,
By the glittering Sound that their borders laves —
They look on its waves.

The sun shines bright over sea and land,
Sparkles the sail-laden Sound in its ray ;
Dolphins gambol and hornbeaks play,
Fishermen lay out their nets from the strand.

[1] The *Ironbearing* land, one of the ancient names of Sweden, on account of the iron which is one of its chief productions.

Smoking "dragons" with track of foam
Lash their tails, as snorting they roam
From city to city. But time doth flee;
The sun is setting, the shades grow deep,
The waves are silent, the breezes sleep,
And the barks lie still on the motionless sea;
The fisherman hastes to his cottage the while
To rest from his toil.
The boats lie empty down by the shore,
The butterfly sleeps in the drooping flower,
Every blade has its pearl of dew,
Night birds fly,
Arches of shadows are flung o'er the sky,
Stars peep forth from the heaven's deep blue.

Hark! the evening gun
Tells that the day is done;
While the broad moon o'er the glittering tide
Spangles with silver the sails as they glide,
"God's peace" proclaiming from shore
O'er Sweden and Denmark for evermore.
Labors are ending!
Slumber descending:
Only yon beacon keeps vigil there —
And the silent prayer.

* MY WRINKLES

1845

OH runes, by time's unerring chisel graven!
Ye wrinkles slowly gathering round my eyes,
Thanks for the kindly message ye have brought me;
Thanks, for ye wake no terror in my heart.
I know your meaning well; full soon, ye whisper,
Old age shall come, with silent footstep stealing,
And then comes death — and it is time to bid
A long farewell to this world's vanities,

To flattery, and the idle lust of praise.
Ah, fatal lust! full oft in fond illusion
We deem that we have quenched it, — mounted far
Above it on the wings of lofty thought,
Of feelings glowing for a world's redemption, —
Deem that we 've drown'd it in a higher love,
In prayer and streaming tears at Jesus' feet,
When lo! 't is crawling still as crawled the serpent
Amid th' ambrosial groves of Paradise,
Luring the soul with false, degrading pleasures,
And tainting life with venomed shafts of discord.
But the great Lord of life, who sees our weakness,
Sends us an angel messenger — pale Time;
And lo! Time's angel, grave, yet merciful,
Compassionate even in sternest mood, right gently
Prints on our brow his stamp indelible,
Closes the temple of our former pleasures,
And posts Scorn's grinning demon at its portals.
And all beyond it is a howling desert,
Of uncouth monsters full, that eat men's hearts;
But there are fair and sheltered paths as well,
That lead to blissful homes, long sought, long dreamt of;
And there a voice is heard, all men inviting
To realms of peace, to those blest tabernacles
Where dwells the good, the beautiful forever.
Oh, to those heights I lift my folded hands,
For there *He* dwells, who shall make all things clear
Through the effulgence of His might and mercy;
And in His presence it is good to be:
This do I know, if I know naught besides!
Oh then, my soul, be youthful evermore,
Be strong in faith, be strong in charity,
And follow Him to everlasting mansions,
Undaunted, though this house of clay be shattered,
And through a thousand deaths thy paths should lead
      thee;

Yet follow Him, till thou hast reached the goal
Where He will turn His glorious face upon thee;
Then shalt thou look on Him, the world forgetting,
Forgetting *thine own self* — and oh, thrice happy,
That thou canst thus forget, that thou canst die
Unto thyself, and live alone in Him.
Rejoice, my soul, for then — thus say the Scriptures —
His *own* thou shalt be called, and on thy forehead
The Lord will write *His name*. O thou frail body,
And O ye furrows worn by time and weeping,
And all infirmities of earth, where are ye?
Changed to the glories of a youth eternal,
Changed to *God's image*, to His holy image!
See, " All things are made new " — all save the gracious,
Th' eternal Renovator of the world.

I thank you then, ye runes, Time's noiseless footprints,
That bring such kindly message: " Time is waning."
I will arise and build a tabernacle
That shall endure when Time's frail tents are shattered:
Then will I strive like holy Paul, and tarry,
" 'Till we shall all be changed."

SUMMER EVENINGS.

Eve approaches; cold mist streaming
  O'er the earth will gather soon, —
Hide the stars above me gleaming,
  Hide the smiling, friendly moon.
Yet 't is naught though mists do tarry
  O'er the earth before my eyes,
If the spirit's gaze can carry
  All my hopes beyond the skies.
No — earth's clouds, so dark and dreary,
  Me nor fear nor doubt can bring;

For beyond life's desert weary,
   I can see a heavenly spring.
Draw around, ye clouds, and cover,
   Shroud me; stars! conceal your light;
Yet my home I can discover,
   Clear the way lies in my sight.

M. R. W.

THE GRAVE.
[Probably translated by Fredrika Bremer from the German.]

How dark and cold the grave is,
   And terrible its rand!
It hides as deep the wave is,
   An undiscovered land.

No sound its gateway knoweth;
   The song of birds is still;
And only friendship streweth
   The flowers o'er the hill.

And he who therein sleepeth
   The widow's sigh ne'er hears;
E'en when the orphan weepeth,
   The grave admits no tears.

Yet it in peace exceedeth
   Each spot; 't is truly fair;
The road that homeward leadeth
   Must ever enter there.

And from all storms defended,
   Where storm and conflict cease,
The heart its throbbings ended,
   At last obtaineth peace.

M. R. W.

THE LAST SONG OF THE LONELY ONE.

FALL, gentle snow, fall deep;
Make cold my place of sleep:
The heart that's burning here
Longs for the coolness there.

And when I sleep below,
Fall faster still, kind snow;
No one will mourn for me,
Then hide me deep in thee.

For oh! no mother will
Kneel at the lonely hill,
Nor any father know
Where I am laid so low.

Ah me! no sister dear
Will give my grave a tear;
And there no brother's grief
Will ever seek relief;

And not a single friend
Will ever o'er it bend,
And in remembrance throw
A flower on the snow.

And he who was my all,
His footstep there may fall:
Woe's me! for by his side
She walks,— his chosen bride

Fall, icy snow, fall deep;
Make doubly cold my sleep:
The heart, now burning sore,
When frozen, feels no more.

www.ingramcontent.com/pod-product-compliance
Lightning Source LLC
Chambersburg PA
CBHW022144300426
44115CB00006B/331